# THE SKEPTIC WA

# THE SKEPTIC WAY

## Sextus Empiricus's *Outlines of Pyrrhonism*

☆

*Translated, with Introduction and Commentary,*
*by* BENSON MATES

*New York    Oxford*
OXFORD UNIVERSITY PRESS
*1996*

Oxford University Press

Oxford   New York
Athens   Auckland   Bangkok   Bombay
Calcutta   Cape Town   Dar es Salaam   Delhi
Florence   Hong Kong   Istanbul   Karachi
Kuala Lumpur   Madras   Madrid   Melbourne
Mexico City   Nairobi   Paris   Singapore
Taipei   Tokyo   Toronto

and associated companies in
Berlin   Ibadan

Published by Oxford University Press, Inc.,
198 Madison Avenue, New York, New York 10016

Oxford is a registered trademark of Oxford University Press

Library of Congress Cataloging-in-Publication Data
Sextus, Empiricus.
[Pyrrōneioi hypotypōseis.   English]
The skeptic way : Sextus Empiricus's Outlines of Pyrrhonism /
translated, with introduction and commentary by Benson Mates.
p.   cm.
Includes bibliographical references and indexes.
ISBN 0-19-509212-0
ISBN 0-19-509213-9 (Pbk.)
1. Skepticism—Early works to 1800.
I. Mates. Benson, 1919–
II. Title.
B621.P972E5   1995   186'.1—dc20
94-31486

1357 98642

Printed in the United States of America
on acid-free paper

# Preface

The Skeptic Way was offered by its practitioners, the Pyrrhonean skeptics, as a way of life leading to *ataraxia*, peace of mind, inner tranquillity. In contrast to the religions, with their multifarious mythologies, belief in which was supposed somehow to contribute to well-being or at least the avoidance of disasters, the Skeptic Way required no belief in anything at all; indeed, the very absence of belief was presented as what would be largely responsible for liberation from the worries, fears, confusions and other inner troubles from which ordinary mortals as well as philosophers seek relief.

This renunciation of belief set Pyrrhonism at odds not only with religion but also with the dominant philosophies of the day — those of the Stoics, Epicureans, and later Peripatetics — each of which, while not putting forward a set of crude mysteries or absurdities in which its devotees were to believe, nevertheless had its own special and hard-to-understand philosophical doctrine to advance. These doctrines had in common a certain core, which Sextus calls "the philosophical *logos*," the supposition that on the one hand there are the appearances, which are subjective and mind-dependent, and on the other hand there is an objective and independently existing real world; and, further, that in one way or another (there was no agreement on the details) it is possible to extract from the appearances the information we need about the real world in order to be wise and to live happily. Like the religions, these philosophies would have us striving to cope with a more or less recalcitrant "reality" that pretty much goes its own way regardless of what we do. But in the philosophical story the obstacle with which we are left to contend is not a supernatural god or gods but rather *phusis*, nature itself, the "external world."

Accordingly, the Pyrrhonist sympathizes with the disinclination of sober and reasonable people to believe in the existence of fantastic beings of any sort and with their reluctance to suppose that human happiness can depend in any essential way on such beliefs. He points out, however, that the so-called "external world," as described by the various philosophers and even as accepted in an inchoate way by the common man, seems in effect to be nothing more than just another domain of invented entities with which we imagine ourselves required somehow to get along.

So the Pyrrhonist's message, insofar as he has one, is something like this: "At ease! The notion that in order to live well you have to have beliefs about a supposed reality that transcends all appearances is just a mistake. Go by the appearances; put aside your worries about whether they correspond to that so-called 'external world', which the philosophers never manage to describe in a consistent or fully intelligible way; suspend judgment about all such matters and you will reach the equanimity that we all desire."

Sextus Empiricus, a Greek author of the second century A.D., is the principal source of what we know about the Pyrrhonist philosophy, and his most compact exposition of it is the *Outlines of Pyrrhonism*. For reasons that I have explained at the beginning of the Commentary (pp. 220ff. below), I have decided to incorporate in this study a complete translation of the *Outlines*. This will perhaps serve at least to excuse me from complaints about quoting out of context. Much more important, it may, I hope, encourage epistemologists to take a new look at an old and very powerful form of skepticism.

Hellenistic philosophy in general and in particular the Skeptics and Sextus himself were not treated kindly by great nineteenth-century historians of philosophy such as Eduard Zeller, Carl Prantl, and Wilhelm Windelband. They regarded the Hellenistic age as an age of decline in philosophy, in which mindless copying and imitation replaced the serious philosophizing of Plato and Aristotle. Many years ago, when I was doing a study of Stoic logic, I was impressed by the extent to which this prejudice against the Hellenistic period had prevented historians from appreciating the very significant accomplishments of the Stoics in the field of logic. For instance, it had led them to misunderstand and dismiss as trivial the very texts that show that the Stoics invented and almost formalized the propositional calculus, a portion of logic that is more fundamental than the traditionally revered Aristotelian syllogistic. Regrettably, I did not at that time learn the obvious lesson sufficiently well, and although I saw clearly enough that the Stoics had been drastically misrepresented, I nevertheless carelessly accepted the received disparaging view of Sextus, and read him only as a source—and a not very good one at that—of information about the philosophies against which he was contending. His own argumentation seemed almost worthless—poorly structured and full of fallacies, a kind of logical mess in which, with luck, one might find some useful bits of information about other people's views.

Two very valuable books, Charlotte Stough's *Greek Skepticism* and Arne Naess's *Scepticism*, got me reading Sextus again, this time trying to understand the skepticism he describes. So far as I know, these books are the first published works on ancient skepticism that treat it as really serious philosophy. Both of them give an account of Pyrrhonism that seems to me correct in most essentials, and Naess even goes thoroughly into the question whether, from a mental health point of view, the Pyrrhonist way of life is practicable.

In the 25 years since the publication of these two books, the quality of scholarly work on ancient skepticism, as well as that on Hellenistic philosophy generally, has risen to a level that is an order of magnitude higher than what was usual in the days of Prantl and Zeller. Myles Burnyeat, Michael Frede, Anthony Long, David Sedley, Julia Annas, Jonathan Barnes, and Gisela Striker are among the authors responsible for this, and I gratefully acknowledge the instruction I have derived from their writings as well as from those of Stough and Naess.

My purpose in this book is to set forth, explain, and criticize Pyrrhonean skepticism as clearly as I can. I shall not be treating it as a mere historical curiosity or primarily as a critique of Stoicism and the other Hellenistic philosophies, nor shall I give much attention to its supposed roots and to its well established and determining influence on post-Cartesian skepticism. Instead, I seek to present it as a philosophical viewpoint worthy of consideration on its philosophical merits.

In this endeavor there are a Scylla and a Charybdis to be avoided. On the one side, we do not want to attach to the name "Pyrrhonism" just any philosophically interesting skeptical position that may be suggested to us by reading Sextus and other ancient sources. On the other, we want to avoid the kind of account that was in fact offered by some noted historians in the past, consisting of an assemblage of sentences lifted from a multiplicity of ancient authors, with each quotation duly footnoted but with little or no attention given to the relative reliability of the authors quoted, to their dates (sometimes separated by hundreds of years), or, more important, to the intelligibility and coherence of the resulting story. So a middle course seems called for, even though it may leave us open to the kinds of criticisms that are legitimately brought against both of the extremes.

With the foregoing in mind, I have decided to use the terms "Pyrrhonism" and "Pyrrhonean skepticism" to denote the type of skepticism described as "Pyrrhonist" in the writings of Sextus Empiricus. His account seems to me to present a reasonably unified and consistent point of view, and I shall not attempt to distinguish different strands in it or to discern signs of the development that presumably began with Pyrrho himself (fl. c. 300 B.C.), about whom we know next to nothing, and proceeded through many equally unknown figures down to Aenesidemus (first century B.C.) and eventually, in the second century A.D., to Sextus. I also leave to more capable hands all speculation as to whether and how the Hellenistic philosophies generally, and Pyrrhonism in particular, were occasioned and shaped by the social, economic, and political conditions in the times and places in which they arose. My aim is only to grasp the philosophic content of the Skeptic Way and to examine it for acceptability.

As mentioned, for the most part I have no quarrel with the results of present-day scholarship on Pyrrhonism. All the same, my interpretation does differ in certain essential respects from that of other recent scholars, which of course is why I make bold to present it in this book and to back it up with my own translation of Sextus's *Outlines*. The principal respects in which my view differs are the following:

1. I take very seriously the caveat at the end of section 4 of Book I of the *Outlines* (see p. 89 below). That caveat shows that nothing, *but nothing* —not even the caveat itself—in Sextus's account of Pyrrhonism is to be taken as more than a report of what appeared to him to be the case

when he wrote it. When in the course of argument he seems to be making categorical assertions, he is sometimes explicitly or implicitly using them as abbreviations of the corresponding "it appears to me that" statements, but more often he is simply taking them dialectically as premises which he supposes the Dogmatists have asserted or would grant. My view, therefore, is that we must recognize Sextus's discourse as a unique type of philosophical writing; although we normally expect a philosopher, however skeptical he may be, to assert in an unqualified way at least *something*—something that will serve to distinguish his philosophy from others—Sextus is an exception. He gives us his impression of what the characteristic behavior of the Pyrrhonist is, and to some extent he illustrates that behavior with his own, but everything he says is to be understood as nothing more than an expression of "what appears to me now to be the case."

2.  Further, I do not share the view held by some scholars that Sextus's "message," such as it is, is directed exclusively to philosophers and that he is offering suspension of judgment about the external world, as well as a return to ordinary patterns of talking and thinking, merely as a way to resolve or dissolve philosophers' puzzles. Plainly, the considerations that he raises apply not only to the philosophers, with their more or less intricate explanations of the relation between the human psyche and the external world, but to anyone at all who intends his assertions to be more than reports of what at the moment appears to him to be the case.

3.  As regards the so-called "external world," in my opinion Sextus neither accepts it nor rejects it. Some commentators have interpreted him as granting the existence of external objects but as finding insuperable obstacles to discovering the truth about them. Something like this may have been the view of the Academic skeptics, but the Pyrrhonists, as described by Sextus, would consider it essentially a form of dogmatism.

4.  Finally, it seems to me that the fundamental distinction between the propositions to which the Pyrrhonist will (under the right circumstances) assent and those with respect to which he always suspends judgment is that the former are offered as mere reports of his present state of mind, while the latter purport to describe objects or states of affairs the existence and nature of which are mind-independent. This distinction is encapsulated in the distinction between the sense of sentences of the modal form "It seems to me now that *P*" and that of the corresponding categorical sentences *P*.

In line with the purpose of the book, the primary role of the Commentary is to explain and discuss the philosophical content of the various passages commented upon. Historical and philological information is included only insofar as that information seems to me helpful in understanding the text or is necessary for justifying my translations of certain terms and passages. Similar grounds justify the inclusion of cross-references to places where Sextus discusses the same points in his other works. Other ancient authors are cited only infrequently, as they seldom — or so it seems to me — throw much light on the sense of what Sextus has to say.

Though the Commentary is focused upon relevant philosophical issues, I make no claim to have taken up all such issues as may reasonably be raised in connection with the Outlines. If there were an objective criterion as to what is philosophically important and what is not, I would apologize for the selection I have made; but as it is, I confess simply to have chosen the issues that most interested me. The reader will surely think of others; indeed, that probability was part of what motivated me to include a translation of the entire work rather than to give merely a series of quotations to back up my interpretation.

I am most grateful for all the help I have received in the preparation of this book. In addition to the acknowledgments above, I should mention specifically my indebtedness to Karol Janáček for his immensely valuable analytic index to the Teubner text of Sextus, and to Jürgen Mau for his improvements of that text as well as for his personal kindness to me. Special thanks are due to Richard Epstein for encouragement and very valuable criticism and suggestions he has given me, to Julius Moravcsik and the other participants in my seminar at Stanford for their stimulating and instructive comments on an early draft, and to Tony Long and Jonathan Barnes for pointing out a number of errors and obscurities that needed attention.

*Berkeley*                                                                                                         B. M.
February 1995

# Contents

# THE SKEPTIC WAY

# Introduction

# The Skeptic Way

If philosophic authors were to be ranked in order on the basis of their relative influence on the subsequent history of Western philosophy, Plato and Aristotle would be at the top of the list, no doubt. But a good case can be made that the third place should be assigned to a rather obscure Greek physician of the second century A.D., Sextus Empiricus. Beyond what we can infer from his own writings, which have come down to us under the titles *The Outlines of Pyrrhonism* (*Pyrrōneioi hypotypōseis*, abbreviated PH) and *Against the Mathematicians* (*Pros mathēmatikous*, abbreviated M), we have almost no information about him (see p. 223 below). But his writings were immensely influential. To be sure, their literary quality has been criticized as mediocre or worse, and scholars have generally concluded (though with very meager evidence) that there is little in them that is original. But there is no question about their immense influence. Due largely to the work of Richard Popkin and his students and associates, it is now clear that the rediscovery and publication of these works in the sixteenth and seventeenth centuries led directly to the skepticism of Montaigne, Gassendi, Descartes, Bayle, and other major figures, and eventually to the preoccupation of modern philosophy, right down to the present, with attempts to refute or otherwise combat philosophical skepticism.

That there was probably some connection between Sextus's writings and modern philosophy was quite evident long before Popkin took up the matter, for nearly every argument and many of the examples that have dominated epistemology ever since the Renaissance are to be found in these works. The half-immersed oar, the eyeball pressed from one side, the parallel lines that appear to converge in the distance, the lukewarm water that feels hot if poured on an inflamed place, the jaundiced person to whom everything is supposed to look yellow, the dreamer, the madman — all of them, along with the points they are usually taken to substantiate, are in Sextus's account. But Popkin traced out the connection in detail, and it turned out to be what is probably the clearest case of major influence in the entire history of philosophy.

It must be mentioned that in addition to their importance as a factor affecting the development of epistemology from the Renaissance to the present, Sextus's works are important for our knowledge of Greek philosophy generally, since he is by far the most complete and reliable source of information about the Stoics and the other Hellenistic schools. In addition, he is the source of a significant portion of the pre-Socratic fragments.

None of the foregoing is news to knowledgeable students of the history of philosophy, of course. But what is not yet fully appreciated in some quarters is that Pyrrhonism — by this term I mean the form of skepticism presented by Sextus, regardless of who may have been its true author or authors — deserves serious consideration as a philosophical point of view. Arne Naess (1968) and Charlotte Stough (1969) were probably the first to give Pyrrhonism this sort of attention; their work, and more recently a series of excellent books and papers by Anthony Long, Myles Burnyeat, Michael Frede, Jonathan Barnes, Julia Annas, and a growing number of other scholars, have raised the philosophical study of the subject to a new level.

It has become apparent that, in the course of criticizing the views of his various opponents, Sextus offers a relatively sophisticated account of a form of skepticism that differs in a number of respects from the modern forms that are historically descended from it. These differences are of importance philosophically, for they seem to render ancient Pyrrhonism immune to many of the responses that have been made to the modern forms of skepticism, though of course it may be vulnerable to difficulties of its own.

The differences in question are principally the following:

1. First, Pyrrhonism is presented by Sextus as a *good* thing; above all, it is not a doctrine, which we might accept or try to refute, but rather a way of life (*agōgē*) or disposition (*dunamis*) that is supposed to lead its practitioners through suspension of judgment (*epochē*) to a state of inner tranquillity or peace of mind (*ataraxia*). In modern times, on the other hand, the so-called skeptic is not much more than an imaginary participant in philosophers' debates, a participant who represents a doctrine that nobody takes seriously but that nevertheless is notoriously difficult to refute.

2. Modern skepticism occurs in many forms, but most of them include the doctrine that knowledge in general, or at least knowledge of a so-called "external world," is impossible. Pyrrhonism makes no such assertion; it is not directly concerned with knowledge at all, but only with justified belief.

3. In Pyrrhonism there is no talk of *doubt* (although that term is occasionally and mistakenly used in translating certain passages of Sextus); but doubting is almost definitively characteristic of the modern skeptic. By contrast, the characteristic attitude of the Pyrrhonist is one of *aporia*, of being at a loss, puzzled, stumped, stymied. This state of mind is said to arise from the apparent equipollence of the considerations that can be brought for and against any assertion purporting to describe how things are in an external, mind-independent world. Unlike doubting, *aporia* does not imply understanding; when assertions are made that claim to describe the external world, the Pyrrhonist is at a loss as to whether to classify them as true, as false, or, more important, as neither.

4. The Pyrrhonist's skepticism extends to all statements, regardless of subject matter, that are offered as more than mere reports of what, at the moment, appears to the speaker to be the case. Accordingly, it covers typical value judgments as well as judgments of perception, whereas modern skepticism usually concerns itself only with the latter.

5. Correspondingly, a "phenomenon" or "appearance," for the Pyrrhonist, is whatever seems or appears to be the case, whether this concerns sensory experience, physical objects, ethical questions, or anything else; it is properly expressed by a "that" -clause (as in, e.g., "It appears that the good fare ill and the bad fare well" or "It appears that this wine has gone sour"). Further, there is no suggestion in Pyrrhonism that appearances are entities that may be compared and contrasted with the things of which they are appearances. In most presentations of modern skepticism, on the other hand, appearances are hypostatized as certain special kinds of things — sense-data, perceptions, impressions, ideas, or whatever — that are considered actually to have some of the properties (e.g., colors and shapes) that the external objects appear to have.

6. Pyrrhonism is frankly and consistently self-referential, whereas the modern skeptic has a problem with statements like "I cannot know that I cannot know," "I doubt that I doubt," etc.

In view of point 1 above, my exposition begins on a negative note.

## 1. What Pyrrhonism Is Not

The single most important point to understand about Pyrrhonism — and a point that unfortunately has been overlooked by many otherwise astute commentators ever since antiquity — is that Pyrrhonism is *not* a doctrine or system of beliefs. That is, if we use the words "belief" and "true" as the Pyrrhonist (hereinafter also called "the Skeptic," with a capital "S") does, so that the predicate "true" (*alēthēs*) applies primarily to propositions purporting to describe external objects and states of affairs, and "belief" (*doxa*) refers to a strong and stable affirmative attitude toward such propositions, we can say that there is no proposition or collection of propositions that the Pyrrhonist, as such, believes or holds to be true. This applies not only to the whole collection of what commentators have called "first-order" propositions about the world — for instance, "The honey is sweet" or "There are invisible pores in the skin" — but also to so-called "higher-order" propositions, that is, to propositions about propositions. These last include in particular the Skeptic's own pronouncements or slogans, such as "To every argument an equal argument is opposed," "Every issue is indeterminate," and "I suspend judgment."

However, although the Pyrrhonist does not *believe* anything, that does not imply that he doesn't *say* or *assent to* anything. But the only propositions to which he gives his assent are such as merely express the present state (*pathos*) of his soul — for example, such propositions as "I feel hot," "This tastes sweet to me now," and "It appears to me now that there is no divine providence." These expressions of his inner states are said to be *azētētos*, which means that the question of their truth or falsity does not arise. As Sextus observes,

> Nobody, I think, disputes about whether the external object appears this way or that, but rather about whether it *is* such as it appears. (PH 1.22)

The assertions that *are* open to question (*zētētos*) and would be appropriate subjects for assertion or belief, in the strong sense in which those terms are used by the Pyrrhonist, are such as are offered as descriptions of a so-called "external world," the existence and nature of which is supposed to be independent of our subjective impressions, thoughts, and feelings. It is with regard to propositions of this type that the Pyrrhonist has his characteristic attitude of *epochē*, suspension of judgment (or, more accurately, withholding of assent). He does not believe that they are true; he does not believe that they are false; he does not even believe that they are true or false, that is, that they make sense. And in this attitude he finds *ataraxia*, a kind of intellectual peace of mind.

Strictly speaking, therefore, there is nothing about Pyrrhonism that one could directly "refute," unless we imagine ourselves to be somehow in a position to take issue with the Pyrrhonist's reports of the present state of his own mind. (We are assured at PH 1.13 that, qua Pyrrhonist, he does not lie in reporting these states.) We can question whether he is abusing language when he makes his reports or when he withholds assent from ordinary assertions that are put forward as more than such reports, and we can question whether his way of thinking, talking, and acting would in fact lead to *ataraxia* as he suggests, but, since he only gives assent to propositions that do express how things seem to him at the moment, there is evidently no serious possibility of contradicting him.

Well, one may say, if Pyrrhonism is not a doctrine, what is it? Sextus calls it an *agōgē*, a way of life or, perhaps better, a way of thinking and acting in which presumably the action is led by the thought. The Pyrrhonean skeptic, instead of basing his thoughts and actions on firm beliefs about how things really are in a mind-independent external world, "goes by the appearances." That is to say, he goes by (i.e., uses as a criterion in deciding his course of action) what here and now appears to him to be the case. And he reports that this way of thinking and acting is accompanied by *ataraxia*. Sextus explains (PH 1.25–8):

> As regards belief, the Skeptic's goal is *ataraxia* [peace of mind], and that as regards things that are unavoidable it is having moderate *pathē* [feelings]. For when the Skeptic set out to philosophize with the aim of assessing his *phantasiai* [impressions]—that is, of determining which are true and which are false so as to achieve *ataraxia*—he landed in a controversy between positions of equal strength, and, being unable to resolve it, he suspended judgment. But, while he was thus suspending judgment there followed by chance the sought-after *ataraxia* as regards belief. For the person who believes that something is by nature good or bad is constantly upset [by everything

that happens]; when he does not possess the things that seem to be good, he thinks he is being tormented by things that are by nature bad, and he chases after the things he supposes to be good; then, when he gets these, he falls into still more torments because of irrational and immoderate exultation, and, fearing any change, he does absolutely everything in order not to lose the things that seem to him good. But the person who takes no position as to what is by nature good or bad neither avoids nor pursues intensely. As a result he achieves *ataraxia.*

Sextus continues with a famous simile:

Indeed, what happened to the Skeptic is just like what is told of Apelles the painter. For it is said that once upon a time, when he was painting a horse and wished to depict the horse's froth, he failed so completely that he gave up and threw his sponge at the picture — the sponge on which he used to wipe the paints from his brush — and that in striking the picture the sponge produced the desired effect. So, too, the Skeptics were hoping to achieve *ataraxia* by resolving the anomaly of phenomena and noumena, and, being unable to do this, they suspended judgment. But then, by chance as it were, when they were suspending judgment the *ataraxia* followed, as a shadow follows the body.

(On the distinction between phenomenon and noumenon, see p. 232.)

Thus the Skeptic is said to have started out like everyone else, trying to infer reality from the appearances — trying, that is, to figure out what is really the case by determining to what extent the appearances are veridical. But the more deeply he considered the matter, the more he found that the appearances are anomalous; that is, they do not lead to any clear and consistent picture of the external world concerning which they are supposed to give us information. For the received epistemological theories themselves tell us that the qualities of appearances depend not only upon the supposed condition of the external objects, but also to a large extent upon the time, the place, the person or animal experiencing them, and a host of additional factors. Hence it would seem that we are never in a position to say how things really are, but only at most how they appear to this or that perceiver, at this or that time, in such and such circumstances, etc. In view of this, the Skeptic was led to suspend judgment about reality. But then the intellectual peace of mind he was seeking to achieve came about as a by-product of the suspension of judgment. He found that if he took no position at all as to how things are in the real, "external" world, but simply went by how they appear to him at the moment, he seemed to avoid much intellectual confusion and emotional turmoil. By telling himself on every occasion: "This is only how things seem to me, here and now; who knows how they are in reality, or whether talk about "reality" even makes sense?" he sets himself apart from much of life's controversy and struggle and achieves a measure of *ataraxia.*

So the Pyrrhonist is said to live *adoxastōs* (without belief). Of course, like anybody else he has sensory experience and thoughts. He yields to the compulsion of his *pathē* (affects) — for example, the feelings of hunger and thirst move him to seek food and drink — though in his case these unavoidable *pathē* will not be as intense as they are in the ordinary person, for they are not aggravated by the notion that the experience of hunger and thirst is not only unpleasant but indicative of a state of affairs that is objectively bad. Further, he respects the tradition of customs and laws, even going so far (though without belief) as to "reverence gods and say that they exist and have foreknowledge" (PH 3.2); and he takes instruction in some art or craft, presumably in order to make a living. We can also perhaps infer, from Sextus's own announced practice of often using the words "is the case" as an abbreviation for "appears to me now to be the case," that the Pyrrhonist will adjust his speech patterns as necessary to avoid seeming odd in ordinary conversation. (For more on this see p. 72.)

Whether the Skeptic *agōgē* is psychologically possible (some critics have claimed that it is not), and whether, if it is possible, it would lead to the suggested *ataraxia*, and whether that kind of *ataraxia* would have any relevance for anyone other than those philosophers who are upset, intellectually if not emotionally, by the seemingly unbridgeable gap between appearance and reality, are all questions we shall take up later.

## 2. The Self-referential Aspect of Pyrrhonism

Another feature of Pyrrhonean skepticism that needs to be brought out early in any exposition is its self-referential character. Sextus broaches this subject in Book I, chapter 1 of the *Outlines*—in fact, right at the end of the opening paragraph. At the beginning of that paragraph he distinguishes three kinds of philosophers as regards their attitudes toward the traditional "search for truth." First, he says, there are the Dogmatists, for example Aristotle, Epicurus, and the Stoics; these claim to have succeeded in discovering the truth. Then there are the Academics, including Cleitomachus and Carneades; their claim is that such discovery is impossible. Third, there are the Skeptics, who are described here as "continuing to search." (Sextus later shows that he regards the Academics as not essentially different from the Dogmatists, for there is at least one truth that they claim to have discovered, namely, the truth that no other truth can be discovered.)

Then follows one of the most significant statements in the *Outlines*. It is a kind of caveat:

> Concerning [the Dogmatic and Academic systems] it will best become others to speak; but concerning the Skeptic Way we shall now give an outline account, *stating in advance that as regards none of the things that we are about to say do we firmly maintain that matters are absolutely as stated, but in each instance we are simply reporting, like a chronicler, what now appears to us to be the case.* (PH 1.4; emphasis added)

Thus Sextus warns us to take his entire account of skepticism as nothing more than a report of what appears to him now to be the case. We are not to suppose that anywhere in the *Outlines* he claims to be telling us what is in fact the case, whether concerning knowledge, skepticism, or anything else. Nor is he making any commitment to take a firm stand in support of his account of Pyrrhonism; he is only reporting how all of this seems to him now.

It is significant that the form of words employed in this metatheoretic pronouncement is exactly that which is characteristic of the only (un-abbreviated) propositions to which, it turns out, the Skeptic ever gives his assent, namely, those of the form:

It appears to me now [*phainetai moi nun*] that *P*.

We see also that here, as throughout the *Outlines*, Sextus makes quasi-technical use of the rather out-of-the-way Greek verb *diabebaioumai* (which I translate as "to firmly maintain") to express what the Pyrrhonean skeptic characteristically does *not* do. The Skeptic, as described by Sextus, does not "firmly maintain" anything, including the very proposition, "the Skeptic does not firmly maintain anything." What the Skeptic characteristically does do is to report (*apaggellō*) what appears to him at the moment to be the case. Thus Sextus's choice of terminology here shows that, as a good Pyrrhonist, he is putting forward his *Outlines* as one long statement of the "It appears to me now" form.

It might be thought that Sextus's caveat was nothing more than a dialectical ploy to ward off objectors who were trying to refute skepticism by raising the question of whether it applies to itself. Surely such objections were made in his day, as they are in ours. But many passages throughout Sextus's writings show that this statement is not merely an incidental remark. He reminds us time and again to take his own statements as no more than expressions of what appears to him now to be the case. Although there are, as mentioned above, several places (PH 1.135, 200, 202; M 11.18–19) in which he says that on occasion he may use the unqualified sentence *P* as an abbreviation for "It appears to me now that *P*," he warns us not to be misled by this into supposing that there are some things—for instance, the slogans of the Skeptics—that he is willing to assert flat out as true.

Another way in which Sextus makes the same point is by peppering his text with the little word *isōs* ("perhaps," "I suppose," "I guess"). This word occurs over and over again, sometimes—to the puzzlement of editors and commentators—in places where he might be expected to assert definitely, and not with "perhaps," a conclusion for which he has just presented a battery of arguments. But in my opinion the function of *isōs* in all these many occurrences is just to remind us, in accord with the caveat, that, although the great majority of the statements in his account of Pyrrhonism are superficially of categorical form (i.e., are not qualified by "It seems to me" or an equivalent phrase), none of them is to be taken as anything more than an expression, a "chronicle," of what at the moment appears to him to be the case. To the same effect, he also frequently inserts the words *oimai* ("I think") and *tacha* ("perhaps").

In sum, the caveat should be given much more weight than it has been given heretofore; it should be understood as applying without exception to everything in Sextus's whole story: to the Pyrrhonist slogans, to the so-called "Modes" and all their component statements and arguments, to the reports of what the Dogmatists say on this or that issue, to the frequent observations that the Dogmatists contradict themselves, and so on. Since it is stated without qualification, and since there are so many reinforcing indications of the same point elsewhere, I see no reason not to take Sextus absolutely at his word, to mean exactly what he says.

## 3. Appearances: The Phenomena

Among the very few terms that play a prominent role in Sextus's account of Pyrrhonism and yet manage to escape his skeptical scrutiny are the verb "to appear" (*phainesthai*) and its corresponding verbal noun "the appearance" (*to phainomenon*). In using these terms the Pyrrhonist seems to accept without question, as most of us would, a fundamental distinction between the sense or content of statements having the form

(1)     It appears (to me now) that *P*,

on the one hand, and that of the corresponding categorical (i.e., unmodalized) sentences *P*, on the other. Thus, what has become the paradigm example in discussions of Pyrrhonism contrasts

(2)     It appears that the honey is sweet

with

(3)     The honey is sweet,

the "to me" and the "now" being often omitted but understood. (The Greek counterpart to (3) can also be rendered as the general proposition, "Honey is sweet," but in the present connection it seems better taken as a statement about a specific blob of honey and comparable with "The wine is sour.")

Now it is clear that in ordinary speech we frequently use locutions of form (1) merely as a means of making the substatement *P* in a cautious or diffident way. In this use, the role of the "It appears that ⋯" prefix seems mainly to be that of giving some slight protection to the speaker's ego against the possibility that *P* may turn out to be false. But the Pyrrhonist's use of the prefix is different. For him, if you assert (1) and it is eventually found that *P* is not the case, you are not thereby shown to have said something false, for you were only reporting a *pathos* of your soul or mind. But if under these same circumstances you assert *P*, no matter how diffidently, you have done something more than report your own state of mind; you have made a claim that *P* is true, and if *P* is false there is no getting around the fact that you were mistaken. Thus it is one thing to make a statement of form (1) to report a *pathos* of your own mind, as the Pyrrhonist does, but quite another to employ the same form of words to describe, diffidently and without much commitment, how you consider things to be in a supposedly mind-independent world.

It is evident that the Pyrrhonist uses the phrase "It appears to me now that" as a kind of modal operator. In that respect it resembles the so-called "psychological" verbs — like "wonders whether," "believes that," "knows that," "doubts that," "approves of," "is hunting for," etc. — that were singled out by Frege as generating "oblique" contexts, in which words and other expressions do not have their ordinary denotations but instead denote what in "direct" or "ordinary" contexts is their sense or meaning. Thus from a Fregean point of view we can say that the truth or falsehood of a statement of form (1) does not depend upon the truth or falsehood of the sentence *P*, or upon the attributes or even the existence of any objects ordinarily denoted by names and descriptions occurring in *P*. (Here I am not restricting the application of "true" and "false," as the Pyrrhonist does, to propositions purporting to describe the external world.) It depends instead on the speaker's relation to the concepts and propositions that constitute the meanings of the terms and sentences contained in the "that" clause.

For example, the truth value of (2), unlike that of (3), clearly does not depend upon the existence or attributes of the honey. And if a statement is "about" whatever determines its truth value, statement (2), unlike (3), is not about the honey or other sweet things. Instead, it is about the speaker and his attitude toward the proposition that the honey is sweet. All of this is just another way of making the rather obvious point that statements of form (1), when the introductory phrase is used to express part of the content and not merely to signal to the audience that the speaker is hesitant, depend for their truth or falsehood entirely on the speaker's state of mind and not on how things are in a supposed "external world."

The obvious distinction we are considering could also be characterized simply as that between appearance and reality. But we must be careful not to read into this a Pyrrhonist commitment to the existence of any such thing or domain of things as so-called "reality." Indeed, "nature," "reality," and "the external world," as Sextus finds the Dogmatists using them, are among the terms that, as we shall see later, he does not grant to be meaningful; that is, they are not terms for which there are corresponding concepts that are consistent and coherent.

Accordingly, I suggest that when the Pyrrhonean skeptic says that he "accepts the appearances" and that he "goes by the appearances," where appearances are to be contrasted with a so-called "non-evident" reality, he need only mean that he assents to propositions of the form (1), with these understood as reporting a present state (*pathos*) of his soul. Like the Cyrenaics, as reported by Plutarch (*Against Colotes* 1120C–D), "he withdraws from the external world as in a siege, shutting himself up in his *pathē*, applying the verb 'appear' to the external objects but refusing to add 'are.'" Thus he withholds his assent from the corresponding categorical propositions *P*, since they are frequently put forward, both by philosophers and by the ordinary man, as more than such reports. In an often quoted passage Sextus says:

> We do not reject the things that lead us involuntarily to assent, in accord with a passively received *phantasia*, and these are appearances. And when we question whether the external object is such as it appears, we grant that it does appear, and we are not raising a question about the appearance but rather

about what is said about the appearance; this is different from raising a question about the appearance itself. For example, the honey appears to us to be sweet. This we grant, for we sense the sweetness. But whether it *is* sweet we question insofar as this has to do with the [philosophical] theory, for that theory is not the appearance, but something said about the appearance. (PH 1.19–20)

Here the so-called "philosophical theory" would, I think, involve some such claim as that when we assert (3) we mean that there is an external object, the honey, which has the attribute of sweetness and which is causing us to experience the impression or *phantasia* in accord with which we make that assertion. (The sentence I have translated as "But whether it *is* sweet . . ." could also mean "But we do raise questions concerning the statement that it *is* sweet; for that statement is not the appearance, but something said about the appearance"; see p. 229 below. But either way the passage tells us that the Pyrrhonist assents to propositions expressing his own *pathē* but not to propositions which go beyond that.)

Elsewhere Sextus makes plain that it is the content of what is said, and not the actual form of words, that is important to him. Sometimes what seems to be a categorical statement of fact is actually only a report of what appears to be the case:

The word "is" has two meanings, one being "is really" [*huparchei*, "exists"] — as at the present moment we say "it is day" in place of "it is really day" — and the other being "appears to be" — as some of the astronomers are in the habit of saying that the distance between a pair of stars "is" a cubit, meaning "appears to be" and not at all "is really," for perhaps it is really a hundred stades but appears to be a cubit because of the elevation and the distance from the eye. With the word "is" thus having two meanings, when as Skeptics we say "of things that are, some are good and some are bad and some are intermediate between these two," we use "are" as expressing "appears to be," not "really are." (M 11.18–19)

Thus the Pyrrhonist will not object to someone asserting (3) if he means it only as shorthand for (2); as mentioned above, there are several places in Sextus's writings in which he tells us that he employs that type of abbreviation himself.

It is especially important to get as clear as possible on this whole matter, for some commentators have thought that when it appears to the Pyrrhonean skeptic that the honey is sweet, he will assent to (3) and not, or not only, to (2). These commentators will have him withholding his assent only from such claims as

(4)     The honey really is sweet,
        The honey is sweet by nature,
        The honey is sweet, philosophically speaking,

all of which are to be distinguished in sense from (3).

But I think that such an interpretation cannot be reconciled with either the text or the general Pyrrhonean point of view presented by Sextus. There is no place in the text where a tripartite distinction is introduced between (2), (3), and any of the items (4). It is propositions like (2) to which the Pyrrhonist on occasion gives his assent, and propositions like (3) from which he withholds it. As the Pyrrhonist Timon is supposed to have said, "I do not assert that honey is sweet, but I do agree that it seems sweet" (Diogenes Laertius, 9.105). In general, a Pyrrhonist will assent to reports of his own present *pathē* but never to propositions claiming to describe anything beyond that. So the only circumstance in which we find him asserting (3) is one in which he is using (3) merely as an abbreviation of (2).

Another misunderstanding to be avoided is that when the Pyrrhonist tells us (as at PH 1.21–2) that for those who follow the Skeptic Way, "the criterion, by attention to which in the conduct of daily life we do some things and not others, is the appearance [*to phainomenon*]," he is postulating or presupposing the existence of some special kind of entities, like the sense data, percepts, and the like, of latter-day epistemology. The Greek expression *to phainomenon*, which consists of the definite article *to* together with the present participle *phainomenon* of the verb *phainesthai* ("to appear"), means literally "what appears."

Of course, a very literal-minded reader might infer from this that, according to the Pyrrhonist, when the half-immersed oar appears to be broken, *to phainomenon* (i.e., what appears) is none other than the oar itself. But such an interpretation would be not only obviously absurd but also completely at odds with what Sextus says about the Pyrrhonist point of view. For while Sextus follows ordinary usage in employing such a sentence as

> The oar appears to be broken

interchangeably with

> It appears that the oar is broken,

the latter is in "canonical form," in the sense that it expresses more clearly and explicitly the intention of the Pyrrhonist when he gives his assent. He wants to report, not that an object in the external world, the oar, has the attribute of *appearing broken*, but rather that his soul is in a state (*pathos*) expressible by

(5)     It appears (to me now) that the oar is broken.

As in the case of assertion (2), he makes no commitment whatever about the existence and nature of any object external to the soul. Thus what appears would not be the oar, but rather *that the oar is broken*—not an object but, some might say, a "state of affairs."

To this it will be correctly objected, however, that statement (5) can be true when there exists no such state of affairs as *that the oar is broken*; indeed, that is precisely why Sextus and all the rest of the epistemologists bring up the example of the oar. Therefore we cannot very well identify appearances with states of affairs, any more than with the objects said to "appear".

If we analyze (5) along the Fregean lines mentioned above, so that (5) is about the speaker's attitude toward the proposition that the oar is broken, we may be led to identify the appearance with the proposition. And it is true that for Sextus *ta phainomena* are most typically expressed by "that" clauses, not only in such cases as "that the honey is sweet" and "that the oar is broken" but also in cases like "that there is divine providence" and "that tattooing of children is shameful," which have nothing directly to do with "looks," "tastes," "heard sounds," and the like. The "that" clause may be of arbitrary length and complexity; indeed, we have seen that at PH 1.4 Sextus in effect offers his whole treatise as one long "that" clause, to be preceded by "It appears to me now...." This again suggests that the appearance — "what appears to be the case" — is a proposition.

But for Sextus appearances cannot be identified with propositions any more than with states of affairs. For when he speaks of propositions (*axiōmata*) he gives that term its Stoic meaning, in which a proposition is a particular kind of *lekton* or sense; and his remarks about *lekta* (PH 2.109ff.) make it clear that he is unconvinced that any such things exist. Consequently, when he says that *to phainomenon* is "the criterion by attention to which in the conduct of daily life we do some things and not others," we cannot very well interpret him as ascribing that role to propositions. In other words, Sextus does not even grant existence to the entities that nowadays are called "propositions" (i.e., the senses of declarative sentences); therefore, we can hardly maintain that he uses *ta phainomena* ("appearances") to refer to these entities.

A better possibility, it seems to me, is to regard the Pyrrhonists as using *to phainomenon* ("the appearance") as an expression that is syncategorematic, that is, one that contributes to the meaningfulness of more complex expressions in which it occurs but that does not by itself have any denotation or reference. It is a term like the noun "sake" — to borrow an old example from Morton White; obviously we can grant meaning to a sentence like "He did it for the sake of his grandmother" without presupposing the existence of entities called "sakes." Thus, as suggested earlier, discourse nominally about appearances may be understood as reducible to discourse involving sentences of form (1), so that, for example, when the Pyrrhonist says that he uses the appearances as criteria for action, he means only that at every time he goes by what appears to him to be the case and does not concern himself with any question of what really is the case. This is just to say that under the right conditions he is disposed to give his assent to relevant sentences of form (1) but not to the corresponding categorical sentences *P*.

Thus, whereas in typical versions of post-Cartesian skepticism appearances are hypostatized as certain entities that are taken to possess at least some of the qualities (for instance, colors and shapes) that the represented objects appear to have, no such hypostatization need be read into Pyrrhonism. We have noted earlier that Sextus's usage permits the transformation of

It appears that *A* is *B*

into

*A* appears to be *B*,

not to mention

There is an appearance that *A* is *B*

and

> What appears is that *A* is *B*,

and this may invite the thought that in uttering such sentences the Pyrrhonist commits himself to the existence of entities that are somehow intermediate between the external object *A* (or the state of affairs that *A* is *B*) and the person to whom it appears that *A* is *B*. But Sextus makes it abundantly clear that the Pyrrhonean skeptic, by whatever form of words he uses in such cases, intends only to report the present state of his soul and is saying nothing at all about the existence and nature of anything beyond that. So the Pyrrhonist can be excused, I think, from the charge often brought against modern epistemologists; that they invent entities placed between us and the objects perceived, thereby complicating the task of explaining how knowledge of those objects can be acquired.

There is, however, another aspect of the Pyrrhonist's use of the verb "it appears that" (*phainetai*) which is more troublesome. Myles Burnyeat (1983) draws our attention to what seems to be a philosophically important ambiguity in Sextus's use of this verb. For it is one thing to say

> It appears to me that the oar is broken,

which describes what Burnyeat calls "a genuine experience"—it looks as though the oar were broken—and it is quite another to say something like

> It appears to me that the good fare ill and the bad fare well,

(not Burnyeat's example), which seems to mean that we think, or are inclined to think, that this is the case. Thus there would be no self-contradiction or even oddity in saying,

> The oar appears to me to be broken, but I do not believe that
> it is,

whereas

> It appears to me that the good fare ill and the bad fare well, but I do
> not believe that they do,

does seem inconsistent.

No doubt Sextus does run together these two uses of "It appears that." Whether in doing so he is fallaciously trading on an ambiguity or is referring to some property that the two kinds of case seem to him to have in common, is a problem I discussed in Mates (1992b). Here I shall simply note that, as Burnyeat pointed out, this feature of Sextus's usage is crucially relevant to his obvious assumption that

> It appears to me that *P*

and

> I do not believe that *P*

are in general logically consistent.

## 4. The External World

Modern formulations of epistemological skepticism nearly always involve the term "external world" or some other term (e.g., "reality" or "nature") that plays essentially the same philosophical role. The main problem with which epistemologists wrestle is thus typically described as that of explaining how we can acquire "our knowledge of the external world."

The world of "external objects" played an essential role in ancient epistemology, too. The Stoics, Epicureans, and Peripatetics, with whose views Sextus is principally concerned, seem to have agreed that the basic problem of knowledge is twofold: on the one hand there is the soul or mind, with its various states, and on the other there are the external objects, the properties of which are independent of the states of the soul; the soul somehow gets information about the external objects by means of certain so-called *phantasiai*, whether these are taken to be impressions on it (as the Stoics said), or changes of its state, or whatever. Moreover, for the most part these philosophers seem also to have agreed that it is possible, at least in principle, for our *phantasiai* to be just as they are even if the external objects do not have the properties we take them to have, or, in the extreme case, even if the external objects do not exist at all. Thus there is need of an explanation of how it is possible, when we have only these *phantasiai* to go on, to acquire knowledge or even justifiable belief about the external world.

In his critique of the various Dogmatic philosophies Sextus constructs arguments using their terminology and many of their premises. But when we read his whole account, as contrasted with the bits and pieces usually quoted by historians, it gradually becomes clear that he is by no means really adopting this terminology and these premises as his own; indeed, he does not even grant that they are meaningful. Instead, he proceeds dialectically: using the Dogmatist's own vocabulary, principles, and logic, he seeks to draw conclusions that the Dogmatist will find unacceptable. For his own part, as he warns us at the beginning of his discourse, he asserts nothing more than what appears to him at the moment to be the case. In particular instances the dialectical aspect of his argumentation makes it difficult or impossible even to decide whether he is agreeing that something appears to be the case—for example, that the half-immersed oar appears to be broken—or is not agreeing but is simply making dialectical use of a premise that he supposes the Dogmatist will grant.

Accordingly, when Sextus speaks of "what exists externally," we must not assume that he accepts the existence of any such things, or even that he concedes the meaningfulness of the word "external" (i.e., that there is a coherent concept associated with it). In several passages it is evident that he is not only raising questions about the Dogmatists' various characterizations of the external world and about their account of how we achieve knowledge of it, but he is also challenging its very existence. Of course, this is not to say that he, like Berkeley, denies absolutely the existence of the so-called "external objects"—in Berkeley's vocabulary, the "external bodies." Instead, he withholds assent on this, as on all other claims that go beyond the domain of appearance. His official attitude, if I am not mistaken, is one of open-mindedness toward all assertions as to what is really, and not merely apparently, the case. We gather that he has not yet heard an account that strikes him as true, or even as fully intelligible, but he is not prepared to say that he never will.

(I should mention that the Greek phrase I am translating as "the external object" is *to ektos hupokeimenon*. It is also sometimes translated as "the externally existing object." Frequently Sextus uses just the shorter phrase *to hupokeimenon* in contexts in which it is clearly an abbreviation of *to ektos hupokeimenon*, and accordingly I have regularly translated the shorter phrase, too, as "the external object." Since these Greek phrases contain no word corresponding to "object," perhaps a more literal rendering would be "what exists externally" or "what there is externally." However, *to ektos hupokeimenon* may itself be an abbreviation of the longer phrase *to ektos hupokeimenon pragma* ["the externally existing thing"], which occurs occasionally [e.g., at PH 2.51].)

One may wonder what "external" means here. External to what? And in what sense external?

The answer to the first question is plainly that the external objects are supposed to be external to our minds or souls, and not necessarily external to our bodies. To conjecture an answer to the second, we may go to a famous passage in Aristotle's *Categories* (1a20f.). There, preparing to define the terms "primary substance" and "secondary substance" by means of the phrases "predicable of" and "present in," Aristotle says (as I understand this much-discussed passage) that he is using the word "in" in such a way that the meaning of '$X$ is in $Y$' is not '$X$ is a part of $Y$' but rather 'The existence of $X$ depends upon that of $Y$', that is, '$X$ cannot exist unless $Y$ exists.' This is the sense, he tells us, in which a particular bit of grammatical knowledge is "in" a mind, for its existence depends upon the existence of the mind it is "in." Since "external to" presumably means the same as "not in," to say '$X$ is external to $Y$' would be to say 'The existence of $X$ is independent of that of $Y$'.

Thus if, as it seems to me, Sextus and the Dogmatists are following this Aristotelian use of "in," the defining characteristic of an object's being external to me will not be that it is spatially located outside the boundary surface of my body, or outside my head, heart, or wherever else my mind might be thought to be located, but rather that its existence and attributes do not depend upon the existence and attributes of my mind, that is, they are not mind dependent.

This interpretation of the externality of the so-called "external world" is a commonplace nowadays. Berkeley, Hume, and most subsequent epistemologists (Kant seems to have been an exception) have obviously considered that what is essential is mind-independence, not spatial location. The external world is supposed to include not only what is literally "out there," but also every bit of the physical world, no matter where located.

One very important difference, however, between the ancient and modern views is that whereas most modern epistemologists seem to assume that the external world is made up of individual entities to which it makes sense to ascribe spatiotemporal coordinates — things like books, tables, rivers, mountains, clouds, shadows — the ancients applied the term "what exists externally" much more widely. Any assertion whatever, the truth value of which is taken to be independent of what the soul perceives or thinks — in other words, which does not merely express *pathe* of the soul but purports to describe something beyond these, something that is *really so* regardless of what may or may not seem to be the case — is taken to assert the existence of a component or components of the external world.

Therefore, when the Pyrrhonist suspends judgment about the existence and attributes of external objects, it must be understood that he is suspending judgment not only on such questions as whether there are invisible pores in the skin or whether the wine is sour or the number of the stars is even, but also as to whether, for example,

> There is divine providence,
> Zeus is the father of gods and men,
> Children should be cared for,
> Homicide is wrong,
> Hercules' way of life was onerous.

He will have no objection to asserting the result of prefixing "It seems to me now that" to any of these propositions, provided that he has the appropriate *pathe*. But when they are offered as descriptions of how things *are*, no matter how they may seem to be, he withholds assent.

So it is reasonably clear that in Sextus's argumentation, and presumably in that of the Dogmatists with whom he is contending, the denotation, if any, of the phrase "the externally existing objects" consists not only of the kinds of things we would initially suppose that phrase to denote, but also of so-called "states of affairs." In other words, the external world, in the view of the philosophers with whom Sextus is arguing, consists not only of a number of individuals but also, as Wittgenstein suggested, of "everything that is the case."

We may say, therefore, that *ta ektos hupokeimena*, for a given person at a given time, would include any and all things and states of affairs that he takes to exist or to be the case independently of the present *pathe* of his soul.

But what about the *pathe* of his neighbor's soul, or the past and future *pathe* of his own? Are they part of his external world, too? Some evidence on this matter is to be found in Sextus's comments on the Cyrenaics (PH 1.215). There he compares the Cyrenaic Way with Pyrrhonism. Some people say, he tells us, that the two philosophies are alike in that both regard only *pathe* as apprehensible, but that they differ in two respects. First, instead of postulating *ataraxia* as the goal, the Cyrenaics propose "pleasure and the smooth transition of the body from state to state;" second, whereas the Pyrrhonists suspend judgment as regards the philosophic account of the so-called "external objects," the Cyrenaics claim that these objects have a nature that is not apprehensible. What is most noteworthy about this comparison, in my opinion, is that Sextus has so few differences to mention. This lends some probability to the conjecture that in his opinion Pyrrhonism and Cyrenaicism agree in most other respects.

Now, one important Cyrenaic thesis that Sextus does not mention as a difference is the view that each person's *pathē* are private to that person (M 7.196–8). Although we have a common language, say the Cyrenaics, and we apply the same terms—for example, "white" or "sweet"—in similar circumstances, none of us has any way of discovering whether on any given occasion his neighbor is having the same sort of *pathē* as he is, for he would have to have his neighbor's *pathē* in order to make the comparison. If the Pyrrhonist follows the Cyrenaic down this path, his "external world" would, if there were any such thing, contain not only "all the choir of heaven and furniture of the earth" and "everything that is the case," but also all the *pathē* of his neighbors and even his own *pathē* of the past and future. And since, if I am not mistaken, he assents only to reports (*apaggelliai*) of the form

It appears to me now that *P*,

which are nothing more than expressions of his own present *pathē*, it would indeed seem that claims about what appears to his neighbor, or even about what appears to himself at another time, would be among the matters upon which he suspends judgment.

On the other hand, much of Sextus's argumentation does suggest a more public interpretation of the word "external" and its related terminology. For him, the distinction between the external and the internal seems to match the distinction between the evident and the non-evident. In other words, the non-evident and the externally existing objects are treated as one and the same. And he frequently infers, from the fact that there is disagreement (usually disagreement among the Dogmatists) about some matter, that that matter is non-evident. In at least one place he argues explicitly that (1) if *X* were evident, it would be evident to everybody; but (2) it is not evident to everybody (as is shown by the fact that there is disagreement about it); ergo (3).... However, this may only be one of his typically dialectical arguments, in which the premises are those of the Dogmatists and not his own. He never offers an example of something that is supposed, even by the Dogmatists, to be evident to everybody, although at M 8.8 we are told, for whatever it is worth, that the followers of Aenesidemus hold that some appearances appear to just one particular person, but some appearances are common to everybody. It is difficult to tell, therefore, what Sextus's own attitude would be toward the internal-external status of *pathē* other than his own *pathē* of the present moment.

I have been characterizing the Pyrrhonists' "externally existing objects" as objects that are external to the mind or soul. But I must note also that there are grounds for thinking that the Pyrrhonist philosophy, unlike post-Cartesian skepticism, does not accept a fundamental distinction between the soul and a material external world. In fact, Sextus even questions whether there are acceptably clear concepts of soul and body, and this amounts to questioning whether there is any coherent meaning attached to the words "soul" and "body." One supposes, therefore, that he would also question the meaningfulness of any other words, such as "external" and "internal," that are defined in terms of the words "soul" and "body." Therefore, the distinction ultimately most fundamental to Pyrrhonism is best described, I suspect, not even as that between what is mind-dependent and what is not, but simply as that between what now appears to one to be the case and what supposedly is the case, or between what now appears to one to exist and what supposedly does exist. The frequently occurring phrase "to suspend judgment concerning the externally existing objects" seems to mean nothing more than to withhold assent from all propositions purporting to be more than reports of what appears to one to be the case.

Closely related to the internal-external distinction is the distinction between what is the case by nature (*phusei*) and what is the case by convention (*thesei*). At PH 2.214 Sextus says:

> [The Dogmatists] say that the sciences [branches of knowledge] always deal with what is the case by nature, not by convention—and they say this with good reason, for scientific knowledge aims to be firm and unchanging, while the conventional is easily changeable, being altered when there is a shift in the conventions, which is in our power.

Thus the crux of the distinction between nature and convention is that what is the case by convention is in our power (*en hēmin*), in some sense "up to us," whereas what is the case by nature is supposed to be the case independently of us. Note that at PH 1.98 it is taken to be an open question whether there is any such thing as nature, and if nature consists of everything that is the case or exists by nature, this amounts to taking it to be an open question whether there is any such thing as the external world.

In sum, the "externally existing objects" are generally considered external to the soul, not to the body, and they are "external" in the Aristotelian sense of logical independence, not in terms of location. Further, they would include not only individual things, but also states of affairs, that is, counterparts of true declarative sentences. But Sextus's skepticism extends even to the terms "soul" and "body," And so it seems that, for him, all references to things "external" and "internal" will have to be ultimately reducible, insofar as they make sense, to discourse presupposing only the one philosophical distinction he seems not to challenge, namely, the distinction between reporting that something appears to one to be the case and flat-out asserting that it is the case.

## 5. Concepts

In Sextus's critique of the Dogmatists' views we find much talk of concepts. On a wide variety of topics he presents considerations designed to show that there is no consistent or agreed-upon concept of $X$ or that $X$ is "inconceivable." Sometimes — for example, in the description of causation at PH 3.13ff. — he states his point with the qualifier "if we go by what the Dogmatists say"; thus, "if we go by what the Dogmatists say, nobody could have a concept of cause." In other cases he appears to be speaking more absolutely, as at PH 2.70, where he begins his discussion of *phantasiai* with the remark, "The first thing to say on this topic is that one cannot form a concept of *phantasia*." But the context shows that in these cases, too, he is tacitly adding the qualifier "if we go by what the Dogmatists say." He is neither asserting nor denying that he himself can form the concept in question; instead he is drawing consequences, uncomfortable for the Dogmatists, from the definitions they offer and the theories and factual claims to which they subscribe.

It is worth mentioning parenthetically that there are three different Greek terms, *ennoia*, *epinoia*, and *noēsis*, that Sextus employs in the *Outlines* and *Against the Mathematicians* and that in most of their occurrences seem clearly to be synonyms that must be translated as "concept." He uses the three with approximately equal frequency; he applies them, with few exceptions, to the same list of cases; and for each pair of the three there are passages in which the terms of that pair are plainly used interchangeably.

Suppose now that someone were to ask the Socratic-style question, "What *is* a concept?" A standard answer in Sextus's day would be that a concept is a change of state (*kinēsis*) of the intellect (M 8.336a). But a somewhat more informative answer, which can be inferred from the use of the terms in actual practice by Sextus and his opponents, is this: a concept is in effect the meaning of a word or noun phrase. To have a concept of human being (*anthrōpos*) is to know what a human being is (M 8.87ff.); that is, it is to grasp a sense or meaning that is expressed in Greek by the term *anthrōpos*. Thus when Sextus raises the question of whether $X$ is conceivable, he is in effect questioning the very meaningfulness of utterances containing the corresponding word, insofar as that word is to be used in accord with one or another of the Dogmatists' definitions. This aspect of his skepticism has seldom been emphasized, though it fits together nicely with his frequent observations that we are unable to say, of a given assertion by the Dogmatists, whether it is true, false, *or neither*.

However, if we allow that for Sextus and his opponents concepts are in effect the meanings of words, it must be added that these meanings are not to be treated in the Fregean manner as independently existing ideal entities that may be expressed with varying degrees of accuracy by the words we use. Instead, they are to be thought of more "psychologically." Concepts are said to be "formed" by people on the basis of their individual experiences; consequently, since different people will mean different things by a given word, we can expect to be told that they will have different concepts associated with that word.

In various places Sextus mentions some of the most general properties that concepts are supposed to have. We are told that the existence of a concept in no way requires the existence of one or more objects falling under the concept (PH 2.10; M 9.49). A single concept can be associated with two different words (M 9.240), and, of course, different concepts can be associated with the same word. Concepts are compounded of other concepts; for example, the concept of human being is compounded of the concepts of animal, rational, and mortal (M 8.87); and they can also be derived from other concepts by further operations to be mentioned below. We are also told that, at least in some cases, people agree on a common preliminary notion (*prolēpsis*) of X and then go on to expand or revise this into different concepts of X. Thus starting from a preliminary notion or intuition of what a god is — "a creature that is blessed, indestructible, perfect in happiness, and with no evil attributes" — different people or groups of people have proceeded to form different concepts of god (M 9.33).

In addition to his general remarks about concepts, Sextus gives us a large number of examples to consider. At one place or another he speaks in particular of concepts of human being, god, sign, cause, body, surface, motion, time, eternity, number, point, line, plane, solid, boundary, location, dimension, logical consequence, right, left, color, sound, good, bad, and indifferent — not to mention such (perhaps less expected) concepts as those of Socrates, the Cyclopes, the Hippocentaur, "the legendary doings in Hades," the whole man, the happy man, and the Skeptic philosophy.

As regards the formation of concepts, Sextus's account (which, be it remembered, he does not offer as true but only as, at most, what he hears from the Dogmatists and/or what appears to him to be the case) is reminiscent of the British Empiricists' doctrine about so-called "abstract ideas." For instance, he says:

> In general it is not possible to find in conception anything that one does not possess as known in experience. For such a thing will be grasped either by way of resemblance to things that have appeared in experience, or by way of increase or decrease or composition: by resemblance, as when from the seen picture of Socrates we conceive unseen Socrates; by increase when we start with a person of ordinary size and move on to conceive an individual who [as Homer said of the Cyclops] did not resemble "a bread-eating human being but rather a wooded peak in the high mountains"; by decrease when by reducing the size of the ordinary person we get the concept of a pygmy; and by composition when from the concepts of human being and horse we obtain the concept of a thing we have never perceived, the Hippocentaur. Every conception, then, must be preceded by experience through sense perception, and consequently there would be no concepts if there were no objects of sense perception. (M 8.58ff.)

The last point is somewhat expanded in a similar passage:

> And in general, everything that is conceived is conceived either by awareness of things clear to the senses or by derivation from such things, and this last in various ways — in one case through similarity, in another through composi-

tion, in another by analogy, and this again by way either of increase or of decrease. Thus, white and black, sweet and bitter are conceived through awareness of things clear to the senses, for these things, though sensible, are nonetheless conceived. (M 9.393ff.)

According to this account, therefore, every concept is either itself derived directly from sensory experience or else results from the (perhaps repeated) application of the aforementioned operations to these directly derived concepts. Reformulated as a theory about the meanings of words, this is to say that the meanings of a certain basic stock of words—for example, "white," "black," "sweet," "bitter"—are acquired directly from sensory experience, while the meanings of the rest are obtained by combining or altering those basic meanings in various ways.

Thus Sextus follows the principal Dogmatists (Plato is an exception) in expecting that in general there will be several different concepts of *X*, depending upon how the individual person makes the selections and transformations involved in the described procedure for forming concepts. Note, however, that he obviously finds no contradiction in saying, on the one hand, that *X* "cannot be conceived" and, on the other, that there are several concepts of *X*. For example, at M 9.380ff. he considers a number of different concepts of line—as "the flux of a point," "a sequence of points and," and "length without breadth." By offering, for each definition, arguments to show that the proposed concept is incoherent, he tries to establish his conclusion (at 390), that "line is not conceivable." Clearly, for him it is one thing to have a concept of *X*, and quite another to have a satisfactory or consistent concept of *X*; he grants that the Dogmatists have concepts, but he does not find these concepts consistent, either internally or with one another.

Sextus does seem to accept, at least as a basis for argument, that in order to use a given term for communication at any level, the user must associate with it *some* concept—however loose, vague, incoherent, or in other ways unsatisfactory that concept may be. We see this from his treatment of an old puzzle. At the beginning of Book 2 of the *Outlines* he raises the question how it is possible to look for (*zētein*, seek, inquire into, investigate, question) something of which one has no conception. The relevance to his concerns is obvious, for early on in that work he has described the Pyrrhonist as "one who continues to seek" and yet in case after case he concludes that there are no satisfactory concepts corresponding to central terminology in the Dogmatists' assertions. How, therefore, can the Pyrrhonist inquire into issues that he does not understand?

At M 8.337ff., where the same matter is discussed in a somewhat different way, we learn that the puzzle was used by the Epicureans against the Skeptics. But a form of it, framed in the same terminology, occurs in Plato's *Meno* (80D ff.):

MENO. And how, Socrates, will you look for [*zēteseis*] something when you don't know at all what it is [*ho ti esti*]? Or, even if you hit upon it [*entuchois*], how will you know it is the thing you did not know?

SOCRATES. I understand the point you wish to make, Meno. Do you see what a specious argument you are introducing — that a person cannot inquire about [look for, *zētein*] either what he knows or what he does not know? For he would not inquire about what he knows, as he already knows it; nor about what he does not know, since he does not know what he is inquiring about.

Sextus was obviously bothered by the puzzle, for in both of the cited passages he tries to solve it, though not in the same way. In the passage in *Outlines* 2, where he uses it as the occasion for distinguishing two senses of "to apprehend," he concludes that, after all, "the Skeptic is not precluded, I suppose, from a conception that arises during the discussion itself from clear appearances affecting him passively, and which does not at all imply the existence of its object." This seems to mean that as the Skeptic listens to the Dogmatists' discourse he is able to form concepts that, while defective and incomplete, suffice to enable him to take part in the discussion. He "catches on," to some extent, to what the Dogmatists are talking about; or at least he learns, again to some extent, how to talk in their way.

The passage at M 8.337ff. treats the puzzle rather differently. There the topic is the question "Does proof exist?" (which, incidentally, is ambiguous between "Is there a satisfactory concept of proof?" and "Is there any such a thing as a proof?"). We find the following argument:

Either you understand what proof is, or you don't. And if you understand and have a concept of it, proof exists; but if you do not understand, how do you investigate [*zēteite*] a thing of which you have no understanding at all?

Sextus adds (M 8.331a):

In saying this, they [the Epicureans] are pretty well refuted by themselves, since it is agreed that every object of investigation necessarily presupposes a concept or preconception [*prolēpsis*]. For how can anyone even investigate something when he has no concept of the object of the investigation? For if he has hit upon it [*epituchon*] he will not know that he has done so, nor if he has missed it, that he has missed it. (M 8.331a)

Sextus then says that he grants the point,

and, in fact, so far are we from saying that we wholly lack a concept of the object of investigation that, on the contrary, we think that we have many concepts and preconceptions of it, and that it is because of our inability to decide between them and to discover the most cogent among them that we revert to *epochē* and indecision. (M 8.332a)

Thus, both here and in the *Outlines* passage Sextus seems to accept the assumption that in order to investigate or raise questions about $X$ one must have some sort of concept of $X$ (cf. Diogenes Laertius 10.33).

All of this has crucial relevance to the question of how we are to take that very large portion of Sextus's account in which he offers us detailed criticism of Dogmatic theories. Frequently, as at PH 2.27ff., 70ff., and 104ff., his argumentation takes the form of first purporting to establish that there can be no concept of *X*, and then arguing that even if *X* were conceivable, *X*'s could not be apprehended, and that even if they could be apprehended, they could not be used as the Dogmatists propose—and so on. What are we to make of this? How can he continue to use in subsequent argumentation an expression for which he has just pointed out that no corresponding concept can be formed?

It seems to me that the explanation is, once again, the following. Sextus's entire performance should be understood as a feigned dialectical exchange with his opponents, the Dogmatists. He replies to them by deducing—using both their logic and certain premises with which they appear to agree—conclusions that they will presumably find unacceptable. In all cases he is working within the framework of what the opponents say; for the sake of argument he uses their concepts on a temporary basis, or he uses the loose intuitive notions (*prolēpseis*) common to all mankind. But he never puts himself on the line by asserting that one or another of the premises is true, or even by claiming soundness for the types of logical inference—for example, reductio ad absurdum—that he employs. In particular, when he argues that no concept of *X* can be framed, he adds, sometimes explicitly but usually only tacitly, the provision "if we go by what the Dogmatists say." His method is to consider the various concepts of *X* that have been put forward, and for each such concept to show that it is internally inconsistent, or inconsistent with other things the Dogmatists say, or just unintelligible.

Thus in the passage mentioned above (M 9.380ff.), he seeks to show, on the basis of premises that he supposes the Dogmatists will accept, that there can be no concept of Line. His evidence is that each of the three concepts they offer turns out to collide with common assumptions. For example, he argues that the definition of a line as "length without breadth" runs afoul of the principle that in forming one concept from another by diminution or reduction in size, the result of such diminution must be homogeneous with the original, in the way that a part must be homogeneous with the whole. Hence, if you start with the concept of a stripe, by diminution of its width you can get the concept of a narrower stripe; but continued diminution of stripes with respect to width only leads to still narrower stripes, and never to something that has no width at all and thus is not a stripe. For the other concepts of line similar difficulties are raised, and eventually he concludes that "line is inconceivable," which has to mean, I think, not that it is absolutely impossible to form a concept of line, but that no concept can be formed if you go by what the Dogmatists say.

The upshot—if I may harp upon what I take to be crucial in Pyrrhonism—is that the Pyrrhonist does not assent to any propositions other than those expressing a present *pathos* of his soul. This applies in particular to propositions about the meanings of words: Sextus is not prepared even to agree that the assertions of the Dogmatists are meaningful. Indeed, even his own remarks at PH 1.5 and 1.11, concerning the concept of the Skeptic Way, are subject to the caveat of PH 1.4 and thus are to be considered nothing more than expressions of what appeared to him, at the time when he wrote them, to be the case.

There is another problem, or another facet of the same problem, that must be faced before we leave this topic. Sextus seems to grant, as we have seen above, that in order for the Skeptic or anyone else to "investigate" whether it is the case that *P* he must have some concepts, however imperfect they may be, associated with the components of the sentence expressing the proposition that *P*. Thus, to "investigate" or "question" (*zētein*) whether the honey is sweet, he has to attach meaning to the words "honey" and "sweet" and to the sentence "The honey is sweet," or to their counterparts in some other language. Or, to put this in a way that makes the reference to language less obtrusive, he must have in mind some notion of what honey and sweetness are, and of what it would be for the honey to be sweet.

Now if that is true for the verb *zētein*, why is it not also true for the verbs "to appear" and "to be at a loss," which are so central to the Skeptic's own vocabulary? Can the Skeptic honestly report

It appears to me now that *P*

if he does not know what it would be like for it actually to be the case that *P*? Can he honestly say

It appears to me now that the honey is sweet,

if he does not have some understanding of the sentence

The honey is sweet,

that is, unless he attaches appropriate, however imperfect, concepts to the words "honey" and "sweet" and to the whole sentence? How can he simultaneously assent to

It appears to me now that the ship is in motion,

while asserting that "motion is inconceivable," that is, that there is no coherent concept of motion?

But in the case of the Skeptic's own favorite verbs, "to appear" and "to be at a loss," it seems that we do not have the option of explaining away the difficulty by saying that, as in Sextus's discussion of the concept of line, so also here he is simply using the Dogmatists' concepts in a provisional way, without any suggestion that he himself finds them or any improved versions of them acceptable. For this would mean that even in the most fundamental reports of his own *pathē* he is only playing with the Dogmatists' defective concepts. His report about the apparent motion would mean only that "going by the Dogmatists' concept of motion, it appears to me now that the ship is in motion"; and similarly for all the rest of his reports of the form "It appears to me now that *P*." Surely this makes his discourse just too inscrutable.

One proposed solution is this. It is suggested that Sextus, representing the Pyrrhonists, in effect distinguishes two senses or uses for a sentence like "The honey is sweet." One of these is its "ordinary" use, which it has in the discourse of daily life; the other is a "philosophical" use, according to which it means something like "The honey *really* is sweet" and according to which it is loaded with philosophical presuppositions about what honey really is and about how we acquire knowledge of an external world. In line with this distinction, it is theorized that the Pyrrhonist has no quarrel with the ordinary use of the sentence, and that only the philosophical use, with its burden of metaphysics and epistemology, is the object of his critique. Thus the questions we have raised could be answered by saying that in the Skeptic's report,

> It appears to me now that the ship is in motion,

the subsentence and its components—including for example the word "motion"—have their ordinary use, but that when the subsentence has its philosophical use the Skeptic finds himself at a loss as to whether it is true, false, or devoid of sense.

This is undeniably an attractive solution to the problem. It explains how the Pyrrhonist could regard his own canonical reports, "It appears to me now that *P*," to be be meaningful, while at the same time questioning whether there are any sharp and consistent concepts corresponding to the sentence *P* and its components. And it fits in well with Sextus's oftrepeated statement that the Skeptic uses language loosely and does not join the Dogmatists in trying to furnish exact definitions for the most important terms. The Skeptic and the common man, he says, have *prolēpseis* ("preconceptions" or "pre-philosophical concepts") associated with such terms and hence are able to use them in communication. Troubles only arise when the Dogmatic philosopher attempts to sharpen up these rough concepts and include them in his epistemology.

My only reservation about this solution is that it may be thought to imply that Sextus's message is intended for philosophers only, and that he exempts ordinary discourse and the common man totally from his critique. It is of course true that the so-called "Dogmatists," to whom Sextus principally directs his strictures, are not the common people but rather philosophers—for example, Stoics, Epicureans, and Academics, together with Plato and Aristotle and some of the pre-Socratics. Indeed, we are told at PH 1.1–3 that the Dogmatists are those people who think that they have found the truth "as regards what is investigated in philosophy." But this does not imply that

Sextus's skepticism is not also relevant to the language and thought of those of us who do not qualify as Dogmatists "properly so called."

More important, however, is the fact that Sextus never suggests that the common man, in making a statement like "The honey is sweet," presents it as a mere expression of the present *pathos* of his soul. Certainly we can say with assurance that the common man nowadays does not use language in this way. I suppose it could turn out that if our so-called "common man" is asked whether, when he says "The honey is sweet," he means only that the honey tastes sweet to him or he means that it really is sweet, it will appear that he means neither — that he does not usually have this distinction in mind when he makes such statements. But I doubt that this is true. On the contrary, I suspect that nearly everyone, with whatever background, is "philosophical" enough to assume that there is a world "out there" that is the subject of most of our discourse and that exists and goes its own way with its own attributes, regardless of how it may appear to any of us. If this is so, then Sextus has something to say to us all, whether we are "Dogmatists properly so called" or not. In any case, it is at least clear that insofar as ordinary assertions are made with the intention or presumption that their subject matter — that is, what their truth value depends on — is something other than the speaker's state of mind, they are no less open to Sextus's critique than are the philosophical theories of the Dogmatists.

Finally, I must mention one more serious obstacle to understanding what Sextus has to say about concepts. Certain features of the Greek text have the unfortunate effect of making it difficult or impossible to determine in some cases whether he is talking about concepts or about the things that fall under the concepts — for example, about the concept of motion or about the objects that move. There seems to be a genuine ambiguity in the relevant Greek expressions. Typically they consist of a noun with the definite article — for example, *to aition* (the cause) — and such expressions have different senses in different contexts. There is a somewhat similar ambiguity in English. For example, "the tiger" can refer to a class (as in "The tiger is a species of cat") or to a particular animal that is under consideration (as in "The tiger has just retreated behind the tree"), or it can be used in quantifications, where there is reference neither to a class nor to any particular animal (as in "If a lion and a tiger fight, the tiger is sure to win"). Similarly, in Greek the expression *to aition* can be used to denote either a particular cause that has been somehow indicated beforehand, or causes in general (as in "The cause is relative to the effect"), or the concept of cause. This allows Sextus to produce texts in which, on the one hand, we need to understand the term the same way everywhere in order to preserve coherence and consequence, while, on the other, we must treat different occurrences differently in order to preserve local sense.

Thus, for example, in order to make sense of PH 3.13ff. I have had to translate the same expression, *to aition* (which is singular) in some places as "causes," in others as "the cause," and in still others as "cause" (as in "the concept of cause"). Compare also the curious arguments at PH 2.23 and M 7.266–8, where we cannot tell whether the discussion concerns individual human beings, dogs, horses, and plants, or the concepts of human being, dog, horse, and plant, or in some way all of these at once.

## 6. Doubt and Being at a Loss

Modern commentators on Sextus have almost inevitably tended to project some of the features of modern skepticism onto the form of skepticism he describes. The temptation to do so is great because of the historical connections and because so many of the now-standard arguments and examples are to be found in his account. One case in point, in which this tendency is especially obvious and has led to misunderstanding, is the presumption that the characteristic attitude of a Pyrrhonean skeptic is one of doubt. It is an interesting fact, with important philosophical consequences, that in his account of Pyrrhonism Sextus never speaks of doubt. The Greek language is not short of verbs to express that condition (e.g., *endoiazō, distazō*), but he never makes use of any of them. Instead, for the Pyrrhonist's characteristic attitude Sextus uses the verbs *aporō* and *amēchanō*, which mean "to be at a loss."

Henri Estienne (Stephanus, 1528–1598), whose Latin translation of 1562 was so influential in the Renaissance, got things off on the wrong foot by following tradition in rendering the crucial verb *aporō* by the Latin *dubito*. This may well be at least part of the reason why Descartes and consequently Berkeley, Hume, Kant, and epistemologists down to the present day have assumed an essential connection between skepticism and doubting: to be a skeptic is almost "by definition" to be a doubter — a doubter with the kind of doubts that have given rise to the great "scandal" of which Kant spoke, namely, that philosophers are unable to provide a consistent and plausible explanation of how knowledge of an external world is possible.

By contrast, the characteristic attitude of the Pyrrhonean skeptic is, as we have said, not doubt but rather *aporia*, that is, being at a loss, baffled, perplexed, puzzled, stumped, stymied; and his primary concern is with belief, not knowledge. The post-Cartesian skeptic will doubt that we can have knowledge of the external world, and he may even go so far as to doubt that such a world exists; the Pyrrhonist, by contrast, having heard arguments for and against claims that things are thus and so in the external world, is at a loss as to which, *if any*, of the contesting viewpoints is correct. To him the arguments pro and the arguments con seem to be equally strong and equally weak — "to every argument an equal argument is opposed" (PH 1.202) — each conclusion is "no more" worthy of belief than its negation (PH 1.188). Every categorical assertion about the external world, not only by the Dogmatists but even by the common man, creates an *aporia*, an intellectual thicket, through which the Skeptic sees no path. In all such cases he finds himself at a loss (*aporei*); he is unable to decide (*krinein*) one way or the other; he lacks a criterion (*kritērion*), that is, a basis for deciding, and for the most part this lack is due to the fact that the Dogmatists' theories, definitions, and concepts lack consistency. And so, being at a loss, he withholds assent (*epechei*) from all categorical assertions (PH 1.196); he is willing to say how things now seem to him to be, but on the question of how they are in fact, he takes no position (PH 1.192–3).

It may seem that the distinction between doubting and being at a loss is overly fine and has little philosophical significance, and that anyone who is "at a loss" in the aforementioned sense is *eo ipso* in a state of doubt. But care is required here lest we miss the point. It can reasonably be argued, I think, that doubt implies understanding: you are in no position to doubt that *P* if you do not even know what it would be for *P* to be the case. For instance, until a child acquires the relevant concepts, he or she cannot very well doubt that there are infinitely many prime numbers, or that water consists of hydrogen and oxygen. On the other hand, the attitude of being at a loss, as expressed by the Greek verb *aporō*, obviously has no such implication of understanding.

Thus when a philosopher declares, "Being and nothing are one and the same," you may very well find yourself at a loss because you do not understand the sentence he has uttered, whereas in order to doubt that being and nothing are one and the same you have to grasp the sense and be unconvinced that it is true. Berkeley, who did not challenge his opponents' definition of the word "matter," was consequently in a position to doubt that matter exists, and even to believe that it does not. But the Pyrrhonist cannot very well be said to doubt that our beliefs about an external world are true, for, as was mentioned above, he finds no coherent concept corresponding to the word "soul," or, by implication, any corresponding to "external world" (i.e., to "what exists independently of the soul"); indeed, he does not even agree that there is a coherent concept associated with the word "true." The concepts of god, cause, motion, and many other things are similarly challenged.

From a Fregean point of view, it would seem that a principal difference between doubting and being at a loss is that the objects of doubting are propositions or thoughts (*Gedanken*), whereas the objects of being at a loss are sentences. He who doubts that the honey is sweet entertains the thought that the honey is sweet, but he is unconvinced that this thought is true; while the Pyrrhonist, at a loss about the sentence, "The honey is sweet" (and even about the sentence "The sentence 'The honey is sweet' is true"), leaves open the possibility that these sentences and their components are devoid of cognitive content.

In any case, we find that there are several ways in which Sextus presents the Skeptic as being at a loss with respect to a given assertion. Sometimes Sextus provisionally accepts the definitions and other explanations that the Dogmatists give for the component terms of the assertion, and on that basis he tries to show that the arguments pro and con are equally balanced. Or he attacks the definitions and explanations themselves, arguing in effect that the explanations are inconsistent and the terms, as thus defined, are meaningless.

Or he simply surveys the true-false-meaningless alternatives for the assertion and explains that the Skeptic will be at a loss because there is no plausibility in any of them.

In the translation I have left the word *aporia* untranslated, in order that its many occurrences may remind the reader that the state of being-at-a-loss, not that of doubt, is central to Pyrrhonean skepticism. Like the verb *aporō*, *aporia* is derived from *poros* (a passage, or way through), with the privative prefix *a*, so that in general it denotes a state or situation through which there is no passage or way. In its philosophical use, established principally by Aristotle, an *aporia* is a kind of conundrum in which there are plausible arguments for both sides of a philosophical issue, or it is the state of an intellect baffled by such a conundrum. Thus the extensions of the terms *aporia* and "doubt" may overlap, but they are not identical. "Doubt," unlike *aporia*, implies understanding; but *aporia*, unlike "doubt," involves the (futile) consideration of conflicting claims. At least, that is how I hear the two terms.

Note also that the Skeptic's *aporia*, as a state of mind, is consistent with his *epochē*; consequently, although for the most part I have followed tradition in translating the latter term as "suspension of judgment," I perhaps should have used the more accurate phrase "withholding of assent." For one can withhold assent from an assertion without granting that it makes sense, whereas "suspension of judgment" suggests, at least to me, that one knows what the issue is but has not yet made up one's mind as to which of the opposing views is correct.

The Skeptic's *aporia*, leading through *epochē* to *ataraxia*, is also consistent with his "continuing to search" (see PH 1.3), for the "searching" that the Skeptic does turns out to be, in most cases, nothing more than the raising of questions about the meaning and seeming implications of Dogmatic assertions purporting to be true.


## 7. Phantasiai

The term *phantasia* plays an absolutely essential role in the epistemology and the philosophical psychology of most of the Dogmatists whose doctrines Sextus examines. But the question of what it means is surely a perplexing one. As Sextus is happy to point out, the different schools of Dogmatists did not agree with one another on how to define it, and, as we shall see, there was much disagreement even within the schools. Obviously this gives rise to a problem for translators, since in a very real sense we do not know what these people were talking about. Under the circumstances I have decided to add *phantasia* to the terms left untranslated. Of course, a reader can properly expect that an English translation will be in English, but in the case of *phantasia* any term I would choose would have to be treated as a technical term anyway. Keeping the word in Greek will at least identify its occurrences and thus permit readers to see for themselves how it functions in the arguments that Sextus directs against his adversaries.

Most of the relevant scholarly literature in English renders the term as "impression." Bury's translation uses both "impression" and "presentation." Annas and Barnes use "appearance." (For *to phainomenon*, which I am translating as "appearance," they have "what appears)." Hossenfelder, in his German translation, uses *Vorstellung*, which corresponds to "presentation." Other possibilities in English would be "perception," "idea," "representation," or, in a few contexts, "image." Estienne, in the Latin translation of 1572, keeps *phantasia*, as I have done.

No doubt the principal justification for "impression" is that the Stoics, as Sextus reports at several places (e.g., PH 2.70; M 7.228, 372), said that a *phantasia* is a *tupōsis*—an impression on, or a shaping of, the ruling part of the soul. But "impression" has several drawbacks as a translation of *phantasia* in Sextus. One is that the meaning of this word in modern epistemology has been largely determined by Hume, who, in the famous passage at the beginning of *A Treatise of Human Nature*, said:

> All the perceptions of the human mind resolve themselves into two distinct kinds, which I shall call Impressions and Ideas.... Those perceptions, which enter with most force and violence, we may name *impressions*; and under this name I comprehend all our sensations, passions, and emotions, as they make their first appearance in the soul. By *ideas* I mean the faint images of these in thinking and reasoning.

In a translation of Sextus, however, the use of "impression" would have to extend to such cases as "the impression that the bad fare well and the good fare ill" and "the impression that no impression is credible," which are hardly to be described as "sensations, passions, or emotions." In general, the term *phantasia* takes a "that" clause, and the phrase "the *phantasia* that *P*" seems intended to denote whatever state of mind can be honestly reported or expressed by saying "It appears to me now that *P*."

There are good reasons for not using "impression" even in connection with the Stoics. Sextus tells us (M 7.228) that whereas Cleanthes took the word *tupōsis* to refer to raised and depressed areas, such as would be produced in wax by a signet ring, Chrysippus regarded this as absurd in the case of the soul. So Chrysippus conjectured that in defining *phantasiai* as *tupōseis* Zeno had only used the word *tupōsis* figuratively, in the sense of "alteration," and thus had intended to characterize *phantasiai* as certain alterations of the soul. Sextus remarks that the other Stoics did not accept that version either, and he describes and examines several additional possibilities that were suggested.

What is perhaps more to the point here, however, is that apparently the other Dogmatic schools used the term *phantasia* in their own ways. Thus Sextus gives an extended account (M 7.217ff.) of the Peripatetic use, described as quite different from that of the Stoics. According to the Peripatetics, he says, a *phantasia* is a change of state—a "motion" (*kinēma*), presumably in the very wide sense of that word, in which nearly every alteration is called a "motion" (cf. PH 3.63ff.). And the Academics defined the term in still another way. The several definitions are, all of them, much too vague to permit a serious judgment as to whether they are actually inconsistent with one another. It is nevertheless clear, I think, that all three schools agreed on the central role of these *phantasiai*, however characterized, in the acquisition of knowledge or justified belief.

Of course there is no use asking what Sextus himself means by the word *phantasia*, for, as would be expected from a Pyrrhonist, he is not convinced that the word, as used by the philosophers with whom he is arguing, means anything at all. When the Stoics offer their "apprehensive *phantasiai*" as the criteria for determining whether what appears to us to be the case is in fact the case, he comments:

> The first thing to say on this topic is that one cannot form a conception of *phantasia*. For they define a *phantasia* as an impression on the ruling part of the soul. But since the soul is either breath or something even more subtle than breath, as they say, nobody will be able to conceive of an "impression" on it, whether by way of raised and depressed areas, as we see in the case of seals, or by way of the mystical alteration they talk about. And certainly the soul would not be able to keep memories of all the principles that constitute an art [*technē*], since the previously existing alterations would be wiped off by the succeeding ones. But even if one could form a conception of it, the *phantasia* would not be apprehensible for, since it is a *pathos* of the ruling part, and the ruling part, as we have shown, is not apprehensible, we shall not apprehend a *pathos* of it, either.
>
> And further, even if we were to grant that the *phantasia* is apprehended, it would not be possible to make determinations about objects and states of affairs on the basis of it. For, as the Dogmatists say, the intellect does not of itself get in contact with external objects and receive *phantasiai* from them, but it does so by means of the senses; and the senses do not apprehend the external objects but only their own *pathē*, if anything. And so the *phantasia* will be of a sensory *pathos*, which is not the same thing as the external object. For example, the honey is not the same as my experiencing a sweet taste, nor the wormwood the same as my experiencing a bitter taste, but something different. And since this *pathos* differs from the external object, the *phantasia* will not be of the external object but of something different. So if the intellect makes determinations in accord with the *phantasia*, it does so foolishly and not in accord with the external object. Consequently, it is absurd to say that determinations about external matters are made according to *phantasiai* (PH 2.70–3).

Thus Sextus finds it impossible to form a conception of *phantasia* that coheres with the rest of what the Dogmatists believe, and for good measure he adds that even if it were conceivable it would not be apprehensible, and that even if apprehensible it would be epistemologically useless. It is true that in this passage he is referring explicitly to the Stoics only, but there is no reason to suppose that his view of the Peripatetic and Academic accounts would be any less skeptical. Hence we have to assume in this case, as in so many others, that when Sextus employs the Dogmatists' terminology he is not committing himself as to whether it makes sense, but is simply trying, as best he can, to use it in accord with what he takes to be the practice of the school in question.

Let us now look more closely at the Stoic, Peripatetic, and Academic definitions of the term in question. But first, for the sake of completeness, we may briefly note how Plato and Aristotle use it. Both of them do use it, though relatively infrequently and in such a way, unfortunately, as to throw very little light on what it may mean for Sextus or his opponents.

Socrates (at *Republic* 382e), arguing a point with Adeimantus, says that "a god is truthful in word and deed and does not deceive others, either in dreams or in waking moments, by *phantasiai*, by talk [*logoi*], or by signs." In the *Theaetetus*, discussing the doctrine of Protagoras, he observes that "in matters of warmth and everything of that sort," *phantasiai* and sensory perceptions (*aisthēseis*) are one and the same thing," since in such cases "to appear" denotes the same as "to be perceived" (152b–c). Later in the same discussion (160e) he argues that if Protagoras's doctrine is true, it is blatant folly for people to attempt to refute one another's *phantasiai* and opinions (*doxai*).

In the *Sophist* (at 263d ff.), the Stranger sets about distinguishing intelligent thought (*dianoia*), opinion or belief (*doxa*), and *phantasia*. He first says that intelligent thought is a particular kind of rational discourse (*logos*), namely, the silent inner discourse (*dialogos*) of the soul with itself. Affirmation or denial occurring in this silent discourse is called *doxa* (opinion or belief), "and when such a *pathos* [i.e., the opinion] occurs in somebody, not spontaneously but through sensory perception [*aisthēsis*], can that be correctly called anything but *phantasia?*" Continuing, he says that what we mean by "It appears that" is a mixture of sensory perception and opinion. So a *phantasia* is an appearance in which belief is mixed with sensory perception.

(In these texts the Loeb translator, H. N. Fowler, neatly translates *phantasia* as "fancy," with the footnote: "The English word 'fancy', though etymologically identical with the Greek *phantasia*, has lost the close connection with 'seeming' (*phainesthai*) which the Greek retains. The Greek word is therefore more comprehensive than the English, denoting that which appears to be, whether as the result of imagination or of sensation." [pp. 428–9n.].)

Aristotle (at *Metaphysics* 1010b3ff. and in many other places) contrasts a *phantasia* with a sensory perception (*aisthēsis*). *Phantasiai* may be true or false, but a sensory perception is never false. When the same wine seems sweet at one time and not sweet at another, it is not the senses but the *phantasia* that is telling us that the same thing both "is so and not so." In the cited passage the term *phantasia* is used continually in connection with the verb *phainesthai* (to appear), and in such a way as to suggest that *phantasiai* and appearances (*phainomena*) are one and the same. At *De caelo* 294a7 and 297b31 the identification is made explicit.

In the *De anima*, too, Aristotle seems for the most part to use *phantasia* in the sense of "appearance," but the analysis he gives of it is not very illuminating. He says (428a1ff.):

> If the *phantasia* is that with regard to which we say that some image or appearance [*phantasma*] occurs to us (and we are not speaking metaphorically), it is a capacity or state of mind by which we make judgments and true

or false assertions. Sensory perception [*aisthēsis*], belief [*doxa*], knowledge [*epistēmē*], and intelligence [*nous*], are such capacities.

He then explains that a *phantasia* is neither identical with any of the four capacities named, nor is it any compound of them. Yet in the same section he seems to contradict himself by accepting the Platonic analysis of it as a compound of sensory perception and belief; he says that for something to appear to a person is essentially for that person to believe what he has perceived with his senses. He gives an example: a *phantasia* that a thing is white is a combination of the sensation of white with the belief that the thing is white. As a general definition of the term he offers only "a *kinēsis* produced by sensation actively operating" (429a1).

Let us return now to the Hellenistic philosophers. The Stoics, as we have stated earlier, considered that knowledge is based on so-called "apprehensive *phantasiai*." They defined an apprehensive *phantasia* as "one that is derived from, and stamped and impressed in accord with, an existent object or state of affairs, and is such as would not arise from an object or state that was not existent" (PH 2.4). It "grabs you," and "drags you off to assent" (M 7.257). We shall discuss the apprehensive *phantasiai* further in the next section.

For the Peripatetics, too, *phantasiai* are essentially involved in the acquisition of knowledge and justified belief, but the emphasis is less on "force and vivacity" and more on the causal history and representative quality of the *phantasiai* concerned. Sextus explains:

> Aristotle, Theophrastus, and the Peripatetics generally, seeing that at the highest level the nature of things is two fold (for some things, as I said before, are sensible objects and others are objects of thought), give a twofold criterion: sense for the sensible objects and thought for the objects of thought, plus evidence in both cases, as Theophrastus said. First in order of time comes sense, the criterion that is independent of discourse and demonstration; but thought is first in order of potency, though in time it seems to come second as compared to sense. For the sense undergoes a change [*kineitai*] by the sensible objects, and as a result of this evident change [*kinēsis*] in the sense there supervenes a kind of change in the souls of those creatures that are superior and better and capable of initiating changes in themselves. This latter change is termed by the Peripatetics both a "memory" and a *phantasia*—a memory of the *pathos* relating to the sense and a *phantasia* of the sensible object producing the *pathos* in the sense. Hence they say that such a change is like a footprint, and just as that (I mean, the footprint) comes into being both by something and from something—by something, for instance, the pressure of the foot, and from something, for instance, Dion—so also the aforementioned change in the soul comes into being by something, the *pathos* relating to [*peri*] the sense, and from something, the sensible object, to which it preserves a kind of similarity. And this change, again, which is termed both a "memory" and a *phantasia*, contains in itself yet a third and supervenient change, that of the *logikē phantasia*, which occurs consequent to our decision and choice. (M 7.217–21).

If we spell out the footprint analogy, we get: just as Dion, by the pressure of his foot, produces a footprint, so also the sensible object, by the *pathos* of (or relating to) the sense, produces the *phantasia*. The footprint results from the pressure of the foot; so, presumably, the *phantasia* is something that results from the *pathos*, that is, from what happens to the soul. But while it is easy to distinguish the footprint from the pressure of the foot, it is not so easy to distinguish the *phantasia* from the *pathos*. Perhaps this is because we are inclined to treat both *pathos* and *phantasia* as categorematic terms, denoting entities that need to be distinguished from one another.

Sextus gives no illustrative examples, but let us try to construct one for ourselves. Suppose that from a distance we see Dion approaching. Sextus's account suggests that, according to the Peripatetics, what goes on in us is something like the following. First, our sensory apparatus undergoes a change. From this there results (via a *pathos* of the soul) a change of state in the soul, a *phantasia* that something—not yet determined—is approaching. As we gradually recognize what it is and who it is, there "supervenes" another change in the soul, another *phantasia*. This one is called a *logikē phantasia* (a discourse-ready *phantasia*), that is, a *phantasia* the content of which is fit to be expressed in words (M 8.70). In accord with it we may say "There's a man" or "There's Dion"; we have made a choice as to who it is and what it is, and are experiencing a somewhat different *phantasia*. Presumably the first kind of *phantasiai* are experienced by all animals, but only human beings have *logikai phantasiai*; just to see Dion is one sort of experience, which even a chicken could have, but seeing him *as* Dion and as a man is another, bound up with the capacity for discourse (*logos*) (cf. M 8.269ff.).

Diogenes Laertius, at 7.51, says that the *phantasiai* that are not *logikai* are *alogoi*, which R. D. Hicks, the Loeb translator, translates as "irrational." But obviously there is nothing irrational about such a *phantasia*; it merely lacks a content that can be expressed in speech (*logos*). The "irrational" (*alogoi*) animals are not crazy; their deficiency is that their *phantasiai* are not fit to be expressed in words. This is part of the Dogmatists' doctrine, as is attested by Sextus:

> They [the Dogmatists] say that it is not by uttered speech [*logos prophorikos*] that man differs from the non-rational animals, for crows and parrots and jays utter articulate sounds, but he differs by internal speech; nor does he differ merely by having *phantasiai*, for they have *phantasiai* too, but by having *phantasiai* that are produced by inference and combination. (M 8.275)

Unlike the Stoics and Peripatetics, the Academics (or, more properly, the members of the New Academy) considered that there is no criterion of truth, no way at all to reach the truth, whether by reason, sense perception, or *phantasiai* (M 7.158). In other words, their view was that nothing is apprehensible (PH 1.226, but cf. 1.235).

They defined a *phantasia* as "a kind of *pathos* of a living creature, one that is capable of bringing before the mind both itself and something else."

For example, says Antiochus, when we look at something our sense of sight is conditioned in a certain way, and not in the same way as it was before we looked; and in accord with such an alteration we perceive two things, one the alteration itself, and secondly that which produces the alteration, that is, the object seen. And similarly in the case of the other senses. For, just as light shows both itself and all the things that are in it, so also the *phantasia*, which is the leading factor in the cognition of living creatures, must, after the manner of light, both manifest itself and be indicative of the evident object that produced it. (M 7.162–3)

Being of such a nature, the *phantasia* will have two aspects, one pertaining to the object, and the other pertaining to the subject experiencing it. In relation to the former aspect, the *phantasia* is either true or false, true when it accords with the object and false when it does not. But in relation to the aspect pertaining to the experiencing subject, one kind of *phantasia* is apparently true and another is not apparently true; of these, the apparently true is called by the Academics... a "plausible" [*pithanē*] *phantasia*. (M 7.168–9)

Moreover, according to these Academics not all "plausible" *phantasiai* are equal. Some are just plausible, some are plausible and "tested" (*periodeumenai*), and some are plausible, tested, and "stable" (*aperispastoi*). Sextus shows the difference between a merely plausible *phantasia* and a *phantasia* that is plausible and tested in an example:

For example, when a rope is lying coiled up in a dark room, a person who enters the room suddenly gets a simply plausible *phantasia* that it is a snake, but to the person who has looked carefully around and considered the circumstances—for example, that it does not move, that it is of such and such a color, and so on—it appears to be a rope, in accord with a *phantasia* that is plausible and tested. (PH 1.227–8; cf. M 7.187–8)

In addition, a *phantasia* is stable if it is part of a coherent chain or concurrence of plausible *phantasiai*. Sextus gives another example to illustrate this. *Phantasiai* are said not to occur in isolation but connected with one another, like the links in a chain. Thus,

Anyone experiencing a *phantasia* of a man must necessarily have a *phantasia* both of his personal qualities, such as color, size, shape, motion, speech, dress, footgear, and of things external to him, such as air, light, daytime, sky, earth, friends, and all the rest. And whenever none of these *phantasiai* disconcert us by appearing false, but all with one accord appear true, we are the more inclined to have belief. (M 7.176–7)

Hence a stable *phantasia* is one that, concurring with the others in its associated collection, produces belief in this way (M 7.182). (At PH 1.228 a quite different example of a stable *phantasia* is offered, but something appears to be wrong with the text at that point; cf. also M 7.254ff.). Sextus says that the adherents of the New Academy prefer the plausible and tested *phantasia* to the simply plausible, and to both of these the *phantasia* that is plausible, tested, and stable (PH 1.229).

In the corresponding passage at M 7.174f. a somewhat different account is given, implying that the ascending order is: plausible, plausible and stable, plausible and stable and tested. But the two accounts are consistent if, as I think likely, what is meant is that, while both the plausible-stable and plausible-tested combinations are more credible than the simply plausible, only *phantasiai* that have all three attributes are sufficient to produce seriously justified belief.

So much for what the Stoics, Peripatetics, and Academics say about *phantasiai*. However, their actual employment of the term, as reflected in Sextus's argumentation against them, exhibits some additional features that need to be pointed out.

We have seen earlier that in Sextus's account of Pyrrhonism and its competing philosophies, as well as in Greek philosophy generally, such phrases as "the externally existing objects" (*ta ektos hupokeimena*) and "the things that are" (*ta onta*) must be understood to refer not only to individuals but also to states of affairs. Thus, an "external object" may be a tower, an oar, or an invisible pore in the skin, but it may also be the fact that the tower is square or the fact that the oar is not broken. Similarly, expressions like *to on* and *to hupokeimenon* ("what is," "being") cover both "what exists" and "what is the case." Thus, that Socrates is alive is given as an example of a nonexistent object (M 7.391). In the next section we shall see that the term "apprehension" has a similarly wide use. One may be said to apprehend a thing, like a boat or a city or a person, but one is also said to apprehend that such and such is the case.

The same breadth of use (or shall we characterize it as an ambiguity?) applies to the term *phantasia*. That of which the *phantasia* is a *phantasia*, or that from which the *phantasia* arises, is called the *phantaston*. In a given case the *phantaston* may be a thing, like a person, an egg, a bow, an arrow (M 7.406). But there are also *phantasiai* of states of affairs, such as are expressed by the phrases "This thing is white" and "This thing is sweet."

> For in order to grasp what is true in the external objects one must not only be affected by a sensation of whiteness or sweetness but must also be brought to a *phantasia* of such a fact [*pragma*] as "this thing is sweet" or "this thing is white." And similarly in the case of the other senses. (M 7.344)

Further, it is clear that *phantasiai* need not be pictorial or connected in any simple way with sensory perception. Some *phantasiai* (and appearances) are immediately derivable from sense perception, but others, more abstract, are ascribable to the intellect. For example, at M 7.243 Sextus mentions a pair of *phantasiai*, one that the number of the stars is even, and the other that it is odd. At PH 2.76 we read that Xeniades of Corinth had a *phantasia* in accord with which he asserted that no *phantasia* is worthy of credence. In the same vein, at M 7.390 there is mention of a *phantasia* according to which not every *phantasia* is true. At M 7.418 Sextus speaks of an apprehensive *phantasia* that "Fifty is a few" and a non-apprehensive *phantasia* that "Ten thousand is a few." There is even a discussion of whether, when a dog is chasing a wild animal by following its tracks, the dog has a *phantasia* of "If this is its footprint, then the animal is in that direction." Sextus argues that the dog cannot have such a *phantasia*; the reason is not that there are no *phantasiai* corresponding to conditional sentences, but simply that the dog is *alogos*, that is, he does not possess the use of language (M 8.269ff.).

*Phantasiai* are said to arise "from" (*apo*) things and to be "of" (genitive case) things. It is initially tempting to find in this a distinction between that which causes the *phantasia* and that which the *phantasia* is "of." Thus, in the rope-snake example, the *phantasia* would be from the rope and of a snake. But alas, in the relevant contexts Sextus seems to use the preposition *apo* and the genitive construction interchangeably.

As to whether there can be *phantasiai* from nonexistent objects, Sextus represents both the Stoics and the Academics as agreeing that this is in principle possible, but as differing on the crucial question of whether a *phantasia* from a nonexistent object could be indistinguishable from one that is from an existent object. On the other hand, in an argument at M 11.220 Sextus uses as a premise the flat-out assertion that the nonexistent cannot excite a *phantasia*, and elsewhere he argues that there cannot be a *phantasia* of a proof because a proof is composed of propositions (*axiōmata*), and propositions are *lekta*, and *lekta* do not exist. Thus the evidence on this particular question seems contradictory.

In short, what all this seems to show is that the term *phantasia* is an early but typical member of that large and very suspect collection of quasi-technical words that epistemologists have used as names of certain entities that we are supposed to experience directly and through which we obtain knowledge or justified belief about the external world. Modern additions to this class are "impressions," "ideas," "perceptions," "sense-data," "sensa," "images," "intentional objects," "the given," "the sensible manifold," and perhaps the word "experience" itself. I think it fair to say that while, on the one hand, none of these terms has ever been satisfactorily defined or even introduced with reasonably clear conditions governing its use, on the other hand it would be disingenuous to pretend that we have no grasp whatever of what they are supposed to mean. All of them are clearly rooted in the questionable notion that when it appears to us that such and such is the case, what "directly" appears is something that is mind dependent, and that on the basis of the attributes of this mental entity we conclude that such and such is the case (or, if we are cautious, that such and such appears to be the case) in the mind-independent world. For example, we are invited to believe that when it appears to us that the sweater is blue, there is present to our mind an entity that may be called a "sweater appearance" or "sense datum" and that really is blue; and that in this situation the conventions of language allow us properly to assert, looking to this appearance, that 'The sweater is blue' or 'It appears that the sweater is blue'. Admittedly, the mental entity will not in all cases have qualities identical with those that the external object appears to have, but the latter qualities are to be inferred in some way from the former, or from the former plus other "data" of the same kind, or, perhaps, from the other "data" alone.

It is striking that when we read modern epistemologists we find that every one of the aforementioned quasi-technical terms, like our ancient term *phantasia*, is brought in explicitly or implicitly in connection with the verb "to appear" or one of its synonyms. A good example is the introduction of the term "sensa" by C. D. Broad (1923), who was surely one of the more astute and careful workers in this vineyard.

> Whenever I truly judge that *x* appears to me to have the sensible quality *q*, what happens is that I am directly aware of a certain object *y*, which (a) really does have the quality *q*, and (b) stands in some peculiarly intimate relation, yet to be determined, to *x* . . . . Such objects as *y* I am going to call *Sensa*. Thus, when I look at a penny from the side, what happens, on the present theory, is at least this: I have a sensation, whose object is an elliptical, brown sensum; and this sensum is related in some specially intimate way to a certain round physical object, viz., the penny. (Broad, 1923, pp. 239–40)

Broad gives a familiar example:

> Consider, e.g., the case of looking at a stick which is half in water and half in air. We say that it looks bent. And we certainly do not mean by this that we mistakenly judge it to be bent; we generally make no such mistake. We are aware of an object which is very much like what we should be aware of if we were looking at a stick with a physical kink in it, immersed wholly in air. The most obvious analysis of the facts is that, when we judge that a straight stick *looks* bent, we are aware of an object which really *is* bent, and which is related in a peculiarly intimate way to the physically straight stick. The relation cannot be that of identity; since the same thing cannot at once be bent and straight, in the same sense of these words. (Broad, 1923, p. 241)

Nowadays this type of account is frequently attacked by challenging the presumption that whenever it appears to us that such and such is the case, there must be present some sort of entity — an "appearance" or "datum" — with qualities of which we are directly aware and on the basis of which we make our judgment of what is, or at least appears to be, the case. But this kind of attack is ineffectual against the Pyrrhonist, for it is by no means clear that Sextus, or even the Dogmatists he criticizes, made any such assumption in their use of the term *phantasia*. A more likely hypothesis, I think, is that they used this term, like the term *phainomenon*, syncategorematically. Thus, to say that a person *A* has a *phantasia* that *P* may be nothing more than to say that *A*'s soul is in the kind of state normally describable by the sentence 'It appears to *A* that *P*.' If this is so, it would justify our using "appearance" as a translation for *phantasia*, as Annas and Barnes have done. (But that would leave us with "what appears" as a translation for *to phainomenon*, and, as was explained earlier, this would carry the misleading suggestion that *to phainomenon* was part of the external world.)

## 8. Apprehension

Closely related to the term *phantasia* in the Dogmatists' epistemologies is the verb *katalambanō*. The literal meaning of this verb is "to grasp" or "to catch hold of". Some texts (e.g., Cicero *Academica* 2.145) suggest that what is supposed to be "grasped" is the external object or the *phantasia*; others (e.g., M 7.257) indicate that it is the perceiver, who is "practically grabbed by the hair and dragged off to assent." So we do not quite understand the metaphor, but from Sextus's usage and that of his opponents we can see that in any case there is no really satisfactory English equivalent for the term. With misgivings I have decided to follow Bury and most of the critical literature in English by translating it as "apprehend," even though the reader can hardly be expected to wring very much of its meaning out of that vague word.

As would be expected, *katalambanō* and its various cognate forms play a conspicuous role in Sextus's critique. In argument after argument he draws the conclusion that, if you go by what the Dogmatists say, this or that is not apprehensible. The list of items for which he reaches such a conclusion is long; it includes criteria, signs, meanings, propositions, arguments, proofs, causes, bodies, intellects, and human beings — not to mention the so-called "art of living" and the existence of gods. And from the non-apprehensibility he usually draws the further conclusion that (again going by what the Dogmatists say) the various items listed simply do not exist.

The adjective *kataleptos*, which I am ordinarily rendering as "apprehensible," can also mean "apprehended." In most of Sextus's argumentation involving this term and its corresponding privative, *akataleptos*, the difference turns out to be relatively unimportant; for to prove, by a philosophical argument that employs no empirical premises and relies on meanings alone, that something is not apprehended is in effect to prove that it is not apprehensible. But occasionally the difference does seem to make a difference, as at M 7.156, where, arguing within the Stoic framework, Sextus defines *doxa* (belief) as "assent to *akatalepta*," that is, "assent to what is not apprehended."

Although Sextus regards apprehension as an essential element in the epistemologies of all three of the principal Dogmatic schools, he gives explicit attention primarily to what the Stoics say about it. He tells us, first, that they describe it as something "in between" knowledge (*epistēmē*) and belief (*doxa*):

> For they [the Stoics] say that three things are connected with one another: knowledge, belief and, midway between these two, apprehension; and of these, knowledge is apprehension that is steadfast and firm and not liable to change by argument, belief is weak and false assent, and apprehension, being between them, is assent to an apprehensive *phantasia*; and an apprehensive *phantasia*, according to them, is one that is true and of such a kind as would not be false. Moreover, they say that, of these, knowledge is found only in the wise and belief only in the less capable, but apprehension is common to both and is the criterion of truth. (M 7.151–2)

I take this to mean that knowledge is steadfast, firm, unchanging assent to a *phantasia* that is true and is of a kind that would not be false. Belief is weak assent to a *phantasia*, which may be true or may be false. Apprehension is any kind of assent, steadfast or not, to an apprehensive *phantasia*.

The Stoic definition of apprehension, according to Sextus, was "assent to an apprehensive [*kataleptike*] *phantasia*," and an apprehensive *phantasia* was defined as "a *phantasia* that is from [*apo*] an existent object and has been imprinted and impressed in accord with the existent object, and is such as would not come about from a nonexistent object." (Here, as usual, the so-called "objects" must include states of affairs.) Cicero (*Academica* 2.77) indicates that Zeno's original definition of "apprehensive *phantasia*" did not contain the last of the above clauses and that this clause was added later in response to his Academic opponent, Arcesilaus, who claimed that a *phantasia* from a nonexistent object might be just like (*eiusdem modi*) one from an existent object. Cicero's remark is confirmed by Sextus in the following passage:

> An apprehensive *phantasia* is one that is from an existent object and has been imprinted and impressed in accord with the existent object, and is such as would not come about from a nonexistent object. For, holding that this *phantasia* is to the highest degree perceptive of the external objects and exactly reproduces all their peculiarities, they [the Stoics] say that it possesses each of the following features as an attribute. The first is that it comes about from an existent object; for many *phantasiai* occur from what is nonexistent, as in the case of madmen, and these *phantasiai* would not be apprehensive. The second is that it is both from and in accord with the existent object. For some, again, are from an existent object but do not resemble it, as we showed a little while ago in the case of the mad Orestes. For he got a *phantasia* from an existent object, Electra, but not in accord with that object, since he supposed that she was one of the Furies.... [Pentheus], too, was affected by an existent object, Thebes, but not in accord with that object [he saw it double; cf. Euripides, *Bacchae* 918], whereas the apprehensive *phantasia* must be in accord with the object itself. And it must also be imprinted and impressed, in order that all the distinguishing features of the objects of the *phantasiai* be exactly embossed. For just as sculptors apply themselves to all parts of what they are sculpting, and the seals on rings always imprint all their distinctive marks exactly on the wax, so also anyone apprehending external objects must attend to all their properties. And they [the Stoics] added "and is such as would not come about from a nonexistent object," since the Academics, unlike the Stoics, did not suppose it impossible that a *phantasia* will be found that is exactly similar in all respects. For the Stoics say that he who has an apprehensive *phantasia* attends with exactitude to the distinctive differences in the objects, especially since such a *phantasia*, as compared with the others, has a kind of special character.... But the Academics say that, on the contrary, a false *phantasia* that is exactly similar to an apprehensive *phantasia* can be found. (M 7.248–52)

Sextus adds that later Stoics said that the apprehensive *phantasia* is not always a criterion of truth, but only "when it has no obstacle." He gives a couple of examples of such "obstacles"; in both cases they are general considerations that led the person who had the *phantasia* to conclude that "in spite of all appearances, that just *could not* be the case."

Obviously the Stoic definition of "apprehensive *phantasia*," while it is better than nothing, leaves much to be desired as regards clarity. Even the division of the clauses is not clear. In the definition at section 248 the second condition is given as "and has been imprinted and impressed in accord with the existent object," while in section 249 the second condition is "is both from an existent object and in accord with the existent object." And in section 250 the phrase "it must be imprinted and impressed" is treated separately.

At any rate the second condition, however formulated, requires that the *phantasia* be "in accord with [*kata*] the existent object." Why was Orestes' *phantasia* not "in accord with" Electra? We are told that it was because "he believed [M 7.170] or supposed [M 7.249] her to be one of the Furies," or because "the *phantasia* was taken as being of a Fury" (M 7.245). "It seemed to him that he was seeing the Furies" (M 9.63). The presumed cause of the *phantasia*, Electra, did not have the attributes that Orestes, going by the *phantasia*, thought she did.

It is unclear whether the Stoics meant that in this case there was something wrong with the *phantasia* itself. That is, they may have meant that what Orestes had to go on was, as it were, a defective picture of Electra, or they may have thought that although the *phantasia* was a satisfactory enough picture of Electra, Orestes in his madness took it to be a picture of a Fury. In the former case, the "picture," if we keep this questionable metaphor, must itself have had features that prevented it from being apprehensive and that perhaps could have been detected if he had been in a condition to "attend to it with the exactitude of a skilled craftsman." On the other hand, Sextus says (M 7.245) that "insofar as the *phantasia* affected Orestes as being from an existing object, it was true, but insofar as it affected him as being from a Fury, it was false, for there was no Fury." This suggests that the fault was not in the *phantasia* but in the way in which, because of his madness, Orestes was affected by it. In that case, the apprehensiveness of a *phantasia* would be relative to the condition of the apprehending person, and additional parameters would have to be built into the definition; instead of a definition of "*phantasia F* is apprehensive" we would need one for "*phantasia F* is apprehensive for person *A* in condition *C*."

For the "imprinted and impressed" clause in the Stoic definition we are unfortunately not given a relevant example, but Michael Frede, in his classic study of this entire matter ("Clear and Distinct Impressions," in Frede [1987], 151–76) is probably right when he suggests (164) that it amounts to the requirement that the *phantasia* be clear and distinct.

In the last of the conditions, namely, "and is such as would not come about from a nonexistent object" (*hopoia ouk an genoito apo mē huparchontos*), most commentators read "could not" instead of "would not"; the Greek can be taken either way. The difference seems to me to be of crucial philosophical importance, at least if the occurrence of "could not" in the definition is understood to imply that it is absolutely impossible, "by definition," for an apprehensive *phantasia* to be just like a false *phantasia*.

The "could not" interpretation is supported not only by the references to possibility in the M 7.248–52 passage we have quoted above, but also by

Cicero, who recounts an imaginary dialogue between the Stoic Zeno and the Academic skeptic Arcesilaus. Arcesilaus is questioning Zeno:

> What if the wise man, who is not supposed to have mere opinions, were unable to apprehend anything? Zeno no doubt replied that the wise man wouldn't have to opine, because there is indeed something that he could apprehend. What would that be? A *phantasia*, no doubt. What sort of *phantasia*? At this point Zeno defined it [the *phantasia kataleptike*] as one that is impressed and sealed and moulded from something that exists, exactly as it exists. The next question was whether this would apply even if a true *phantasia* could be just like a false one. At this point Zeno was smart enough to see that if a *phantasia* from an existent object were such that one from a nonexistent object could be exactly like it, no *phantasia* could be apprehended. Arcesilaus agreed that this addition to the definition was appropriate, for neither a false *phantasia* nor a true one could be apprehended if the latter were just like what a false one would be; however, he pushed the discussion forward with determination in order to establish that no *phantasia* from a true object was such that it could not have been from a false one. (*Acad.* 2.77)

Now if part of the very definition of an apprehensive *phantasia* is that it *cannot* be false, then when on the basis of an apprehensive *phantasia* you judge that *P*, you *cannot*—by definition—be wrong. But of course this is of no help to the epistemologist in his struggle with the problem of knowledge. It simply pushes the problem around, for whereas previously the difficulty was to explain why experiencing certain relevant apprehensive *phantasiai* justifies beliefs about the external world, now it is to explain how one is to recognize these *phantasiai* as apprehensive. Furthermore, Hume has taught us that "whatever is distinguishable is separable in thought, and whatever is separable in thought is separable in fact"; and the whole discussion surely presupposes that the occurrence of *phantasiai* is at least "distinguishable in thought" from the existence of corresponding external objects; it seems, therefore, that we ought to infer that there can be no necessary connection between the two, and hence that there is literally no such thing as a *phantasia* that *must* be from an existent object or that *must* be true (cf. M 7.154).

If, on the other hand, we read the condition as "and is such as *would* not come from a nonexistent object," as I recommend, we no longer put the Stoics in the position of trying to solve by definition the fundamental problem of finding a criterion for distinguishing true *phantasiai* from false. All kinds of factual matters, such as the clarity and distinctness of the given *phantasia*, the fate of judgments based on past *phantasiai* of that kind, the perceiver's own condition and the external conditions during his experience of the *phantasia*, the testimony of others, and so on, would be relevant to a claim on the perceiver's part that "*that* kind of *phantasia* would never be just a product of my imagination."

It also seems to me that if the Stoics had meant to tell us that it is by definition impossible for a false *phantasia* to be just like an apprehensive *phantasia*, the verbs *dunatai* and *endechetai* were available in philosophical Greek to express that thought. I think their claim is rather that, as a matter of fact and not merely by definition, any *phantasia* that was intrinsically just like an apprehensive *phantasia* would nevertheless be distinguishable in other ways from mere hallucinations or other kinds of illusory experience not derived (in a "natural" way) from the external world.

It has been objected that the added condition, thus interpreted, is already a consequence of the first and second conditions. That this is not so can be illustrated from the Academic example about the snake and the coil of rope (see PH 1.227–8, M 7.187–8). The *phantasia* of the snake was from an external object, the rope, and it might have resembled in every noticeable respect a *phantasia* that would arise from a snake coiled up in the corner of the dark room. In other words, each apparent feature common to the appearance of a coil of rope and to that of a coiled snake in that situation was "imprinted and impressed" on the perceiver. So the *phantasia* may have satisfied the first two Stoic conditions. But afterwards the perceiver, by looking for motion and by poking with a stick, finds that the *phantasia* fails the added condition; it is indeed such as would under such circumstances come from a nonexistent object. In short, it might be that a *phantasia* from an existent object could depict a nonexistent object so faithfully that no amount of scrutiny of it alone would reveal its deceptiveness. As suggested by the New Academy, further information about other *phantasiai*, the perceiver, and the external world would be required.

To all of this it needs to be added, however, that in substituting "would" for "could" and thereby excusing the Stoics from trying to define the criterion problem out of existence, we do not extricate them from the Skeptic's net. For the Skeptic is not only pointing out the difficulty of distinguishing apprehensive *phantasiai* from those that are not apprehensive; he is challenging the claim that there are any apprehensive *phantasiai* at all, given the Dogmatists' characterizations of these *phantasiai*. He argues that without even having a consistent concept of *phantasia* there is no way for anyone to support a claim that a particular *phantasia* is "such as would not come about from a nonexistent object or state of affairs."

Before we leave this subject, there are several features of the grammar of "to apprehend" that deserve mention because they will draw our attention to a philosophically significant aspect of the matter that might otherwise escape our notice. We see that in general the verb is used in such a way that sometimes one is said to apprehend the *phantasia* and sometimes the external object or state of affairs, and sometimes both. (The last would fit well with the claim by some of the Dogmatists that the nature of *phantasiai* is to "reveal" both themselves and the objects that produce them). For the most part "to apprehend" takes a "that" clause, as in "to apprehend that pleasure is the good" (PH 2.5), and this seems to be the fundamental use. But frequently we find expressions of the form "to apprehend an $X$"; for example, "to apprehend a cause" (PH 3.23ff.), "to apprehend a *pathos*" (PH 1.215), "to apprehend Socrates." Usually this form seems reducible to the form "to apprehend $Y$ as an $X$" or to "to apprehend that $Y$ is an $X$."

However, the reduction can be made in either of two non-equivalent ways, giving rise to a bothersome ambiguity. In most of its occurrences, "*A* apprehends an *X*" appears to be equivalent to "A apprehends something as being an *X*." In this use, "to apprehend a man" means to apprehend something — for example, Socrates — as being a man, while to apprehend a cause is to apprehend something as being a cause, and to apprehend Socrates is to apprehend something as being Socrates. But there are also a number of instances, like the aforementioned "to apprehend a *pathos*," in which "*A* apprehends an *X*" seems to mean "*A* apprehends an *X* as being something." Accordingly, "to apprehend a *pathos*" would not mean "to apprehend something as being a *pathos*," but rather "to apprehend a *pathos* as being something" — for example, as being a sweet taste or a pain or the color green, or whatever. Thus, while Sextus apparently requires that in order to apprehend a cause one must apprehend something as being a cause (which cannot be done without having a concept of cause), he does not, I think, require that in order to apprehend a *pathos* one must have a concept of *pathos*. After all, we are told that we all apprehend our own *pathē* — indeed, nothing but our own *pathē* — but presumably not everybody has a concept of *pathos*. The frequently occurring phrase "to apprehend a *phantasia*" seems to be like "to apprehend a *pathos*"; it would have to mean "to apprehend a *phantasia* as being *of* something."

It thus appears that there are at least two senses of "to apprehend," one of which implies possession of a concept while the other does not. There is, however, still another complication. In a very interesting though somewhat puzzling passage at the beginning of Book 2 of the *Outlines*, where Sextus is arguing against the Stoics and the Epicureans, he distinguishes a pair of senses both of which imply possession of a concept. In the first of these, '*A* apprehends an *X*' amounts to 'There is something, an *X*, that *A* apprehends as an *X*'; this seems to be the same as the first of the two senses noted above. In this sense, Sextus stresses, apprehending involves the existence of what is apprehended; to say that Smith apprehends a donkey would be to imply that there exists something, a donkey, that Smith takes to be a donkey. But in the other, much weaker and rather odd, sense that Sextus now describes, '*A* apprehends an *X*' does not imply that there exists anything, let alone an *X*, that *A* takes to be an *X*; only *A*'s having a concept of *X* is said to be necessary. In this weaker sense, if we say that *A* apprehends a donkey we do not imply the existence of a donkey or of anything else that he takes to be a donkey, but only that *A* knows what a donkey is. Sextus considers it obvious that the stronger sense is required if apprehension is to justify belief, but he finds that this stronger sense leads to *aporia*. Here he does not object to apprehension in the weaker sense, but elsewhere he raises questions as to whether there are coherent concepts corresponding to most of the principal terms used in the Dogmatists' philosophies, and consequently whether in these cases apprehension is possible at all.

Thus we end up with at least three senses of "to apprehend." In all three, if I am not mistaken, *A*'s apprehending an *X* (or that *X* is the case) involves

*A*'s having a *phantasia* of (or that) *X*. In one sense — by far the most common — '*A* apprehends an *X*' amounts, as we have said, to 'There is something, an *X*, that *A* takes to be an *X*'. Thus '*A* apprehends a cause', as used in Sextus's argumentation about causes, seems equivalent to 'There is something that is a cause and that *A* takes to be a cause'. This requires that *A* have a concept of cause, that is, that he know what it is to be a cause, so that he can recognize one when he meets it. In the second sense, in order for *A* to apprehend an *X* it is only necessary that he have a concept of *X* (and presumably be experiencing a *phantasia* of *X*). Macbeth could be apprehending a dagger even when there was no dagger before him. But, as Sextus points out, this kind of apprehension does not justify assent to propositions about the external world. In the third sense, which Sextus never discusses explicitly but nevertheless appears to use in certain cases, *A* can apprehend an *X* without having any concept of *X*; everyone apprehends *phantasiai* and his own *pathē*. I have conjectured that even in this case the underlying notion is "to apprehend *X* as being *Y*," and that although one does not need concepts of *phantasia* and *pathē* in order to apprehend these items, they cannot be apprehended without being apprehended as something.

It needs to be repeated, however, that most of the time "to apprehend" is used by Sextus in such a way as to imply that the possession of a satisfactory concept of *X* is a necessary, though not sufficient, condition for apprehending an *X*. Indeed, in one passage he states this condition without qualification:

> If then, this criterion [i.e., human beings, proposed by the Dogmatists as the "by whom" criterion; cf. PH 2.21] is to be apprehended, it must be conceived well beforehand, inasmuch as conception in every case precedes apprehension. But up to now human beings have turned out to be inconceivable, as we shall establish. Therefore, human beings are certainly not apprehensible. (M 7. 263–4)

The logic of "to apprehend," as well as its grammar, throws a certain amount of additional light on its meaning. There are several ways in which Sextus attempts to refute a claim that a person *A* apprehends that *Y* is an *X* or apprehends *Y* as an *X*. The principal one of these, as we have seen, is to show that *A* does not even have an acceptable concept of *X* (i.e., does not know what it would be for something to be an *X*); this may be ascribed to some inadequacy of *A*, or, more likely when philosophical matters are under discussion, it is inferred from there being no such concept because the definitions given are incoherent. A second way in which Sextus tries to refute an apprehension claim is to argue that, even if *A* had a satisfactory concept, there would be insuperable obstacles (e.g., *A* might have to examine an infinite number of cases) to his discovering that something is an *X*. In still other cases Sextus presents arguments of the following form: since *X* is by definition *YZ* and *Y* or *Z* is not apprehensible, neither is *X*. For example,

> Even if one could form a concept of the *phantasia*, the *phantasia* would not be apprehensible; for since it is a *pathos* of the ruling part [of the soul] and the ruling part, as we have shown, is not apprehensible, we shall not be able to apprehend a *pathos* of it either. (PH 2.71)

Note that the principle involved here is more than a simple consequence of the presumed fact that you cannot have a concept of $YZ$ without having concepts of $Y$ and $Z$.

Consider some of Sextus's examples. One cannot apprehend that this or that object is a human being, or apprehend it as a human being, if one does not even know what a human being is. Similarly, in order for a person to apprehend a cause, that is, to apprehend something as being a cause, that person must at least know what a cause is; this amounts to knowing what it would be for something to be a cause, or equivalently, it amounts to grasping the sense of the word "cause" or that of one of its synonyms in some language. Accordingly, in his arguments Sextus presents a number of considerations indicating that ("going by what the Dogmatists say") nobody could have a conception of human being or of cause, and he infers from this that nobody could apprehend a human being or a cause; he seems also to think that this implies that, if we go by what the Dogmatists say, there is no such thing as a human being or a cause. (At the same time, however, in accord with the Skeptic methodology of balancing argument against argument, he tips his hat to common belief by agreeing that of course it is also plausible that there do exist human beings and that there do exist causes.)

On the other hand, when considering the proposition "The number of the stars is even" (PH 2.90), he does not suggest that the concept or concepts involved are incoherent and that we therefore do not understand what is being asserted. Rather, he observes that there is no way of determining whether the proposition is true. He argues that it is not "evident" and that attempts to prove it will have to be based on other nonevident propositions and will lead to an infinite regress. Whatever we may think of this argument, we can see that here the non-apprehensibility of $Y$ being an $X$ is inferred from the claim that even if no question is raised about the concept $X$ (even number), there are insuperable obstacles to ascertaining that $Y$ (the number of the stars) falls under it.

A further example of this latter tack is to be found at PH 1.126, where it is argued that (again "going by what the Dogmatists say") we cannot accurately apprehend by the sense of sight that $Y$ is an $X$ — for example, that the rose is red — for the physiology of vision is supposed to be such that we always see not only $Y$ but the combination or "mixture" of $Y$ and the membranes and liquids contained in our eyes. Once more, it is not for the moment challenged that we have such concepts as that of "red"; instead it is observed that, on the Dogmatists' account of sensory perception, what we see when we look at the rose to ascertain its color is not the rose alone but the combination of the rose and the fluids and lens of the eye, so that the color perceived depends not only on the color of the rose but on the properties of the membranes and liquids in the eye.

What seems philosophically most significant in all this is that the logic of "to apprehend" is essentially different from that of "to see" and the various other perception verbs, such as "to hear" and "to taste," that serve as basic undefined terms in modern epistemologies, especially those in the Anglo-American tradition. These epistemologies usually treat "to see" and all the other perception verbs as extensional and thus, in effect, as subject to the laws of ordinary predicate logic. Seeing is treated as a direct relation between a perceiver and an object perceived; whether the relation holds in a given case is it is independent of any thought or judgment the perceiver may have about the nature of what he is perceiving. Thus it is considered perfectly possible for you to see an $X$ even if you do not know what an $X$ is. And if an $X$ is a $Y$, and you are seeing an $X$, then you are seeing a $Y$ whether you know it or not; and if you are seeing an $X$, then there exists something that you are seeing; and so on. But none of this applies to the verb "to apprehend" when it is used for the Stoic *katalambanein*. Instead, its logic will be more like that of the expressions "to see as" and "to see that." If you do not know what it is to be an $X$ — or, in other words, if you do not have a concept of $X$ — then you cannot see something as an $X$, in the sense of seeing that something is or looks like an $X$.

In the Anglo-American tradition we rely so heavily on the extensionality of perception verbs that when the perceived object does not exist we are strongly inclined to invent an "intended object" for the perceiver to be related to. If Jones sees a pink rat, and there is no pink rat, we feel pressure to supply an object, whether an "intended pink rat," a sense datum, a sensum, or whatever, so that he will stand in the seeing relation to *something*. We are very reluctant to agree that in such a case "he sees nothing," for that locution has by convention a far different and more complex meaning.

It has to be granted, I think, that for the epistemologists' purposes the intensional notion of "apprehending *as*" promises, at least at first glance, to be more useful than the extensional notions that figure in modern accounts. After all, the epistemologists' goal is to give an acceptable account, in a vocabulary that is not question-begging, of what must be true of an individual $A$ and the rest of the world if

$A$ knows that $P$

or

$A$ believes, with good grounds, that $P$

is to be true. But in these sentences the subsentence $P$ occurs obliquely, so that their truth value depends in part on $A$'s attitude toward the proposition or thought expressed by $P$. Thus intensionality is involved, and there will always be a gap in any argument that tries to infer, even with probability rather than with strict logic, one of these sentences from premises expressing only an extensional relation between $A$ and certain objects external to $A$ — whether these objects are things denoted by the components of $P$ or are sense data or other items "directly" perceived by $A$. By contrast, there is no parallel logical difficulty (though no doubt there are plenty of other problems) in supporting one of the above sentences by

$A$ apprehends a *phantasia* that $P$.

Suppose, for example, that $A$ remarks to $B$: "The bus has gone by." $B$ asks, "How do you know that?" and $A$ replies, "Because I saw it as we were rounding the corner." The modern epistemologist interprets this last to mean that *A* saw the bus, or, perhaps, that *A* directly perceived a bus-type visual sense datum or something like that. But notice that in this extensional sense of "see," *A* could perfectly well have seen the bus without realizing that it was the bus, or even that it was *a* bus, and he could have intuited the sense datum even if it had had no special significance for him and were just part of the passing scene. Thus there is a logical gap between his answer to the "How do you know?" question and the knowledge claim that answer was supposed to justify.

Clearly, if knowledge or justified belief is ever to be validly concluded, the intensionality has to come in at some point. *A* has to see *that* the bus is going by, or think *that* "there goes the bus." It is not sufficient that light reflected from the bus excite *A*'s properly functioning sensory apparatus, or that part of *A*'s visual field be a kind of "picture" of a bus. What the Hellenistic epistemologists have done is, as it were, to load the required intensionality into the terms *phantasia* and "apprehend," while most of the moderns keep it unexplained in the background and try to deal only with the individual's relation to the external objects and the various other items that are supposed to represent them.

Let us then summarize the general features of what Sextus apparently takes to be common to the various Dogmatic accounts of the role of *phantasiai* and apprehension in the acquisition of knowledge or justified belief about the external world.

Suppose that a given human being, *A*, experiences a *phantasia* of *X* as being a *Y*, i.e., a *phantasia* that *X* is a *Y*. The *phantasia* is described by some of the Stoics as an "impression" on the ruling part of the soul; other Stoics, and also members of other schools, prefer to describe it as just a change of state of the soul, not explaining what features of this change of state make it a *phantasia* of one thing rather than of another. All schools seem to agree that *A* acquires the *phantasia* either through the senses (*aisthēseis*) or the intellect (*dianoia*).

If the *phantasia* satisfies certain conditions, the specification of which differs from school to school, *A* is said to apprehend that *X* is a *Y*. For the Stoics, the condition is that the *phantasia* must be "apprehensive" or "gripping"; for the Peripatetics, the *phantasia* must have a certain causal history and representative quality; for the Academics, it should be "plausible," "tested," and "stable," which are determined by the consistency and other features of the sequence of relevant *phantasiai* to which it belongs.

(If in this way *A* apprehends that *X* is a *Y*, *A* is also said to "determine" that *X* is a *Y*, "in accord with" his *phantasia* that *X* is a *Y*.)

Finally, it is in relation to this view of the epistemological process that the Dogmatists distinguish three "logical criteria," that is, elements involved in apprehending that *X* is a *Y*: first, the human being *A* (the "by whom" criterion); second, the senses or the intellect (the "by means of which" criterion); and thirdly the *phantasia* that *X* is a *Y*, or the "application" (*prosbolē*) of this *phantasia* (the "according to which" criterion).

## 9. Truth and the Criterion of Truth

At PH 2.80ff. Sextus begins his discussion of truth by mentioning a curious Stoic distinction between "truth" and "the true":

> The true [*to alēthes*] is said [by the Stoics] to differ from truth [*hē alētheia*] in three respects, namely, in essence, in composition, and in power. They differ in essence, since the true is not a body (for it is a proposition and thus a *lekton*), whereas truth is a body (for it is knowledge assertoric of all truths, and knowledge is the ruling part [of the soul] in a certain state, just as a fist is a hand in a certain state; and the ruling part is a body, for according to them it is breath). They differ in composition, since the true is something simple, like "I am conversing," but the truth consists of many true items of knowledge. And they differ in power, since the truth involves knowledge, but in general the true does not. Consequently they say that the truth exists only in wise people, while the true occurs also in the stupid, for it is possible for a stupid person to say something true.

In the parallel passage at M 7.38ff. Sextus offers an analogy to illuminate the Stoic distinction further:

> Just as the deme is one thing and the citizen is another—that is, the deme is the aggregate of the citizens and the citizen is one individual—so on the same basis truth is distinguished from the true; truth is like the deme and the true is like the citizen, because the one is composite and the other is simple.

Note, however, that the analogy does not fit very well, for how could the Stoics agree that an aggregate of incorporeal entities is a body?

In any case, after this introduction Sextus says that for the time being he will restrict his discussion to the true, for in so doing he will also deal with the truth, since the latter is defined as "the systematized knowledge of things true." And in fact he pays no further attention to the Stoic distinction, instead using the word "truth," as we all would, simply for the attribute of being true. He recognizes that the Dogmatists differ among themselves as to what the truth bearers are, with the Stoics usually assigning that role to propositions and arguments while the Epicureans assign it to sentences.

From M 8.9ff. and many other passages it appears that both the Stoics and the Epicureans predicated "true" of *phantasiai* as well as of propositions or sentences, and there are also texts in which "is true" seems used as a synonym for "exists." Thus, at PH 3.253, where Sextus is giving arguments to show that nothing can be taught, we read:

> Now what is taught is either true or false; and if false, it could not be taught; for they say that the false is the nonexistent, and the nonexistent could not be an object of teaching. But neither would it be taught if it were claimed to be true; for in our discussion of the criterion we pointed out that the true does not exist. If, then, neither the false nor the true is taught, and aside from these there is nothing that can be taught (for nobody will claim that while these cannot be taught, he teaches things that are objects of *aporiai*), then nothing can be taught.

"True" is also predicated of appearances (e.g., at PH 2.88) and of things generally (PH 1.12, 2.42).

I suppose that Sextus allows the predicate "true" to slide around the metaphysical landscape in this way—from *phantasiai* to appearances to external objects—because he takes the Dogmatists to agree with one another at least on the notion that acquiring knowledge involves having *phantasiai* that adequately represent corresponding states of affairs and that also possess content expressible in propositions, which then can be asserted on the basis of the occurrence of those *phantasiai*; so that when everything goes right, all three elements are involved and they can all be appropriately said to be true.

Now, what was principally of interest to the epistmologists and consequently to the Skeptics was not the concept of truth per se, but rather the problem of finding a "criterion" of truth: in the process of acquiring knowledge or even grounded beliefs, how shall we to decide which *phantasiai* (or appearances, propositions, etc.) are true? This is the central topic considered in PH 2 and in M 7 and 8.

At PH 2.14 (cf. M 7.29) Sextus tells us that the word "criterion" has two senses:

> We must first mention that the word "criterion" [*kritērion*] means either that by which, as they say, we decide [*krinesthai*] questions about existence and nonexistence, or that with regard to which we conduct our lives. We should now examine what is called "the criterion of truth," since we have already discussed the criterion in its other sense in our discourse [HP 1.21ff.] on Skepticism.

Thus the criterion of truth is "that by which the Dogmatists say we make decisions about existence and nonexistence." This is one of many texts in which it is implied, though not stated explicitly, that for the Dogmatists truth is a property of assertions purporting to describe what is in fact the case, as contrasted with assertions that are offered merely as expressions of what now appears (to the person in question) to be the case. That is, truth is predicable of claims about the world of externally existing objects and states of affairs, as contrasted with reports of a present *pathos* of the speaker's mind or soul.

We see from the very first section of the *Outlines* that the principal activity of philosophers is described as "searching" for the truth, or, equivalently, as "questioning" truth claims (the same verb, *zēteō*, covers both); truth is what the Dogmatists think they have found, and truth claims are what the Skeptics continue to question. People do not question, we are reminded, whether things appear this way or that, but only whether they are as they appear to be:

> The appearance, ⋯ since [it] lies in feeling and involuntary *pathos*, ⋯ is not open to question [*azētētos*]. Thus nobody, I think, disputes about whether the external object [or state of affairs] appears this way or that, but rather about whether it is such as it appears to be. (PH 1.22)

Hence the question of truth or falsehood does not arise for propositions that only express a present *pathos* of the speaker.

Charlotte Stough, I believe, was the first to point out (Stough, 1969, 142–3) that Sextus thus restricts the application of "true" and "false" to propositions about the external world. Myles Burnyeat, too, draws our attention to this feature of Sextus's usage:

> When the skeptic doubts that anything is true (PH 2.88ff., M 8.17ff.), he has exclusively in view claims as to real existence. Statements which merely record how things appear are not in question — they are not called true or false — only statements which say that things are thus and so in reality. In the controversy between the skeptic and the dogmatists over whether any truth exists at all, the issue is whether any proposition or class of propositions can be accepted as true of a real objective world as distinct from mere appearance. For "true" in these discussions means "true of a real objective world"; the true, if there is such a thing, is what conforms with the real, an association traditional to the word *alēthēs* since the earliest period of Greek philosophy (cf. M 11.221). (Burnyeat, 1980, p. 121)

And other scholars have made the same point (see, for example, Long, 1974, p. 85).

As applied to the Dogmatists, the point is surely correct. Everything that Sextus reports them to have said concerning truth indicates that they all — or at least the Stoics, Epicureans, and Peripatetics — regarded it as essentially involving a relation between propositions, sentences, or *phantasiai*, on the one hand, and an external, mind-independent world, on the other. There is no hint that any of them, possibly excepting Protagoras, ever implicitly or explicitly held any "theory" of truth other than, perhaps, what is nowadays called the "correspondence theory" (cf. M 7.168: "a *phantasia* is true when it is in accord with the *phantaston*, and false when it is not in accord"). The idea of defining truth as "what is useful to believe, in the long run and on the whole" or as "what is consistent with the most encompassing consistent system of common beliefs," or in any other way that would sidestep the well known skeptical difficulties inherent in the "correspondence" view, seems not to have occurred to philosophers in antiquity.

However, in my opinion it is not quite correct to attribute this usage to the Pyrrhonists themselves. There is every reason to doubt that Sextus, as a Pyrrhonist, accepts the existence of so-called "external objects" and "states of affairs," or even that he considers the phrase "external object," as used by the Dogmatists, to be meaningful. After all, since he not only challenges the existence of bodies and souls but does not even admit that there are consistent and coherent concepts of them, and since the term "external object" seems to mean "object that exists independently of the soul," he can hardly have agreed that there is an acceptable concept of "external object." Thus I do not share the view that the Pyrrhonist's position is in effect:

> I understand what the Dogmatist means when he asserts that there exist certain external objects with such and such attributes, but I am at a loss as to how one could find out whether the objects have the attributes in question.

It is, rather, more like this:

> I am at a loss as to whether the Dogmatist's assertions are, in their intended
> senses, true, false, or neither, for truth and falsehood are supposed to obtain
> with respect to so-called "external objects", and the Dogmatists do not furnish
> us a satisfactory concept of "external object," nor even one of "true."

Thus it seems to me that the texts that have led commentators to conclude
correctly that Sextus applies the predicates "true" and "false" only to such
*phantasiai* or statements as purport to describe the external world are once
again to be understood as texts in which Sextus is following his practice of
employing philosophically important terms in accord with what he takes to be
either the usage of the Dogmatists generally or the usage of whichever
Dogmatists he is criticizing at the moment. His own deep skepticism leaves him
in a state of *epochē*, not only as to whether there are any such things as
"external objects," but even as to whether these terms of the Dogmatists have
any intelligible meaning at all.

Sextus's attack on the notion of truth, both in *Against the Mathematicians*
and in the *Outlines*, takes the form of questioning whether anything—a
*phantasia*, an appearance, a criterion, proposition, proof, meaning, utterance,
or just a *pragma* (thing)—is ever true. In M 8 he begins his account by
observing that, of those Dogmatists who have examined the matter,

> Some say that nothing is true and some say that there is something that is
> true; and of those who say that something is true, some claim that only objects
> of thought, others that only objects of sense, and still others that both objects
> of thought and objects of sense are true. Thus Xeniades of Corinth, as we
> pointed out earlier, said that nothing is true; and so also, perhaps, Monimus
> the Cynic, when he said that the whole matter is a confusion, i.e., a supposition
> that what is not the case is the case. The followers of Plato and Democritus
> considered that only objects of thought are true; but whereas Democritus did
> so on the ground that no object of sense exists by nature, since the atoms that
> compose everything have a nature devoid of every sensible quality, Plato did
> so because sense objects are always becoming and never being.... 
> Aenesidemus's people (in accord with Heraclitus) and also Epicurus fell back
> on sense objects, but they differed as to details. For Aenesidemus's people
> speak of a difference among the appearances, and they say that some of them
> appear in common to everybody but others appear to just one particular
> person, and that those which appear to all in common are true, while the other
> sort are false.... But Epicurus says that all objects of sense are true, i.e.,
> existent. For there is no difference between saying that something is true and
> saying that it exists. Also, in defining "is true" and "is false" he says "That is
> true which is in the state in which it is said to be" and "That is false which is
> not in the state in which it is said to be." And he says that sense perception...
> always reports truly and grasps the existent object as it really is by na-
> ture.... But the Stoics say that some objects of sense and some objects of
> thought are true, the sense objects not directly so but through the thought
> objects that accompany them. For, according to the Stoics, that is true which
> is the case and contradicts something...which, since it is an incorporeal
> proposition [*axiōma*], is an object of thought. (M 8.4–10)

This is followed by an oft-cited passage in which Sextus ascribes to the Stoics a sign-sense-denotation distinction and the view that while signs and denotations are physical objects, senses or meanings (*lekta*) are not.

> The first disagreement about truth, then, was something like the foregoing. But there was also another controversy, according to which some people placed the true and the false in what is meant, others in the utterance, and others in the change of state of the intellect. Those proposing the first opinion are the Stoics, who said that three things are connected with one another: that which is meant, that which means, and that which is denoted; of these, that which means is the sound [*phōnē*], for example, "Dion"; that which is meant is the actual entity indicated or revealed by the sound and which we perceive coexisting with our intellect, while the barbarians, although hearing the sound, do not understand it; and the thing denoted is the external object, such as Dion himself. Of these three things, two are bodies, namely the sound and the object denoted, but one, the thing meant, i.e., the *lekton*, is incorporeal; the *lekton* is what is true or false.
>
> The followers of Epicurus and Strato the Physicist, accepting only two of these, namely, that which means and the object denoted, appear to hold the second view and to assign the true and the false to the sound. The last opinion (I am speaking of the one that locates truth in the change of state of the intellect) seems to be a fabrication of the schools. (M 8.11–3)

In a later passage (M 8.63ff.) Sextus criticizes the doctrine of Epicurus, which he there depicts as the claim that (1) every sense object is true, (2) every *phantasia* is of an existent object and is of the same quality as that which excites the sensation, and (3) those who say that some *phantasiai* are true and some are false are led astray by not being able to separate questions of belief from those of clarity and distinctness. According to this, when Orestes seemed to see the Furies, the sensation excited by the images was true (for the images existed), but the mind, thinking the images substantial, formed a false belief.

It is initially bothersome that this account of Epicurus's views is apparently confused, for within the space of a few lines it has him ascribing truth to (1) the uttered sound, (2) the *phantasia* of the existent object, and (3) the existent object itself, provided that "it is in the state in which it is said to be." But, in accord with what we have noted earlier, perhaps there is essential consistency here after all, and the point is simply that when, on the basis of what nowadays might be called a "veridical" *phantasia*, a sentence is uttered that correctly describes an external object or state of affairs, Epicurus would call the *phantasia*, the sentence, and the external object — all of them — "true".

At any rate, Sextus's criticism is that Epicurus's doctrine provides no way of distinguishing a *phantasia* that comes from a substantial body and one that comes from an image (M 8.65). He makes a similar criticism of the Stoics (M 8.67–8). They claim, he says, that some *phantasiai* are "empty" (e.g., those that occurred to Orestes from the Furies), others are "defectively impressed," coming from externally existing objects but not "in accord" with those objects (e.g., the *phantasia* that came in his madness to Heracles from his own children but as though from those of Eurystheus); and some are "apprehensive" and true. But, of course, the rub is that there seems to be no way of telling which are which.

Sextus finds further that the Stoics get into special difficulties of their own when they tell us that truth and falsehood apply to a certain subclass of the *lekta*, namely propositions (ax*iōmata*). For they define a *lekton* as "that which exists in accord with a *logikē phantasia*," where a *logikē phantasia* is "one the content of which can be expressed in speech"; and a proposition is defined as "a complete *lekton* that by itself can be asserted" (i.e., which, unlike, e.g., the predicate "walks" or the command "Walk!," can be used without supplement-ation to make an assertion [M 8.70, PH 2.104]); and they explain further that a proposition is a compound *lekton*—for example, the proposition "Dion is walking" is a compound of the *lekta* corresponding to "Dion" and "is walking." Noting that the Stoics also say that *lekta* are incorporeal, Sextus objects that composition and division apply only to bodies, not to incorporeal things, and so he infers (M 8.80, 83) that, if we go by the Stoic account, we must conclude that there is no such thing as a proposition. Indeed, he offers further considerations to indicate that there are no such things as *lekta* in general.

Once again, the upshot is that Sextus finds the Dogmatists' accounts, on this topic as on many others, essentially unintelligible. Their explanations of what truth is and of how it can be discovered involve such terms as "external object", *lekton*, and *phantasia*, for which they offer no consistent, coherent, or useable definitions. Consequently, while he does not exclude the possibility that these Dogmatists may in the future present an account that makes sense and might even be acceptable to him, Sextus finds that for the present he must withhold assent from all their claims to have found the truth.

## 10. The Modes of *Epochē*

The various groups of considerations called the "Modes" or the "Tropes" of *Epochē* (see PH 1.36–1.86) constitute the portion of Sextus's account that had the greatest influence on Descartes and subsequent figures in seventeenth and eighteenth century philosophy. These Modes include practically all the ingredi-ents of what nowadays is called "the argument from illusion," together with a lot of similar observations, some true and some false, some deserving serious treatment and others simply ludicrous. They are described by Sextus as "modes [*tropoi*] by which *epochē* seems to be brought about" (PH 1.36). Three series are given, containing ten, five, and two modes, respectively. Of these, the series of ten, which Sextus ascribes to Aenesidemus, is by far the most interesting, at least in relation to later developments. The five and the two are in effect metatheoretical, summarizing the ten and explaining how attempts to respond to them will be futile.

It is important to clarify what these modes actually are, for some scholars find in them a doctrine that can be ascribed to the Skeptics. Sextus says that in addition to being called "modes" they are also "synonymously" called *logoi* and *topoi*. Unfortunately, the word *logos* is a candidate for the honor of being the most ambiguous word in the entire Greek language. In the present context it might mean argument, as it plainly does in Sextus's exposition of Stoic logic, but it can also denote an explanation or an account or just any portion of discourse. Similarly, the word *topos*, as used here, could refer to anything from a topic, in the Aristotelian sense of that term, to simply a passage in a book. So we do not get much help from these "synonyms" that Sextus offers.

However, even a casual reading of the Modes shows that they certainly are not arguments, if an argument is defined in Stoic fashion as a system of propositions, one of which is the conclusion, while the others are premises from which the conclusion is supposed to follow logically. They are more aptly described as considerations that tend to leave us in a state of *aporia* or *epochē* about some matter.

For instance, why do we think that a particular blob of honey is sweet? Because it tastes sweet. But, according to the received theory of perception, whether the honey tastes sweet at any given time depends in part on the condition of our sense organs at that time. We have every reason to suppose not only that other animals, with different sense organs, will experience it quite differently, but also that we ourselves in different circumstances will be differently affected. So why should we attribute to the real honey, which is supposed to have an independent existence "out there," the particular qualities with which *we* are affected at this moment, in this condition, rather than the qualities experienced at other times and in other conditions, by other animals or by ourselves? Why should we suppose that it really is the color it looks to us, rather than, say, the color it looks to our dog? And so on. No firm "conclusion" about these matters is drawn by the Skeptic, but the questions he raises leave us at a loss, with the feeling that we lack any good reason for our common presumption that on the whole the external world really is as it looks, sounds, feels, smells, and tastes to us, rather than as perceived through the quite different sensory apparatus of other creatures. Our original assertion, that the honey is sweet, has not been refuted, but our basis for supposing it true has been undermined. Thus the Modes are not arguments, in any fairly strict sense of that term, and we cannot do much better than to follow Sextus in characterizing them as *logoi* which seem to have the effect of bringing about a state of *epochē* (PH 1.36–7).

It was inevitable that, as suggested earlier, some would-be refuters of Pyrrhonean skepticism would think that in the various assertions that constitute the Modes there is a handle by which to get a critical hold on Pyrrhonism. They notice that many, if not most, of these assertions have categorical form. So they say:

> Aha! Here we have caught the Skeptic making all sorts of confident state-ments—some of them obviously true, such as that things taste differently after one has eaten something bitter, and many of them false or absurd, such as that you can paralyze a poisonous snake by touching it with an oak twig, or that elephants are afraid of billy goats and lions are afraid of roosters, or that Alexander the Great's butler used to shiver when he was in the sun or a hot bath, but felt warm in the shade.

I formerly thought that the answer to this refutation was simply that the various categorical statements constituting the substance of the Modes should be understood as assertions taken from the Dogmatists and that they give no hint as to what may seem to Sextus to be the case. And indeed he often indicates, both in the *Outlines* and in *Against the Mathematicians*, that he is only recounting what "they say," referring to the Stoics or some of the other Dogmatists. Thus the general point of the Modes would be simply that the Dogmatists' account of the connection between the way things are and the way they appear to be is such that no categorical assertions can be justified by the kind of evidence which that account accepts as justification. The Skeptic would not be reporting or revealing his own *pathē* regarding any of the details, but only as regards this general point.

But now I am inclined to think that there is somewhat more to it than that. Sextus's initial caveat, that in his whole story he is just chronicling what now seems to him to be the case, must not be lost sight of. In the Modes he is telling us, I think, that it does seem to him that the same things look, taste, feel, smell, and sound differently to the same person under different circumstances, and to different people or animals under the same circumstances, and so on. His *pathē* are also probably not neutral with regards to at least some of the particular cases, such as whether or not the half-immersed oar looks broken, or whether the architectural lines of the Stoa, viewed from one end of the building, appear to converge. I think also that his statements reporting the opinions of other people are similarly to be understood as reports of what seem to him to be those opinions. If this is correct, he is not only drawing our attention to the fact that the Dogmatists' accounts lead to inconsistent decisions about what is the case and what is not; in some instances (admittedly not easy to distinguish) he is telling us about various relevant things that appear to him to be the case. What he is clearly *not* doing is telling us that any of the above-mentioned propositions is true. However, he must suppose that much of what seems to him to be the case will also seem so to us, his reading audience; otherwise he would hardly go to the trouble of reciting to us all the various facts and fictions which he says "seem to lead to *epochē*" and eventually to *ataraxia*.

I need to explain what I mean when I say that certain things appear to Sextus to be the case but that nothing appears to him to be true, for one might well suppose that "to be true" and "to be the case" were synonymous. My meaning is that there are some sentences of the form

It appears to me that *P*

to which Sextus would give assent, but that there are none of the form

It appears to me that *X* is true,

(where the letter '*P*' is to be replaced by a categorical sentence, and '*X*' by a quotation name or other designation of such a sentence). Thus, in the present context I am using "true" in the principal sense in which I believe it was used by Sextus and the Dogmatists, and in which it refers to a relation between a proposition and the external, mind-independent world.

## 11. Belief and Dogma

There is also the related question, argued at some length by Burnyeat, Frede, and many others, as to whether the Pyrrhonean skeptic believes anything. In my opinion Sextus is clear enough on this point. Over and over again he presents the Skeptic as living, thinking, and talking *adoxastōs*, that is, without believing, free of *doxa*. He never describes the Skeptic as believing (*doxazein*) anything whatever. But his commentators have frequently objected that it is humanly impossible to get along without at least a few beliefs. Consequently, some of them have concluded that he is just mistaken, while others explain in one way or another that he does not really mean what he seems so clearly to say.

Now of course the Greek word *doxa* and the English word "belief" have many different senses, none of them very precise. Some people, in some circumstances, use "belief" in such a way that certain kinds of external behavior simply *constitute* believing; according to this use, perhaps, my sitting down on my chair in a confident manner just *is* all there is to my believing, on that occasion, that the chair will support me; no particular mental goings on, or even dispositions to have such goings on if suitably stimulated, are required. If something like this were the sense of *doxa* that Sextus has in mind when he says that the Skeptic lives *adoxastōs*, his account would indeed be unacceptable, even inconsistent; for he also tells us that in all ordinary circumstances the Skeptic will behave in the same way as anyone else. Belief, for the Pyrrhonist, is a state of the soul, and is not to be identified with or even completely reliably inferred from particular patterns of ordinary behavior.

Furthermore, for the Pyrrhonist not just any transitory whim or inclination to acquiesce when *P* is asserted counts as a belief that *P*. What is required is a disposition to "take a stand on," "stick to," "maintain firmly," "hold with certainty" (*diabebaiousthai*) the proposition believed, through time and against objections; a belief is an attitude that is relatively solid or settled. As mentioned in section 2 above, this verb *diabebaiousthai*, with the connotations suggested by its etymology (from *bebaios*, "firm," "steady," with *dia*, "through time"), expresses for Sextus an essential difference between the attitude of the Dogmatist and that of the Skeptic. (Attempting to signal its quasi-technical status for the Pyrrhonists, I have translated it uniformly as "to maintain firmly"). The typical Dogmatist has a number of propositions, most of them categorical, to which he subscribes, not just for the moment or as a whim, but with conviction. But the Skeptic has no such list; there is no proposition—not even, I think, reports expressive of his own present *pathē*—that he undertakes to maintain firmly, over time and against objections. It is thus in this strong sense of "belief," in which a belief is a firmly maintained affirmative attitude toward a proposition purporting to describe some feature of the external world, that we can say with assurance that the Pyrrhonean skeptic has no beliefs.

One may wonder what the relation is between a "dogma" and a "belief."
At PH 1.13 Sextus describes the kind of dogmatizing that the Pyrrhonist
avoids: "when we assert that he [the Skeptic] does not dogmatize, we use
'dogma' in the sense...of assent to one of the non-evident matters [*adēla*]
investigated by the various branches of science." When the relevant implications of this definition are worked out, dogmatizing and believing turn out to
be one and the same. For, according to Sextus's usage, to believe is to believe
that something is true; and truth, as we have seen, has to do with claims about
the so-called "external world," as contrasted with mere reports of the present
*pathos* of the speaker's mind or soul; and finally, objects and states of affairs
qualify as "external" if and only if they are also describable as "non- evident."
Thus, to believe is to dogmatize and to dogmatize is to believe; saying that the
Skeptic lives *adoxastōs*, that is, without belief, is just another way of saying that
the Skeptic does not dogmatize.

In section 15 below I shall consider the question of whether in order to
conduct his daily life the Pyrrhonist *must* have at least a few beliefs, in the
strong sense in which that word denotes a firm and steady affirmative attitude
toward propositions purporting to describe a world that exists and has its
attributes independently of the believer. It is clear enough that Sextus does not
think that such beliefs are necessary, and surely it is not obvious that he is
wrong about this.

## 12. *Ataraxia*

As regards matters of belief, the goal (*telos*) of the Skeptic is *ataraxia* ("peace
of mind," "imperturbability"); as regards things that are forced upon him, it is
to have moderate *pathē* (PH 1.25, 29, 3.235). *Ataraxia* is not to be pursued
directly; instead, it arises as a byproduct of *epochē*, which in turn follows upon
the state of *aporia* that results from the Skeptic's attempts to resolve the
anomaly (*anōmalia*) of phenomena and noumena by discovering what *is* the
case, as contrasted with what merely *appears to be* the case.

*Ataraxia* is defined at PH 1.10 as an "untroubled and tranquil condition
of the soul"; it is freedom from *tarachē*, that is, from being disturbed or upset.
However, Sextus does not suggest that the Skeptic achieves *ataraxia* in so
unrestricted a sense, but only "as regards matters of belief":

> We do not suppose, of course, that the Skeptic is wholly untroubled, but we
> do say that he is troubled only by things unavoidable. For we agree that
> sometimes he is cold and thirsty and has various feelings like those. (PH 1.29)

In its promise of *ataraxia*, therefore, Pyrrhonism offers no general panacea for
life's troubles, such as might be held out by religion or perhaps by a
Seneca-style stoicism. Instead, the Skeptic's *ataraxia* is, in the first instance at
least, only a relief from whatever unpleasant puzzlement one might have about
what is really the case in a supposedly mind-independent external world. Of
course it is possible that this special kind of relief might in some way produce
a more general equanimity in the Skeptic.

We are told that the kind of upset or perturbation that the Skeptic eventually gets rid of is caused by "anomaly" in the phenomena and noumena, in the *phantasiai*, in "the facts" (*ta pragmata*). (See the discussion of "anomaly" in the next section.)

> Certain talented people, upset by anomaly in "the facts" and at a loss as to which of these "facts" deserve assent, endeavored to discover what is true in them and what is false, expecting that by settling this they would achieve *ataraxia*. (PH 1.12)

The Skeptic, of course, is one of these "talented people." His attempt to discover which of the alleged facts are true and which are false involves philosophizing about how to distinguish true *phantasiai* from false (PH 1.26). But in view of the considerations raised in the Modes of *Epochē*, the arguments for and against the various positions on this subject, as well as on particular issues (such as, e.g., whether this wine is sweet or bitter) seem to him to be indecisive. As a result, he is brought to a state of *epochē*, and by good fortune *ataraxia* follows the *epochē*, "as a shadow follows the body" (PH 1.29).

We are given very little specific explanation of how in general the skeptical considerations and the *epochē* are supposed to lead to peace of mind — at least a peace of mind that might matter to anyone besides those few philosophers who are really upset by the difficulty of explaining how, when all we have to go on are the appearances, we can acquire knowledge or even justifiable belief about an external world. Only in the case of beliefs as to what is good and what is bad does Sextus offer any details about why the person who lives free of belief leads a more tranquil life than the believer.

> For the person who believes that something is by nature good or bad is upset by everything that happens; when he does not possess the things that seem to be good, he thinks he is being tormented by things that are by nature bad, and he chases after the things he supposes to be good; then, when he gets these, he falls into still more torments because of irrational and immoderate exultation, and, fearing any change, he does absolutely everything in order not to lose the things that seem to him good. But the person who takes no position as to what is by nature good or bad neither avoids nor pursues intensely. As a result, he achieves *ataraxia*. (PH 1.27–8)

This point is elaborated in M 11. Discussing the relation of happiness and unhappiness to the belief that certain things are good by nature, Sextus says:

> All unhappiness comes about because of some perturbation [*tarachē*]. But in human beings every perturbation is due either to intense pursuit of certain things or to intense avoidance of certain things. All people intensely pursue what they believe to be good and avoid what they assume to be bad. Thus, all unhappiness arises from pursuing good things on the assumption that they are good, and avoiding bad things on the assumption that they are bad. Since, then, the Dogmatist feels sure that this thing is good by nature and that thing is bad by nature, he will always be pursuing the one and avoiding the other, and being perturbed because of this, he will never be happy. (M 11.112–3)

The Skeptic, on the other hand, is better off:

> But if a person should say that nothing is by nature any more to be desired
> or avoided than to be avoided or desired, then since whatever occurs is relative
> and, according to different times and circumstances, is now desirable and now
> to be avoided, he will live happily and unperturbed, being neither elated at the
> good nor depressed at the bad, bravely accepting what befalls him of necessity,
> and free from the distress due to a belief that something bad or something
> good is at hand. This will accrue to him from not believing that anything is
> good or bad by nature. (M 11.118)

Such is the explanation of how freedom from belief in the objective truth or
falsehood of propositions about good and evil is supposed to contribute to
happiness and peace of mind.

It is hard to find much plausibility in the general claim that the person
who, on a given occasion, thinks "this *appears* to me to be very, very bad" will
be any less upset than if he thought "this *is* very, very bad," especially if he also
entertains the philosophical reflection that, after all, in the end the appearances
are all that matter to one. And it is even less clear how freedom from belief in
the objective truth or falsehood of propositions contributes to *ataraxia* when
those propositions are concerned, not with values, but with such value-neutral
topics as, for example, whether the number of the stars is even or whether there
are invisible pores in the skin.

I have known a few — very few — philosophers to whom the problem of
"our knowledge of the external world" was seriously upsetting; such individuals
might indeed find relief in the kind of reflections that constitute the Pyrrhonist
point of view. And I can imagine someone being so caught up in certain moral
questions of the day — such as whether abortion or suicide under such and
such conditions is a bad thing — that he or she would find comfort in
suspending judgment, with the thought that the arguments on both sides seem
more or less evenly balanced and that the issues seem never to have been
satisfactorily defined. But as to the common man, on such questions as whether
it is really the case that the honey is sweet or that the wine is sour, it is hard
to see why he would be particularly upset by the conflicting evidence, or, if he
were, how Pyrrhonism could offer any more help than, perhaps, the advice to
stop worrying about that and be content with the appearances.

## 13. Further Special Terminology

**Anomaly.** The Greek *anōmalia* means irregularity, or, more generally,
seeming incapability of being brought under a coherent account. Sextus speaks
of the *anōmaliai* of phenomena and noumena, or of *phantasiai*, or of *ta
pragmata* (whether these last are "things," objects, states of affairs, or propositions; see "Objects or states of affairs" below). He means thereby that different
items from these classifications seem to lead us to inconsistent assertions: the
snow that looks white is arguably dark in color; the tower that looks round
from one point of view looks square from another; customs differ from one

country to another; what one group of people think ought to be done under given circumstances is the opposite of what another group proposes; and so on. Thus, the *anōmaliai* are irregularities and incongruities that bring us to a state of *aporia*, that is, of being at a loss as to which, if any, of the various seemingly inconsistent alternatives is true.

**Art.** The only justification I have for following the usual practice of translating *technē*, in its philosophical use, as "art" is that this translation is very widely employed and no alternative seems fully satisfactory. But a *technē* is not necessarily an art; rather it is any regular method of making something, or, more generally, of accomplishing some practical task. Thus it is the kind of skill that is based on a set of rules or principles; it cannot be just a knack or some sort of natural gift. Sculptors, painters, and musicians may indeed be "artists" in this sense, but only insofar as their activity is based on theory. More clearly included are all craftsmen, as well as physicians, engineers, and even skilled politicians (like Plato's philosopher-king). Thus the term has very wide scope; on one extreme, it seems to exclude only what might be called "pure science," and on the other, only such skills as do not involve any theoretical basis whatever.

Consequently, when Sextus raises the question (PH 3.239 ff.) of whether there is an "art" of living, he is not asking whether there is some way of dancing through life with grace and aplomb so as to avoid the slings and arrows of outrageous fortune, or the whips and scorns of time; rather, he is asking whether there is any system of rules or principles for achieving success in this activity.

Cognate with *technē* is *technitēs*, which is usually translated as "artist." But in some texts (e.g., PH 3.259ff., where the *technitēs* is contrasted with the *atechnos*) "skilled" and "unskilled" seem better than "artist" and "non-artist." Annas and Barnes (1985) get around this by using "expert" (and "expertise") everywhere, and I would have followed them in this if "art" and "artist" were not so customary.

Obviously the trouble with "art" as a translation for *technē* is that we have a tendency to contrast art with science — to say such things as that "medicine is an art, not a science" — whereas everything that we would call "applied science" would fall under the term *technē*, while any activity that just proceeds "intuitively" would not. Also, unless we are trying to be humorous or flattering, we do not apply the term "artist" to such artisans as the plumber and the carpenter, though each of these is definitely a *technitēs*.

**Motion.** I translate *kinēsis* in the regular way, as "motion," despite the fact that at PH 3.64ff. we are told that "those who seem to have given a more complete account of *kinēsis* distinguish six kinds," of which only one, "local transition," turns out to be what we would call "motion." It is thus clear from that passage that *kinēsis* is used by Sextus and his opponents at least some of the time in a sense that is much wider than that of our word "motion," to include changes of size, color, hardness, etc., and even creation and annihilation. This use seems to be more or less in line with that of Aristotle in the *Physics*, where, however, although the sense of *kinēsis* is much wider than that of "motion" it nevertheless is said to be narrower than that of *metabolē* (change). (See also the Commentary, at 3.63–81.)

**Objects or states of affairs.** *Ta pragmata* are whatever our statements (*logoi*) are about (cf. PH 1.8; M 1.313), in other words, everything there is. The corresponding *logoi* will consist not only of nouns and noun phrases, but also of full sentences and systems or sequences of these. That honey is sweet, that it is day, and that the number of the stars is even are just as much examples of *pragmata* as are the city of Athens, the pores of the skin (cf. PH 2.51–2, 2.97–9), and all our *phantasiai*.

I have not found an English expression that seems appropriate, even when supplemented by the foregoing remarks, for all occurrences of *pragma*. Consequently, whenever in the translation there is talk of "things," "objects," "matters," "facts," and "states of affairs," the reader should suspect that some form of the word *pragma* occurs in the Greek.

**Pathos.** *Pathos* comes from the verb *paschō*, ("to be acted upon"). So when *B* acts upon *A*, the resulting state of *A* is a *pathos* of *A*.

However, while it is usually presumed that a *pathos* of a thing *A* is always the result or effect of the action of some *B* on *A*, Sextus clearly does not accept this presumption. He tells us that our *pathē* are "in" us (M 7.241) and that they "reveal" only themselves (M 7.194), but he nowhere agrees that there must be something "external" that produces them. Further, as we see from PH 1.19 and 21, and M 8.316 and 397, he is primarily interested in such *pathē* as are involuntary (*abouleta*). The appearances, which are the Pyrrhonist's criteria and are not open to question, are said to "lie in" these involuntary *pathē*.

Thus, so far as I can see, the *pathē* of the soul are simply states of the soul, which the Dogmatists, but not the Pyrrhonist, suppose to be brought about in some cases by the action of external objects or states of affairs.

**Slogans.** For want of a better word, I use the word "slogan" for the Greek word *phōnē* as applied by Sextus to such Skeptic formulae as, "not more this than that," "I do not apprehend anything," "to every argument an equal argument is opposed." However, the word *phōnē*, in its fundamental sense, refers to the sound of the voice, whether of man or of any other animal with a larynx and lungs; and therefore translating it as "slogan" misses the somewhat deprecatory connotation deriving from this. Thus the slogans are noises; make of them what you will; the Skeptic takes no responsibility for their having any defensible meaning.

**Soul.** The received view, repeated by Sextus in a number of places (PH 2.29, 3.229; M 8.101, 11.46, and elsewhere) was that a human being is a compound of soul and body, with the soul the cause of life. (However, Sextus makes it clear that he himself does not accept this; see M 10.338, 7.263ff. and 287ff.). The body was supposed to be a kind of image or expression (*tupos*) of the soul, as was allegedly shown by the fact that we can judge a person's character by his outward look (PH 1.85, 2.101; cf. M 8.155). Both the Stoics and the Epicureans thought that the soul consisted of tiny particles, but the Stoics believed that this "vapor" retained its identity after death, while the Epicureans held that it was "dispersed like smoke" (M 9.71–2). The soul was said to have "parts," especially the senses and the intellect (sometimes called "the ruling part"); these "parts," however, are not separate or disjoint from one another but rather exist coextensively throughout the soul in the same way in which sweetness and liquidity exist throughout the honey (M 7.359). The goods of the soul are the virtues — courage, justice, wisdom, etc. (M 11.142).

It is the soul that is supposed by the Dogmatists to apprehend external objects, but Sextus argues that the soul itself is not apprehensible. He nowhere states explicitly that no satisfactory conception of the soul can be formed, but the evidence he gives for its non-apprehensibility — namely, that the various definitions given by the Dogmatists are inconsistent and incoherent — is the same sort of evidence from which he elsewhere infers inconceivability. As I have suggested earlier, if the so-called "external world" is by definition that which exists and has its attributes independently of the soul and its *pathē*, then if there is no concept of soul, there is no concept of external world.


## 14.  Summary

Pyrrhonism is not a doctrine, but a way of intellectual life, a way of thinking, talking, and acting. The Pyrrhonist contents himself with how things seem to him to be, here and now; he withholds his assent from assertions about how things are in fact, insofar as such assertions purport to state that something is the case in the external world, the world of objects and states of affairs that are supposed to exist and go their ways independently of what may seem (to minds or souls) to be the case. If he has the relevant *pathos*, he will assent to a modal proposition of the form "It seems to me now that *P*" — for instance, to "It seems to me now that the honey is sweet" — but not to the corresponding categorical subproposition *P* — in this example, "The honey is sweet" — when the latter is taken as describing the external world. We are told that a state of *ataraxia* comes over him as a side effect of his withholding assent from all such categorical propositions. Free of beliefs, he no longer worries and argues about how things are in the supposedly "real" world, and he finds that he gets along well enough just by thinking, talking, and acting on the basis of how things seem to him to be.

As regards other people's statements that are offered as more than mere reports of inner *pathē*, the Pyrrhonist finds himself in a condition of *aporia* — that is, he is utterly at a loss as to whether they are true, false, or neither, or even (because of the haziness of the concepts of truth and falsehood) both. His difficulties arise in different ways in different kinds of cases. Sometimes there seems to be a clash of appearances; for, as the Dogmatists' theories agree, the nature of the appearances depends not only on the properties of the supposedly underlying external objects or states of affairs but also on many other factors. As a result, according to these theories, conflicting appearances can arise from a single external object or state of affairs. When such a conflict occurs, there seems to be no acceptable way of deciding which of the appearances are to be accepted as representing the external reality and which are to be rejected. There are also collisions between appearances and theory; thus, on the one hand, nobody denies that motion appears to exist, but, on the other, when we examine the relevant definitions and explanations it appears to be impossible. And there are collisions within theory. What the Dogmatists say about causation, for example, leads one to suspect that there is no consistent concept of Cause that the disputants share, and again we can find no criterion for deciding among them.

So the Pyrrhonist, unable thus far to straighten out these "anomalies", lives *adoxastōs*, that is, he believes nothing (remember that, a "belief" [*doxa*] is a relatively settled disposition to maintain, over time and against objections, some thesis about the external world). Instead of trying to conduct his life on the basis of supposed "facts" about that external world, he "goes by the appearances." Philosophers have often argued that this is simply not practicable, but that thought seems not to have bothered Sextus. To the contrary, he considers that by getting free of beliefs about a supposed "reality" the Pyrrhonist not only avoids various unnecessary evils but also is less drastically affected by the necessary ones. Behaving in conformity with the laws and customs of his society, he follows the common course of life, even going so far as to say some things that he does not believe—for example, "that there are gods and that we reverence gods and ascribe to them foreknowledge"—but presumably he will always be silently adding to such statements the modal phrase "It seems to me now that." Or, of course, he may be merely uttering the words in the way that schoolchildren often mouth compulsory prayers or pledges of allegiance without attending in any way to their content. In any case, it seems that by keeping a low profile, including using categorical sentences *P* as abbreviations for 'It seems to me now that *P*' in his speech, he will not only reap the aforementioned benefits, but presumably will also avoid the unpleasant consequences usually visited upon people who depart from the ordinary in any conspicuous way.

An initially puzzling feature of Sextus's argumentation is that he regularly employs important terminology that, in the same contexts, he challenges as meaningless. We are thus left to wonder how he can expect us to follow an argument in which there occur crucial terms for which, he is suggesting, there are no corresponding concepts that are consistent and coherent. The explanation, in my opinion, is that when examining the views of a particular group of Dogmatists Sextus endeavors to use their own terminology in the way he thinks they do, even though he himself is not convinced that sense can be made of this use; and his technique is to exhibit difficulties within the Dogmatists' views by temporarily adopting, for the sake of argument, much of their language and some of their principles, and then by employing their logic to deduce consequences they will find unsatisfactory. Thus, while such terms as *phantasia*, "apprehension", "nature", "external objects", and "truth" play central roles in his arguments, Sextus is not convinced that any clear meanings attach to them, nor, consequently, that the so-called "philosophical *logos*" containing these terms has any validity at all.

Modern commentators and critics have struggled to find at least *something* that the Pyrrhonist, as depicted by Sextus, is "committed to." It has been suggested that at least he has to believe the "second-order" skeptical slogans, such as "contrary claims are equal." More recently, it has been proposed that, insofar as he is a Pyrrhonist, he at least has to recommend Pyrrhonism as a route to *ataraxia*. And it is said that in any case he is stuck with some principles of logic, for example, the law of noncontradiction (else his reductio ad absurdum arguments would not go through). But in view of the dialectical technique described above, it is next to impossible to find clear support in the text for any such claims. When all is said and done, perhaps what is called for is a rereading of the caveat at the beginning of the *Outlines*: "Concerning the Skeptic Way we shall now give an outline account, *stating in advance that as regards none of the things that we are about to say do we firmly maintain that matters are absolutely as stated, but in each instance we are simply reporting, like a chronicler, what now appears to us to be the case.*"

## 15. Some Responses to Pyrrhonism

When the modern skeptic asserts that knowledge of the external world is impossible, the critic can engage him head-on by arguing that, on the contrary, such knowledge *is* possible. Indeed, the critic will usually argue that knowledge of the external world not only is possible but also is obviously actual.

Almost nobody takes seriously the possibility that the skeptic may be right. Descartes allows himself only a so-called "methodological skepticism" as a device that is supposed to help him establish the foundations of knowledge more securely. Berkeley, for all his skepticism about the existence of an external world, was at great pains to dodge the label of "skeptic" (for "skeptic" was a very bad word); indeed, he presented his philosophy as a *remedy* for skepticism. In modern times, even so sober and sympathetic an expositor as A. J. Ayer states flat-out (Ayer, 1956, p. 78) that "No doubt we do know what [the skeptic] says we cannot know." And some philosophers have denied that there really is any such person as "the skeptic"; they consider skepticism to be nothing more than a philosophers' puzzle that has little or no importance or even amusement value for anyone else.

Until recent times, attacks on the modern form of skepticism have characteristically involved an attempt to analyze the concept of knowledge, with the aim of establishing that, for instance, if the probability of a proposition *P* relative to the supporting evidence is sufficiently high, *P* can be known even if it is not strictly a logical consequence of that evidence. Thus the skeptic's worry that "I might be wrong" is put down as irrelevant; "I know it, but it is possible that I am wrong," although an odd thing to say, is deemed not to be a contradiction. However, Hume and others have pointed out that skepticism challenges the very data — especially data obtained by observation of correlations and relative frequencies — upon which probability judgments have to be based. Thus the retreat to probability seems no more effective as a response to modern skepticism than to Pyrrhonism. (In this connection, see Mates, 1981, pp. 109ff.)

Another approach has been to deny the existence of such things as the sense data, sensa, sensations, percepts, impressions, etc., which seem to screen off the would-be knower from the objects of his hoped-for knowledge, and which thus play a prominent role in most formulations of modern skepticism. But this approach, too, has won less than universal acceptance, because (among other reasons) the skeptical puzzle can be formulated without resorting to the disputed kinds of entities. (I have done this in Mates, 1981, pp. 132ff.)

More recent attacks have developed from the idea that the root of skepticism is to be found in the misuse of language. The alleged misuse may be exhibited by considering, step-by-step, the typical "argument from illusion" that leads to the skeptical conclusion. (J. L. Austin [1962] does an admirable job of this.) Or, in place of explicit argument, we may simply be given confident assertions like: "*Of course* we all know red when we see it; it's *unmistakeable*," or "*Of course I do* sometimes know Tom is angry," where the point is that there is really no problem about how knowledge is acquired; rather, it is just a matter of getting clear on the proper use of the verb "to know." When G. E. Moore attempted to refute idealism by establishing that "Here is a hand, and here is another hand," he was probably making a similar point ("If that is not a physical object, *I don't know what is*" ). On closer examination, however, it appears that the possibility of making the kinds of "stretches" and other "abuses" singled out by Wittgenstein, Ryle, Austin, and others as responsible for the philosophical "cramps" is in fact essential to the functioning of language as a tool for communication. (That this is so should have been suspected when we noticed that many of the very things we were authoritatively told "You can't say" are things that the majority of native speakers of the language frequently and successfully do say.)

A still more recent refutation of skepticism is the interesting argument that it is in principle impossible for the users of a working language to be "massively mistaken." Such a refutation suggests that meaning and truth are so intimately connected that any evidence suggesting that most of what a group of language users say is false will show instead that we have not understood what they mean. The point becomes more apparent, perhaps, if we imagine how one would go about learning a totally alien language for which there were no bilingual helpers or other aids. Obviously the procedure would have to involve making a large number of observations establishing that speakers are willing to utter a given expression affirmatively when and only when such-and-such is the case. Thus the very process of discovering meaning would seem to involve essentially the assumption that most of what is said affirmatively is in fact true. And that leads us to the conclusion that when the skeptic raises the possibility that anybody and everybody who makes an assertion of the form 'I know that *P*' is mistaken he only shows that he has not yet caught on to the mean-ing—that is, the use—of the word "know."

Now whatever the worth of criticisms like these may be, it is clear that ancient Pyrrhonism cannot be confronted in this direct way, for the Pyrrhonist, unlike the post-Cartesian skeptic, makes no categorical assertions and ad-vances no doctrine whatever, whether concerning knowledge or anything else. He assents only to statements that report his own *pathē* of the present moment, and on these matters it seems that we are hardly in a position to take issue with him.

In view of this, critical responses to Pyrrhonism have usually taken one of two forms. Either the critic claims to have found certain things that the Pyrrhonist asserts (or "has to assert") after all, or he abandons the search for such propositions and instead offers the pragmatic argument that a practicing Pyrrhonist simply could not carry on a normal life. But critics have been singularly unsuccessful in catching Sextus, who is our principal authority on Pyrrhonism and who was a Pyrrhonist himself, making any claims of knowledge or even making any confident assertions that are intended to be more than reports of his own *pathē*. So most of the responses have been of the pragmatic type. It is suggested, for example, that since the Pyrrhonist is not sure of even the most elementary facts about the external world, he will be paralyzed or hesitant in many circumstances in which confident behavior is called for; and that even if he somehow overcomes this handicap, he will, at the very least, talk in odd ways and thus suffer the consequences of being considered eccentric or worse. In other words, the Pyrrhonist will be in great difficulty if he tries really to live *adoxastōs*, as he proposes to do.

Let us then consider the puzzling question of whether the *agōgē* of Pyrrhonism, fully and properly understood, would indeed make a noticeable difference to a person who followed it.

Early in the *Outlines* Sextus tells us that although the Skeptics have no philosophical "system," in the sense of an organized collection of beliefs about the external world, they do not treat life haphazardly as just a series of random occurrences. Instead,

> We do follow a certain rationale that, in accord with appearances, points us toward a life in conformity with the customs of our country and its laws and institutions, and with our own particular *pathē*. (PH 1.17)

He then explains that there are four aspects to the Skeptic's day-to-day life: first, there are the sensations and thoughts that come to him naturally, that is, that arise without any positive mental activity on his part; second, some of his *pathē*—for example, hunger and thirst—compel him to take appropriate action; third, he follows the laws and customs of his country (even going so far as to say, despite his suspension of judgment, that the gods exist and have foreknowledge of human affairs); and fourth, he learns an art or craft in order to be able to make his living. Sextus emphasizes that he does all of this *adoxastōs*, free of belief (PH 1.23–4, 226; 2.246; 3.2, 235–7).

It would thus appear that, so far as his behavior in daily life is concerned, the Skeptic will be hard to distinguish from the common man. (Here I am distinguishing the Skeptic's daily-life behavior from what might be called his "philosophical" behavior, in which he keeps questioning assertions made by the Dogmatists. But of course he can keep questioning their dogmas without giving any external indications that he is so doing.) However, most scholars who have considered the matter seem to feel that there *must* be some distinguishing features of the Skeptic's behavior because it is just *impossible* to have no beliefs and yet act completely normally.

There are few, if any, passages in Sextus that can be taken to support this view. One that has been cited occurs at M 11. 166–7. Here he is considering a claim by certain opponents that if the Pyrrhonist is confronted with a really drastic practical dilemma — such as whether to obey when a tyrant orders him to do something "unspeakably" bad, or to resist and by his resistance incur torture or death — he will be unable to follow his program of living *adoxastōs* and will have to make a firm decision that one course of action is really choiceworthy and the other is really to be avoided. To this, Sextus makes the rather puzzling response:

> Now in arguing thus they do not comprehend that the Skeptic does not conduct his life according to philosophical theory (for so far as regards this he is inactive), but as regards the non-philosophic regulation of life he is capable of choosing some things and avoiding others. And when compelled by a tyrant to commit any forbidden act he will perchance [*tuchon*] choose the one course and avoid the other owing to the preconception [*prolēpsis*] due to his ancestral laws and customs; and as compared with the Dogmatist he will certainly endure hardship more easily because he has not, like the other, any additional beliefs beyond the actual suffering. (M 11.165–6, Bury's translation)

This has been taken to mean that the Pyrrhonist, faced with an order from a tyrant to do something really bad, perhaps will do it and perhaps will not, for he is not sure of anything. Thus he would compare very unfavorably with Socrates, who, when ordered by the Thirty to bring in Leon of Salamis for execution, responded by just going home.

But the last part of the passage in question is rather dark, and it can be interpreted in a radically different way. The words *tuchon* and *prolēpsis* are important here. We have seen earlier that Sextus sprinkles his texts with parenthetical occurrences of the words *isōs*, *tacha*, *oimai*, all of which mean "perhaps" or "I suppose," and we have conjectured that his purpose in doing so is to remind the reader that as a Pyrrhonist he asserts nothing categorically, not even when he is expounding Pyrrhonism. That may also be the only role of *tuchon* in the present passage. Further, *prolēpseis* (somewhat misleadingly rendered by Bury as "preconceptions") are the common "prephilosophical" concepts and assumptions of all mankind (M 9.124), as contrasted with the philosophic concepts and beliefs of the Dogmatists (M 7.443); they are needed if discourse containing the corresponding terms is to be intelligible at any level. For example, we are told that there are *prolēpseis* of "human being" and "motion," so that the ordinary use of those terms for communication is possible, but that when the philosophers try to formulate precise concepts for them, incoherence and inconsistency result.

If this understanding of *tuchon* and *prolēpsis* is correct, the crucial sentence can be rendered as follows:

> And when required by a tyrant to do something forbidden, he will, I suppose, choose the one course and avoid the other on the basis of the common understanding of the laws and customs of his country; and, as compared with

the person who holds dogmas, he will certainly bear suffering more easily, since, unlike the other, he does not believe additionally in anything external to it.

Sextus would thus be (tentatively) ascribing to the Pyrrhonist nothing more sinister than that, when confronted with the alternatives, he will indeed make a choice, not on the basis of a philosophical theory to the effect that something is really choiceworthy, but rather in accord with the laws and customs of his country as commonly (or prephilosophically) understood. Therefore, in these circumstances, too, it would seem that the Skeptic's behavior will be indistinguishable from that of the common man. I think that the same is the case as regards all the rest of the Skeptic's nonlinguistic behavior.

But now what of his speech? Will he not at least stand out by talking in odd ways — for instance, by saying such things as "It appears to me now that my name is Sextus Empiricus" and "It appears to me now that I live in Rome" when "My name is Sextus Empiricus" and "I live in Rome" are called for?

Sextus does not comment specifically on this matter, but there are indirect indications that here, too, he expects the Skeptic's behavior to tend toward the norm. At M 11.18–9, which I have quoted previously, he observes that the word "is" has two meanings, one of which is "appears to be." (Compare Berkeley's note in his *Commonplace Book* [ed. Fraser, p. 24]:

> My positive assertions are no less modest than those that are introduced with
> "It seems to me," "I suppose," etc.; since I declare, once for all, that all I write
> or think is entirely about things as they appear to me. It concerns no man else
> any further than his thoughts agree with mine.)

Hence the Skeptic may well on occasion say "*A* is *B*" and mean "*A* appears to be *B*"; in fact, on a number of occasions Sextus remarks that he himself is doing just that. Further, we are told in several places (e.g., PH 1.191, 194, 207) that the Skeptic uses language (*katachrēstikōs*) "loosely" and does not join the Dogmatists in fighting over words or in seeking to use them with philosophic precision (*kuriōs*). In view of this we may conjecture that a sophisticated Pyrrhonist, following the ancient maxim of *lathe biōsas* ("live in such a way as to escape notice"), would also be inclined to follow the advice to "think with the learned, but speak with the vulgar."

The question of whether Pyrrhonism would make a practical difference also calls to mind Berkeley's treatment of a similar (and, in fact, closely related) matter. The comparison is instructive. It will be remembered that Berkeley had to contend with people who, like Samuel Johnson, thought that they could refute him by kicking stones or by inviting him to leave the room by passing through the wall instead of using the door. He devoted a considerable portion of the *Principles* to explaining that if you give up blind matter, which is his version of the "external world," you will really never miss it.

> First, then, it will be objected that by the foregoing principles, all that is real
> and substantial in nature is banished out of the world: and instead thereof a
> chimerical scheme of ideas takes place.... What therefore becomes of the sun,
> moon, and stars? What must we think of houses, rivers, mountains, trees,

stones; nay, even of our own bodies? Are all these but so many chimeras and illusions on the fancy? To all which, and whatever else of the same sort may be objected, I answer, that by the principles premised, we are not deprived of any one thing in nature. Whatever we see, feel, hear, or any wise conceive or understand, remains as secure as ever, and is as real as ever. There is a *rerum natura*, and the distinction between realities and chimeras retains its full force. (*Principles*, section 34).

The only thing whose existence we deny, is that which *philosophers* call Matter or corporeal substance. (*Principles*, section 35)

If any man thinks this detracts from the existence or reality of things, he is very far from understanding what hath been premised in the plainest terms I could think of. (*Principles*, section 36)

In short, be not angry. You lose nothing, whether real or chimerical. Whatever you can in any wise conceive or imagine, be it never so wild, so extravagant, and absurd, much good may it do you. You may enjoy it for me. I'll never deprive you of it. (*Commonplace Book*, ed. Fraser, v. 1, p. 20)

We are to understand, therefore, that the Berkeleyan phenomenalist's doubts about the existence of a material external world will not lead him to try to exit rooms through the wall, nor to place his hand in the fire, nor to walk especially cautiously lest the floor give way, nor to act in any other similarly bizarre manner. For the kinds of appearances that occasion and justify the behavior of the average man in given situations will give rise to the same sort of behavior in the phenomenalist. He has as much reason as anybody else to expect that the experience of placing his hand in the fire will be accompanied by an experience of pain, and that if he has the visual, tactual, and other experiences of walking into a wall, he will then have some disagreeable *pathē*. The nub of the matter is that we all "go by the appearances" anyway; indeed, it is hardly more than a truism to say that the best we can do in life is to make our decisions rationally on the basis of what seems to us, all things considered, to be the case. Nothing more can be expected. There is really no practical difference between the person who says "I am bringing my umbrella because it appears to me, on the basis of everything I see, hear, read, remember, etc., that it will rain" and the person who just says, "I am bringing my umbrella because it is going to rain"; both of them, whatever they may say, are acting on the basis of what seems to them to be the case. It will therefore be difficult, if not impossible, to recognize a thoroughgoing phenomenalist by his behavior, at least if we exclude his linguistic behavior.

But Berkeley also deals at some length with the charge that his philosophy would lead to odd ways of talking:

But, say you, it sounds very harsh to say we eat and drink ideas, and are clothed with ideas.... I acknowledge it does so,... and it is certain that any expression which varies from the familiar use of language will seem harsh and ridiculous. But this doth not concern the truth of the proposition.... I am not for disputing about the propriety but the truth of the proposition. (*Principles*, section 38)

We must no longer say upon these principles that fire heats, or water cools, but that a spirit heats, and so forth. Would not a man be deservedly laughed at, who should talk after this manner? I answer, he would so; in such things we ought to think with the learned and speak with the vulgar. They who to demonstration are convinced of the truth of the Copernican system, do nevertheless say the sun rises, the sun sets, or comes to the meridian; and if they affected a contrary style in common talk, it would without doubt appear very ridiculous. (*Principles*, section 51)

In the ordinary affairs of life, any phrases may be retained so long as they excite in us proper sentiments, or dispositions to act in such a manner as is necessary for our well-being, how false soever they may be, if taken in a strict and speculative sense. Nay, this is unavoidable, since propriety being regulated by custom, language is suited to the received opinions, which are not always the truest. Hence it is impossible, even in the most rigid philosophic reasonings, so far to alter the bent and genius of the tongue we speak, as never to give a handle for cavillers to pretend difficulties and inconsistencies. But a fair and ingenuous reader will collect the sense from the scope and tenor and connexion of a discourse, making allowances for those inaccurate modes of speech which use has made inevitable. (*Principles*, section 52)

Hence the Berkeleyan will not insist on using words "in a strict and speculative sense" but instead, like the Pyrrhonist, he will not hesitate in ordinary situations to employ the "inaccurate modes of speech which use has made inevitable," thereby escaping the adverse attention that expressing himself in "canonical" form would occasion.

Thus any distinctive difference between the phenomenalist and other people will lie at most in how he *thinks*, as contrasted with how he *talks and acts*. From the Berkeleyan point of view, each individual person acts on the basis of how things appear to him, and therefore if he embraces the doctrine that there is no external, mind-independent world beyond the appearances, it should make no difference whatever to his actions. The difference will be in the realm of thought. Berkeley sums this up nicely in his remark:

My speculations have the same effect as visiting foreign countries; in the end I return where I was before, but my heart at ease, and enjoying life with new satisfaction. (*Commonplace Book*, ed. Fraser, v. 1, p. 92)

I conjecture that the Pyrrhonist, if pressed on these matters, would take a position similar to that of Berkeley: he would insist that adopting Pyrrhonism should make no difference to action, and that in particular it need make no difference to patterns of speech. If it makes any difference at all, the difference will be an "internal" one, relating specifically to a protophilosophical belief in a so-called "external world" of things and facts — a world the existence and nature of which is supposedly independent of the states of the soul. Hence there is some reason to hold that Pyrrhonism, like Berkeleyan phenomenalism, is to be understood as another one of those philosophic positions which at first reading strike us as utterly absurd but which, after all the explaining is done, turn out to claim nothing more than what we have in effect accepted all along; in the words of J. L. Austin, "There's the bit where you say it and the bit where you take it back" (1962, p. 2).

In any case, Sextus not only does not expect the Pyrrhonist Skeptic to have practical troubles in consequence of his skepticism; on the contrary, he says that the Pyrrhonist, free of all beliefs about a supposedly external world, will indeed "enjoy life with new satisfaction," being released from certain fears and worries that are allegedly a by-product of such beliefs. The Skeptic's soul will not be entirely free of perturbation, of course, because some types of distress are unavoidable. But since he does not assume that his troubles are anything other than appearances, his "perturbation" is said to be more moderate than that of the person who supposes that such troubles derive from objectively evil facts in the external world. Sextus tries to support his point with an observation derived from medical practice:

> For do we not observe frequently, in the case of those who are being cut, that the patient who is being cut manfully endures the torture of the cutting... because he is affected only by the hurt due to the cutting; whereas the man who stands beside him, as soon as he sees a small flow of blood, at once grows pale, trembles, gets in a great sweat, feels faint, and finally falls down speechless, not because of the pain (for he does not experience it), but because of the belief he has about pain being an evil? Thus the perturbation due to the belief about an evil as evil is sometimes greater than that which results from the so-called evil itself. (M 11.159–60, following Bury)

He concludes:

> He, then, who suspends judgment about all objects of belief enjoys the most complete happiness [*eudaimonia*], and, during involuntary and instinctive affections, although he is perturbed... yet his *pathē* are moderate. (M 11.160–1)

I have to confess that several features of this account of how the Skeptic will achieve *ataraxia* and happiness through *epochē* are very puzzling. For one thing, we are told at the beginning of the *Outlines* (PH 1.12, 27) that what was initially upsetting to the "talented people" who eventually became Skeptics was "anomaly in the facts" about the external world; the alleged facts did not fit together, and the future Skeptics were at a loss as to which of them were true and which false. In each case, investigation turned up equally strong and equally weak arguments pro and con. So the next step was retreat to a condition of *epochē*, of withholding assent from all propositions taken to be more than reports of the soul's *pathē*. Then, to the Skeptics' surprise and as if by accident, the desired *ataraxia* supervened.

Now the so-called "Modes of *Epochē*" give us an overview of the kinds of considerations that supposedly lead the Skeptics to adopt a pattern of life in which they live by the appearances and do not believe any assertions or theories about an external world. But it is striking that all but one of these Modes are concerned with questions having no immediate relevance to the domain of values; instead they have to do with such questions as whether the honey is really sweet, whether there really are invisible pores in the skin, whether things really have the shapes they appear to have, and so on. Only Aenesidemus's tenth Mode offers the sort of considerations that presumably bring the Skeptics to *epochē* as to whether things or actions are good, bad, or indifferent.

Yet when (at PH 1.27f. and, much more fully, in M 11) Sextus gets down to the business of explaining in detail how *epochē* about the external world leads to *ataraxia* and happiness, he considers only value judgments. The Skeptic gives up any belief that judgments about good and evil have objective validity, and through his *epochē* in this limited area he achieves his *ataraxia*. Not even a hint is given of how the state of *epochē* on such matters as are considered in most of the Modes contributes to peace of mind. For these kinds of case we are left to conjecture that the relevant discomfort is perhaps the kind of frustration a biological scientist might feel at being unable to find the cause of cancer, or a physicist might feel at being unable to find a unified theory for all types of force. And it is hard to see how such discomfort will be in any way alleviated if the scientist suspends judgment as to what is really the case and realizes that ultimately all he has ever had to go on is appearance. It is even hard to understand why that sort of "upset" is something that one would seriously want to get rid of. Only those very rare persons who are seriously worried by what philosophers call "the problem of our knowledge of the external world" would seem to be potential beneficiaries of such *ataraxia* as may be induced by the kind of *epochē* involved in most of the Modes.

Equally bothersome is the fact that there is so little apparent plausibility in Sextus's explanation of why the Skeptic, by giving up the notion that certain things are objectively good and others are objectively bad, will be happier than other people. After all, it is a platitude of Greek philosophy that everyone seeks to acquire what appears to him to be good, and to avoid what appears to him to be bad. Therefore, it would seem that if the Skeptic keeps in mind that he was "going by" the appearances all along, even before he reached the state of *epochē*, he will realize that he still has every bit as much reason to be upset by what he sees, hears, or feels, as he ever had. If, for example, in one of life's emotionally wrenching situations — such as watching the battlefield death of a comrade in arms — he were to tell himself:

> This is only an appearance; what the reality is, or even
>     whether there *is* a "reality" here, I do not know,

any likelihood that his *pathē* will be more moderate would seem to depend on his inferring from this some such totally unjustified conclusions as:

> Maybe it will turn out that I have been dreaming,

or

> Maybe this is all a hallucination,

or

> Maybe things will look quite differently to me five minutes
>     from now.

For, according to a thorough Pyrrhonism, it is *just* these kinds of appearances that, in the context of the totality of appearances he had experienced, have occasioned whatever emotional turmoil beset him during the time before he reached the Pyrrhonist state of *epochē*. He will have as much reason as he ever had to expect and fear that the present unhappy appearances will be followed by more of the same, and that it will not later seem to him that he was only dreaming or having a hallucination.

Sextus says, "The person who takes no position as to what is by nature good or bad neither avoids nor pursues intensely; as a result, he achieves *ataraxia*." It has been suggested that the Pyrrhonean prescription amounts psychologically to the advice to "hang loose" and "don't worry; be happy!" But again, it would seem that suspension of judgment about whether there is an external world should properly have no effect on our expectations that future experiences will be similar in quality and order to those of the past. So the beneficial effect, if any, of following the advice to hang loose and not worry would be entirely independent of reaching a state of *epochē* regarding the external world.

We therefore seem forced to the paradoxical conclusion that only by being misunderstood would Pyrrhonism lead to peace of mind or any other practical difference for anyone.

In recent times the favored antidote to philosophical skepticism has been (and probably still is) the claim that the whole puzzle rests ultimately on abuse of language. Ryle, Austin, Wittgenstein, the Logical Positivists, and many others have tried in their various ways to show us how this is so. The Positivists pointed out that most of the crucial assertions in the so-called "argument from illusion" are absolutely unverifiable (nor even confirmable) in experience; and from this they inferred that such assertions are "devoid of cognitive content." Gilbert Ryle (1949) argued that the whole sense-datum/material-object distinction, upon which typical formulations of modern skepticism rest, arises from "the logical howler...of assimilating the concept of sensation to the concept of observation," that is, from misusing the verb "observe" and its synonyms and cognates. J. L. Austin, in his classic *Sense and Sensibilia* (1962) and elsewhere, gave many examples that show how we stumble into philosophic perplexity when we run roughshod over the fine distinctions embedded in ordinary language. And Wittgenstein, whose appreciation of philosophic tangles was second to none, tried to show how things go wrong when the underlying conventions that govern the successful use of language are disregarded or misapplied.

The general idea that all these philosophers shared, then, is that if you use the language properly, as it is used when it serves its purposes well, you will find that you cannot even formulate the considerations that lead to skepticism. The problem of "our knowledge of the external world" disappears, because in order to raise it the terms "knowledge," "external world," and a host of other expressions have to be used in ways that violate the very conventions that make language work.

In view of the essential differences between Pyrrhonean and modern skepticism, it is not possible simply to take over these considerations lock, stock, and barrel and apply them unchanged to Pyrrhonism. Indeed, the

Pyrrhonist accepts so little of the standard philosophical vocabulary of his time that it is not easy to find cases in which he can be accused of misusing crucial terms. Almost the only philosophically important expression that he seems to use uncritically is the quasi-modal operator "It appears to me now that" and if his skepticism is vulnerable to the abuse-of-language charge, it will have to be so with respect to this phrase. Accordingly, let us consider the possibility that this is where he goes wrong.

Prima facie it would seem that the essential difference between the Pyrrhonean Skeptic and the non-Skeptic is no more than this: in those and only those kinds of situation in which the non-Skeptic would assert the categorical proposition *P*, the Skeptic would assent only to 'It appears to me now that *P*.' When the ordinary man and the Dogmatist will say (let us temporarily use "say" for "say or think") "The honey is sweet," the Skeptic says "It appears to me now that the honey is sweet"; when the non-Skeptics say "Tattooing babies is shameful," the Skeptic says "It appears to me now that tattooing babies is shameful"; and so on.

Of course this circumstance would be seen by the Skeptic and his opponents in rather different ways. As the opponents would describe it:

> When the honey is sweet, we say "The honey is sweet," but
> the Skeptic proposes to say only "It appears to me now
> that the honey is sweet,"

whereas presumably the Skeptic would instead put it this way:

> When it appears to him that the honey is sweet, the Dogma-
> tist philosopher or the ordinary man will say "The honey
> is sweet," but a Skeptic will say "It appears to me now that
> the honey is sweet."

Either way, however, it looks as though the difference were largely a matter of how to use the language, whether in express statements or in thought.

Now it has been argued with some plausibility that the ordinary man and the Dogmatist philosopher are the ones who use the language correctly, while the Skeptic goes astray. For probably the single most important part of learning one's native language involves witnessing, primarily in early childhood but also later on, the use of linguistic expressions in reference to the objects and states of affairs to which they refer. Even if we adopt the Skeptic's way of describing the matter, we can say that—employing the "honey" example once again—the child learns that when it appears to him that the honey is sweet the appropriate descriptive comment in English is "The honey is sweet." Somewhat later, it will be suggested, the child learns derivatively the conditions for using the sentence "It appears to me now that the honey is sweet," which are quite different and often include the intent to express lack of certainty.

Thus this objection to Pyrrhonean skepticism can be put as follows. We learn the correct descriptive use of the words, phrases, and sentences of our language by discovering their association with the kinds of objects and states of affairs they denote. This discovery sometimes occurs through explicit instruction by parents and others, but for the most part it is the result of the child's witnessing the more or less successful use of the language by others, and of his trying it out for himself. No doubt the process is extremely complex, but it seems clear that the Pyrrhonist is in the untenable position of suggesting that we should no longer apply a certain class of linguistic expressions to the very kinds of situations upon which, as paradigms, their use has been learned. The oddity is analogous, it is suggested, to teaching your child the use of a color word—for example, "red"—by showing him a number of objects to which it is supposed to apply, as well as a number to which it is supposed not to apply, and then trying to tell him later that as a matter of fact none of those paradigms was really red.

One is reminded of Susan Stebbing's well-known response (1937) to Sir Arthur Eddington (1928) on the solidity of tables. Eddington had observed that, whereas such things as tables and similar objects are ordinarily considered to be solid, modern physics has established that actually this is not so and that in fact they consist of swarms of tiny particles separated by relatively huge amounts of empty space. To this, Stebbing replied that *of course* modern science can have made no such discovery as that tables are not solid, for by the word "solid" we ordinarily *mean* "of a consistency such as that of tables." Thus, she argued, to say that tables are not solid is to say something unnecessarily mystifying, involving in Eddington's case a new use of the word "solid."

The objection to Pyrrhonism we are at present considering is in effect that the Pyrrhonist is making a mistake similar to that ascribed to Eddington, except that the linguistic expressions involved are categorical sentences and not single words like "solid." We have learned, it is said, the use of categorical sentences by witnessing their application to certain states of affairs that we take as paradigmatic. Then the Pyrrhonist comes along and tries to tell us that these sentences do not really apply to those paradigmatic cases after all. But in so doing he, like Eddington, only shows that he does not understand the ordinary (and correct) use of the expressions in question. Just as the native speaker of English knows that the word "solid" applies to such things as tables, he will also know that the sentence "The honey is sweet" applies in the very situation in which the Pyrrhonist refuses to use it and proposes instead to say only "It appears to me now that the honey is sweet."

Now it seems to me that in the Stebbing-Eddington disagreement Eddington was clearly right. When the physicist tells us that tables are not really solid there is no abuse of the word "solid" nor any departure from its ordinary sense. For although we have doubtless learned "solid" on paradigms like tables, any dictionary of the English language will confirm that the relevant sense of this word involves the property of "having its interior completely filled with matter." (The first sense given by the *Oxford English Dictionary* is "free from empty spaces, cavities, interstices, etc.; having the interior filled completely in or up.") And science has in fact established that the interiors of such material objects as tables are not, as was previously supposed, completely filled with matter. Thus the example shows that it is indeed possible to learn the use of a term $Y$ on certain paradigms $X$ and later make sense of and even agree to such a statement as "No $X$ is $Y$."

Let us try to see in greater detail how this is possible. The Pyrrhonist case is forbiddingly complex, since the linguistic expressions concerned are not just one or two words but rather all the categorical statements in the language, and the paradigms allegedly denoted are not objects but states of affairs. So let us attempt to construct and analyze a simpler case, with the hope that our analysis may then be applied to the objection to Pyrrhonism.

Accordingly, imagine a very young child who, through some rather unusual circumstances, is frequently left to roam the halls of a natural history museum. (Perhaps he has working parents who cannot afford a full-time sitter and must somehow divide this duty among themselves; the father is an attendant in the museum, and on the days when it is his turn to take care of his son, he brings the boy with him to work.) The child amuses himself by looking at the exhibits, and he hears what the adult visitors are saying to their children — such things as "Look at the lion," "That's a zebra," "These are animals of the African savanna," and so on, apparently with reference to the lifelike stuffed animals at which they are pointing. So, on these objects as paradigms he learns (at least part of) the use of the words "lion," "zebra," "animal," and related terms, and he adopts this use as his own. This fits in pretty well with what he sees in his picture-books at home; for although he is aware that a picture only resembles and is not identical with the real thing, what are presented to him as pictures of lions or zebras do indeed look like the paradigms in the museum, and hence in this regard he has no cause to suspect that something is awry. (Unfortunately, I have to add to this story the completely implausible supposition that this child has never been to a zoo and so has never witnessed the relevant words being applied to real animals.)

Then one day he does realize, again from what he hears people saying, that the objects in the museum are not really lions, zebras, or animals after all, but are only stuffed lions, stuffed zebras, and other examples of the taxidermist's art.

The question is: how can he make sense of this? How can he understand it when he is told that the object in the museum exhibit is not a zebra? Why is he not in the situation that Russell used to describe in connection with so-called "logically proper names," or words that have been "ostensively defined"? Recall Russell's old argument that if, for example, the proper name "Socrates" were a logically proper name for us, introduced into our vocabulary by an "ostensive definition" in which somebody pointed at Socrates and said, in an instructive mode, "That's Socrates," we would not be able to make sense of such a statement as "Socrates does not exist." For the proposition, if true, would have no subject. Even its negation, "Socrates exists," is regarded by Russell as devoid of sense, for, he says, "the word 'exists' is only significant when applied to a description as opposed to a name; we can say 'The author of Waverley exists', but to say 'Scott exists' is bad grammar, or rather bad syntax" (Russell, 1945, p. 831). Accordingly, he held that statements with the word "Socrates" in their subject position only make sense because for us this word is not really a logically proper name but rather an abbreviation of a description. A similar puzzle would affect such statements as "Actually Socrates was somewhere else that day" and "You have never seen Socrates." So when our museum attendant's son is told that what he sees in the exhibits are not really lions, zebras or other animals, why does he not respond with puzzlement, incredulity, or with some such Austinian remark as "If that's not a zebra, I don't know what is."

The immensely complex process by which children learn their native language is obviously a subject for scientific study by experts in the field, but even the layman can notice certain broad features of it. According to recent tradition, the kinds of information that a native speaker, as such, possesses about his native language can be classified roughly according as they concern either the syntax, the semantics, or the pragmatics of the language. Thus he is able to recognize, within reasonable limits, which expressions are grammatically correct and which are not; he knows, again within reasonable limits, what grammatically correct expressions mean; and he is aware of the conventions governing appropriateness of use — for example, the conventions that mandate relevance in conversation or discourage the use of certain words and phrases in certain social situations.

Of course, we are dealing here with interrelated aspects of the learning process, rather than with a sharp division of it into mutually exclusive elements. Thus, syntax cannot be cleanly separated from semantics, since even in as relatively regimented a natural language as Latin many of the "rules" of syntax refer to meanings. And semantics and pragmatics overlap because the pragmatic circumstances of use are among the principal sources of evidence as to what people mean by what they say. But nevertheless the syntax-semantics-pragmatics distinction is conceptually useful in the present connection.

Thus our concern here is primarily with semantics, for the Pyrrhonist is not accused of systematic violation of the rules of syntax, nor of disregard for such conventions as have to do with maintaining relevance in conversation or using a vocabulary appropriate to the kind of audience one is addressing. The charge is rather that he is making a mistake in the domain of meaning; for it is argued that the meaning is the use and that such a sentence as "The honey is sweet" is generally and properly used in the very kind of circumstance in which the Pyrrhonist declines to use it.

However, in considering the semantics of a language we must keep in mind another distinction, that between sense and denotation. It is one thing to know which objects a given expression denotes and quite another to know its sense or meaning. The distinction was most clearly set forth by Frege, but it is an ancient one and it appears in various forms (e.g., as connotation/denotation or intension/extension) throughout the history of semantics.

With this in mind we can divide into two categories the semantic information that is acquired in the course of learning one's native language:

first, there is information as to which objects or states of affairs the various linguistic expressions denote, and second, there is information as to what these expressions mean. The former kind of information has primarily to do with the relation between the linguistic expressions and their (for the most part extra-linguistic) subject matter, or what they are "about"; the latter concerns such relations as synonymy and implication among the expressions themselves. Obviously the two types of information are intimately connected. Thus a common (but risky) way of forming an hypothesis about what a given predicate $X$ means involves surveying that part of its denotation or extension that may be accessible, and then "seeing what is common" to those items, that is, finding another predicate $Y$ that is true of just those things, and finally concluding that $X$ means the same as $Y$.

Another distinction that is relevant in the present connection concerns the way semantic information is acquired. In some cases, we find out about the denotation or sense of an expression directly, by being shown or told; in other cases, we acquire the information indirectly, by "inferring" or "gathering" it from observing what happens as the language is used by ourselves and other people.

Thus as regards denotation, the very young child may in a few cases receive explicit instruction, as when first-time parents, eager for their child to acquire the language as soon as possible, introduce a few color terms by something like what philosophers have called "ostensive definitions." And language users continue to receive, throughout their lives, occasional instruction of this form, often by means of pictures—for example, "This is an adz," "This is an example of a mortise-and-tenon joint." But when later children come along, the weary parents no longer have much time or energy for the game with color words, and the much more important "indirect" type of learning takes over almost completely. The requisite information is acquired without such explicit instruction; instead, by being present when the language is in use, and by noticing what is said in what circumstances, the learner catches on to what is being talked about.

The process of acquiring semantic information in this "indirect" way is no doubt much more complicated, requiring much more intellect, than what is involved in the more direct way. For even a rat can be taught in certain cases, by a procedure remotely analogous to ostensive definition, to recognize one kind of thing as a sign for another; and I suppose that some "higher" animals—for example, dogs—can be taught this for a few cases in which the sign is a linguistic expression. But "gathering," just from overhearing a body of discourse, that such-and-such objects are what are being talked about, probably requires the full resources of the human brain. It is hard to imagine any of what Sextus calls "languageless [*alogoi*] animals" accomplishing this. For it seems to depend on a background assumption—usually not consciously made, of course—that most of what people say is true: "they must be talking about *that*, since otherwise what they are saying wouldn't be true." (And why would anyone suppose that most of what people are saying is true? Because we all—even the very young child—see language as a tool by means of which desirable results are obtained, and plainly it would not work if what is asserted did not for the most part correspond to fact.)

Information about sense or intension, too, may be acquired both directly and indirectly — directly when we are given an explicit definition of a term or we look it up in the dictionary or someone corrects our misuse of it, and indirectly when, from what we hear and read, we gather that its sense must be such and such. Some limitations on the sense can be inferred from knowledge of the denotation: "It can't mean *that*, or it wouldn't apply to those things." And further information about the semantic interconnections of expressions will be obtained in the course of discovering what they denote; thus our young child, by observing that the word "animal" may be applied to everything to which the word "zebra" applies — and this not after further inspection of the object in question, but "automatically," as it were — learns a connection between these two words, a connection that will later support the confident assertion of such propositions as "Zebras are animals" and "If that's not an animal, it can't really be a zebra." Here again here seems to be a crucial background presumption that, at least when the language appears to be functioning descriptively, most of what is said corresponds to fact.

With these distinctions in mind, I return to the question how our museum attendant's son can understand it when he is told that the paradigms on which he learned the words "lion," "zebra," "animal," and so on, are not really lions, zebras, or animals after all. The answer is that he will inevitably have acquired a great deal more semantic information about these words than that which merely associates certain objects with them as their presumed denotations. He will have learned that lions roar, zebras run, lions bring down zebras and eat them, animals in general are capable of spontaneous movement, and so on. From his early experience in the museum he formed, correctly enough, the idea that "zebras are things like those"; now he discovers that while indeed zebras are things like those in certain respects, they are very unlike those in certain other respects that are crucial for standard application of the word.

In general, the additional information he acquires will concern not only the relation between language and the world, so to speak, but also relations internal to the language. The language learner is always in the position of having to reconcile his impression that "this term refers to these things" with his other, equally demanding, impression that "this term means the same as, or implies, that term." And at the same time he must try to preserve to the maximum extent the body of statements that are considered true by the speakers of the language, for otherwise it will be impossible for him to communicate successfully in that language. Some of the semantic interrelations among the terms will be mediated by the relations of those terms to the extralinguistic world. For example, he may have observed the application of verbs "run" and "roar" to various cases, and he may have noticed that such sentences as "Zebras run" and "Lions roar" are taken as true — so that, since the objects in the museum do not run and roar, something has to give.

It seems that learning a language is a process somewhere between learning a technique, like how to swim, and learning a body of principles or facts, like geometry. Wittgenstein has usefully compared it with learning how to play such a game as chess. There are rules, and if you do not play according to those rules you are not playing chess, whatever else you may be doing.

But while following rules is important in the use of language, too, in this case the matter is much more complicated. For although using language is indeed like playing a game, it is also very different. Language is a tool for getting things done, and its principal use is not to provide amusement. Along with its various rules, there is clearly also a second-order rule to the effect that, within reason, first-order rules may be bent or stretched as necessary to get the job done. When the skilled carpenter occasionally uses his screwdriver as a chisel, our attitude is: if it works, fine. In a game, the goal is to achieve a desirable result while following the rules; in the use of language, it seems, the rules need be followed only insofar (apart from aesthetic considerations) as to do otherwise would render the tool ineffective. Thus when the so-called "ordinary-language" philosophers used to claim that "you *can* say" this but "you *can't* say" that, they were often faced with the awkward fact that language users often do say precisely the kinds of things they allegedly "can't say," and they do manage to communicate.

Perhaps more relevant to our present concern is the fact that the process of learning our native language can, with certain important reservations, be conceptualized as one in which we tacitly make a series of hypotheses regarding syntax, semantics, and pragmatics. What the language learner learns is always "provisional," in that it is subject to revision in the light of further data. When the data do not cohere, a kind of balancing act results. Sometimes hypotheses about denotation (including truth) are given up or revised; sometimes hypotheses about meaning; sometimes both. The museum attendant's son gives up the hypothesis that "zebra," "lion," "animal," and so on, denote objects in the exhibits, in order to preserve the hypothesized sense and denotation of "run," "roar," "zebras run," "lions roar," and so on. A very rough governing principle seems to be that resolution of conflict among hypotheses must be made in such a way as to preserve to the maximum the body of propositions considered true by the language users.

I think that this is what we do in the case of the word "solid," too. When Eddington says "Tables are not solid" and gives us his reason, we do not simply declare his statement false on the ground that it is the negation of a statement generally accepted as true by the speakers of the English language. Nor do we classify "solid" as ambiguous and achieve a kind of consistency by saying that the scientist uses the word in one sense and the ordinary man uses it in another. For there is a lot more to the ordinary man's semantic information about the word "solid" than that it is regularly applied to objects of the consistency of tables. As mentioned earlier, the relevant ordinary sense of the word is not that of "of a consistency such as that of tables," but rather of something like "having its interior completely filled with matter." The ordinary man does not reject the scientist's statement that "tables are not really solid" as absurd, as though it were a statement like "squares are not quadrilaterals,",", but rather he accepts it as new information requiring a change of mind on his part.

The case with the imagined objection against Pyrrhonism is similar. To be sure, we probably do learn to use a categorical sentence like "The honey is sweet" in the very kind of situation in which the Pyrrhonist will think or say only "It seems to me now that the honey is sweet." But we also learn a great deal about the ordinary sense of these categorical sentences and their components, which is to say that we learn how they are related semantically to the other expressions of the language. In the process we learn to distinguish the sense of "The honey is sweet" from that of "It seems to me now that the honey is sweet"; we find that in every case in which the former is seriously asserted, the speaker could truthfully assert the latter, while on the other hand, the former can be false even when the latter is true. And just as we did not feel that the physicist does violence to the language when he says that tables are not in fact as solid as the non-scientist may think them to be, so we see that the Pyrrhonist is not abusing the language when he suggests that the philosophers and some ordinary people regularly use the categorical sentence *P* when only 'It seems to me now that *P*' is justified.

In sum, I conclude that, on the one hand, Pyrrhonism survives the charges that it abuses the language and that it cannot be put into practice, but that, on the other, it has a fatal flaw: only by being misunderstood to some extent would it have any possibility of leading to the *ataraxia* that is its principal goal and justification.

# Sextus Empiricus
# Outlines of Pyrrhonism

# Outlines of Pyrrhonism

*Book 1 of Three*

## Contents of Book 1

## 1. The Main Difference between the Philosophies

When people search for something, the likely outcome is that either they find 1
it or, not finding it, they accept that it cannot be found, or they continue to
search. So also in the case of what is sought in philosophy, I think, some people 2
have claimed to have found the truth, others have asserted that it cannot be
apprehended, and others are still searching. Those who think that they have 3
found it are the Dogmatists, properly so called—for example, the followers of
Aristotle and Epicurus, the Stoics, and certain others. The followers of
Cleitomachus and Carneades, as well as other Academics, have asserted that
it cannot be apprehended. The Skeptics continue to search. Hence it is with 4
reason that the main types of philosophy are thought to be three in number:
the Dogmatic, the Academic, and the Skeptic. Concerning the first two it will
best become others to speak; but concerning the Skeptic Way we shall now
give an outline account, stating in advance that as regards none of the things
that we are about to say do we firmly maintain that matters are absolutely as
stated, but in each instance we are simply reporting, like a chronicler, what now
appears to us to be the case.

## 2. The Accounts of Skepticism

One account of the Skeptic philosophy is called "general"; the other, "specific". 5
In the general account we set forth the characteristic traits of Skepticism,
stating its basic idea, its origins, arguments, criterion and goal, as well as the
modes of *epochē* [suspension of judgment], and how we take the Skeptic
statements, and the distinction between Skepticism and the competing philosophies. In the specific account we state objections to each part of so-called 6
"philosophy." Let us, then, first take up the general account, beginning the
exposition with the various terms for the Skeptic Way.

## 3. The Nomenclature of the Skeptic Way

The Skeptic Way is called Zetetic ["questioning"] from its activity in question- 7
ing and inquiring, Ephectic ["suspensive"] from the *pathos* that arises concerning the subject of inquiry, Aporetic ["inclined to *aporiai*"] either, as some say,
from its being puzzled and questioning about everything or from its being at
a loss as to whether to assent or dissent, and Pyrrhonean because it appears
to us that Pyrrho applied himself to Skepticism more vigorously and conspicuously than his predecessors did.

## 4. What Skepticism Is

The Skeptic Way is a disposition to oppose phenomena and noumena to one 8
another in any way whatever, with the result that, owing to the equipollence
among the things and statements thus opposed, we are brought first to *epochē*

9  and then to *ataraxia*. We do not apply the term "disposition" in any subtle
sense, but simply as cognate with "to be disposed." At this point we are taking
as phenomena the objects of sense perception, thus contrasting them with the
noumena. The phrase "in any way whatever" can modify both the word
"disposition" (so as to make us take that word in a plain sense, as we said) and
the phrase "to oppose phenomena and noumena"; for since we oppose these in
various ways—phenomena to phenomena, noumena to noumena, or *alternando* phenomena to noumena, we say "in any way whatever" in order to
include all such oppositions. Or we can apply "in any way whatever" to
"phenomena and noumena," in order that we may not have to inquire how the
phenomena appear or the noumena are thought, but may take these terms in
10 their plain senses. By "opposed" statements we simply mean inconsistent ones,
not necessarily affirmative and negative. By "equipollence" we mean equality
as regards credibility and the lack of it, that is, that no one of the inconsistent
statements takes precedence over any other as being more credible. *Epochē* is
a state of the intellect on account of which we neither deny nor affirm anything.
*Ataraxia* is an untroubled and tranquil condition of the soul. In our remarks
on the goal of Skepticism we shall come back to the question of how *ataraxia*
enters the soul along with *epochē*.

## 5. The Skeptic

11 The definition of the Pyrrhonean philosopher is implicitly contained in that of
the Skeptic Way: he is the person who has the aforementioned disposition.

## 6. The Origins of Skepticism

12 We say that the causal origin of the Skeptic Way is the hope of attaining
*ataraxia*. Certain talented people, upset by anomaly in "the facts" and at a loss
as to which of these "facts" deserve assent, endeavored to discover what is true
in them and what is false, expecting that by settling this they would achieve
*ataraxia*. But the main origin of Skepticism is the practice of opposing to each
statement an equal statement; it seems to us that doing this brings an end to
dogmatizing.

## 7. Does the Skeptic Dogmatize?

13 When we say that the Skeptic does not dogmatize we are not using the term
"dogma" as some do, in its more common meaning, "something that one
merely agrees to", for the Skeptic does give assent to the *pathē* that are forced
upon him by a *phantasia*; for example, when feeling hot (or cold) he would not
say "I seem not to be hot (or cold)." But when we assert that he does not
dogmatize, we use "dogma" in the sense, which others give it, of assent to one
of the non-evident matters investigated by the sciences. For the Pyrrhonist
14 assents to nothing that is non-evident. Not even in putting forward the Skeptic
slogans about nonevident things does he dogmatize—slogans like "Nothing

more" or "I determine nothing" or any of the others of which we shall speak later. For the dogmatizer propounds as certainty the things about which he is said to be dogmatizing, but the Skeptic does not put forward these slogans as holding absolutely. He considers that, just as the "All things are false" slogan says that together with the other things it is itself false, as does the slogan "Nothing is true," so also the "Nothing more" slogan says that it itself is no more the case than its opposite, and thus it applies to itself along with the rest. 15 We say the same of the other Skeptic slogans. So that since the dogmatizer is one who posits the content of his dogmas as being true, while the Skeptic presents his skeptical slogans as implicitly self-applicable, the Skeptic should not be said to dogmatize thereby. But the most important point is that in putting forward these slogans he is saying what seems to him to be the case and is reporting his *pathos* without belief, not firmly maintaining anything concerning what exists externally.

## 8. Does the Skeptic Have a System?

We proceed in the same way when asked whether the Skeptic has a system. If 16 one defines a system as an attachment to a number of dogmas that agree with one another and with appearances, and defines a dogma as an assent to something non-evident, we shall say that the Skeptic does not have a system. But if one says that a system is a way of life that, in accordance with 17 appearances, follows a certain rationale, where that rationale shows how it is possible to seem to live rightly ("rightly" being taken, not as referring only to virtue, but in a more ordinary sense) and tends to produce the disposition to suspend judgment, then we say that he does have a system. For we do follow a certain rationale that, in accord with appearances, points us toward a life in conformity with the customs of our country and its laws and institutions, and with our own particular *pathē*.

## 9. Does the Skeptic Theorize about Nature?

We reply in the same vein if asked whether the Skeptic needs to theorize about 18 nature. On the one hand, if there is a question of making an assertion with firm confidence about any of the matters dogmatically treated in physical theory, we do not theorize; but, on the other hand, in the course of opposing to every statement an equal statement, and in connection with *ataraxia*, we do touch upon physical theory. This, too, is the way we approach the logical and ethical parts of so-called "philosophy."

## 10. Do the Skeptics Deny Appearances?

Those who claim that the Skeptics deny appearances seem to me not to have 19 heard what we say. For, as we stated above, we do not reject the things that lead us involuntarily to assent in accord with a passively received *phantasia*, and these are appearances. And when we question whether the external object is such as it appears, we grant that it does appear, and we are not raising a question about the appearance but rather about what is said about the appearance; this is different from raising a question about the appearance itself.

20 For example, the honey appears to us to be sweet. This we grant, for we sense the sweetness. But whether it *is* sweet we question insofar as this has to do with the [philosophical] theory, for that theory is not the appearance, but something said about the appearance. And even when we do present arguments in opposition to the appearances, we do not put these forward with the intention of denying the appearances but by way of pointing out the precipitancy of the Dogmatists; for if the theory is so deceptive as to all but snatch away the appearances from under our very eyes, should we not distrust it in regard to the non-evident, and thus avoid being led by it into precipitate judgments?

## 11. The Criterion of the Skeptic Way

21 That we hold to the appearances is obvious from what we say about the criterion of the Skeptic Way. The word "criterion" is used in two ways: first, for the criterion that is assumed in connection with belief about existence or nonexistence, and that we shall discuss in our objections; and second, for the criterion of action, by attention to which in the conduct of daily life we do some

22 things and not others; it is of the latter that we are now speaking. Accordingly, we say that the criterion of the Skeptic Way is the appearance — in effect using that term here for the *phantasia* — for since this appearance lies in feeling and involuntary *pathos* it is not open to question. Thus nobody, I think, disputes about whether the external object appears this way or that, but rather about whether it is such as it appears to be.

23      Holding to the appearances, then, we live without beliefs but in accord with the ordinary regimen of life, since we cannot be wholly inactive. And this ordinary regimen of life seems to be fourfold: one part has to do with the guidance of nature, another with the compulsion of the *pathē*, another with the handing down of laws and customs, and a fourth with instruction in arts and

24 crafts. Nature's guidance is that by which we are naturally capable of sensation and thought; compulsion of the *pathē* is that by which hunger drives us to food and thirst makes us drink; the handing down of customs and laws is that by which we accept that piety in the conduct of life is good and impiety bad; and instruction in arts and crafts is that by which we are not inactive in whichever of these we acquire. And we say all these things without belief.

## 12. What Is the Goal of Skepticism?

25 After these remarks, our next task is to explain the goal of the Skeptic Way. Now the goal or end is that for the sake of which everything is done or considered, while it, in turn, is not done or considered for the sake of anything else; or, it is the ultimate object of the desires. We always say that as regards belief the Skeptic's goal is *ataraxia*, and that as regards things that are

26 unavoidable it is having moderate *pathē*. For when the Skeptic set out to

philosophize with the aim of assessing his *phantasiai*—that is, of determining which are true and which are false so as to achieve *ataraxia*—he landed in a controversy between positions of equal strength, and, being unable to resolve it, he suspended judgment. But while he was thus suspending judgment there 27 followed by chance the sought-after *ataraxia* as regards belief. For the person who believes that something is by nature good or bad is constantly upset; when he does not possess the things that seem to be good, he thinks he is being tormented by things that are by nature bad, and he chases after the things he supposes to be good; then, when he gets these, he falls into still more torments because of irrational and immoderate exultation, and, fearing any change, he does absolutely everything in order not to lose the things that seem to him 28 good. But the person who takes no position as to what is by nature good or bad neither avoids nor pursues intensely. As a result, he achieves *ataraxia*.

Indeed, what happened to the Skeptic is just like what is told of Apelles the painter. For it is said that once upon a time, when he was painting a horse and wished to depict the horse's froth, he failed so completely that he gave up and threw his sponge at the picture—the sponge on which he used to wipe the paints from his brush—and that in striking the picture the sponge produced the desired effect. So, too, the Skeptics were hoping to achieve *ataraxia* by 29 resolving the anomaly of phenomena and noumena, and, being unable to do this, they suspended judgment. But then, by chance as it were, when they were suspending judgment the *ataraxia* followed, as a shadow follows the body. We do not suppose, of course, that the Skeptic is wholly untroubled, but we do say that he is troubled only by things unavoidable. For we agree that sometimes he is cold and thirsty and has various feelings like those. But even in such cases, 30 whereas ordinary people are affected by two circumstances—namely by the *pathē* themselves and not less by its seeming that these conditions are by nature bad—the Skeptic, by eliminating the additional belief that all these things are naturally bad, gets off more moderately here as well. Because of this we say that as regards belief the Skeptic's goal is *ataraxia*, but in regard to things unavoidable it is having moderate *pathē*. But some notable Skeptics have added "suspension of judgment during investigations" to these.

## 13. The General Modes of *Epochē*

Since we have been saying that *ataraxia* follows on suspending judgment about 31 everything, the next thing would be to explain how we reach this suspension. Roughly speaking, one may say that it comes about through the opposition of things. We oppose phenomena to phenomena or noumena to noumena, or *alternando*. For instance, we oppose phenomena to phenomena when we say 32 that the same tower appears round from a distance but square from close up; and noumena to noumena when, in reply to one who infers the existence of divine providence from the order of the heavenly bodies, we oppose the fact that often the good fare ill and the bad fare well, and deduce from this that divine providence does not exist; and noumena to phenomena, as when 33 Anaxagoras argued, in opposition to snow's being white, that snow is frozen

water and water is dark in color, and therefore snow is dark in color. Or, with a different concept of opposition, we sometimes oppose present things to present things, as in the foregoing examples, and sometimes present things to things past or to things future; for example, when somebody brings up an
34 argument that we are not able to refute, we say to him: "Just as before the birth of the person who introduced the system which you follow, the argument supporting that system did not yet appear sound although it really was, so also it is possible that the opposite of the argument you now advance is really sound despite its not yet appearing so to us, and hence we should not yet assent to this argument that now seems so strong."
35 But in order that we may more accurately understand these oppositions, I shall set down the modes or arguments by means of which suspension of judgment is brought about, without, however, maintaining anything about their number or their force. For they may well be unsound, and there may be more than the ones I shall mention.

## 14. The Ten Modes

36 The older Skeptics, according to the usual account, have handed down some modes, ten in number, through which it seems that suspension of judgment is brought about, and which they also synonymously call "arguments" or "points." And these modes are as follows: first, there is the one based on the variety of animals; second, the one based on the differences among human beings; third, that based on the differences in constitution of the sense organs; fourth, on the circumstances; fifth, on positions, distances and locations; sixth,
37 on admixtures; seventh, on the quantity and constitution of the external objects; eighth, on relativity; ninth, on the frequency or infrequency of occurrence; and tenth, on ways of life, customs and laws, mythic beliefs and dogmatic
38 opinions. We adopt this order without prejudice.

Superordinate to these are three modes, one based on what does the judging, another based on what is judged, and a third based on both. The first four of the ten modes are subordinate to the mode based on what does the judging, for that is either an animal or a human being or a sense and is in some circumstance; the seventh and tenth modes are referred to the mode based on what is judged; and the fifth, sixth, eighth, and ninth are referred to the one
39 that is based on both. These three in turn are referred to the relativity mode, making it the most generic, with the three as specific and the ten as subordinate. We offer the foregoing comments, as plausible, concerning their number; concerning their content, we say the following.
40 The first argument, as we were saying, is that according to which the same *phantasiai* do not arise from the same things because of the difference of animals. This we conclude from the difference in the ways animals are
41 produced and from the variety in the structures of their bodies. As concerns the ways they are produced, some animals are produced without sexual union, and others from intercourse. And, of those produced without sexual union, some come from fire, like the tiny creatures that appear in ovens, some from

stagnant water, like mosquitoes, some from wine that is turning, like gnats, some from earth, like [...], some from slime, like frogs, some from mud, like worms, some from donkeys, like dung-beetles, some from greens, like caterpillars, some from fruit, like the gall insects in the wild fig tree, some from rotting 42 animals, like bees from bulls and wasps from horses. Of animals produced by intercourse, some, the majority, come from homogeneous parents, and others, like mules, from heterogeneous parents. Again, of animals in general, some are born viviparously, like human beings; others oviparously, like birds; and still 43 others just as lumps of flesh, like bears. So one would expect these dissimilarities and differences of origin to result in great contrariety of *pathē*, contributing incompatibility, disharmony, and conflict.                                                44

However, it is the differences among the most important parts of the body, especially those naturally fitted for judging and sensing, that can produce the greatest conflict of the *phantasiai*. Thus, things that appear white to us are said to be yellow by people with jaundice, and reddish by those with bloodshot eyes. Since, then, some animals have yellow eyes, others bloodshot eyes, others white, and still others some other color, it is likely, I think, that their perception of colors will be different. Further, if we look long and fixedly at the sun and 45 then stoop down to a book, the letters seem to us golden and moving around. Since, then, some animals have by nature a luster of the eyes and emit a fine and quick stream of light, so as even to be able to see at night, we should expect that external objects would not affect them and us in the same way. And 46 illusionists, by treating lamp wicks with copper rust and cuttle fish ink, make the bystanders appear now copper-colored and now black, just by a slight sprinkling of the mixture. It is surely all the more reasonable that, since differing humors are mixed in the eyes of animals, these animals will have differing *phantasiai* of the external objects. Also, when we press the eyeball on 47 one side, the forms, shapes and sizes of the things seen appear elongated and narrowed. So it is likely that those animals that have elongated and slanting pupils (e.g., goats, cats, and such) will in their *phantasiai* experience the external objects as different from and unlike what animals with round pupils take them to be. Mirrors, too, because of their differing construction, sometimes show the 48 external objects as very short, when the mirror is concave, and sometimes as long and narrow, when it is convex. And some show the head of the reflected person at the bottom, and the feet at the top. Since, then, some of the organs 49 of sight are bulging with convexity and others are quite concave, while still others are in a flat plane, it is likely that because of this the *phantasiai*, too, are various, and that dogs, fish, lions, human beings, and locusts do not see the same things as equal in size or similar in shape, but in each case what is seen depends on the imprint created by the eye that receives the appearance.

The same argument holds for the other senses as well. For how could one 50 say, with regard to touch, that animals are similarly affected whether their surfaces consist of shell, flesh, needles, feathers, or scales? And, as regards hearing, how could one say that perceptions are alike in animals with a very narrow auditory canal and in those with a very wide one, or in those with hairy ears and those with ears that are hairless? Indeed, even we find our hearing affected one way when our ears are plugged and another way when we use

51 them ordinarily. Smell, too, will differ according to the variety of animals. For if we ourselves are affected in one way when we have a cold with a lot of phlegm, and in another way when the parts about the head are filled with an excess of blood (in the latter case being repelled and feeling virtually assaulted by things that seem to others to smell sweet), then, since some animals are flabby and phlegmatic by nature, others very rich in blood, and still others have a predominant excess of yellow or black bile, it is reasonable to suppose

52 that this makes odiferous things appear differently in each case. So, too, with the objects of taste, since some animals have rough and dry tongues and others very moist. And when in a fever we ourselves have relatively dry tongues, we consider the food offered to us to be earthy, bad tasting, and bitter, and we feel thus because of the differing strength of the humors said to be in us. Since, then, the animals too have differing organs of taste, with different humors predomi-

53 nating, they would get differing taste *phantasiai* of the external objects. For, just as the same food, when digested, becomes in one place a vein, in another an artery, in another a bone, and in still another a tendon, and so on, showing a differing disposition depending on the difference of the parts receiving it; and just as water, one and the same in form, when applied to trees becomes bark in one place, branch in another, and blossom in another and thus finally fig,

54 pomegranate, and each of the other fruits; and just as one and the same breath of the musician, when blown into a flute becomes here a high note and there a low note, and the same stroke of the hand on the lyre produces here a bass sound and there a treble one; so, too, it is likely that the external objects are perceived differently depending on the differing makeups of the animals having the *phantasiai*.

55 But one can see this more clearly from the preferences and aversions of animals. Thus, perfume seems very pleasant to human beings but intolerable to dung beetles and bees, and the application of olive oil is beneficial to human beings but kills wasps and bees. And to human beings sea water is unpleasant

56 and even poisonous to drink, while to fish it is most pleasant and potable. And pigs bathe more happily in the worst stinking mud than in clear and pure water. And, of animals, some eat grass and others eat bushes, some eat wood and others seeds or meat or milk, some like their food aged and others fresh, and some like it raw and others like it prepared by cooking. And in general the things that are pleasant to some animals are unpleasant, repugnant and

57 even poisonous to others. Thus, hemlock fattens quails and hyoscyamus fattens pigs, and pigs enjoy eating salamanders, as the deer enjoy eating poisonous creatures and swallows enjoy blister-beetles. Ants and mosquitoes, when swallowed by human beings, produce discomfort and stomach ache, whereas the she-bear, if she feels somehow weak, is strengthened by licking them up.

58 The adder is stupefied by the mere touch of a branch of oak, and the bat by a leaf of the plane tree. The elephant fears the ram, the lion the rooster, sea-monsters the crackling of bursting beans, the tiger the sound of a drum. And it is possible to give further examples, but — that we may not seem more prolix than necessary — if the same things are unpleasant to some but pleasant to others, and if the pleasure and unpleasantness lie in the *phantasiai*, then differing animals receive different *phantasiai* from the external objects.

But if the same things do appear differently because of the difference of 59
animals, then we shall be in a position to say how the external object looks to
*us*, but we shall suspend judgment on how it is in nature. For we shall not be
able to decide between our *phantasiai* and those of the other animals, since we
are part of the dispute and thus are in need of someone to make the decision, 60
rather than competent to pass judgment ourselves. Besides, we shall not be able
to give preference, whether with or without proof, to our *phantasiai* over those
of the non-rational animals. For in addition to the possibility of there being
no such thing as a proof, as we shall point out, any purported proof will either
be apparent or not apparent to us. And if, on the one hand, it is not apparent,
then we shall not accept it with confidence. But if, on the other, it *is* apparent
to us, then since what is apparent to animals is the very matter in question,
and the proof is apparent to us animals, the proof itself will be in question as 61
to whether, as apparent, it is true. But it is absurd to try to settle the matter
in question by means of the matter in question, since the same thing will be
both credible and not credible, which is impossible—credible insofar as
tending to prove, not credible insofar as needing proof. Therefore, we shall not
have a proof justifying us in preferring our own *phantasiai* to those of the
so-called "non-rational" animals. If, therefore, the *phantasiai* differ because of
the difference of animals, and it is impossible to decide between them, then it
is necessary to suspend judgment concerning the external objects.

But for good measure we go on to match up the so-called "non-rational" 62
animals with human beings as regards *phantasiai*. For, after our serious
arguments, we do not consider it unseemly to poke a little fun at the
Dogmatists, wrapped, as they are, in the fog of their discussions with themselves. We usually take the non-rational animals as a group when comparing
them with human beings, but since in groping for an argument the Dogmatists 63
say that the comparison is unfair, we shall for even more good measure carry
our joking still further and base the argument on just one animal—the dog, if
you will—which seems to be the humblest of all. For we shall find that even
in this case the animals that are the subject of the argument are not inferior to
ourselves as regards the credibility of the appearances.

So, then, the Dogmatists acknowledge that this animal differs from us in 64
sensation; for it perceives more by the sense of smell than we do, being able by
this sense to track wild animals that it cannot see, and with its eyes it sees them
more quickly than we do, and its sense of hearing is more acute. Next let us 65
consider reasoning. One kind of reasoning is internal, the other is expressed.
Let us first look at the internal kind. This, according to those Dogmatists who
at the moment are our chief opponents—namely, the Stoics—seems to
involve the following: acceptance of the familiar and avoidance of the alien,
knowledge of the arts related to this, possession of the virtues pertaining to
one's proper nature and of those having to do with the *pathē*. Now then, the 66
dog, the animal upon which as an example we decided to base the argument,
chooses what is congenial to him and avoids the harmful, hunting for food and
withdrawing before the raised whip. Furthermore, he has the art, namely
hunting, to provide the congenial. Nor is he without virtue. For certainly if 67
justice is giving to each according to his deserts, the dog, who fawns on and

guards his family and benefactors but wards off strangers and malefactors,
68  would not be lacking in justice. And if he has this virtue, then in view of the
unity of the virtues he has them all, which the wise tell us is not the case with
the majority of mankind. And we see him valiant and smart in his defending,
to which Homer bears witness when he depicts Odysseus as unknown to all
the people of the household but recognized by the dog Argus alone. The dog
was not deceived by the physical changes in the man, nor had he lost his
"apprehensive *phantasia*," which he clearly retained better than the human
69  beings did. And according to Chrysippus, who was certainly no friend of
non-rational animals, the dog even shares in the celebrated Dialectic. In fact,
this author says that the dog uses repeated applications of the fifth undemonstrated argument-schema when, arriving at a juncture of three paths, after
sniffing at the two down which the quarry did not go, he rushes off on the third
without stopping to sniff. For, says this ancient authority, the dog in effect
reasons as follows: the animal either went this way or that way or the other;
he did not go this way and he did not go that; therefore, he went the other.
70  Furthermore, the dog is aware of and can deal with his own *pathē*. For when
a thorn has got stuck in him, he hastens to remove it by rubbing his foot on
the ground and by using his teeth. And when he has a wound anywhere he
gently licks off the accumulated pus, since dirty wounds are hard to cure, while
71  clean ones are easily healed. Indeed, he follows very well Hippocrates' prescription; since "immobility cures the foot," whenever his foot is injured he holds it
up and keeps it undisturbed so far as possible. When he is troubled by humors
that do not agree with him, he eats grass, and then regurgitates the uncongenial
72  material along with it and gets well. Since, then, it is apparent that the animal
upon which as an example we have rested the argument chooses what is
congenial and avoids what is troublesome, and possesses the art of obtaining
the congenial, and is aware of and able to deal with his own *pathē*, and
furthermore is not without virtue—in which elements consists the perfection
of internal reasoning—the dog would thus far be without deficiency. Which, I
suppose, is why certain philosophers [the Cynics] have honored themselves
with the name of this animal.

73      Concerning reasoning as expressed externally it is not necessary at present
to inquire, for even some of the Dogmatists have deprecated it as counter-
productive to the acquisition of virtue, and for this reason they used to practice
silence during their schooling. And anyhow, supposing that a person is unable
to speak, no one will infer that he is non-rational. But leaving these points
aside, we certainly observe animals, the subject of our discussion, uttering quite
74  human sounds—jays, for instance, and others. And letting this too pass, even
if we do not understand the utterances of the so-called "non-rational" animals
it is not at all improbable that they are conversing although we do not
understand. For when we hear the talk of barbarians we do not understand
75  that either, and it seems to us undifferentiated sound. Moreover, we hear dogs
making one sound when they are keeping people away and another when they
are howling, and one sound when they are beaten and a different one when
they are fawning. In general, if somebody were to study the matter he would

find a great difference of sounds uttered by this and the other animals according to different circumstances, and so for that reason it may fairly be said that the so-called "non-rational" animals have their share of externally 76 expressed reasoning. And if they are neither inferior to human beings in the acuteness of their senses nor in internal reasoning, nor, on top of that, in externally expressed reasoning, then as concerns *phantasiai* they are not less 77 worthy of belief than we are. It is also possible to show this, I think, by basing the argument on each kind of non-rational animal. For instance, who would not say that birds excel in shrewdness and employ externally expressed reasoning? For they have knowledge not only of things present but also of the future, and by prophetic sounds or some other signs they reveal these things in advance to people who can understand them.

As I previously indicated, I have made this comparison for good measure, 78 having sufficiently shown, I think, that we cannot prefer our own *phantasiai* to those of the non-rational animals. But if the non-rational animals are not less worthy of belief than we are when it comes to deciding about *phantasiai*, and the *phantasiai* differ depending on the variety of animals, then although I shall be able to say how each of the external objects appears to me, I shall be forced, for the reasons stated above, to suspend judgment as to how it is in nature.

Such, then, is the first mode of *epochē*. We said that the second was the 79 one based on the differences among human beings. For even if it were granted, by way of supposition, that human beings are more to be believed than the non-rational animals, we shall find that even consideration of our own differences leads to suspension of judgment. For human beings are said to be composed of two elements, the soul and the body, and we differ from one another in respect to both of them. As regards the body, we differ in form and constitution. The body of a Scythian differs in form from that of an Indian, and 80 the variation is produced, they say, by the differing relative strengths of the humors. Depending on this difference in relative strength of the humors there arise differing *phantasiai*, as we pointed out in the first mode. So, too, these humors produce a great difference in the choice and avoidance of things external. Indians like some things and we like others, and liking different things is an indication of receiving differing *phantasiai* from the external objects. In 81 consequence of our peculiarities of makeup, we differ in such a way that some of us digest beef better than rock fish or get diarrhea from the weak wine of Lesbos. There was, it is said, an old woman of Attica who safely drank thirty drams of hemlock, and Lysis took four drams of opium without trouble. And 82 Demophon, who waited table for Alexander, used to shiver in the sun or the bath, but felt warm in the shade; the Argive Athenagoras felt no pain when stung by scorpions and venomous spiders; the Psyllaeans, as they are called, are not harmed when bitten by asps or other snakes; nor are the Egyptian Tentyritae harmed by crocodiles. Further, the Egyptians who live along the 83 Astapous river opposite Lake Meroe safely eat scorpions, snakes, and the like. And Rufinus of Chalcis, when he drank hellebore, neither threw up nor suffered any laxative effect, but he took it and digested it as though it were something to which he was accustomed. Chrysermus the Herophilean, if he ever used 84 pepper, risked a heart attack. And Soterichus the surgeon, whenever he smelled fried fish, got diarrhea. Andron the Argive was so immune to thirst that he even traveled through the Libyan desert without needing anything to drink. Tiberius Caesar could see in the dark, and Aristotle tells of a certain Thasian to whom it seemed that a human phantom was all the time leading him around.

85     Since there is so much variation among human beings as regards the body — and it suffices to mention only a few of the cases that the Dogmatists provide — it is likely that human beings will also differ among themselves as regards the soul. For the body is a kind of image of the soul, as indeed the art of Physiognomy shows. But the greatest indication of the vast and limitless difference in the intellect of human beings is the inconsistency of the various statements of the Dogmatists concerning what may be appropriately chosen,

86     what avoided, and so on. The poets, too, have expressed themselves appropriately about these things. For Pindar says:

> The crowns and trophies of his storm-foot steeds
> Give joy to one; yet others find it joy
> To dwell in gorgeous chambers gold-bedecked;
> Some even take delight in voyaging
> O'er ocean's billows in a speeding barque.
>
> Frag. 221 Snell, as translated by Sir J. E. Sandys

And the poet says:

> One person delights in one activity, another in another.
>
> *Odyssey* 14.228

Tragedy, too, is full of such things:

> If the same things were beautiful and wise for everybody,
> There would be no disputatious strife among mankind.
>
> Euripides, *Phoenissae* 499–500

And again,

> It is strange that the same thing should be pleasing to some
> mortals and hateful to others.
>
> Anon., frag. 462 Nauck

87     Since, then, choice and avoidance are in pleasure and displeasure, and pleasure and displeasure lie in sense and *phantasia*, when the same things are chosen by some people and avoided by others it is logical for us to infer that these people are not affected alike by the same things, since if they were they would alike have chosen and avoided the same things. But if the same things produce different affects depending on the difference of human beings, this too would reasonably lead to suspension of judgment and we would, perhaps, be able to say what each of the external objects appears to be, relative to each

88     difference, but we would not be able to state what it is in nature. For we shall either have to give credence to all human beings or to some. But if to all, we shall be attempting impossibilities and accepting contradictory statements. And if to some, let the Dogmatists tell us to whom we should give assent. The Platonist will say "to Plato" and the Epicurean "to Epicurus," and the others

analogously, and thus with their unsettled disputes they bring us again to 89
suspension of judgment. Anyone who says that we ought to give assent to the
majority view is making a childish proposal, for no one is able to approach the
whole human race and by talking with them find out what pleases the majority.
Indeed, there may be peoples of whom we know nothing but among whom
attributes that are most rare among us are common, while the attributes most
common among us are rare among them; so that, for example, most of them
feel no pain when bitten by spiders, while a few, on rare occasions, do; and
analogously with the other "idiosyncracies" previously mentioned. Of necessity,
therefore, suspension of judgment comes in again, via the differences of human
beings.

While the Dogmatists egoistically claim that in deciding the facts prefer- 90
ence ought to be given to themselves above all other human beings, we realize
that this claim of theirs is inappropriate since they themselves are part of the
dispute. And if, giving preference to themselves, they make a decision about the
appearances, by entrusting the decision to themselves they beg the question
before the deciding is begun. In any case, in order to arrive at suspension of 91
judgment by an argument dealing with only one person — their Ideal Sage, for
example, who is expert at interpreting dreams — we take up the third mode in
the list.

This mode is the one that we say is based on the difference of the senses.
That the senses differ from one another is obvious from the start. For instance, 92
to the eye it seems that paintings have hollows and prominences, but not to
the touch. And for some people honey seems pleasant to the tongue but
unpleasant to the eye; consequently, it is impossible to say without qualification whether it is pleasant or unpleasant. And likewise in the case of perfume,
for it pleases the sense of smell but displeases the taste. So too with spurge 93
juice: since it is painful to the eyes but painless to all the rest of the body, we
will not be able to say without qualification whether, insofar as its nature is
concerned, it is painful or painless to bodies. And rain water is beneficial to the
eyes, but it is rough on the wind pipe and lungs, as is olive oil despite its being
soothing to the skin. The sting-ray, when it touches the extremities, produces
numbness, but it can touch the rest of the body harmlessly. Hence we shall not
be able to say how each of these things is in its nature, but only how it appears
to be in each instance.

More examples can be given, but in order not to delay carrying out the 94
purpose of our essay, the following point needs to be made. Each thing that
appears to us in sensation seems to affect us as complex; for example, the apple
seems smooth, fragrant, sweet, yellow. But it is not evident whether it really
has these and only these qualities, or whether, having only one quality, it
appears differently depending on the different constitutions of the sense organs,
or again whether it has more qualities than are apparent but some of them do
not affect us. That it has one quality could be argued on the basis of what we 95
previously said about the food taken up by the body and the water taken up
by the tree and the air breathed into flutes and pipes and similar instruments;
for the apple, too, may be of one form but appear differently because of the
difference of the sense organs through which it is perceived. And that the apple 96

has more qualities than those that appear to us, we can reason as follows. Suppose that someone is born having the senses of touch, smell, and taste, but can neither hear nor see. Then he will assume that the origin of his perceptions is not something visible or audible, but that it has only those three types of
97   quality which he is capable of perceiving. And it is possible that we, with only our five senses, perceive only those qualities of the apple that we are fitted to perceive, and that perhaps there are other qualities, affecting other sense organs which we lack and for which we consequently cannot perceive any corresponding objects.

98        But nature, someone may say, has made the senses exactly proportionate to the objects of sense. But what is this "nature", seeing that there is so much unresolved controversy among the Dogmatists concerning its very existence? For anyone who decides this question, that is, whether nature exists, will have no credibility with them if he is an ordinary person, while if he is a philosopher he will be part of the controversy and instead of being a judge will be subject
99   to judgment himself. So that if it is possible that only those qualities exist in the apple which we seem to perceive, or that there are more than these, or again that there are not even the ones that affect us, what the apple is like will be nonevident to us. The same argument holds also in the case of the other objects of sense. And since the senses do not apprehend the external objects, the intellect is not capable of doing so either, so that this argument, too, seems conducive to suspension of judgment concerning the external objects.

100       In order that we shall be able to reach suspension of judgment when basing the argument on each single sense or even disregarding the senses, we take up further the fourth mode of *epochē*. This is the one described as "based on circumstances," where by "circumstances" we mean conditions. We say that it is concerned with being in a natural or unnatural condition, with being awake or asleep, with dependence on age, on being in motion or at rest, on hating or loving, on being in need or satisfied, on being drunk or sober, on predisposi-
101   tions, on being courageous or fearful, on being distressed or cheerful. Thus, things affect us in dissimilar ways depending on whether we are in a natural or unnatural condition, as when people who are delirious or possessed by a god seem to hear spirits but we do not. Similarly, those people often say that they perceive odors of storax or frankincense or some such thing, and much else, too, although we do not sense them. And the same water that seems to us to be lukewarm seems boiling hot when poured on an inflamed place. And the same coat appears tawny-orange to people with bloodshot eyes but not to me.
102   Also, the same honey appears sweet to me but bitter to the jaundiced. Further, if someone says that an intermingling of certain humors produces, in persons who are in an unnatural condition, odd *phantasiai* of the external objects, it must be replied that since healthy people, too, have intermingled humors, it is possible that the external objects are in nature such as they appear to those persons who are said to be in an unnatural state, but that these humors are making the external objects appear to the healthy people to be other than they
103   are. For to give the power of altering the external objects to some humors but not to others is arbitrary; since just as the healthy in a natural state have the nature of the healthy and in an unnatural state that of the sick, so too the sick

in an unnatural state have the nature of the healthy and in a natural state that of the sick; so that credence should be given to these last, too, as being in a relatively natural state.

Different *phantasiai* come about, too, depending on whether we are asleep 104 or awake. For when we are awake we do not imagine [*ou phantazometha*] what we imagine when we are asleep, nor when we are asleep do we imagine what we imagine when awake, so that whether the *phantasiai* are the case or are not the case is not absolute but relative, that is, relative to being asleep or awake. It is fair to say, then, that when asleep we see things that are not the case in the waking state, though not absolutely not the case. For they are the case in our sleep, just as what we see in our waking state is the case, though not in our sleep.

Depending on age, too, different *phantasiai* arise, since the same air seems 105 cold to the aged but temperate to those who are in their prime, and the same color appears faint to older people but vivid to those in their prime, and likewise the same sound appears faint to the former but clearly audible to the latter. And people of differing ages are moved in different ways depending on 106 their choices and aversions. For instance, children are interested in balls and hoops, but people in their prime prefer other things, and the elderly still others. From this we conclude that, also depending on differences of age, differing *phantasiai* arise from the same external objects.

Objects appear differently, too, depending on whether one is in motion or 107 at rest. For things that we see as stationary when we are at rest seem to be moving when we are sailing by. Depending on liking and disliking, also: for 108 some people are completely repelled by pork, while others eat it with the greatest of pleasure. Whence Menander, too, said:

> Look how his face appears now that he
> has come to this — like an animal!
> It is acting justly that makes us fair.
>
>                     Frag. 518 Kock

And many people who have ugly mistresses think them beautiful. Depending 109 on hunger and satiety, too: since the same food seems very pleasant to the hungry but unpleasant to the sated. And depending on being drunk or sober: since things we consider shameful when we are sober appear to us not to be shameful when we are drunk. And depending on predispositions: since the 110 same wine that appears sour to people who have previously eaten dates or figs seems sweet to those who have eaten nuts or chickpeas; and the vestibule of the bathhouse is warm to those entering from outside and cold to those leaving, if they have spent some time in it. And depending on being afraid or 111 feeling courageous: since the same thing seems frightful and terrible to the timid but not at all so to the bold. And, finally, depending on being distressed or cheerful: since the same things that are annoying to people who are distressed are pleasant to those who are cheerful.

Since, therefore, there is so much anomaly depending on conditions, and 112 human beings are in one condition at one time and another at another, how each external object appears to each person is easy to say, I suppose,

but not how it is, since the anomaly is unresolved. For anyone resolving it is either in one of the aforementioned conditions or is in no condition at all. But to say that he is in no condition at all — for example, neither healthy nor sick, neither in motion nor at rest, nor of any particular age, and devoid
113    of the other conditions as well — is completely absurd. But if he, being in some condition, makes a decision about the *phantasiai*, he will be part of the dispute and in other ways not a pure or fair judge of the external objects, because he has been contaminated by the conditions he is in. The waking person cannot compare the *phantasiai* of sleepers with those of people who are awake, nor can the healthy person compare those of the sick with those of the healthy. For we assent to things that are in the present and move us in the present, more than to things that are not in the present.

114        In another way, too, the anomaly of such *phantasiai* is unresolved. For anyone preferring one *phantasia* to another or one circumstance to another either does this without making a decision and without giving proof, or by making a decision and giving proof. But he will not do it without these means, for then he will not be credible, nor will he do it with them, either. For if he makes a decision about the *phantasiai*, he will certainly decide by means of a
115    criterion. And certainly he will either say that this criterion is true or that it is false. But if he says that it is false, he will not be credible. And if he says that the criterion is true, either he will say this without proof or he will say it with proof. Again, if he says it without proof, he will not be credible; but if with proof, the proof will certainly need to be true if he is to be credible. When he affirms the truth of the proof which he is taking to establish the credibility of
116    the criterion, will he have made a decision about this or not? If he has not made the decision, he will not be credible; and if he has made the decision, then it is obvious that he will say that he has decided by means of a criterion, in order that it may be maintained, and the criterion has need of a proof, in order that it may be shown to be true. And neither is it possible for a proof to be sound without the prior existence of a true criterion, nor for a criterion to be true
117    without the previously confirmed proof. And thus the criterion and the proof fall into the circularity type of *aporia*, in which both are found not to be credible; for each, while it awaits the credibility of the other, is equally incredible with the other. Therefore, if nobody, with or without a proof and criterion, is able to give one *phantasia* preference over another, then the differing *phantasiai* that arise depending on the different conditions will be undecidable; so that this mode, too, leads to suspension of judgment concerning the nature of the external objects.

118        The fifth argument is that depending on positions, distances, and locations. For, depending on each of these, the same things appear different — for example, the same stoa viewed from either end appears tapering but from the middle completely symmetrical, and from afar the same boat appears small and stationary but from close up large and in motion, and the same tower appears round from afar but square from close up.

119        These depend on distances. But depending on locations: the same lamp-light appears dim in the sunshine but bright in the dark, and the same oar

appears broken when it is in the water and straight when it is out, and the egg soft when it is in the bird but hard when it is in the air, and the ligure liquid in the lynx but hard in the air, and coral soft in the sea but hard in the air, and sound appears one way in a pipe, another in a flute, and still another when it is simply in the air.

And depending on positions: the same portrait appears smooth when tilted  120 back, but when tilted forward a certain amount it seems to have depths and prominences. And the necks of pigeons appear different in color depending on the different angles of inclination.

Therefore, since everything apparent is viewed in some location and from  121 some distance and in some position, each of which produces a great deal of variation in the *phantasiai*, as we have remarked above, we shall be forced also by this mode to have recourse to suspension of judgment. And anyone wishing to give preference to some of these *phantasiai* will be attempting the impossible. For if he makes his assertion simply and without proof, he will not be credible;  122 whereas, supposing that he wishes to use a proof, if he says that the proof is false he will confute himself, while if he says that it is true he will need a proof of its being true, and again a proof of that, since it too must be true, and so on ad infinitum. But it is impossible to produce infinitely many proofs; and so  123 he will not be able by means of a proof to give one *phantasia* preference over another. And if one cannot decide about the aforementioned *phantasiai* either with or without a proof, suspension of judgment results; for, I suppose, of any given thing we are able to say of what sort, relative to its particular position, distance, and place, it appears to be, but for the above reasons we cannot state of what sort it is in its nature.

The sixth mode is the one that depends on admixtures and according to  124 which we conclude that, since none of the external objects affects us by itself but always in combination with something, it is perhaps possible to say what the mixture of the external object and that together with which it is observed is like, but we cannot do the same for the external object considered by itself. It is obvious from the start, I think, that none of the external objects affects us by itself, but always does so in combination with something, and that depending on this it is observed as different. Thus, our own complexion is seen  125 as of one hue in warm air and as of another in cold air, and so we cannot say how our complexion is in nature, but only how it looks together with each of the two kinds of air. Further, the same sound appears one way in thin air and another in dense air, and spices are more pungent in the bathhouse and in the sun than in very cold air, and the body is light when immersed in water, but heavy in air.

In order to get away from just external admixtures: our eyes contain within  126 themselves both membranes and liquids. Since things seen are not observed without these, they will not be accurately apprehended, for it is the mixture that we perceive, and because of this the jaundiced see everything yellow, while those with blood in the eyes see things as bloodred. And since the same sound appears of one quality in open places and of another in places that are narrow and winding, and of one quality in clear air and another in murky air, it is

likely that we do not perceive the sound in and of itself; for the ears have narrow and winding passages and are contaminated by vaporous effluvia said
127  to be conducted from places around the head. Moreover, since there are substances in the nostrils and in the areas of taste, we perceive the objects of taste and of smell together with these and not in and of themselves. Therefore, because of the admixtures the senses do not perceive precisely how the external objects are.

128  Nor does the intellect do so either, especially since its guides, the senses, go wrong; perhaps it too contributes some special admixture of its own to the reports of the senses; for we observe that there are humors situated around each of the places in which the Dogmatists suppose that the ruling part of the soul is located, whether the brain or the heart or whatever part of the animal anyone wants to put it in. And so by this mode also we see that, being unable to say anything about the nature of the external objects, we are forced to suspension of judgment.

129  The seventh mode, we said, is that depending on the quantity and constitution of the external objects, giving "constitution" its common meaning, namely, combination. It is obvious that by this mode, too, we are forced to suspend judgment about the nature of the objects. For example, shavings off a goat's horn appear white when observed by themselves and not in combination, but when they are combined in the substance of the horn they look black. And individual filings of a piece of silver appear black, but when united with
130  the whole they affect us as white. And pieces of Taenarean marble look white when they are polished, but combined in the whole stone they appear yellow. And grains of sand when scattered appear rough, but when gathered together in a dune they affect our senses as soft. And hellebore, taken when fine and
131  light, tends to choke one, but not when coarse. And wine, when drunk in moderation, strengthens us, but when taken in excess, disables the body. And food, similarly, exhibits different powers depending on the amount; often, indeed, by being taken in too great quantity it brings the body down with
132  indigestion and diarrhea. So here, too, we shall be able to say of what quality the shaving of horn is, and of what quality the combination of many shavings is, and the same for the particle of silver and the combination of many particles, and for the bit of Taenarean marble and the combination of many bits, and we can make relative statements in the case of the grains of sand and the hellebore and the wine and the food, too, but we still cannot state the absolute nature of the things because of the anomaly of *phantasiai* depending on combination.

133  It seems that in general even beneficial things become harmful when they are used in immoderate quantities, and the things that seem hurtful when taken in excess are harmless in small quantities. The best indication of this point is what is observed in regard to the powers of medicines, in which the exact mixing of the simple drugs produces a compound that is beneficial, but the occasional slightest error in weighing, when overlooked, makes it not only not beneficial but even quite hurtful and often poisonous.

134  So the argument relating to quantities and constitutions muddles the existence of the external objects. Consequently this mode too may be expected

to lead us around to suspension of judgment, for we are unable to say anything without qualification about the nature of the external objects.

The eighth mode is the one based on relativity, where we conclude that, 135 since everything is in relation to something, we shall suspend judgment as to what things are in themselves and in their nature. But it must be noticed that here, as elsewhere, we use "are" for "appear to be," saying in effect "everything appears in relation to something." But this statement has two senses: first, as implying relation to what does the judging, for the object that exists externally and is judged appears in relation to what does the judging, and second, as implying relation to the things observed together with it, as, for example, what is on the right is in relation to what is on the left. And, indeed, we have taken 136 into account earlier that everything is in relation to something: for example, as regards what does the judging, that each thing appears in relation to this or that animal or person or sense and in relation to such and such a circumstance; and as regards the things observed together with it, that each thing appears in relation to this or that admixture or manner or combination or quantity or position.

But it is also possible to prove by a special argument that everything is in 137 relation to something, as follows. Do the things that are what they are by virtue of a difference differ from the things that are in relation to something, or not? If they do not differ, then they too are in relation to something; if they do differ, then, since whatever differs is in relation to something (for it is called what it is in relation to that from which it differs), the things that are what they are by virtue of a difference are in relation to something. And, according to the 138 Dogmatists, of things that are, some are *summa genera*, others are *infimae species*, and others are genera and species. But all these are relative. Again, of things that are, some are pre-evident and others are non-evident, as they say; the appearances signify, and the non-evident things are signified by the appearances. For, according to them, "the appearances are a view of the non-evident." But what signifies and what is signified are relative. Therefore, 139 everything is relative. Moreover, of things that are, some are similar and others are dissimilar, and some are equal and others are unequal; but these things are relative; therefore, everything is relative. And even the person who says that not all things are relative confirms the relativity of all things, for by the arguments he opposes to us he shows that the very relativity of all things is relative to us and not universal.

Now, when we have shown that all things are relative, the obvious result 140 is that as concerns each external object we shall not be able to state how it is in its own nature and absolutely, but only how, in relation to something, it appears to be. It follows that we must suspend judgment about the nature of the objects.

In connection with the mode based on the constancy or infrequency of 141 occurrence, which we say is the ninth in order, we consider such items as the following. The sun is certainly a much more marvelous thing than a comet. But since we see the sun all the time but the comet only infrequently, we marvel at the comet so much as even to suppose it a divine portent, but we do nothing

like that for the sun. If, however, we thought of the sun as appearing
infrequently and setting infrequently, and as illuminating everything all at once
and then suddenly being eclipsed, we would find much to marvel at in the
142  matter. And earthquakes are not equally troublesome to the person who is
experiencing one for the first time and to the person who has become
accustomed to them. And how marvelous is the sea to the person who sees it
for the first time! And a beautiful human body that is seen suddenly and for
143  the first time excites us more than if it were to become a customary sight.
Things that are rare seem precious, but things that are familiar and easy to get
do not. Indeed, if we thought of water as rare, how much more precious it
would appear than all the things that do seem precious! And if we imagine gold
simply scattered on the ground like stones, to whom do we think it would then
be precious and worth hoarding away?

144      Since, then, the same things, depending on whether they occur frequently
or infrequently, seem at one time marvelous or precious and at another time
not, we infer that we shall perhaps be able to say how each of these appears
when it occurs frequently or when it occurs infrequently, but that we shall not
be able to state without qualification how each of the external objects is. And,
accordingly, via this mode too we withhold assent as regards them.

145      The tenth mode, which is principally concerned with ethics, is the one
depending on ways of life and on customs, laws, mythic beliefs, and dogmatic
suppositions. A way of life is a chosen basis for living or for some particular
action, adopted by one person or many—for example, by Diogenes or the
146  Laconians. A law is a written agreement among the citizens, the violator of
which is punished; a custom or common practice (for there is no difference) is
the joint acceptance by a number of people of a certain way of acting, where
the violator is not in all cases punished; thus, there is a law against adultery,
147  and for us it is a custom not to have intercourse with a woman in public. A
mythic belief is the acceptance of things that are not the case and are
fictional—such as, among others, the myths about Cronus—and in which
many people place credence. And a dogmatic supposition is the acceptance of
something that seems to be established by analogy or some kind of proof, such
as that there are atomic elements of things, or homoeomeries [ultimate
particles of matter], or *minima*, or other things.

148      And we oppose each of these items sometimes to itself and sometimes to
each of the others. For example, we oppose custom to custom thus: some of
the Ethiopians tattoo their babies, but we do not. And the Persians think it
becoming to wear brightly colored garments that reach to the feet, but we
consider it unbecoming; and whereas the Indians have intercourse with women
149  in public, most others consider this shameful. We oppose law to law thus:
among the Romans, he who gives up his patrimony does not pay his father's
debts; but among the Rhodians he always pays them; and among the Tauri of
Scythia there was a law that foreigners were to be sacrificed to Artemis, but
150  with us it is forbidden to kill a human being at the temple. And we oppose a
way of life to a way of life when we set Diogenes's way of life in opposition to
that of Aristippus, or that of the Laconians to that of the Italians. We oppose

a mythical belief to a mythical belief when in one place we say that according to myth Zeus is the father of men and gods, while in another we say that it is Oceanus, referring to the line:

Oceanus, the source of the gods, and Tethys, the mother.

Iliad 14.201

And we oppose dogmatic opinions to one another when we say that some 151 people assert that there is just one element and others that there are infinitely many, and that some assert that the soul is mortal and others that it is immortal, and that some assert that our affairs are arranged by divine providence while others assert that they are not.

We also oppose custom to the other items — to law, for example, when we 152 say that among the Persians sodomy is customary but among the Romans it is prohibited by law; and with us adultery is prohibited, but among the Massagetae it is by custom treated as a matter of indifference, as Eudoxus of Cnidos reports in the first book of his *Travels*; and with us it is forbidden to have intercourse with one's mother, whereas with the Persians this sort of marriage is very much the custom. And among the Egyptians men marry their sisters, which for us is prohibited by law. Custom is opposed to way of life 153 when, whereas the majority of men have intercourse with their wives in some place apart, Crates did it with Hipparchia in public; and Diogenes went around with shoulders bare, while we dress in the usual way. And custom is opposed 154 to mythical belief, as when the myths say that Cronus ate his own children, it being customary among us to take care of children; and whereas with us it is customary to worship the gods as being good and immune from evil, they are presented by the poets as being wounded by and envious of one another. 155 Custom is also opposed to dogmatic opinion when with us it is the custom to pray to the gods for good things, whereas Epicurus says that the divinity does not care about us; and when Aristippus thinks it a matter of indifference whether one wears women's clothing, while we think this shameful.

We oppose way of life to law when, though there is a law against striking 156 a free and well-born man, the pancratiasts hit one another because of their way of life, and when, though homicide is forbidden, the gladiators kill one another for the same reason. Further, we oppose mythical belief to way of life when we 157 point out that the myths say that Heracles in the house of Omphale "carded wool and endured slavery" and did these things which nobody would choose to do, even to a moderate degree, whereas Heracles's way of life was noble. We 158 oppose way of life to dogmatic supposition when athletes undertake an onerous way of life for the sake of glory, on the supposition that glory is good, while many philosophers dogmatize that it is an evil thing. And we oppose law 159 to mythical belief when the poets present the gods as practicing adultery and sodomy, while with us the law prohibits doing these things; and we oppose law 160 to dogmatic opinion when the Chrysippeans say that intercourse with mothers or sisters is a matter of indifference, while the law prohibits these things. 161 Further, we oppose mythical belief to dogmatic supposition when the poets say that Zeus came down and had intercourse with mortal women, whereas this is

162 deemed by the Dogmatists to be impossible; and the poet says that Zeus,
because of grief over Sarpedon,

> Let fall a shower of blood upon the earth,
>                                          Iliad 16.459

while it is a dogma of the philosophers that the divinity is impassive; and when
the philosophers reject the myth of the hippocentaurs, while offering us the
hippocentaur as a paradigm of nonexistence.

163      For each of the foregoing oppositions it was possible to take many other
examples, but in an outline these will suffice. At any rate, since by this mode,
too, so much anomaly in "the facts" has been shown, we shall not be able to
say how any external object or state of affairs is in its nature, but only how it
appears in relation to a given way of life or law or custom, and so forth. And
so because of this mode, too, we must suspend judgment about the nature of
the external "facts." Thus, via all ten modes we end up with suspension of
judgment.


## 15. The Five Modes

164 The more recent Skeptics hand down the following five modes of *epochē*: the
first is the mode based on disagreement; the second is that based on infinite
regress; the third, that based on relativity; the fourth, on hypothesis; and the
165 fifth is the circularity mode. The one based on disagreement is that according
to which we find that, both in ordinary life and among philosophers, with
regard to a given topic there has been reached an unresolvable impasse on
account of which we are unable to reach a verdict one way or the other, and
166 we end up with suspension of judgment. The one based on infinite regress is
that in which we say that what is offered as support for believing a given
proposition is itself in need of such support, and that support is in need of other
support, and so on ad infinitum, so that, since we have no place from which to
167 begin to establish anything, suspension of judgment follows. The one based on
relativity is, as we said before, that in which the external object appears this
way or that way in relation to the judging subject and the things observed at
168 the same time, but we suspend judgment as to how it is in its nature. And the
one based on hypothesis comes into play when the Dogmatists, involved in an
infinite regress, begin with something that they do not establish but that they
deem worthy of acceptance as agreed upon without question or demonstration.
169 And the circularity mode occurs when what ought to make the case for the
matter in question has need of support from that very matter; whence, being
unable to assume either in order to establish the other, we suspend judgment
about both.
      That every matter of inquiry can be brought under these modes we shall
170 show in brief as follows. Anything proposed for consideration is either a sense
object or a thought object, but whichever it is, there is a disagreement

concerning it. For some people say that only the sense objects are true, others that only the thought objects, and still others that some of each. Now, will they say that the disagreement can be decided or that it cannot? If it cannot, we have the conclusion that one must suspend judgment, for concerning disagreements that are not decidable one cannot make an assertion. On the other hand, if it is decidable, then we want to know how it is to be decided. Shall we decide 171 about a sense object, for example (for first we shall base the argument on this case) by a sense object or a thought object? If by a sense object, then, since the sense objects are what our inquiry is about, this object too will need something else as support. And if that also is a sense object, it again will need support from another one, and so on ad infinitum. But if we are to decide about the 172 sense object by a thought object, then, since there is a disagreement about the thought objects, too, and this is a thought object, it also will be in need of decision and support. But by what will it be supported? If by a thought object, it will similarly involve an infinite regress; but if by a sense object, then, since a thought object was used as support for a sense object and a sense object for a thought object, the circularity mode of *epochē* comes in.

But if, to avoid these points, our interlocutor should think to assume 173 something, by consent and without demonstration, as a basis for demonstrating what follows, the hypothesis mode comes into play and allows no way out. For if the hypothesizer is worthy of credence, we shall be no less worthy of credence whenever we hypothesize the opposite. And if what the hypothesizer hypothesizes is true, he makes it suspect by taking it as a hypothesis instead of establishing it; but if it is false, the underpinnings of the things being established will be rotten. Further, if hypothesizing contributes something to credibility, we 174 might as well hypothesize what is in question and not something else from which the hypothesizer is going to establish the point at issue; and if it is absurd to hypothesize what is in question, it will also be absurd to hypothesize a proposition superordinate to this.

That all sense objects are relative is evident, for they are relative to whoever 175 does the sensing. It is therefore plain that any sense object that is proposed to us is easily brought under the five modes. And we reason in the same way about thought objects. For if it is said that the dispute is not decidable, the necessity of suspending judgment about it will be granted us. And if the dispute 176 is going to be decided, then if by means of a thought object, we shall produce an infinite regress, while if by means of a sense object, a circular inference. For when the dispute is about the sense object and cannot be decided by means of a sense object because of an infinite regress, there will be need of a thought object, just as for the thought object there will be need of a sense object. For 177 these reasons, again, anyone who assumes something as a hypothesis will be acting absurdly. Furthermore, the thought objects, too, are relative; for they are so named with respect to the people who think them, and if they were in nature as they are said to be, there would be no dispute about them. Hence the thought objects, too, are brought under the five modes, so that in all cases it is necessary for us to suspend judgment about any matter proposed for consideration.

Such, then, are the five modes handed down by the later Skeptics; they are not put forward by way of throwing out the ten modes, but in order to combat the precipitancy of the Dogmatists in greater detail by means of both together.

## 16. The Two Modes

178 They also hand down two other modes of *epochē*. For since everything that is apprehended is either apprehended through itself or through something else, by pointing out that what is apprehended is apprehended neither through itself nor through anything else they produce *aporiai*, as they suppose, about everything. That nothing is apprehended through itself is apparent, they say, from the dispute among the physical scientists concerning not only all sense objects but also, I think, all thought objects — a dispute that is not decidable since we cannot use either a sense object or a thought object as a criterion, for
179 anything we take will be in dispute and hence not credible. And the following is the reason why they do not agree that something can be apprehended through something else. If that through which something is apprehended must in every case be apprehended through something else, they encounter the circularity or infinite regress modes of *epochē*. But if somebody should wish to take as apprehended through itself something through which something else is apprehended, he runs up against the fact that for the aforementioned reasons nothing is apprehended through itself. So we are at a loss as to how the thing in question could be apprehended either on the basis of itself or on that of something else, since there is no apparent criterion of truth or of apprehension and since signs, even apart from proof, are eliminated, as we shall show later.

It will suffice for the present to have said thus much about the modes leading to suspension of judgment.

## 17. Some Modes for Refuting People Who Give Causal Explanations

180 Just as we hand down the modes of *Epochē*, so some people set forth modes by which we produce *aporia* about particular causal explanations, thereby giving a jolt to the Dogmatists since they pride themselves especially on these. Aenesidemus, indeed, hands down eight modes by means of which he thinks to
181 refute and expose as unsound every dogmatic causal explanation. The first of these, he says, is the mode according to which causal explanations in general, concerned as they are with what is nonevident, get no agreed-upon confirmation from the appearances. The second is that according to which, although there is often a plethora of ways of giving a causal explanation of what is in
182 question, some people give such an explanation in one way only. According to the third, they refer orderly things to causes that exhibit no order. According to the fourth, when they have apprehended how the appearances come about, they think they have apprehended how the things that are not appearances come about, whereas although it is possible that these latter come about

similarly to the appearances, it is also possible that they come about, not similarly, but in a way peculiar to themselves. The fifth mode is that according 183 to which practically all the causal explainers give accounts based on their own particular hypotheses about the elements and not on common and generally agreed approaches. The sixth is that according to which they often accept what fits in with their own particular hypotheses but reject what is equally credible but does not so fit in. According to the seventh, they assign causes that conflict 184 not only with the appearances but even with their own hypotheses; while according to the eighth it frequently happens that when the things under investigation and the things seemingly apparent are equally puzzling, they construct their doctrine about the equally puzzling on the basis of the equally puzzling. Nor is it impossible, Aenesidemus says, that some should fail with 185 their causal explanations on the basis of certain mixed modes dependent on the foregoing ones.

Possibly, too, the five modes of *epochē* suffice against the causal explanations. For any cause that somebody proposes will either be compatible with all philosophical systems and with Skepticism and with the appearances, or it will not. And that it will be thus compatible is impossible, I suppose, for there is disagreement about all the appearances and nonevident things. But if there is 186 disagreement about the proposed cause, the proponent will be asked for the cause of it, and if he takes an appearance as the cause of an appearance or a non-evident thing as the cause of a non-evident thing, he will land in an infinite regress, and in a circular inference if he takes them *alternando*. And if he makes a stand somewhere, either he will say that he has established the cause as such in relation to what was said before, thus introducing "in relation to" and eliminating "in nature," or else he will take something as an hypothesis and will be brought to a standstill. So, by these modes too it is possible, I think, to combat the precipitancy of the Dogmatists in their causal theories.

## 18. The Skeptic Slogans

Since, in using each of these modes and those leading to suspension of 187 judgment, we utter certain slogans expressive of the Skeptic temper of mind and of our *pathē*— for example, "not more," "nothing is to be determined," and the like— it would be reasonable to take up these next. Let us begin with "not more."

## 19. The "Not More" Slogan

We say this sometimes in the form I have just mentioned, but sometimes in the 188 form "nothing more"; for we do not, as some people suppose, employ the "not more" in specific investigations and the "nothing more" in general ones; rather, we say either "not more" or "nothing more" indifferently, and now we shall discuss them as though they were identical. This slogan, then, is elliptical. Just as when we say "a duplex" we are saying in effect "a duplex house," and when we say "a wide" [*plateia*, a square] we are saying in effect "a wide street," so also when we say "not more" we are saying in effect "not more this than that, up than down." Some of the Skeptics, however, in place of the "not" adopt "what" — "what more this than that" — taking the "what" to refer to the cause, so that the meaning is "because of what [i.e., why] this more than that?" For it is common practice to use questions instead of assertions, as in the line

189

> What mortal doesn't know the bride of Zeus?
>
> Euripides, *Hercules* 1

and assertions instead of questions, such as "I want to know where Dion lives" and "I ask why one should marvel at a poetic person." Also, the use of "what" instead of "why" [i.e., "because of what"] is found in Menander:

> [Because of] what was I left behind?
>
> Frag. 900 Kock

190 And the slogan "not more this than that" also makes evident our *pathos* with respect to which we reach equilibrium through the equipollence of the opposed things — where we use the term "equipollence" for equality as regards what appears persuasive to us, and "opposed things" in the everyday sense of things that conflict, and "equilibrium" for the absence of assent to either alternative.

191 Even if the slogan "nothing more" exhibits the character of assent or denial, we do not use it in that way, but rather we take it in an imprecise and not strictly correct sense, either in place of a question or instead of saying "I don't know to which of these I ought to assent and to which I ought not to assent." For our goal is to make evident what appears to us, and we do not care with what expression we do it. And this also should be noticed: that in uttering the "nothing more" slogan we are not maintaining that it is entirely true and firm, but in its case, too, we are speaking in accord with what appears to us.

## 20. "Non-assertion" (*Aphasia*)

192 Concerning non-assertion we say the following. The term "assertion" has two senses, a wider and a narrower. In the wider sense an assertion is an expression indicating affirmation or denial, such as "It is day," "It is not day"; whereas in the narrower sense it is an expression indicating affirmation only; in this sense people do not call negative statements "assertions." Non-assertion, then, is the avoidance of assertion in the wider sense, in which we say that both affirmation and negation are covered; so that non-assertion is a *pathos* of ours in view of

193 which we say that we do not affirm or deny anything. From this it is evident that we adopt the "non-assertion" slogan, too, not on the assumption that things are in their nature such as to produce non-assertion in every case, but simply as making evident that we, now, when we are uttering it, and in the case

of the particular matters in question, are experiencing this *pathos*. And this, too, must be kept in mind: it is dogmatic statements about the non-evident that we say we neither affirm nor deny; we grant the things that stir our *pathē* and drive us by force to assent.

## 21. "Perhaps," "It Is Possible," "Maybe"

The slogans "perhaps," and "perhaps not," and "possibly" and "possibly not," 194 and "maybe" and "maybe not" we take in place of "perhaps it is the case" and "perhaps it is not the case," and "possibly it is the case" and "possibly it is not the case," and "maybe it is the case" and "maybe it is not the case" — for brevity's sake using "possibly not" for "possibly it is not the case" and "maybe not" for "maybe it is not the case," and "perhaps not" for "perhaps it is not the case." But here again we do not fight over words, nor are we raising the issue 195 of whether the slogans make evident the nature of these matters; rather, as I said before, we employ them imprecisely. Nevertheless, I think, it is evident that these slogans are expressive of non-assertion. Certainly the person who says "perhaps it is the case," by not firmly maintaining that it is the case, is in effect also asserting the seemingly inconsistent "perhaps it is not the case;" similarly for the remaining slogans.

## 22. "I Withhold Assent"

We use "I withhold assent" as short for "I am unable to say which of the 196 alternatives proposed I ought to believe and which I ought not believe," indicating that the matters appear equal to us as regards credibility and incredibility. As to whether they are equal, we maintain no firm opinion, but we do state what appears to us to be the case about them when that appearance affects us. And withholding assent [*epochē*] is so called from the intellect's being held back [*epechesthai*] in such a way as neither to assert nor deny, because of the equipollence of the matters in question.

## 23. "I Determine Nothing"

Concerning "I determine nothing" we say the following. We think that 197 "determining" is not simply saying something but rather is putting forward and assenting to something non-evident. Thus, I suppose, the Skeptic will be found not to be determining anything, not even the slogan "I determine nothing" itself. For that slogan is not a dogmatic opinion, that is, an assent to the non-evident, but rather it makes evident our *pathos*. Whenever the Skeptic says "I determine nothing," he is saying this: "I am now in such a state of mind as neither dogmatically to affirm nor deny any of the matters in question." And this he says, reporting what appears to him concerning the matters at hand, not dogmatically and confidently, but just as a description of his state of mind, his *pathos*.

## 24. "Everything Is Indeterminate"

198   Indeterminateness is a *pathos* of the intellect in accord with which we take neither a negative nor an affirmative position on the matters of dogmatic inquiry, that is, the non-evident. Whenever the Skeptic says "Everything is indeterminate," he uses "is" in place of "appears to me to be," and with "everything" he does not refer simply to all there is, but rather to the Dogmatists' non-evident objects that are under his consideration; and by "indeterminate" he means "not standing out as superior, as regards credibility and incredibility, among the things that are opposite or mutually inconsistent."

199   And just as the person who says "I'm walking around" is in effect saying "I am walking around," so, according to us, the one who is saying "Everything is indeterminate" means also "as relates to me" or "as appears to me"; consequently, what is said comes down to this: "all the matters of dogmatic inquiry that I have considered appear to me to be such that not one of them seems to me superior, as regards credibility and incredibility, to anything inconsistent with it."

## 25. "Everything Is Non-apprehensible"

200   And we adopt a similar stance, too, when we say "Everything is non-apprehensible." For we explain "everything" in the same way, and we add "to me," so that what is said amounts to this: "All of the non-evident matters of dogmatic inquiry that I have considered appear to me to be non-apprehensible." This is not the assertion of one who is firmly maintaining that the things investigated by the Dogmatists are of such a nature as to be non-apprehensible, but rather of one who is reporting his own *pathos*, in accord with which he says: "I take it that up to now, because of the equipollence of the opposites, I have apprehended none of them; and consequently everything that is brought forward by way of refutation seems to me to be irrelevant to what we are reporting."

## 26. "I Am Non-apprehensive" and "I Do Not Apprehend"

201   Both of the slogans "I am non-apprehensive" and "I do not apprehend" express a personal *pathos*, in accord with which the Skeptic declines for the present to take an affirmative or negative position on any of the non-evident matters of inquiry, as is evident from what we have previously said about the other slogans.

### 27. "To Every Argument an Equal Argument Is Opposed"

When we say "To every argument an equal argument is opposed," by "every 202 argument" we mean "every argument that has been considered by us," and we use "argument" not in its ordinary sense but for that which establishes something dogmatically, that is to say, concerning the non-evident, and which establishes it in any way at all, not necessarily by means of premises and conclusion. We say "equal" as regards credibility and the lack of it, and we use "opposed" in its common meaning of "conflicting"; and we tacitly supply "as appears to me." Thus, when I say "To every argument an equal argument is 203 opposed," I say in effect this: "for every argument that I have examined and that establishes something dogmatically, there appears to me to be opposed another argument that establishes something dogmatically and is equal to it as regards credibility and lack of credibility," so that the utterance of the statement is not dogmatic but is just a report of a human *pathos*, which is apparent to the person experiencing it.

But also some people state the slogan thus: "To every argument an equal 204 argument is to be opposed," intending to give this admonition: "To every argument establishing something dogmatically let us oppose some conflicting argument that proceeds dogmatically and is equal to it as regards credibility and lack of credibility"; they are addressing the statement to the Skeptic, although they use the infinitive "to be opposed" in place of the imperative "let us oppose." And they address this admonition to the Skeptic lest he be tricked 205 somehow by the Dogmatist into ceasing to raise questions about the arguments and through precipitancy should miss out on the *ataraxia* that appears to them and that they, as we mentioned before, think follows on suspension of judgment about everything.

### 28. More about the Skeptic Slogans

This will be a sufficient number of the slogans to discuss in an outline, 206 especially since, on the basis of what we have already said, it is possible to give an account of the rest. For concerning all the Skeptic slogans it is necessary for this to be understood first of all: we absolutely do not firmly maintain anything about their being true, especially since we say that they can be confuted by themselves, as they are included among the cases to which they apply—just as cathartic drugs not only flush out the bodily humors but expel themselves as well. Also, we do not put them forward as sharply expressing the 207 points with which they have to do, but we employ them imprecisely and, if you like, not strictly correctly; for it does not befit the Skeptic to fight about slogans, and besides it works in our favor that not even these slogans are said to have signification absolutely, but only relatively, that is, relative to the 208 Skeptics. In addition, it must be borne in mind that we do not apply them to all things in general but only to things that are non-evident and are investigated dogmatically, and that we are saying what appears to us and are not asserting, as something firmly maintained, anything about the nature of the external objects. On the basis of these points I think it possible to fend off every sophism against a Skeptic slogan.

209    And now that we have elucidated the character of Skepticism, reviewing its basic idea, parts, criterion, and goal—and the modes of *Epochē*, too—and have discussed the Skeptic slogans, we consider that the next thing to do is to go over concisely the distinction between it and the alternative philosophies, in order that we may understand more clearly the Ephectic Way. Let us begin with the Heraclitean philosophy.

## 29. That the Skeptic Way Differs from the Heraclitean Philosophy

210 Now it is evident from the start that the Heraclitean philosophy differs from our Way, for Heraclitus makes dogmatic assertions about many non-evident things, but, as has been said, we do not. It is true that Aenesidemus and his followers used to say that the Skeptic Way was a road to the Heraclitean philosophy, since opposites appearing to be the case about the same thing leads into opposites being the case about the same thing, and the Skeptics say that opposites appear to be the case about the same thing, while the Heracliteans move from this to their being the case. But we reply to them that opposites' appearing to be the case about the same thing is not a dogma of the Skeptics but a matter occurring not only to the Skeptics but also to the other philosophers, and, indeed, to all mankind. For surely nobody would bring

211 himself to say that honey does not taste sweet to healthy people and that it does not taste bitter to the jaundiced. So the Heracliteans, just as we and perhaps the other philosophers, start from an assumption common to everybody. Therefore, if the Heracliteans had got their "opposites are the case about the same thing" from one or another of the Skeptic slogans—such as, for example, "Everything is non-apprehensible," "I determine nothing," or the like—perhaps Aenesidemus and his followers might have validly drawn their conclusion. But since what the Heracliteans start from is something observed not only by us but by the other philosophers and the plain man as well, why would anyone claim that our Way, any more than the other philosophies or the plain man's view, is a road to the Heraclitean philosophy, since we all utilize the same materials in common?

212    Indeed, not only does the Skeptic Way not promote acceptance of the Heraclitean philosophy, but it actually works against it, for the Skeptic rejects all Heraclitus's dogmatic assertions as precipitate pronouncements, opposing his "world conflagration" and his "opposites are the case concerning the same thing"; and, as I was saying before, in regard to each dogma of Heraclitus he derides the dogmatic precipitancy and reiterates "I do not apprehend" and "I do not determine anything," all of which conflicts with the Heracliteans. Now it is absurd to say that a conflicting Way is a road to the system with which it

conflicts; therefore, it is absurd to say that the Skeptic Way is a road to the Heraclitean philosophy.

## 30. Wherein Skepticism Differs from the Democritean Philosophy

But the Democritean philosophy, too, is said to have something in common  213 with Skepticism, since it seems to use the same material as we do. For from honey's appearing sweet to some people and bitter to others, Democritus, as they say, reasons that it is neither sweet nor bitter, and in view of this he joins in sounding the Skeptic slogan "not more." But the Skeptics and the followers of Democritus use the slogan "not more" differently, since the latter apply it in reference to neither alternative being the case, whereas we apply it in reference to our not knowing whether both or neither of the appearances is the case. So  214 that we differ also in respect to this, and the difference becomes most evident when Democritus says "Truly, [there are] atoms and the void"; for he says "truly" instead of "in truth"; and it is superfluous to state, I think, that he differs from us when he says that in truth atoms and the void exist, although he does start from the anomaly of the appearances.

## 31. Wherein Skepticism Differs from the Cyrenaic Way

Some people say that the Cyrenaic Way is the same as the Skeptic Way, since  215 it too says that only *pathē* are apprehensible. But it differs, for it says that pleasure and the smooth transition from state to state of the body are the goal, while we say that it is *ataraxia*, which is incompatible with their goal. For the person who firmly maintains that pleasure is the goal undergoes torments whether or not pleasure is present, as I have argued in the section on the Goal. Further, we suspend judgment as regards the philosophic theory about the external objects, whereas the Cyrenaics assert that these objects have a nature that is not apprehensible.

## 32. Wherein Skepticism Differs from the Protagorean Way

Protagoras thinks that man is the measure of all things; of things that are, that  216 they are; and of things that are not, that they are not. And by "measure" he means the criterion, and by "things" he means objects or facts. So in effect he says that man is the criterion of all objects or facts; of those that are, that they are; and of those that are not, that they are not. And for this reason he posits only what appears to each person, and thus he introduces relativity. Wherefore  217 he too seems to have something in common with the Pyrrhoneans. But he differs from them, and we shall see the difference when we have properly set forth what Protagoras thinks.

He says that matter is in flux and that as it flows additions are continuously made, replacing the effluvia; and that the senses are restructured and altered depending on the age and the other structural features of our bodies.

218 He says also that the explanations of all appearances are founded on matter, as matter in itself is capable of being in all respects such as it appears to anyone. And [he says] that people apprehend different things at different times depending on the different conditions they are in. For the person who is in a natural condition apprehends those features of matter that can appear to people who are in a natural condition, while those who are in an unnatural condition apprehend what can appear to people in an unnatural condition.

219 And the same account applies in relation to age and as regards being asleep or awake and for each type of condition. For him, therefore, man becomes the criterion of existence, since whatever appears to somebody exists, and what does not appear to anybody does not exist.

We see, therefore, that he dogmatizes both about matter being in flux and about the explanations of all appearances being founded on it, while these are nonevident matters concerning which we suspend judgment.

### 33. Wherein Skepticism Differs from the Academic Philosophy

220 Some, of course, claim that the Academic philosophy is the same as Skepticism, and so the next step will be to discuss this, too.

According to most people, there have been three Academies. The first and most ancient is the school of Plato and his followers; the second, or Middle Academy, is that of Arcesilaus, the pupil of Polemo; and the third, or New Academy, is that of Carneades and Cleitomachus. Some add a fourth, the school of Philo and Charmidas, and some even reckon the school of Antiochus

221 as a fifth. Beginning, then, with the Old Academy, let us see how these philosophies differ from ours.

Some people have said that Plato was dogmatic, others that he was aporetic, and still others that he was aporetic in some respects and dogmatic in others. For he shows, they say, a "gymnastic" and aporetic character in his "gymnastic" discourses, where Socrates is introduced either as making sport of someone or as contending with the sophists, but a dogmatic character where he speaks seriously through Socrates or Timaeus or some such personage.

222 Concerning those who say that he is dogmatic or that he is dogmatic in some respects and aporetic in others, it would be superfluous to say anything now; for they concede his difference from us. The question whether he is, strictly speaking, skeptical, we treat more fully in our commentaries; but now we shall argue in brief, against the school of Menodotus and Aenesidemus (for these most of all advanced this position), that whenever Plato makes statements about the Ideas or about the existence of providence or about the virtuous life being more choiceworthy than the wicked, if he assents to these as being more

plausible than not, he also abandons the Skeptic character since he gives preference to one thing over another as regards credibility and incredibility. From what has been said before it is very evident that this is alien to us.

And if he does put forward some points skeptically whenever, as they say, 223 he is doing "gymnastics," that does not make him a Skeptic; for he who dogmatizes about any single thing or prefers any *phantasia* at all to any other as regards credibility and incredibility, or makes an assertion about something nonevident, acquires the dogmatic character, as Timon, too, shows by what he says about Xenophanes. For, after praising him in many respects and even 224 dedicating his *Satires* to him, he portrays him as making this lamentation:

> I, too, should have had wisdom of mind when I was vacillating. But, being old and not completely versed in Skepticism, I was deceived by the treacherous pathway. For in whichever direction I turned my mind, everything was resolved into one and the same; and everything, continually drawn in all directions, wound up in a single common nature. (Diels *Vorsokt.* 11*A*35)

By reason of this, indeed, Timon describes him as more or less free from delusion, but not completely free, where he says:

> Xenophanes, fairly free from delusion, mocker of Homer's fiction, invented a god far removed from human kind, spherical in shape, unshakeable, unblemished, and surpassing thought in his thinking. (Diels *Vorsokt.* 11*A*35)

He calls him "fairly free from delusion" as being on some points not deluded, and "mocker of Homer's fiction" because he ridiculed Homer's stories about [divine] tricks. But Xenophanes, contrary to the preconceptions of the rest of 225 mankind, asserted dogmatically that everything is one, and that god coalesces with everything and is spherical in shape, devoid of *pathē*, unchangeable and reasonable; whence it is easy to show the difference between Xenophanes and us. In any case, it is very evident from what has been said that even if Plato is aporetic about some things, he is not a Skeptic because in some respects he appears to be making assertions about the existence of non-evident things or to be preferring one non-evident thing to another as regards credibility.

The members of the New Academy, although they say that all things are 226 non-apprehensible, differ from the Skeptics, it appears, even in the very statement that all things are non-apprehensible (for they firmly maintain this, while it seems to the Skeptic that maybe something can be apprehended); but they differ from us very evidently in the judgment of things good and evil. For the Academics say that something is good or evil, not as we do, but having been persuaded that what they call good *is* good more likely than not, and similarly in the case of evil; whereas we say such things, not with the thought that what we are saying is plausible, but, without any belief, following the common course of life in order not to be incapable of action. And we say that, 227 so far as the philosophic theory is concerned, *phantasiai* are equal as regards credibility and incredibility, but they say that some are plausible and others the reverse.

And they draw distinctions among the plausible *phantasiai*: some, they think, are just plausible, some are plausible and tested, and some are plausible, tested and stable. For example, when a rope is lying coiled up in a dark room, a person who enters the room suddenly gets a simply plausible *phantasia* that
228 it is a snake; but to a person who has looked carefully around and considered the circumstances — for example, that it does not move, that it is of such and such a color, and so on — it appears to be a rope, in accord with a *phantasia* that is plausible and tested. And a *phantasia* that is in addition stable is such as the following. After Alcestis had died, Heracles is said to have brought her up again from Hades and to have shown her to Admetus, who got a plausible and tested *phantasia* of Alcestis; but since he knew that she had died, his
229 intellect withdrew the assent and leaned toward disbelief. Accordingly, the New Academics prefer the plausible and tested *phantasia* to the simply plausible, and to both of them the *phantasia* that is plausible, tested, and stable.

And although both the Academics and the Skeptics say that they are persuaded of certain things, here too the difference of the philosophies is very
230 evident. For "to be persuaded" has different senses: on the one hand, it means not to resist but simply to follow without much proclivity or strong pro feeling, as the child is said to be persuaded by or obedient to his teacher; but sometimes it means to assent to something by choice and with a kind of sympathy due to strong desire, as when a profligate man is persuaded by one who approves of living extravagantly. Since, therefore, the followers of Carneades and Cleitomachus say both that they are strongly persuaded and that things are strongly persuasive, whereas we say that we simply make a concession without any pro feeling, we would differ from them in this respect, too.

231 But we also differ from the New Academy as regards the goal; for whereas the gentlemen who say that they conduct themselves in accord with the plausible employ it in everyday life, we live without belief, following the laws, customs, and our natural *pathē*. And if we were not aiming at brevity, we could say still more about this distinction.

232 Arcesilaus, however, who we said was the head and founder of the Middle Academy, does indeed seem to me to share the Pyrrhonean arguments, so that his Way is almost the same as ours. For one does not find him making any assertion about the existence or nonexistence of anything, nor does he prefer one thing to another as regards credibility or incredibility; rather, he suspends judgment about everything. And he asserts that the goal is suspension of
233 judgment, which, we were saying, is accompanied by *ataraxia*. He further says that individual cases of suspension are good and that individual cases of assent are bad. One might note, however, that while we say these things in accord with what is apparent to us, and we do not firmly maintain them, he says them as holding in nature, so as to mean that the suspension itself *is* good and the
234 assent *is* bad. And if one is to believe what is said about him, he appeared at first glance to be a Pyrrhonean, they say, but in truth he was a Dogmatist; and since he undertook to test his associates by the aporetic method, to see whether they were naturally fitted to receive the Platonic dogmas, he seemed to be aporetic, but in fact he did pass on the Platonic dogmas to those of his

associates who were naturally fitted. And this was why Ariston said of him: "He is Plato in front, Pyrrho in back, and Diodorus in the middle," for he made use of the dialectic of Diodorus, but he was an outright Platonist.

The followers of Philo say that, insofar as it depends on the Stoic criterion, 235 that is, the apprehensive *phantasia*, objects and facts are not apprehensible, but that insofar as it depends on the nature of the objects and facts themselves, they are apprehensible. Antiochus even transferred the Stoa to the Academy, so that it was said of him that in the Academy he did Stoic philosophy; for he showed that the Stoic dogmas are in Plato. So the difference between the Skeptic Way and the so-called Fourth and Fifth Academies is quite evident.

## 34. Whether Medical Empiricism Is the Same as Skepticism

Since some say that the empiricism of the empirical medical system is the same 236 as the Skeptic philosophy, it needs to be recognized that inasmuch as empiricism firmly maintains the inapprehensibility of the non-evident, it is not the same as Skepticism; nor would it befit a Skeptic to take up that system. He might better adopt the so-called Method, it seems to me, for it alone of the 237 medical systems seems not to make precipitate assertions about non-evident things by self-assuredly telling us whether they are apprehensible or not apprehensible; and following the appearances, it takes from them what seems beneficial, in accord with the Skeptic practice. For we said above that everyday life, in which the Skeptic shares, has four parts: one involving nature's guidance, another involving the compulsion of the *pathē*, still another the tradition of laws and customs, and a fourth the teaching of arts. Accordingly, 238 just as the Skeptic, in accord with the compulsion of the *pathē*, is led by thirst to drink and by hunger to food and similarly in the other cases, so too the Methodic physician is led by the *pathē* to what is appropriate — by tightness to loosening up, as when one seeks refuge in heat from a cold-induced attack of cramping; and by secretion to drying up, as when people in a sauna, relaxed and sweating profusely, come to the end of the session and with that in mind betake themselves to the cold air. It is also very evident that conditions that are naturally alien impel us to their removal, seeing that even the dog, when stuck by a thorn, proceeds to pull it out. And so in sum — in order not to 239 depart from the outline form by taking up each point individually — I consider that all the things thus said by the Methodics can be classed as instances of the compulsion of the *pathē*, whether these *pathē* are natural or unnatural.

Also common to the two Ways is the undogmatic and relaxed use of words. For just as the Skeptic uses the slogans "I determine nothing" and "I 240 apprehend nothing" undogmatically, as we have said, so also the Methodic physician employs "common features" and "pervade" and the like in an uncomplicated way. So, too, he uses the word "indication" undogmatically, as short for "the guidance of the apparent *pathē*, both natural and unnatural, to the seemingly appropriate remedies," analogous to what I said in the case of hunger and thirst and the rest. Thus it must be said, on the basis of these and 241 similar significant features, that the Methodic physician's Way has a kinship with Skepticism. And indeed, when considered not simply in itself but in comparison with the other medical systems, it has more kinship than they do.

With this much said about the seeming alternatives to the Skeptic Way, we here complete both the general account of Skepticism and Book 1 of the Outlines.

# Outlines of Pyrrhonism

## Book 2 of Three

### Contents of Book 2

## 1. Can the Skeptic Question What Is Said by the Dogmatists?

Since our inquiry is directed against the Dogmatists, let us go over, briefly and in outline, each part of what is called "philosophy", after first having answered those Dogmatists who constantly proclaim that the Skeptic is not in a position to raise questions about or even comprehend in any way the issues concerning which they dogmatize. For they declare that either the Skeptic apprehends what the Dogmatists say or he does not; and if he does apprehend, how can he be at a loss about what he claims to apprehend? But if he does not

apprehend, then he will not even know how to discuss what he has not
3 apprehended. For just as the person who does not know what, say, the
theorems called "reduced with the respect to" and "by means of two conditionals" are is not able to discuss them, so the person who does not understand
the particular things said by the Dogmatists is unable to raise objections to
what he does not understand. Therefore, the Skeptic is in no way able to
question the statements of the Dogmatists.

4      Now let those who say this tell us what they mean here by "to apprehend"
—whether they mean "to conceive" *simpliciter*, that is, without also maintaining the existence of the things under discussion, or they mean "to conceive"
and also "to establish the existence of" those things. For if they are saying that
in their account "to apprehend" means "to assent to an apprehensive *phantasia*," where an apprehensive *phantasia* is "one that is derived from, and
stamped and impressed in accord with, an existent object or state of affairs, and
is such as would not arise from something nonexistent," then perhaps not even
they themselves will want to claim inability to raise questions about things that
5 they have not apprehended in *this* sense. For example, when the Stoic raises
questions in opposition to the Epicurean's statement that Being is divided, or
that god does not have foreknowledge of events in the Cosmos, or that pleasure
is good, has he apprehended or not? If he has apprehended, then by saying that
these states of affairs exist he has completely abrogated the Stoa, while if he
has not apprehended them, he cannot say anything against them.

6      And a similar point will have to be made against people who subscribe to
other systems, whenever they wish to question the views of those with whom
they have doctrinal differences. So they are not even able to raise questions
against one another. Or rather, to be more serious about it, if it is once granted
that it is impossible to raise questions about what is not in this sense
apprehended, the whole Dogmatic philosophy, so to say, will be confuted and
7 the Skeptic philosophy firmly established. For he who makes a dogmatic
assertion about something nonevident either does so having apprehended that
about which he is talking, or not having apprehended it. But if he has not
apprehended it, he will not be worthy of belief; while if he has apprehended it,
he will say either that he has apprehended it affecting him directly, through
8 itself and with clarity, or else by means of some research and inquiry. Now, if
he says that the nonevident thing has affected him and been apprehended
immediately through itself and with clarity, then that thing would not be
nonevident but, instead, would be equally apparent to everybody, that is, a
matter agreed upon and not disputed. But there has been endless controversy
among the Dogmatists about every single nonevident matter, so that he who
firmly maintains and asserts something about the existence of a nonevident
thing or state of affairs cannot have apprehended it affecting him through itself
9 and with clarity. But if he has apprehended it by means of some research, how,
on the hypothesis before us, was he able to conduct the inquiry before he had
accurately apprehended its object? For since the inquiry requires the prior
accurate apprehension of, and thus an inquiry into, what is going to be
inquired about, while in turn the apprehension itself of the object of inquiry

certainly requires an inquiry into that object beforehand, it becomes impossible (because of the circularity mode of *aporia*) for the Dogmatists to inquire into and dogmatize about things non-evident. If any of them wish to begin with the apprehension, we refer them to the necessity of inquiring about the object before apprehending it, while if they wish to begin with the inquiry, we refer them to the necessity of apprehending the object before it is inquired about. So that for these reasons it is impossible for them either to apprehend any of the nonevident things or to maintain firmly an assertion about them. These considerations, I think, will result directly in the confutation of the Dogmatic sophistry and the introduction of the philosophy of suspending judgment.

If, however, they are going to say that it is not this kind of apprehension 10 that they are claiming should precede inquiry, but rather conception *simpliciter*, then it is not impossible for those who suspend judgment to inquire about the existence of non-evident things. For, i suppose, the Skeptic is not precluded from a conception that arises during the discussion itself from clear appearances affecting him passively, and that does not at all imply the existence of its objects; since, as the Dogmatists say, we conceive not only of things and states of affairs that exist, but also of those that do not. Hence, the person who suspends judgment remains in the Skeptic state both when he is inquiring and when he is forming conceptions; for it has been shown that he assents to whatever things affect him in accord with a passively received *phantasia*, insofar as that *phantasia* appears to him. But notice that even in this case the 11 Dogmatists are precluded from inquiry. For inquiring about objects and states of affairs is not inconsistent in those who agree that they do not know how these things are in nature, but only in those who think they have accurate knowledge of them, since for the latter the inquiry has already reached its end, as they think, whereas for the former the supposition on which every inquiry is based still holds — namely, that they have not already found out the facts.

Accordingly, we must now inquire, briefly and in outline, into each part of 12 so-called "philosophy." And since there has been a great deal of controversy among the Dogmatists about the parts of philosophy, with some saying that there is only one part, some two, and some three, and it would not be convenient to go into this at greater length just now, we shall continue our account by setting forth fairly the doctrine of those who seem to have considered the matter most fully.

## 2. Where the Criticism of the Dogmatists Should Begin

Now the Stoics and some others say that there are three parts of philosophy, 13 namely, the logical, the physical, and the ethical; and they begin their instruction with the logical part, even though there has been much dispute about the proper place to begin. Without subscribing to any doctrine we shall follow them, and, since the things said in the three parts have need of testing and a criterion, and discussion of the criterion seems to belong to the logical part, let us begin with discussion of the criterion and the logical part.

### 3. The Criterion

14 But we must first mention that the word "criterion" means either that by which they say that we decide questions about existence and nonexistence, or that with regard to which we conduct our lives. We should now examine what is called the criterion of truth, since we have already discussed the criterion in its other sense in our discourse on Skepticism.

15        "Criterion," then, in the present account has three senses — the general, the specific, and the most specific. In the general sense, it is any standard of apprehension; in this sense even physical features — for example, eyesight — are called criteria. In the specific sense, it is any technical standard for apprehension — for example, the mason's rule and chalk line. In the most specific sense, it is any technical standard for the apprehension of a non-evident object or state of affairs; in this sense the standards of ordinary life are not called criteria, but only logical standards and those that the Dogmatists apply in deciding

16 about truth. We propose, therefore, to lead off with a discussion of the logical criterion. But "logical criterion," too, is used in three senses, to refer to the "by whom," the "by means of which," and the "according to which." Thus the "by whom" criterion would be a human being; the "by means of which" would be the senses or the intellect; and the "according to which" would be the application of the *phantasia* in accord with which the human being tries to reach a decision by means of the senses or the intellect.

17        It was appropriate, I think, to make these remarks in advance, in order that we may understand what our discussion is about; it remains to proceed to the refutation of those who precipitately assert that they have apprehended the criterion of truth; we begin with the controversy about this.

### 4. Does There Exist a Criterion of Truth?

18 Of those who have considered the matter, some, for example, the Stoics and others, have asserted that there is a criterion; others, including the Corinthian Xeniades and Xenophanes of Colophon, who said "opinion holds sway over everything," have asserted that there is not; while we have suspended judgment

19 as to whether there is or not. This dispute, then, they will either declare to be decidable or to be undecidable; if undecidable, they will be granting at once that judgment should be suspended; but if decidable, let them say with what it is to be decided, seeing that we do not have any agreed-upon criterion and do

20 not know — indeed, are inquiring — whether one exists. And anyhow, in order to decide the dispute that has arisen about the criterion, we have need of an agreed-upon criterion by means of which we shall decide it; and in order to have an agreed-upon criterion it is necessary first to have decided the dispute about the criterion. Thus, with the reasoning falling into the circularity mode, finding a criterion becomes aporetic; for we do not allow them to adopt a criterion hypothetically, and if they wish to decide about the criterion by means of a criterion we force them into an infinite regress. Further, since proof

requires a criterion that has been proved, while the criterion has need of what has been determined to be a proof, they land in circularity.

We think, therefore, that these points are sufficient to show the precipi- 21 tancy of the Dogmatists as concerns their account of the criterion; but in order to be able to refute them in detail, it will not be inappropriate to expatiate on the subject. We do not, however, undertake to combat every single doctrine concerning the criterion (for by so doing even we would necessarily sink into unsystematic talk, as the controversy has grown out of all proportion), but since the criterion in question seems to be threefold — the "by whom" and the "by means of which" and the "according to which" — we shall take up each of these in turn and establish that it is not apprehensible; in this way, our argument will be systematic and complete. Let us begin with the "by whom," the agent; for the rest seem somehow to share the perplexity attached to this.

## 5. The "By Whom" Criterion

Now it seems to me that human beings, if we go by the statements of the 22 Dogmatists, are not only non-apprehensible but are even inconceivable. Indeed, we hear the Platonic Socrates expressly agreeing that he does not know whether he is a human being or something else. And when the Dogmatists wish to define the concept, they first disagree and then talk nonsense.

Thus Democritus says that human beings are "what we all know." But if 23 we go by this we shall not know human beings, since we also know a dog and consequently the dog will be a human being. Further, there are some human beings whom we do not know; therefore, they will not be human beings. What is more, if we go by this concept, nobody will be a human being. For since Democritus says that human beings must be known by all, and no human being is known by all human beings, no one, according to him, will be a human being.

Further, that we are not making these remarks sophistically is apparent 24 from their relevance to him. For this gentleman says that in truth there exist only atoms and the void, which are the existential basis not only of animals but of all compounds, so that as far as these [atoms and the void] are concerned we cannot form a conception of the individuality of the human being, since they are common to everything. And besides these there is no other substrate; therefore, we shall have no means of distinguishing human beings from the other animals and thus of forming a precise concept.

Epicurus, on the other hand, defines a human being as "*this* sort of shape, 25 plus animation." According to him, then, since human beings are ostensively defined by pointing, what is not pointed at is not a human being. And if somebody points at a woman, a man will not be a human being, while if he points at a man, a woman will not be a human being. We shall also argue for the same conclusions on the basis of the differences of circumstances, which we know from the fourth mode of *Epochē*.

26      Others used to assert that a human being is a rational mortal animal, capable of thought and knowledge. But since it is shown in the first mode of *Epochē* that no animal is non-rational and all are capable of thought and knowledge, we shall not know what these people have in mind if we go by what
27  they say. And the attributes in the definition are meant either as actual or as potential. If, on the one hand, they are meant as actual, then a person will not be a human being unless he has perfect knowledge and perfect reason and is in the very act of dying—for that is *actual* mortality. But if, on the other hand, they are meant as potential, then no one who has perfect reason and has already got intelligence and knowledge will be a human being; but this is even
28  more absurd than the previous conclusion. By this, therefore, the concept of human being has shown itself impossible to frame.

When Plato deems a human being to be a "wingless biped with flat nails, capable of political knowledge," even he does not think to put this forward as something he firmly maintains. For since human beings are among those things that, as he puts it, are always becoming and never really exist, and since further it is impossible, according to him, to assert and firmly maintain anything about that which never really exists, not even Plato will want to seem to propose this definition as something he firmly maintains, but only, in his usual way, as a statement of what is plausible.

29      But even if we should grant for the sake of argument that human beings are conceivable, they will be found not to be apprehensible. For a human being is compounded of soul and body, but neither the body nor the soul, it seems,
30  is apprehensible; therefore the human being is not apprehensible, either. And that the body is not apprehensible is evident as follows: the attributes of something are other than that of which they are attributes. Thus, whenever a colored surface or something like that affects us, it is probably the attributes of the body that affect us, and not the body itself. Besides, they say that the body is extended in three directions; therefore, we ought to apprehend its length, breadth, and depth if we are to apprehend the body. But if depth affected us, we would perceive the silver interiors of gold coins. Therefore, we do not apprehend the body, either.

31      But, not to linger over the dispute about the body, human beings will be found not to be apprehensible also because the soul is not apprehensible. That this is not apprehensible is evident as follows: of those who have discussed the soul—leaving to one side the extensive and interminable battle over it—some, like the followers of Dicaearchus the Messenian, say that there is no such thing as the soul; some say that there is such a thing; and some have suspended
32  judgment. Now if the Dogmatists are going to say that this dispute is not decidable, they will be admitting right off that the soul is not apprehensible; while if they will say that it is decidable, let them tell us by what they will decide it. They cannot say "by the senses," for according to them the soul is an object of thought. But if they will say "By the intellect," we shall reply that since the intellect is the most non-evident part of the soul, as is shown by the fact that those who agree about the existence of the soul disagree about the
33  intellect, if they propose to use the intellect to apprehend the soul and to decide the dispute about it, they will be proposing to decide and establish the less

questionable by the more questionable, which is absurd. Hence, the dispute about the soul will not be decided by the intellect, either. Therefore, it will not be decided by anything. And if that is the case, the soul is not apprehensible, so that human beings would not be apprehensible either.

But even if we grant that human beings are apprehensible, it would not be 34 possible, I think, to show that determinations about things and issues should be made by them. For anyone who says that determinations about things and issues should be made by a human being will say this either without proof or with proof. But he will not say it with proof, for it is necessary that the proof be true and have been determined to be such, and, in view of this, that it have been determined *by someone* to be a true proof. Since, therefore, we are not able with general agreement to say by whom the proof can be determined to be such (for we are in the midst of our inquiry into the "by whom" criterion), we shall not be able to decide about the proof, nor, in view of this, to prove that the criterion with which the argument is concerned is a criterion. But if, 35 on the other hand, it will be said without proof that determinations about things and issues should be made by human beings, the statement will not be worthy of belief. Consequently, we shall not be able to maintain firmly that human beings are the "by whom" criterion. Moreover, by whom will it be determined that human beings are the "by whom" criterion? For if they just say this without making a determination, they will not be believed. And if they say "by a human being," the point at issue will have been assumed. But if by 36 another animal, how do they light upon that animal to determine whether human beings are the criterion? For if they do so without making a determi- nation, they will not be believed, while if with a determination, that again will have to be determined by something. But if by itself, the same absurdity will remain (for the determination about what is in question will be made by means of what is in question), and if by a human being, we have the circularity mode; and if by something other than these two, we shall again demand in its case the "by whom" criterion, and so on ad infinitum. For this reason, therefore, we shall not be able to say that things and issues should be determined by a human being.

But let it be the case and let it be believed to be the case that determina- 37 tions about things and issues should be made by human beings. Then, since human beings differ a great deal, let the dogmatists first agree with one another that *this* is the human being to whom one should pay attention, and then, and only then, let them tell us to agree with him. But if they are going to dispute about this "as long as water flows and trees grow," as the saying goes, how can they urge us to be quick about assenting to anyone? For if they say that we 38 must give credence to the person who is wise, we shall ask them "What sort of wise person? — The wise Epicurean? The wise Stoic? The Cyrenaic? The Cynic?" They will not be able to agree upon an answer.

If somebody thinks that we should desist from raising such questions, and 39 simply believe the most sagacious person of all, then, in the first place, the Dogmatists will disagree about who is most sagacious of all, and next, even if it be granted that it is possible to agree on someone as the most sagacious of all people present and past, still this will not make that person more worthy

40 of belief. For since sagacity is subject to great, almost infinite, variation in degree, we declare that it is possible for another person to turn up who is more sagacious than this person whom we are saying is the most sagacious of all people past and present. Thus, just as we are told to give credence, because of his sagacity, to the person who is now said to be wiser than the others present and past, so one ought to give even more credence to the more sagacious person coming after him. And when that successor has appeared, we must expect another one to show up who is more sagacious than he, and so on ad

41 infinitum. Nor is it evident whether these people will all agree with one another or will give accounts that disagree. Wherefore, even if someone is agreed to be more sagacious than other people past and present, since we are not able to say with firm assurance that nobody will be more clever than he (for it is nonevident), it will always be necessary to await the determination by the wiser person of the future, and not to assent to the aforementioned "best" one.

42      But even if we grant for the sake of argument that nobody is, was, or will be more sagacious than our hypothetical sage, even then it does not make sense to believe him. For since it is above all the sagacious who, in arguing about the facts, love to defend unsound ones and make them seem to be sound and true, when this clever fellow says something we shall not know whether perhaps the matter is in nature as he says or whether he is defending as true what is really false and is persuading us to think it true on the ground that he is more sagacious than all other existing people and for that reason is not subject to refutation by us. So we shall not even give assent to this person as one who determines the facts truly, since, though we think it possible that he may be telling the truth, we also think it possible that he says what he says while wishing, because of an excess of cleverness, to defend the false as true. For these reasons, in determining the facts we have no obligation to believe even the most clever of all existing people.

43      If anyone says that we ought to pay heed to the consensus of the many, we shall reply that that is foolish. For, first of all, the truth is a rare thing, I think, and for that reason it is possible for one person to be wiser than the many. And next, for any given criterion there are more people who disagree than agree about it, since all the people who accept any criterion, whatever its kind, other than the one that seems to some to be generally agreed upon, will oppose this latter one and are much more numerous than those who agree

44 about it. But apart from these considerations, those who agree are either in different conditions or in one and the same condition. Now they are certainly not in different conditions so far as what is being spoken about is concerned; else how can they have said the same things about it? But if they are in one and the same condition, then, since not only the individual person who makes a different statement is in a single condition but also those who are agreeing, no difference will be found (insofar as it is a matter of the conditions

45 in which we find ourselves) even on the basis of numbers. Consequently, there is no more need to pay attention to the many than to the one; in addition to which, as we pointed out in the fourth mode of Skepticism, the classification of determinations on the basis of numbers is not apprehensible, since there exist innumerable human beings and we cannot go through the determinations of

all of them and say which are asserted by more people and which by fewer. Thus, according to this, it is absurd to choose among determinations on the basis of numbers.

But even if we disregard numbers, we shall not find anyone by whom  46 things and issues are to be determined, despite our having granted so much for the sake of argument. Therefore, for all these reasons, the criterion "by whom" things and issues are to be determined will be found not to be apprehensible.

And as the other criteria are encompassed in this one (for each of them is  47 either a part or a *pathos* or an action of a human being), the next thing, I suppose, would be to go on to one of the topics coming next in order in our account, on the assumption that the other criteria have been adequately covered by the present remarks. But in order that we may not seem to be avoiding giving a specific refutation for each case, we shall say a few things about these, too, for good measure. However, first we shall discuss the so-called "by means of which" criterion.

## 6. The "By Means of Which" Criterion

Concerning this criterion there has been a huge and almost endless controversy  48 among the Dogmatists. But we, again with a view toward systematic treatment, say that since according to them the human being is the one "by whom" objects and issues are determined, and since he has, as they also agree, only his senses and intellect by means of which to make determinations, if we show that he will not be able to make them by the senses alone, nor by the intellect alone, nor by both of them, we shall have concisely rebutted all the particular doctrines; for it seems that they all can be reduced to these three positions. Let  49 us begin with the senses.

Since, then, some people say that the senses provide "empty" *pathē*, —that is, that nothing the senses seem to perceive exists—while others say that everything by which they suppose them to be moved exists, and still others say that some of it exists and some of it does not, we shall not know to whom we should assent. For we shall not decide the dispute by the senses, since we are questioning whether they produce "empty" *pathē* or apprehend truly, nor by something else, since on the hypothesis before us there is no other criterion by means of which one ought to make the determination. Therefore, whether  50 sensation produces "empty" *pathē* or apprehends anything is not decidable and not apprehensible; and a corollary to this is that in making determinations about things and issues we ought not give heed to sensation alone, since in regard to it we cannot assert that it even apprehends anything at all.

But suppose, for the sake of argument, that the senses do serve to perceive  51 things; even so, they will be found no less unworthy of belief in relation to making determinations about the external objects and states of affairs. For certainly the senses are moved in opposite directions by things external—for example, taste perceives the same honey sometimes as bitter and sometimes as sweet, and to sight the same color seems sometimes blood red and sometimes white. Not even smell agrees with itself, for myrrh is found unpleasant by the  52 person who has a headache, but pleasant by the one who is not in that condition. And those who are divinely possessed or raving seem to hear people conversing with them, while we do not. Further, the same water seems

53 unpleasantly hot to people in a fever, but lukewarm to others. Thus, there is no way of saying whether one is to deem all *phantasiai* true, or some true and some false, or all false, since we have no agreed-upon criterion by means of which we shall make our proposed determinations, nor are we even provided with a true proof that has been determined to be such, since we are still in search of the criterion of truth by means of which the purported true proof

54 should be appraised. Also, for these reasons, any person who thinks that we should believe those who are in a natural condition and not believe those who are not is being absurd, for he will not be believed if he says this without proof, nor, for the reasons given above, will he have a true proof that has been determined to be such.

55      And even if someone were to agree that the *phantasiai* of people who are in a natural condition are worthy of belief, while those of people who are in an unnatural condition are not, it will still be found impossible to make determinations about the external objects by means of the senses alone. For certainly sight, even when it is in the natural condition, at one time calls the same tower round and at another time calls it square; and taste declares the same food unpleasant for the sated but pleasant for the hungry; and hearing

56 similarly perceives the same sound as loud at night but faint by day; and the sense of smell fancies the same things malodorous in the case of the many but not so in the case of the tanners; and by the same sense of touch we feel warm when we are entering the bathhouse by the vestibule, but cold when we are leaving. Wherefore, since the senses contradict themselves even when they are in the natural state, and the disagreement is undecided because we have no criterion by means of which it can be decided, the same *aporiai* follow of necessity. And, to establish this conclusion it is possible to carry over still more points from what we have said before in connection with the modes of *Epochē*. Hence it would not be true, I think, that it is possible to make determinations about the external objects and states of affairs by means of the senses alone.

57      In our account, then, let us proceed to the intellect. Those who claim that in making determinations about objects and states of affairs we should pay heed to the intellect alone are, in the first place, unable to show that the existence of the intellect is apprehensible. Gorgias, when he claims that nothing exists, implies that not even the intellect exists, while others assert that it does exist, so how shall we resolve this dispute? Not by the intellect, since that would beg the question; nor by anything else, for according to the present hypothesis there is nothing else, as they claim, by means of which determinations about objects and states of affairs are made. Therefore, whether the intellect exists or does not exist is neither decidable nor apprehensible; a corollary to which is that in making determinations about objects and states of affairs one ought not attend only to the intellect, which has not as yet been apprehended.

58      But suppose that the intellect has been apprehended, and let it be agreed by hypothesis that it exists; I still say that it is not able to make determinations

about objects and states of affairs. For if it does not even discern itself accurately, but disputes with itself concerning its own existence and the manner of its genesis and the location where it is, how would it be able accurately to apprehend anything else? And even granting that the intellect is able to make  59 determinations about objects and states of affairs, we shall not find out how to make such determinations in accord with it. For since there is much controversy regarding the intellect, with one intellect being that of Gorgias, in accord with which he says that nothing exists, and another that of Heraclitus, in accord with which he says that everything exists, and still another that of those who say that some things exist and others do not, we shall have no way of resolving this controversy of the intellects, nor shall we be able to say that one should heed the intellect of this person but not that of that one. If we take a  60 chance on making the determination by any one intellect, we shall be assenting to one party of the dispute and thus begging the question; but if by anything else, we shall be making false the assertion that one should make determinations about objects and states of affairs by the intellect alone.

Another thing: from what was said about the so-called"by whom" criterion  61 we shall be able to show that we are not able to find the most clever of all the intellects, and that even if we did find the most clever of all past and present intellects, one ought not to pay attention to it, for whether in the future there  62 will be another intellect more clever than it is nonevident; and further, that even if we hypothesize an intellect that is more clever than any that will arise, we shall not give assent to the person who is making determinations by means of it, lest, putting forward some false proposition, he is able by means of his sharp intellect to fool us into believing that it is true. Consequently, we should not make determinations about objects and states of affairs by the intellect alone.

The remaining possibility is to say that it should be done by means of both  63 the senses and the intellect. But again this is impossible. For not only do the senses not lead the intellect to apprehension, but they even oppose it. Democritus, as we know, on the basis that honey appears bitter to some people and sweet to others, said that it is neither sweet nor bitter, while Heraclitus said that it is both. And the same account may be given in the case of the other senses and sensory objects. Thus the intellect, moved by the senses, is forced to make differing and inconsistent statements; and this is alien to an apprehensive criterion.

Then there is also the following to be said. The Dogmatists will make  64 determinations about objects and states of affairs either by all the senses and by everybody's intellect, or by some. But if someone will say "by all," he will be claiming what is impossible, with so much inconsistency apparent among the senses and among the intellects; and in particular, his statement will be turned back on itself because of the assertion of the intellect of Gorgias that one should not pay heed either to the senses or to the intellect. And if they say "by some," how will they determine, not having an agreed-upon criterion by means of which to make determinations about the differing senses and intellects, that we should hold to these senses and this intellect and not to those? And if they are going to say that we shall make determinations about  65 the senses and intellects by the intellect and the senses, they will be begging the question; for whether it is possible for anyone to make determinations by means of these is precisely what we are questioning.

66    And this, too, needs to be said: either they will make determinations about both the senses and the intellects by the senses, or both by the intellects, or the senses by the senses and the intellects by the intellects, or the intellects by the senses and the senses by the intellect. If, then, they prefer to make determinations about both by either the senses or the intellect, they will not do so by both sense and intellect but by one of these, whichever they may choose; and

67    consequently the previously mentioned *aporiai* will dog their steps. But if they are going to decide about the senses by the senses and the intellects by the intellect, then, since the senses are inconsistent with the senses and the intellects with the intellects, whichever of the battling senses they take for making the determinations about the other senses, they will be begging the question. For they will be taking as credible one party to the dispute, in order to decide about others that are no more questionable than it. And the same argument applies

68    in the case of the intellects. But if they will decide about the intellects by the senses and the senses by the intellect, we have circularity, since in order that a determination be made about the senses it is necessary that one have been made about the intellects beforehand, and in order that the intellects be tested there must first be a decision about the senses. Since, therefore, we cannot

69    decide about criteria of the same type by means of those of the same type, nor about both types by means of one type, nor, *alternando*, about each type by the other type, we shall not be able, in making determinations, to prefer one intellect to another or one sense to another. And for this reason we shall not have anything by means of which to make determinations, for if we are neither able to do so by means of all the senses and intellects, and if we do not know by which we should do so and by which we should not, then we shall not have anything by means of which to make determinations about things and issues.

So that for these reasons, too, the "by means of which" criterion would be nonexistent.

## 7. The "According to Which" Criterion

70    Next, let us take a look at the criterion "according to which" they say determinations about objects and states of affairs are reached. The first thing to say on this topic is that one cannot form a conception of *phantasia*. For they define a *phantasia* as an impression on the ruling part of the soul. But since the soul is either breath or something even more subtle than breath, as they say, nobody will be able to conceive of an "impression" on it, whether by way of raised and depressed areas, as we see in the case of seals, or by way of the mystical alteration they talk about. And certainly the soul would not be able to keep memories of all the principles that constitute an art [*technē*], since the

71    previously existing alterations would be wiped off by the succeeding ones. But even if one could form a conception of it, the *phantasia* would not be apprehensible, for, since it is a *pathos* of the ruling part, and the ruling part, as

we have shown, is not apprehensible, we shall not apprehend a *pathos* of it, either.

And further, even if we were to grant that the *phantasia* is apprehended, it 72 would not be possible to make determinations about objects and states of affairs in accord with it. For, as the Dogmatists say, the intellect does not of itself get in contact with external objects and receive *phantasiai* from them, but it does so by means of the senses; and the senses do not apprehend the external objects but only their own *pathē*, if anything. And so the *phantasia* will be of a sensory *pathos*, which is not the same thing as the external object. For example, the honey is not the same as my experiencing a sweet taste, nor the wormwood the same as my experiencing a bitter taste, but something different. And since this *pathos* differs from the external object, the *phantasia* will not be 73 of the external object but of something different. So if the intellect makes determinations in accord with the *phantasia*, it does so foolishly and not in accord with the external object. Consequently, it is absurd to say that determinations about external matters are made according to *phantasiai*.

Nor again can one say that the soul apprehends the external objects by 74 means of the sensory *pathē* because the *pathē* of the senses are similar to the external objects. For from whence will the intellect know whether the *pathē* of the senses are similar to the objects of sense, when it has not itself met with these external objects, and when the senses do not reveal to it the nature of those objects, but only their own *pathē* (as I have argued from the modes of *Epochē*)? For just as the person who does not know Socrates but has seen a 75 picture of him does not know whether the picture is like Socrates, so also the intellect, looking at the *pathē* of the senses but not having observed the external objects, will not know whether the *pathē* of the senses resemble the external objects. Therefore, not even on the basis of similarity will the intellect be able to judge these objects in accord with the *phantasia*.

But by way of concession let us grant that, in addition to being conceived 76 of and apprehended, the *phantasiai* are such that determinations can be made about objects and issues according to them, even though the argument points to the complete opposite of this. Then either we shall give credence to every *phantasia* and make determinations according to it, or to some. But if to every *phantasia*, it is clear that we will give credence also to that of Xeniades, according to which he said that no *phantasiai* are worthy of credence, and our statement will be turned back on itself to imply that not all *phantasiai* are such that determinations about objects and issues can be made according to them. But if to some, how shall we determine that to these *phantasiai* we should pay 77 heed, and to those, not? And if they say that we are to do so without a *phantasia*, they will be granting that *phantasiai* are superfluous for making determinations, since they will be saying that it is possible to do this about objects and issues without them. But if they say "with a *phantasia*," how will they select the *phantasia* which they are using to decide about the other *phantasiai*? Once again, they will need another *phantasia* for judging the other 78 one, and still another for that, and so on ad infinitum. But it is impossible to make an infinite number of determinations. Consequently, it is impossible to discover which sort of *phantasiai* should be used as criteria and which not. Since, therefore, even if we grant that determinations about objects and issues should be made in accord with *phantasiai*, the argument is overturned whether we give credence to them all or only to some; it follows that we should not use *phantasiai* as criteria for making such determinations.

79   At this point in our outline these remarks will suffice as regards the criterion according to which determinations about objects and states of affairs are said to be made. Nevertheless, it must be understood that we have no intention of asserting that a criterion of truth does not exist, for that would be dogmatic; but since the Dogmatists seem to have established plausibly that there is a criterion of truth, we have set up some seemingly plausible counter-arguments—not, however, firmly maintaining that they are true or more plausible than the opposing ones, but arriving at suspension of judgment on the basis of the apparent equipollence, as regards plausibility, of these arguments and those of the Dogmatists.

## 8. The True and Truth

80   However, even if we were to grant, as an hypothesis, that there is a criterion of truth, it is revealed as useless and idle when we recall that, going by what is said by the Dogmatists, truth is nonexistent and the true is unreal.

81   What we have in mind here is the following. The true is said to differ from truth in three respects, namely, in essence, in composition, and in power. They differ in essence, since the true is not a body (for it is a proposition and thus a *lekton*), whereas truth is a body (for it is knowledge assertoric of all truths, and knowledge is the ruling part in a certain state, just as a fist is a hand in a certain

82   state; and the ruling part is a body, for according to them it is breath). They differ in composition, since the true is something simple, like "I am conversing,"

83   but the truth consists of many true items of knowledge. And they differ in power, since the truth involves knowledge, but in general the true does not. Consequently they say that the truth exists only in wise people, while the true occurs also in the stupid, for it is possible for a stupid person to say something true.

84   The foregoing is what the Dogmatists say. In deference once again to the plan of our treatise, however, we shall restrict ourselves for the present to arguments about the true, for they also cover the truth since it is defined as "the systematized knowledge of things true." Furthermore, while some of these arguments (namely, those whereby we call in question the very existence of the true) are more general, while others (by means of which we show that the true is not to be found in the sound or in the *lekton* or in the movement of the intellect) are specific, we think it sufficient on this occasion to set out the more general. For just as when the foundation of a wall is destroyed, all the superstructure is destroyed along with it, so also, when the subsistence of the true is challenged, the particular subtleties of the Dogmatists will be included.

## 9.  Is There Anything True by Nature?

There is a controversy among the Dogmatists regarding the true, since some  85
of them say that there is something true and others say that nothing is true.
But it is not possible to resolve the controversy, because the person who says
that there is something true will not, in view of the controversy, be believed
without proof, while if he wishes to give a proof, then if he agrees that it is false
he will not be credible; whereas if he says that it is true he falls into a circular
argument and will be required to give a proof that it is in fact true, and another
proof of that, and so on ad infinitum. But it is impossible to prove an infinite
number of things. Therefore, it is impossible to know even that there is
something true.

Further, the "something," which they say is the highest genus, is either true  86
or false, or neither true nor false, or both false and true. If, then, they are going
to say that it is false, they will be agreeing that everything is false. For just as
since Animal is animate all particular animals are animate, so, if the highest
genus of all, the "something," is false, all the particular things will be false and
nothing will be true. But along with this there follows also the conclusion that
nothing is false, for the very statements "everything is false" and "something is
false," being included among the "all," will be false. And if the "something" is
true, then everything will be true — from which it will follow again that nothing
is true, for since this statement itself (I mean "nothing is true") is something, it
is true. And if the "something" is both false and true, each of the particulars  87
will be both false and true. From this it follows that nothing is true by nature.
For that which has such a nature as to be true would in no way be false. But
if the "something" is neither false nor true, it is conceded that all the
particulars, being said to be neither false nor true, will not be true. And for
these reasons, it will be nonevident to us whether there is something true.

In addition to these considerations, either the true are appearances only,  88
or nonevident only, or, of the true some are nonevident and some are
appearances; but none of these alternatives is true, as we shall show; nothing,
therefore, is true. For if the true are appearances only, the Dogmatists will say
either that all or that some of the appearances are true. And if they say "all,"
the argument is turned around, for it appears to some that nothing is true. But  89
if they say "some," nobody can assert without a criterion that these are true
and those are false, while if he employs a criterion he will say either that this
criterion is an appearance or that it is nonevident. But it is certainly not
nonevident, for it is now being assumed that appearances only are true. But if
it is an appearance, then, since the point at issue is which appearances are true
and which are not, the appearance that is taken for the purpose of judging the
appearances will need again another apparent criterion, and this another, and
so on ad infinitum. But it is impossible to decide an infinite number of things.
Therefore, it is impossible to apprehend whether the true things are appearances only.

Similarly, the person who says that the non-evident only are true will not  90
say that all of them are true (for he will not say both that the number of the

stars is even and that it is odd); and if he says that only some are true, by what shall we decide that these non-evident matters are true and those are false? Certainly not by an appearance. But if by something non-evident, then, since we are investigating which of the non-evident are true and which are false, this non-evident point will itself require another to decide about it, and that one another, and so on ad infinitum. Therefore, it is not the case that the non-evident only are true.

91    The remaining alternative is to say that of the true, some are appearances and some are non-evident, but this possibility, too, is absurd. For either all the appearances and the non-evident are true, or some of the appearances and some of the non-evident. Now if all, the statement will once again be turned around, as it will be granted true that nothing is true; and it will be said to be

92 true both that the number of the stars is even and that it is odd. But if only some of the appearances and some of the non-evident are true, how shall we determine that of the appearances these are true and those are false? If by some appearance, the argument will go on ad infinitum. And if by something non-evident, then since the non-evident also require determining, by means of what will this non-evident point be determined? If by some appearance, we have the circularity mode, and if by something non-evident, an infinite regress.

93 Similar things must also be said about the non-evident. For the person who tries to make a determination about them by something non-evident falls into the infinite regress, while the one who tries to do so by an appearance either gets into an infinite regress (if he again and again employs something apparent) or into circularity (if he switches over to something non-evident). It is false, therefore, to say that of the true things some are appearances and some are non-evident.

94    So if neither the appearances only nor the non-evident only are true, nor are some of the appearances and some of the non-evident, then nothing is true. But if nothing is true, and the criterion is supposed to be useful for making determinations about the true, the criterion is useless and idle even if we grant for the sake of argument that it has some sort of existence. And if one must suspend judgment as to whether there is anything true, it follows that those who say that dialectic is the science of things false or true or neither are getting ahead of themselves.

95    Further, since the criterion of truth has appeared to be aporetic, it is no longer possible, if we go by the statements of the Dogmatists, to make any confident assertion either about the things that seem clear or about the non-evident, for seeing that the Dogmatists think that they apprehend these latter on the basis of the "clear" things, how shall we dare to assert anything about the non-evident if we are forced to suspend judgment about these

96 so-called "clear" things? But for very good measure we shall raise some objections applying against the non-evident objects and states of affairs in particular. And since these seem to be apprehended and confirmed by means of sign and proof, we shall point out briefly that one ought also to suspend judgment about those. Let us begin with signs, for proof seems to be a species of sign.

## 10. Signs

Of objects of discourse [*ta pragmata*], some, according to the Dogmatists, are 97
pre-evident and some are non-evident; and of the non-evident, some are
non-evident once and for all, some are temporarily non-evident, and some are
non-evident by nature. And they call "pre-evident" those things that come to
our awareness directly, such as that it is daytime;"non-evident once and for all"
are those which do not naturally fall within our apprehension, such as that the
number of the stars is even; "temporarily non-evident" are those which, though 98
they are by nature clear, are temporarily non-evident to us because of external
circumstances, as, for example, the city of Athens is at the moment non-evident
to me; and "non-evident by nature" are those which are not of such a nature
as to fall within our clear view, such as the intelligible pores, for these never
appear of themselves but may be thought to be apprehended, if at all, by means
of other things, such as perspiration or something like that. Now the pre- 99
evident things, they say, have no need of a sign, for they are apprehended by
means of themselves. Nor do the once-and-for-all non-evident things have need
of a sign, since they are never apprehended at all. But, say the Dogmatists, the
temporarily non-evident and the naturally non-evident are apprehended by
means of signs, though not by the same ones, for the temporarily non-evident
are apprehended by means of mnemonic signs, and the naturally non-evident
by means of indicative signs.

According to the Dogmatists, then, some of the signs are mnemonic and 100
others are indicative. And they call a sign "mnemonic" if, having been observed
together with the thing signified, it, by its clearness at the time when it occurs
to us (while the thing signified is non-evident), leads us to recall what was
observed together with it and is not occurring clearly now, as is the case with
smoke and fire. A sign is "indicative," as they say, if it is not clearly observed 101
together with what is signified, but it signifies that of which it is a sign by its
own individual nature and constitution; for example, the motions of the body
are signs of the soul. Whence they also define the indicative sign thus: "an
indicative sign is a proposition that is the true antecedent in a true conditional
and serves to disclose the consequent." There being two different kinds of sign, 102
as we said, we do not argue against every sign but only against the indicative
kind, since it seems to have been invented by the Dogmatists. For the
mnemonic sign is relied on in the normal course of life, since fire is signified to
the person who sees smoke, and if he observes a scar he says that there has
been a wound. Hence, not only do we not fight against the normal course of
life, but we are allied with it in that we assent undogmatically to what it relies
on, while opposing the peculiar creations of the Dogmatists.

It was, I think, appropriate to say these things in advance in order to 103
clarify the matter in question. It remains for us to proceed to the refutation,
not being concerned to show completely the nonexistence of the indicative sign,
but only recalling the apparent equipollence of the arguments that are brought
for and against its existence.

## 11. Is There Such a Thing as an Indicative Sign?

104 Now the sign, if we go by what is said about it by the Dogmatists, is not conceivable. Thus, for example, those who seem to have dealt with it careful-ly — the Stoics — in their attempt to set before the mind the notion of sign say that a sign is a proposition that is the true antecedent in a sound conditional and serves to disclose the consequent. And they say that a proposition is a complete *lekton* that is assertoric by itself, and a sound conditional is one that 105 does not have a true antecedent and a false consequent. For the conditional either has a true antecedent and a true consequent, (for example, "If it is day, it is light") or a false antecedent and a false consequent, (for example, "If the earth is flying, the earth has wings") or a true antecedent and a false consequent, (for example, "If the earth exists, the earth is flying") or a false antecedent and a true consequent, (for example, "If the earth is flying, the earth exists"). They say that of these only the one with a true antecedent and a false 106 consequent is unsound, and that the others are sound. They say also that a "guiding proposition" is the antecedent of a true conditional that has a true antecedent and a true consequent. And it serves to disclose the consequent, seeing that "She has milk" seems to disclose "She has conceived" in this conditional, "If she has milk, she has conceived."

107    That is what the Stoics say. But we say, first of all, that it is non-evident whether there is any such thing as a *lekton*. Some of the Dogmatists — the Epicureans — say that *lekta* do not exist, while others — the Stoics — say that they do exist. When the Stoics say that *lekta* exist they employ either mere assertion or a proof as well. But if mere assertion, the Epicureans will counter with the assertion that *lekta* do not exist; and if the Stoics will bring in a proof, then since the proof consists of propositions, that is, of *lekta*, and, itself consisting of *lekta*, cannot be brought in to promote belief in the existence of *lekta* (for how will a person who does not grant the existence of *lekta* agree 108 that there is a *system* of *lekta*?) — it follows that the person who seeks to establish the existence of *lekta* by assuming the existence of a system of *lekta* is trying to make what is in question believable by means of what is in question. Hence, if it is impossible to establish the existence of *lekta* either simply or by a proof, it is non-evident that there is any such thing as a *lekton*.

    Similarly with regard to the question of whether propositions exist, for the 109 proposition is a *lekton*. Further, even if it should be granted for the sake of argument that *lekta* exist, it will be found that propositions do not, for they are composed of *lekta* that do not exist simultaneously with one another. In the case of "If it is day, it is light," when I say "It is day" the proposition "It is light" does not yet exist, and when I say "It is light" the "It is day" no longer exists. And since composite things cannot exist if their parts do not exist simultaneously, and the things of which propositions are composed do not exist simultaneously, propositions do not exist.

110    But, even leaving these points aside, the sound conditional will be found not to be apprehensible. For Philo says that a sound conditional is one that does not have a true antecedent and a false consequent; for example, when it is day and I am conversing, "If it is day, I am conversing"; but Diodorus defines

it as one that neither is nor ever was capable of having a true antecedent and a false consequent. According to him, the conditional just mentioned seems to be false, since when it is day and I have become silent, it will have a true antecedent and a false consequent. But the following conditional seems true: 111 "If atomic elements of things do not exist, then atomic elements of things do exist," since it will always have the false antecedent, "Atomic elements of things do not exist," and the true consequent, "Atomic elements of things do exist." And those who introduce connection or coherence say that a conditional is sound when the denial of its consequent is inconsistent with the antecedent; so, according to them, the above-mentioned conditionals are unsound, but the following is true: "If it is day, it is day." And those who judge by "force" declare 112 that a conditional is true if its consequent is in effect included in its antecedent. According to them, I suppose, "if it is day, then it is day" and every repeated conditional will be false, for there is no way for a thing itself to be included in itself.

So it will seem, I guess, that there is no way of settling the controversy. 113 For whether we give preference to any one of the aforementioned positions with or without proof, we shall not be credible. For a proof is considered sound if its conclusion follows from the conjunction of its premises as a consequent follows from an antecedent; as, for example, with:

> If it is day, it is light.
> But it is day.
> Therefore, it is light.

and

> If, if it is day it is light, and it is day, then it is light.

But when we ask how we shall determine whether the consequent follows from 114 the antecedent, we are met with circularity. For in order that a determination about the conditional be proved, the conclusion of the proof must follow from the premises, as we have said above; and, in turn, in order for this to have any credibility, it is necessary that a determination have been made about the conditional and the relation of following. Which is absurd. Therefore, the true 115 conditional is not apprehensible.

But the "guiding proposition", too, is a subject of *aporia*. For it, they say, is the antecedent in a conditional that has a true antecedent and a true consequent. But if the sign "serves to disclose the consequent," that consequent 116 will either be pre-evident or nonevident. And if it is pre-evident, it will not have any need of what is supposed to do the "disclosing," but will be apprehended along with it and will not be the thing signified, and thus the other will not be a sign of it. On the other hand, if it is non-evident, then since there are undecidable disputes about the non-evident things as to which of them are true and which are false, and even in general whether any one of them is true, it will be non-evident whether the conditional has a true consequent. A corollary to this is that it is also non-evident whether its antecedent is a "guiding proposition."

117    But, leaving these points to one side, it is impossible for the sign to serve
to disclose the consequent if what is signified is relative to the sign and is
therefore apprehended together with it. For relative things are apprehended
together with one another; for example, just as the right cannot be apprehended as the right of the left before the left is apprehended, nor vice-versa, so also
in the case of the other relative things; and thus the sign cannot be apprehended as the sign of the significatum before the significatum is apprehended.
118  And if the sign is not apprehended before the significatum, it cannot really
serve to disclose something that is apprehended together with it and not
after it.

       Thus also, if we go by the usual statements of the Stoics, a concept of sign
cannot be formed. For they say both that the sign is relative and that it serves
119  to disclose the significatum to which they say it is relative. Now, if it is relative,
that is to say, relative to the significatum, it certainly ought to be apprehended
together with the significatum, just as the left with the right and the up with
the down and the rest of the relative things. But if it also serves to disclose
what is signified, it also certainly ought to be apprehended in advance in order
that, being preknown, it may lead us to the notion of the object or state of
120  affairs that becomes known through it. But it is impossible to form a notion of
an object or state of affairs that cannot be known before that [object or state
of affairs] before which it has to be apprehended; therefore, it is impossible to
conceive of something that is relative and serves to disclose that existing thing
relative to which it is thought. But they say both that the sign is relative and
that it serves to disclose the significatum; it is impossible, therefore, to conceive
of the sign.

121    In addition to these points, the following should be said. There has been a
controversy among those who have gone before us, with some claiming that
there is such a thing as an indicative sign and others that there is no such thing.
Now whoever says that there is such a thing as an indicative sign will say this
either simply and without proof, making a bald assertion, or he will say it with
proof. But if he employs mere assertion he will not be credible, while if he tries
122  to prove it he will assume what is in question. For since proof is said to come
under the genus Sign, and it is disputed whether or not there is such a thing
as a sign, there will also be a dispute as to whether or not there is such a thing
as a proof—just as when, for example, it is questioned whether there is any
such thing as an animal, it is also questioned whether there is any such thing
as a human being; for a human being is an animal. But it is absurd to try to
prove what is in question either by means of what is equally in question or by
means of itself; therefore, it will not be possible for anyone by means of a proof
123  to maintain firmly that there is such a thing as a sign. But if one cannot,
whether simply or with proof, make and firmly maintain a positive assertion
about the sign, it is impossible for an apprehensive assertion to be made about
it; and if the sign is not accurately apprehended, it will not be said to be
significant of anything, since it itself is a subject of disagreement, and for this

reason it will not even be a sign. Hence, according to this line of reasoning, too, the sign is nonexistent and inconceivable.

And there is still more to be said. Either all the signs are appearances, or all are non-evident, or some signs are appearances and some are non-evident. But none of these alternatives is true; therefore, there does not exist a sign. 124

Now, that it is not the case that all signs are non-evident is shown as follows. According to the Dogmatists, the non-evident does not appear of itself but affects us by means of something else. And so the sign, if it were non-evident, would require another non-evident sign, since according to the hypothesis before us, no sign is an appearance; and that one would require another, and so on ad infinitum. But it is impossible to grasp an infinite number of signs; therefore, it is impossible for the sign, if it is non-evident, to be apprehended. And for this reason it will also be nonexistent, being unable to signify anything, that is, to be a sign, because it is not apprehensible.

But if all the signs are appearances, then, since the sign is relative—that is, relative to the significatum—and relative things are apprehended together with one another, the things said to be signified, being apprehended together with what is an appearance, will be appearances. For just as, when the right and the left are perceived, the right is no more said to be apparent than the left, nor the left than the right, so too when the sign and the significatum are apprehended together, the sign should no more be said to be apparent than the significatum. And if the significatum is an appearance, it will not be a significatum, since it will not need anything to signify and disclose it. Whence, just as if there is no right, neither is there a left, so if there is no significatum there can be no sign; thus, if one says that all signs are appearances, the sign turns out to be nonexistent. 125

126

It remains to suppose that some signs are appearances and some non-evident; but even so the *aporiai* remain. For the things said to be signified by signs that are appearances will be appearances, as we said before, and not being in need of anything to signify them, will not be significata at all, whence the others will not be signs, either, as they do not signify anything. As to the non-evident signs, which need something to disclose them, if they are said to be signified by non-evident things, the argument goes on to infinity and they are found not to be apprehensible and for that reason nonexistent, as we have said before. But if they are said to be signified by appearances, they will be appearances apprehended together with their signs and for this reason will also be nonexistent. For it is impossible that there exist some object or state of affairs that is both non-evident by nature and yet is apparent, and the signs that the argument is about, having been posited as non-evident, have been found to be appearances because the argument has been turned around. 127

128

If, therefore, it is neither the case that all the signs are appearances nor that they are all non-evident, nor that some of them are appearances and some are non-evident, and besides these, as the Dogmatists themselves say, there is no other alternative, the so-called "signs" will be nonexistent. 129

130     These few arguments, out of many, will suffice for the present to support
the position that there is no such thing as an indicative sign. Next we shall set
forth those supporting the position that signs do exist, in order that we may
show the equipollence of the opposed arguments. Either, then, the expressions
that are uttered against signs signify something or they do not. But if they do
not, how can they have any bearing on the existence of signs? And if they do
131 signify something, there is such a thing as a sign. Furthermore, the arguments
against signs are either probative or they are not. But if they are not probative,
they do not prove that there is no such thing as a sign; while if they are
probative, since a proof, as serving to disclose the conclusion, falls under the
genus Sign, signs will exist. Whence the following sort of argument is also
made:

> If there is a sign, there is a sign; and if there is no sign, there is a sign, for the
> nonexistence of signs is shown by a proof, which is a sign. But either there is
> a sign or there is not; therefore, there is a sign.

132 This argument, however, is matched by the following:

> If there is no sign, there is no sign. And if there is a sign—a sign being what
> the Dogmatists say it is—there is no sign. For the sign under discussion,
> which, in accord with its concept, is said to be both relative and serving to
> disclose the significatum, turns out to be nonexistent, as we have shown. But
> either there is a sign or there is no sign; therefore, there is no sign.

133 Also, with regard to the phrases uttered about the sign, let the Dogmatists
themselves answer whether these signify something or not. For if they do not
signify anything, they do not make credible the existence of a sign; while, if they
do signify, the significatum will follow from them. But this was that there is
such a thing as a sign; from which, as we showed, by a turnaround of the
argument it follows that there is no such thing as a sign.

   So, with such plausible arguments presented both for and against the
existence of signs, it must be said that it is "not more" the case that signs exist
than that they do not.


## 12. Proof

134 From these considerations it is manifest that proof, too, is a matter upon which
there is no agreement; for if we are suspending judgment about signs, and a
proof is a kind of sign, it is necessary to suspend judgment about proofs as
well. And we shall find that the arguments propounded concerning signs can
be adapted to fit proofs as well, since the latter seem to be both relative and
serving to disclose the conclusion, from which has followed all the things we
135 have said about signs. But if it is necessary to say something applying
specifically to proofs, I shall briefly consider the argument concerning them,
after first trying to give a concise clarification of the Dogmatists' definition of
proof.

   A proof, as they say, is an argument that, by means of agreed-upon
premises and a valid inference, discloses a non-evident conclusion. What they

mean will become more clear from the following: An argument is a system consisting of premises and a conclusion. Those propositions that are agreed 136 upon for the establishment of the conclusion are called the premises, and the proposition which is established from the premises is called the conclusion.

For example, in this argument:

> If it is day, it is light.
> It is day.
> Therefore, it is light.

the proposition "It is light" is the conclusion and the others are premises. Some 137 arguments are valid, and some are not valid; they are valid whenever the conditional whose antecedent is the conjunction of the premises and whose consequent is the conclusion, is sound. For instance, the previously mentioned argument is valid, since "It is light" follows from the premise conjunction, "It is day, and if it is day it is light" in this conditional:

> If (it is day and if it is day it is light), then it is light.

Arguments not having this characteristic are invalid.

And of the valid arguments, some are true and some are not true—true, 138 whenever not only is there a sound conditional consisting of the premise conjunction and the conclusion, as we said before, but also both the conclusion and the premise conjunction, which is the antecedent of the conditional, are true. And a conjunction,—for example, "It is day, and if it is day it is light"—is true whenever every conjunct is true. Arguments not having the above-described characteristic are not true. For, supposing that it is daytime, 139 such an argument as the following is valid enough,

> If it is night, it is dark.
> It is night.
> Therefore, it is dark.

since the following conditional is sound:

> If (it is night and if it is night it is dark), then it is dark

but the argument is not true. For the conjunctive antecedent—"It is night and if it is night it is dark"—is false, since it contains the false conjunct "It is night," and a conjunction containing a false conjunct is false. Hence they also define a true argument as one that leads logically from true premises to a true conclusion.

Again, of the true arguments some are probative and some are not 140 probative; the probative are those validly concluding something non-evident from things that are pre-evident, and the non-probative are those that are not of this sort. For example, such an argument as this:

> If it is day, it is light.
> It is day.
> Therefore, it is light.

is not probative, for its conclusion, that it is light, is pre-evident. But such an argument as:

> If sweat flows through the surface, there are intelligible pores.
> Sweat flows through the surface.
> Therefore, there are intelligible pores.

is probative, since its conclusion, "There are intelligible pores" is non-evident.

141      And, of the arguments validly concluding something non-evident, some lead us through the premises to the conclusion simply in the manner of guides, and others lead us not only as guides but also as bringing something hidden to light. Leading us as guides are those that seem to depend upon trust and memory, for example, this one:

> If a god has said to you that this man will be rich, then this
>     man will be rich.
> This god (suppose that I am pointing to Zeus) has said to you
>     that this man will be rich.
> Therefore, this man will be rich.

142 For we assent to the conclusion not so much because of the force of the premises as because we trust the assertion of the god. But some arguments lead us to the conclusion not only as guides but also as bringing something hidden to light, for example:

> If sweat flows through the surface, there are intelligible pores.
> The first.
> Therefore, the second.

For the flowing of the sweat discloses the existence of the pores, given the common notion that water cannot go through a solid body.

143      Thus, a proof should be an argument that is valid and true and has a non-evident conclusion disclosed by means of the force of the premises, and in view of this it is defined as an argument which, by means of agreed-upon premises and valid inferences, discloses a non-evident conclusion.

    It is by means of these considerations, then, that the Dogmatists are accustomed to clarify the notion of proof.

## 13. Are There Proofs?

144 That proof is nonexistent can be inferred from the very things they say, by attacking each ingredient of the concept. For instance, an argument is composed of propositions, and composite things cannot exist unless the things of which they are composed coexist with one another, as is obvious in the case of a bed and similar things. But the parts of an argument do not coexist with one another. For when we state the first premise, neither the other premise nor the conclusion as yet exists; and when we state the second one, the first premise no longer exists and the conclusion has not yet come into being; and, finally,

when we assert the conclusion, its premises are no longer in being. Therefore, the parts of the argument do not coexist with one another, whence it will be apparent that the argument, too, does not exist.

But apart from these considerations, the valid argument is not apprehen- 145 sible. For if its validity is determined on the basis of the soundness of the corresponding conditional, and the truth of the conditional is a matter of unsettled dispute and is perhaps not apprehensible, as we have pointed out in our discussion of signs, then the valid argument, too, will not be apprehensible. Now the logicians say that an argument becomes invalid either by incoherence 146 or by deficiency or by being put forward in an unsound schema or by redundancy. For example, it is invalid by incoherence when the premises are not logically connected with one another and with the conclusion, as in:

> If it is day, it is light.
> Grain is being sold in the agora.
> Therefore, Dion is walking.

It is invalid by redundancy when it contains a premise that is not needed for 147 the validity of the argument, for example:

> If it is day, it is light.
> It is day.
> Dion is walking.
> Therefore, it is light.

And it is invalid by being in an unsound schema whenever the schema of the argument is not valid; for example, while the following, as they say, are syllogisms:

> If it is day, it is light.
> It is day.
> Therefore, it is light.

and

> If it is day, it is light.
> It is not light.
> Therefore, it is not day;

this argument is not valid:

> If it is day, it is light.
> It is light.
> Therefore, it is day.

For since the conditional declares that if its antecedent is the case so is the 148 consequent, it is reasonable, when the antecedent is assumed, to infer also the consequent, and when the consequent is denied, to deny also the antecedent, for if the antecedent were the case, the consequent would also be the case. But

when the consequent is assumed, the antecedent will not in general be implied;
for the conditional did not promise that the antecedent follows from the
consequent, but only that the consequent follows from the antecedent.

149        For that reason, an argument inferring the consequent of a conditional
from the conditional and its antecedent is said to be syllogistic, and likewise
one inferring the negation of the antecedent from the conditional and the
negation of the consequent. But an argument, like the one mentioned above,
that infers the antecedent from the conditional and its consequent is invalid in
that it infers a false conclusion from true premises (when it is uttered at night
while there is lamp light). For the conditional "If it is day, it is light" is true,
and also the second premise, "It is light," but the conclusion, "It is day," is false.

150        An argument is unsound by deficiency if something is lacking that is
needed for inferring the conclusion. For example, while the following argument
is sound, as they suppose:

> Wealth is good or bad or indifferent.
> It is neither bad nor indifferent.
> Therefore, it is good,

this argument is defective by deficiency:

> Wealth is good or bad.
> It is not bad.
> Therefore, it is good.

151 So if I shall show that, going by what the Dogmatists say, no difference can be
discerned between invalid and valid arguments, I shall have shown that the
valid argument is not apprehensible, so that the innumerable arguments that
they bring forward in accord with their logic are useless. And I show it as
follows.

152        It was said that the kind of argument that is invalid by incoherence is to
be recognized by the lack of logical connection of the premises with one
another and with the conclusion. Now since recognizing this connection has to
be preceded by making a determination about the truth value of the corresponding conditional, and since the conditional is not decidable, as I have
argued, it will be impossible to distinguish the arguments that are invalid by
153 incoherence. For anyone who says that a given argument is invalid by
incoherence will, if he just asserts it, receive in opposition the assertion
contradictory to his own; but if he proves it by an argument, he will be told
that this argument must first be valid if it is to prove the lack of logical
connection between the premises of the argument that is allegedly characterized by incoherence. But we shall not know whether it is probative, since we
have no agreed-upon test of that conditional by which we are to determine
whether the conclusion of the argument follows from the conjunction of the
premises. And so, on this basis, too, we shall not be able to distinguish from
the valid arguments those arguments that are invalid by incoherence.

154        We shall say the same things to anyone who claims that a given argument
is invalid by being propounded in an unsound schema. For he who tries to

establish that a schema is unsound will not have an agreed-upon valid argument by means of which he will be able to infer what he claims. By these considerations we have in effect also refuted those who try to show that there are arguments invalid by deficiency. For if the argument that is complete and finished cannot be distinguished from other arguments, then the argument that is deficient will be non-evident. And, further, whoever wishes to show, by means of an argument, that some argument is deficient will not be able to make a tested and correct statement to that effect because for the corresponding conditional he does not have an agreed-upon test by means of which he can make a determination about the inference in the argument he is discussing. 155

Furthermore, the argument said to be unsound by redundancy cannot be distinguished from the proofs. For, as far as redundancy is concerned, even the "undemonstrated" arguments so much talked of by the Stoics will be found defective, and if those are taken away, Stoic logic is overturned. For these, the Stoics say, have no need of demonstration to establish them, and they themselves serve to demonstrate that the other arguments are valid. But that they are redundant will be clear when we have set forth the undemonstrated arguments and then make good what we are saying. 156

Now the Stoics fancy that there are many undemonstrated arguments, but for the most part they put forward the following five, to which all the others, it seems, can be reduced. From a conditional and its antecedent, the first concludes the consequent. For example: 157

> If it is day, then it is light.
> It is day.
> Therefore, it is light.

From a conditional and the contradictory of its consequent, the second concludes the contradictory of the antecedent. For example:

> If it is day, then it is light.
> It is not light.
> Therefore, it is not day.

From the denial of a conjunction and one of the conjuncts, the third concludes the contradictory of the other conjunct. For example: 158

> Not both: it is day and it is night.
> It is day.
> Therefore, it is not night.

From a disjunction and one of the disjuncts, the fourth concludes the contradictory of the other disjunct. For example:

> Either it is day or it is night.
> It is day.
> Therefore, it is not night.

From a disjunction and the contradictory of one of the disjuncts, the fifth concludes the other disjunct. For example:

> Either it is day or it is night.
> It is not night.
> Therefore, it is day.

159  These, then, are the vaunted undemonstrated arguments, but they all seem to me to be invalid by redundancy. To begin with the first, for example, either it is agreed or else it is non-evident that the proposition "It is light" follows from the antecedent "It is day" in the conditional "If it is day, it is light." But if it is non-evident, we shall not concede the conditional as agreed upon; while if it is pre-evident that if "It is day" is the case then necessarily "It is light" is also the case, then in saying "It is day" we imply "It is light," so that this argument will suffice:

> It is day.
> Therefore, it is light.

and the conditional "If it is day, it is light" will be superfluous.

160       We make a similar point in the case of the second undemonstrated argument. For either it is possible or it is not possible for the antecedent to hold while the consequent does not. But if it is possible, the conditional will not be sound; while if it is not possible, then in asserting the negation of the consequent we shall be simultaneously asserting the negation of the antecedent. So once again the conditional will be superfluous, since what is being propounded amounts to:

> It is not light.
> Therefore, it is not day.

161  The same reasoning applies also in the case of the third undemonstrated argument. Either it is pre-evident or it is non-evident that it is impossible for all the conjuncts of the conjunction to hold. And if it is nonevident, we shall not concede the contradictory of the conjunction; while if it is pre-evident, then in asserting one of them we shall be simultaneously denying the other, and the contradictory of the conjunction will be superfluous, as we are saying in effect:

> It is day.
> Therefore, it is not night.

162  We say similar things about the fourth and fifth undemonstrated arguments. For either it is pre-evident or it is non-evident that, of the components of a disjunction, necessarily one is true and the other is false. And if it is non-evident, we shall not concede the disjunction; but if it is pre-evident, then when one of them is asserted it is obvious that the other does not hold, and

when one is denied it is pre-evident that the other does hold, so that the following suffice:

> It is day.                          It is not day.
> Therefore, it is not night.         Therefore, it is night.

and the disjunction is superfluous.

Similar points can also be made about the so-called "categorical" syllo-  163
gisms, which are much used by the Peripatetics. Thus, in the argument:

> The just is fair.
> The fair is good.
> Therefore, the just is good.

either it is agreed upon and pre-evident that the fair is good, or it is disputed and non-evident. But if it is non-evident, it will not be conceded while the argument is being put forward, and for this reason the syllogism will not be valid; while if it is pre-evident that whatever is fair is without exception good, then when it is said that something is fair it is simultaneously implied that it is also good, so that the following form of the argument suffices:

> The just is fair.
> Therefore, the just is good.

and the other premise, in which the fair is said to be good, is superfluous.  164
Likewise, in the following argument:

> Socrates is a human being.
> Every human being is an animal.
> Therefore, Socrates is an animal.

if it is not immediately evident in advance that anything whatever that is a human being is also an animal, the universal premise will not be agreed upon nor shall we concede it when the argument is put forward. But if something's  165
being an animal follows from the fact that it is a human being, and for that reason the premise "Every human being is an animal" is agreed to be true, then when it is said that Socrates is a human being it is simultaneously implied that he is an animal, so that this form of the argument suffices:

> Socrates is a human being.
> Therefore, Socrates is an animal.

and the premise "Every human being is an animal" is superfluous. And, not to  166
spend more time on this, it is possible to use similar methods in the case of the other first-figure categorical arguments.

In view of the fact, however, that these arguments on which the logicians found their syllogisms are redundant, all logic is overturned because of this

redundancy, for we are not able to distinguish from the so-called "valid"
167  syllogisms those arguments that are redundant and consequently invalid. And
if some people disapprove single-premised arguments, they are no more worthy
of credence than Antipater, who does not reject such arguments.

For these reasons, what the logicians call "valid argument" is not deter-
minable. But further, a "true" argument is not discoverable, both for the
foregoing reasons and because it must in all cases end in a true proposition.
For the conclusion that is said to be true is either an appearance or it is non-
168  evident. And it is certainly not an appearance; for then it would not need to
be disclosed by means of the premises, being self-evident and no less an
appearance than its premises. But if it is non-evident, then since there is an
unresolved dispute concerning non-evident things, as we have pointed out
previously, and they are therefore also not apprehensible, the conclusion of the
argument said to be true will not be apprehensible, either. And if this is not
apprehensible, we shall not know whether what is concluded is true or false.
Thus we shall be ignorant as to whether the argument is true or false, and the
"true" argument will not be discoverable.

169      But, passing over these difficulties also, it is impossible to find an argument
that concludes something non-evident by means of things that are pre-evident.
For if the conclusion follows from the conjunction of the premises, and if what
follows and is the consequent is relative, that is, relative to the antecedent, and
if relatives must be apprehended together with one another, as we have
established — then, if the conclusion is non-evident the premises will be
non-evident, and if the premises are pre-evident the conclusion will also be
pre-evident, as it is apprehended together with them and they are pre-evident;
so that no longer is something non-evident being inferred from things that are
170  pre-evident. For these reasons neither is the conclusion disclosed by the
premises, whether it is non-evident and thus not apprehended, or pre-evident
and not in need of anything to disclose it. If, therefore, a proof is said to be an
argument that by inference — that is, validly — discloses a non-evident conclusion by means of some premises agreed to be true, and we have pointed out
that there exists no argument that is valid or true or that validly concludes
something non-evident from things that are pre-evident or that serves to
disclose its conclusion, it is plain that there is no such thing as a proof.

171      From the following line of attack, too, we shall make plain that proof
neither exists nor is even conceivable. The person who says that there is such
a thing as a proof is positing either a generic proof (a "proof in general") or a
particular proof. But, as we shall point out, it is not possible to establish the
existence either of a generic proof or of a particular proof, and besides these
no other can be thought of. Therefore, nobody can establish the existence of
172  proof. For the following reasons the generic proof does not exist. Either it has
some premises and a conclusion or it does not. If it does not, it is not a proof.
If it does have some premises and a conclusion, then, since everything proved
173  and proving is particular, it will be a particular proof. Therefore, there is no

such thing as a generic proof. But neither is there a particular proof. For they will define "proof" either as the system of premises and conclusion, or as the system of premises alone. But neither of these is a proof, as I shall show. Therefore, there is no particular proof. The system of premises and conclusion 174 is not a proof because, first of all, it has a non-evident part, namely, the conclusion, and so will be non-evident. But this is absurd, for if the proof is non-evident, then, rather than serving to prove other things, it will itself be in need of something to prove it [i.e., to prove that it is a proof].

Also, since they say that proof is relative, that is, relative to what is 175 inferred, and things that are relative, as they themselves claim, are thought of in relation to other things, what is proved must be other than the proof; and if indeed the conclusion is what is proved, the proof will not be thought of together with its conclusion. Furthermore, either the conclusion contributes something to its own proof, or it does not; but if it does contribute, it will be serving to disclose itself, and if it does not contribute but is superfluous, it will not even be part of the proof, since we shall say that the latter is defective by redundancy.

But neither would the system of the premises alone be a proof, for who 176 would say that this kind of statement:

If it is day, it is light.
It is day.

is an argument or even completely expresses any thought at all? Thus, a system of premises alone does not constitute a proof. Therefore, no particular proof exists, either. And if no particular proof nor generic proof exists, and no other "proof" is conceivable, then there is no such thing as proof.

One can show the nonexistence of proof also from the following consider- 177 ations. If there is a proof, then either, being itself an appearance, it serves to disclose an appearance, or being itself non-evident, it serves to disclose something non-evident, or being non-evident, to disclose an appearance, or being an appearance, to disclose something non-evident. But it cannot be conceived as disclosing any of these; therefore, it cannot be conceived. For if, 178 being an appearance, it serves to disclose an appearance, what is disclosed will be simultaneously an appearance and non-evident—an appearance, since by hypothesis it is such, and non-evident, since it is in need of something to disclose it and does not of itself affect us in a clear way. And if, being non-evident, it serves to disclose something non-evident, it will have need of something to disclose it and will not serve to disclose other things, which is at odds with the concept of proof. And for these reasons, neither will a non- 179 evident proof serve to disclose something pre-evident. Nor will a pre-evident proof serve to disclose something non-evident. For since they are relatives, and relatives are apprehended together with one another, what is said to be proved will be apprehended together with the pre-evident proof and will be pre-evident, so that the argument is turned back on itself and the proof of the non-evident is found not to be pre-evident. If, therefore, the proof is neither an appearance and of an appearance, nor non-evident and of something non-evident, nor non-evident and of something pre-evident, nor pre-evident and of something non-evident, and they say that besides these there is no other alternative, then it must be stated that the proof is nonexistent.

180    In addition, the following needs to be said. There is a controversy about proof; for some assert that it does not exist — as, indeed, do those who say that nothing at all exists — and some, like the majority of the Dogmatists, claim

181  that it does exist; but we say that it "no more" exists than not. And besides, a proof always includes a dogma, and the Dogmatists have had disputes about every dogma, so necessarily there is controversy about every proof. For if, in agreeing, for example, to the proof that there exists a vacuum, one simultaneously agrees to the existence of the vacuum, then it is evident that those who dispute the existence of a vacuum will also dispute the proof of it. And the same reasoning applies to all the other dogmas proved by the proofs. Therefore, every proof is disputed and is a matter of controversy.

182    Since, then, proof is non-evident because of the controversy concerning it (for objects of controversy, as such, are non-evident), its existence is not manifest of itself but needs to be established for us by a proof. The proof, however, by which proof is established will not be agreed upon and manifest (for we are right now questioning whether there is any proof at all), and being a matter of controversy and non-evident, it will require another proof, and that one another, and so on ad infinitum. But it is impossible to prove an infinite number of things; therefore, it is impossible to show that there is such a thing as proof.

183    But neither can it be disclosed by a sign. For since there is a question whether there is such a thing as a sign, and since signs require proof of their own existence, we have circularity, with the proof requiring a sign and the sign again requiring a proof, which is absurd. And for these reasons it is not possible to resolve the controversy about proof, since the decision requires a criterion and it is questionable whether there is any such thing; and in view of this, the criterion will need a proof showing that there is such a thing as a criterion, so

184  that we have the circularity type of *aporia* once again. Hence, if neither by means of a proof nor by means of a sign nor by means of a criterion is it possible to show that there exists a proof, nor is this of itself pre-evident, as we have shown, then whether there exists a proof will not be apprehensible. For this reason, proof will indeed be nonexistent, for proof and proving are thought of together, and so the proof, not being apprehensible, will not be able to prove anything. Hence, proof will not exist.

185    It will suffice to have said this much, by way of outline, against the existence of proof. The Dogmatists, in support of the opposite point of view, say that either the arguments given against proof are probative, or they are not probative. And if they are not probative, they cannot show that there is no proof; while if they are probative they themselves, by a turnaround of the

186  argument, establish the existence of proof. Whence the Dogmatists also

propound the following argument:

> If there is a proof, there is a proof.
> If there is no proof, there is a proof.
> Either there is a proof or there is no proof.
> Therefore, there is a proof.

With the same force they set forth this argument:

> What follows from contradictory propositions is not only true
>     but necessary.
> But "There is a proof" and "There is no proof" are contradic-
>     tories, from each of which it follows that there is a proof.
> Therefore, there is a proof.

Now in opposition to these points it is possible to state, for example, that 187
since we do not think that any argument is probative, we do not say absolutely
that the arguments against proof are probative, but only that they seem
plausible to us; and plausible arguments are not necessarily probative. Yet if
they are probative (which we do not maintain), they certainly are also true.
And true arguments are those that from true premises validly infer something
true; therefore their conclusion is true. But that conclusion was "Therefore,
there is no such thing as a proof"; consequently, turning the argument around,
"There is no such thing as a proof" is true. And just as cathartic drugs flush 188
themselves out along with the various materials in the body, so these arguments apply to themselves along with the other arguments that are said to be
probative. Nor is this nonsense, for even the slogan "Nothing is true" not only
denies each of the other statements but negates itself as well.

Moreover, the following argument,

> If there is a proof, there is a proof.
> If there is no proof, there is a proof.
> Either there is a proof or there is no proof.
> Therefore, there is a proof.

can be shown invalid in a number of ways, but for the present let the following
method suffice. If the conditional "If there is a proof, there is a proof" is sound, 189
then the contradictory of its consequent, namely, "There is no proof" must be
inconsistent with "There is a proof," for the latter is the antecedent of the
conditional. Now, according to the Dogmatists it is impossible for a conditional made up of inconsistent propositions to be sound. For a conditional says
that if its antecedent is the case, so is its consequent, whereas inconsistent
propositions, on the other hand, say that if either is the case, the other cannot
be so. Therefore, if the conditional "If there is a proof, there is a proof" is
sound, the conditional "If there is no proof, there is a proof" cannot be sound. 190
Conversely, if we agree by hypothesis that the conditional "If there is no proof,
there is a proof" is sound, then the proposition "There is a proof" can hold
simultaneously with "There is no proof." And if it can hold simultaneously with

it, it is not inconsistent with it. Therefore, in the conditional, "If there is a proof, there is a proof," the contradictory of its consequent is not inconsistent with its antecedent, so that, conversely, this conditional will not be sound, since the

191 other one was postulated as sound by hypothesis. And since the proposition "There is no proof" is not inconsistent with "There is a proof", the disjunction "Either there is a proof or there is no proof" will not be sound, for the sound disjunction says that one of its disjuncts is sound and the other or others are false, with inconsistency. Or, conversely, if the disjunction is sound, the conditional "If there is no proof, there is a proof," as composed of inconsistent parts, will be found unsound. Consequently, the premises of the aforementioned argument are inconsistent, that is, they negate one another, and thus the

192 argument is not sound. But the Dogmatists cannot even show that anything follows logically from the contradictory propositions, since, as we have argued, they have no criterion for logical consequence.

But we are going on beyond necessity. For if, on the one hand, the arguments on behalf of proof are plausible (and let them be so), while, on the other hand, the attacks made against proof are also plausible, it is necessary to suspend judgment about proof, saying that it "no more" exists than not.

## 14. Syllogisms

193 I suppose that it is also superfluous to discuss in detail the much vaunted syllogisms since, for one thing, they are included in the refutation of the existence of proof (for it is evident that when proof does not exist there is no place for probative argument either), and for another, we have in effect refuted them by the objections previously made, when in discussing redundancy we mentioned a method by means of which it is possible to show that all the

194 probative arguments of the Stoics and Peripatetics are invalid. Yet perhaps it will not be amiss to consider them separately, for good measure, since these thinkers are much taken with them. Now there is a great deal that one could say by way of showing their nonexistence, but in an outline it suffices to deal with them by the following method. And for the present I shall discuss the undemonstrated syllogisms, for if these are nullified all the remaining arguments are overthrown, since the proof of their validity is based on these.

195 So, then, the proposition "Every human being is an animal" is established by induction from the particulars; for from the fact that Socrates is both a human being and an animal, and Plato, Dion, and each of the particulars likewise, it seems possible to maintain that every human being is an animal — recognizing that if even one of the particulars should appear to be in opposite case with the others, the universal proposition is not sound; for example, although most animals move their lower jaw and only the crocodile moves the upper, the proposition "Every animal moves the lower jaw" is not

true. Thus, when they say:

> Every human being is an animal.
> Socrates is a human being.
> Therefore, Socrates is an animal,

intending to infer from the universal proposition "Every human being is an animal" the particular proposition "Therefore, Socrates is an animal," (which, as we pointed out, is involved in establishing by induction the universal), they fall into a circular argument, establishing the universal proposition inductively by means of each of the particulars, and then syllogistically inferring the particular from the universal. Similarly, in the case of this argument:

> Socrates is a human being.
> No human being is four footed.
> Therefore, Socrates is not four footed,

by proposing to establish inductively the "No human being is four footed" proposition while wishing to infer each of the particular cases from it, they are caught in the circularity *aporia*.

A similar treatment should be given to the remaining arguments called "undemonstrated" by the Peripatetics, and also to such propositions as "If it is day, it is light." For the proposition "If it is day, it is light" is, as they say, involved in proving the proposition "It is light," and the proposition "It is light" together with "It is day" serves to establish the proposition "If it is day, it is light"; for the aforementioned conditional would not have been considered sound if the constantly conjoined truth of "It is light" and "It is day" had not been observed beforehand. But if, in order to establish the conditional "If it is day, it is light," it is necessary to apprehend in advance that whenever it is day it is also always light, while from this conditional it is inferred that whenever it is day it is light — so that the coexistence of its being day and its being light is implied by the conditional "If it is day, it is light" insofar as this just depends on the undemonstrated argument before us, and that conditional in turn is established by the coholding of the aforementioned propositions — then here too the circularity mode of *aporia* destroys the basis of the argument.

> So likewise in the case of the argument:
>
> If it is day, it is light.
> It is not light.
> Therefore, it is not day.

On the basis of day's not being observed without light, the conditional "If it is day, it is light" would be thought sound, assuming that if indeed by hypothesis day should ever appear without light, the conditional would be said to be false. But insofar as the matter just depends on the aforementioned undemonstrated argument, the proposition "There is no day when there is no light" is inferred

from the proposition "If it is day, it is light," so that each of these propositions needs, if it is to be established, the firm establishment of the other in order to
201 become credible through it by circular inference. But also, from the fact that some things — day, say, and night — cannot coexist, the negated conjunction "Not both: it is day and it is night" and the disjunction "Either it is day or it is night" would be deemed true. But the Dogmatists suppose that the non-coexistence is established by means of the negated conjunction and the disjunction, saying:

> Not both: it is day and it is night.
> It is night.
> Therefore, it is not day.

and

> Either it is day or it is night.
> It is night.
> Therefore, it is not day.

or

> It is not night.
> Therefore, it is day.

202 Whence we argue again that if, in order to establish the disjunction and the negated conjunction we need to have apprehended in advance that the propositions contained in them are inconsistent, and the Dogmatists expect to infer that inconsistency from the disjunction and the negated conjunction, the circularity type of *aporia* is introduced; for we cannot place credence in the aforementioned composite propositions without apprehending the incompatibility of the propositions contained in them, nor can we solidly maintain the inconsistency before asserting the syllogisms based on these propositions.
203 Therefore, since because of the circularity we have no place upon which to ground belief, we shall say that, insofar as the matter depends on these points, neither the third nor the fourth nor the fifth undemonstrated argument has any substance.

For the present, then, it will suffice to have said thus much about the syllogisms.


## 15. Induction

204 It is also easy, I think, to find fault with the inductive mode of inference. For when the Dogmatists attempt to lend credence to a universal by induction from the particulars, in doing this they will consider either all the particulars or only

some of them. But if they consider only some, the induction will not be firm, since some of the particulars omitted in the induction may refute the universal; while if they consider all, they will be working at an impossible task, since the particulars are infinite in number and unbounded. So that either way, I think, the induction turns out to be shaky.

## 16. Definitions

But the Dogmatists are also very proud of their logical treatment of definitions, 205 which they include in the logic component of so-called "philosophy." So now let us too make a few observations about definitions.

The Dogmatists think that definitions have many uses, but you will find, I think, that there are two main ones, which they say include all the necessary uses; for they represent definitions as necessary in all cases either for apprehen- 206 sion or for instruction. So if we show that they are not of use for either of these purposes, we shall nullify, I think, all the vain labor of the Dogmatists concerning them.

Coming right to the point, then: If, on the one hand, whoever cannot 207 recognize the object of a definition is unable to define that which he cannot recognize, and, on the other hand, any person who can recognize it and proceeds to define it has not apprehended the object from its definition but has composed a definition for an object that has already been apprehended, then definitions are not necessary for the apprehension of things. And since, if we wish to define absolutely everything we shall define nothing (because of the infinite regress), while if we agree that some things are apprehended even without definitions, then we are asserting that definitions are not necessary for apprehension (for we could apprehend everything without definitions in the same way in which those undefined things were apprehended), either we shall 208 define nothing at all or else we shall assert that definitions are not necessary.

And for these reasons definitions are not necessary for teaching, either, as we shall find. For just as the first person to recognize a thing recognizes it without a definition, so likewise the person who is taught about it can be taught without a definition. Further, the Dogmatists judge definitions by 209 reference to the things defined, and declare defective those definitions that include some property not belonging to all or some of the things defined. Thus, whenever somebody says that a human being is a rational immortal animal or a rational mortal grammatical animal, when none are immortal and some are not grammatical, they declare the definition defective. And hence it is also 210 possible that definitions cannot be judged because the particulars with reference to which they are to be judged are infinite in number; and thus they will not facilitate apprehension and instruction about those things by means of which they are judged, which obviously will have been known beforehand, if at all, and apprehended beforehand.

And how could it not be ridiculous to say that definitions are of use for apprehension or instruction or clarification in general, when they involve us in
211 so much unclarity? For instance, if we may jest, suppose that somebody wished to ask someone else whether he had met a person riding a horse and leading a dog, and he put the question to him as follows: "O logical mortal animal, capable of intelligence and knowledge, have you met a broad-nailed animal capable of laughter and of political knowledge, who has his buttocks seated on a mortal animal capable of neighing and who is leading a four-footed animal capable of barking?" How would he not be utterly ridiculous in thus by his definitions striking the other person dumb concerning so familiar a state of affairs?

212      Therefore it must be said that in view of the foregoing point definitions are useless, whether they are said to be "phrases that, by a brief reminder, lead us to the concept of the objects or states of affairs ranged under the expressions," as is evident (is it not?) from what we said a little beforehand, or a "phrase disclosing the essence," or whatever you like. For, wishing to explain what a definition is, the Dogmatists fall into an endless controversy, which, though it does seem to dispose of definitions, I now pass over because of the plan of my treatise.

It suffices for me at present to have said thus much about definitions.

## 17. Division

213 Since some of the Dogmatists tell us that logic is "the science dealing with syllogisms, induction, definitions, and division," and we have already, after our arguments on the criterion, signs, and proof, discussed syllogisms, induction, and definitions, we think it not amiss briefly to consider division, too. They say, then, that there are four kinds of division: either a term is divided with respect to its meanings, or a whole is divided into its parts, or a genus into species, or a species into particulars. But it is easy, I think, to show that there is no science of division with respect to any of these.

## 18. Division of a Term into Its Meanings

214 To come right to the point: They say that the sciences always deal with what is the case by nature, not by convention — and they say this with good reason, for scientific knowledge aims to be firm and unchanging, while the conventional is easily changeable, being altered when there is a shift in the conventions, which is in our power. Since, therefore, terms have meaning by convention and not by nature (for otherwise everybody, Greeks and barbarians alike, would understand everything meant by our utterances; besides which it is also in our power to point out the things meant and mean them by any other terms we may choose), how can there be a science of the division of terms into their meanings? Or how could logic really be, as some think, a "science of things meaning and meant"?

## 19. Whole and Part

We shall discuss whole and part in our section on physics, but at present the 215 following points need to be made concerning what is called the division of the whole into its parts. When somebody says that a group of ten things is divided into one, two, three, and four, that group is not really divided into these. For as soon as its first part, namely, the one, is taken away (granting for the sake of argument that this can be done), there no longer exists the group of ten but rather a group of nine, that is, something quite other than the group of ten. 216 Thus the subtraction and division of the remaining parts is not from the group of ten but from some other things, a different one each time.

So it is impossible, I think, to divide the whole into what are called its parts. For if the whole is divided into parts, the parts ought to be comprised in the whole before the division, but they seem not to be so comprised. Thus for example—resting our argument once more on the group of ten—they say that the nine things are certainly a part of the ten, for the latter is divided into one and the nine. But similarly the eight are a part of the ten, for it is divided into the eight and two. And likewise with the seven, the six, the five, four, three, two, and one. If, however, all these are comprised in the group of ten, then, 217 since together with it they constitute a group of fifty-five, it follows that fifty-five are included in the ten, which is absurd. Therefore, the things said to be its parts are not comprised in the group of ten, nor can that group be divided as a whole into parts, as they are not to be seen in it at all.

The same objections will also be made in the case of magnitudes—for 218 example, if somebody should wish to divide up a ten-cubit length. So it is impossible, I think, to divide a whole into parts.

## 20. Genera and Species

Now there remains the argument about genera and species; we shall treat it at 219 greater length elsewhere, but for now, in brief, we shall have the following things to say. If, on the one hand, the Dogmatists claim that genera and species are concepts, our critical remarks on the ruling part and on *phantasia* refute them; whereas if they allow them an independent existence, what will they say to the following? If there are genera, either they are equal in number to their 220 species, or there is one genus common to all the species said to belong to it. Now if the genera are equal in number to their species, there will no longer be a common genus to be divided into them. But if the genus is said to be one and the same in all the species of it, either each species will partake of the whole of it, or of a part of it. But certainly it will not partake of the whole; for it is impossible for some one existent thing to be included in two separate things in such a way as to be observed as a whole in each of the things in which it is said to be included. But if the species partakes of a part, then, in the first place, membership in the genus will not in general follow from membership in the species, as they assume, and Human Being will not be Animal, but, like

221 Substance, a part of Animal and not animate or sensitive. Next, all the species would be said to participate either in the same part of their genus or in different parts. But, for the reasons stated above, it is impossible that they all participate in the same part. And if they partake of different parts, the species will not be similar to one another with respect to genus (which they will not accept), and each genus will be infinite because cut up into infinitely many pieces — not into the species only but also into the particulars, in which, no less than in its species, it is found. For Dion is said to be not only a human being but also an animal. But if these consequences are absurd, then the species do not even participate in a part or parts of their genus, it being one single thing.

222    But if each species partakes neither of the whole genus nor of a part of it, how could it be said that the genus is one and the same in all its species, and in such a way as to be divided into them? No one, I think, could say this unless he were inventing some imaginary entities that will be abolished, in accord with the attacks of the Skeptics, by the unresolved controversies of the Dogmatists themselves.

223    In addition, there is this to be said: The species are of this kind or of that kind; and their genera are either of both this kind and that kind, or of this kind but not of that kind, or neither of this kind nor of that kind. For example, when of the "somethings" some are corporeal and some are incorporeal, and some are true and some are false, and some perhaps are white and some are black, and some very large and some very small, and so on with the rest, the genus Something (for the sake of argument), which some say is the most general of 224 all, will either be all of these or some of them or none. But if Something, that is, the genus, is absolutely none of them, the inquiry is terminated. And if it is said to be all of them, then, in addition to the impossibility of that statement, each of the species and of the particulars in which it exists will need to be all of them. For just as when the genus Animal is defined by them as animate sensitive substance, each of its species is said to be a substance and animate and sensitive, so if the genus is both corporeal and incorporeal, false and true, perhaps black and white, very small and very large, and all the rest, each of the species and of the particulars will be all of these — which is contrary to 225 what we find. Therefore, this too is false. But if the genus is some of them only, the genus of these will not be the genus of the rest; for example, if Something is corporeal, it will not be the genus of the incorporeal things, and if Animal is rational, it will not be the genus of irrational things, so that there will not be an incorporeal something nor an irrational animal, and similarly in the other cases. But that is absurd. Therefore, the genus cannot be of both this kind and that kind, nor of this kind but not of that kind, nor of neither this kind nor of that kind; and if such is the case, then the genus does not exist at all.

    And if someone should say that the genus is potentially all things, we shall reply that what is potentially something must also be actually something; for example, one cannot be potentially a grammarian without being actually something. So, too, if the genus is potentially everything, we ask them what it is in actuality, and thus the same *aporiai* remain. For it is impossible to be 226 actually all the opposites. Nor can it be some of them actually and others only potentially, for example, actually corporeal and potentially incorporeal. For it is potentially that which it is capable of being actually, and it is impossible for what is actually a body to become, by actualization, something incorporeal. Thus if (for the sake of argument) the genus Something is actually corporeal, it is not potentially incorporeal, and conversely. Hence it is not possible for the genus to be some things actually and some only potentially. And if it is nothing at all actually, it does not even exist. Therefore, the genus, which they claim to divide into the species, is nothing.

Moreover, here is another point worth looking at. Just as, since Alexander 227 and Paris are identical, it is not possible for "Alexander is walking" to be true while "Paris is walking" is false, so if being human is the same for Theon and Dion, then the term "a human being," when used in the composition of a proposition, will make that proposition true or false of both of them. But that is not what we find. For when Dion is sitting down and Theon is walking around, the proposition "A human being is walking" is true when said of one of them and false when said of the other. Therefore, the appellative "a human being" is not common to them both and the same for both, but applies, if at all, differently to each.

## 21. Common Accidents

Similar things are said also about common accidents. For if the ability to see 228 is one and the same accident in Dion and Theon, then on the hypothesis that Dion perishes but Theon survives and is able to see, either the Dogmatists will say that Dion's ability to see has not perished although he himself has, which makes no sense, or they will say that the same ability to see has both perished and not perished, which is absurd. Therefore, Theon's ability to see is not the same as Dion's, but each ability, if it exists at all, is peculiar to each. And if breathing is the same accident for both Dion and Theon, it is not possible for the breathing of Dion to exist and that of Theon not to exist but this is possible when the one has perished and the other survives. Therefore, breathing is not the same accident for both.

In any case, concerning these matters this concise statement will suffice for the present.

## 22. Sophisms

Perhaps it will not be out of place briefly to consider the topic of sophisms, 229 since those who glorify logic say that it is requisite for explaining them away. Thus, they say, if logic has the ability to distinguish true from false arguments, and if sophisms are false arguments, logic will be capable of discerning these as they abuse the truth with their apparent plausibilities. Hence, the logicians, pretending to be giving assistance to tottering common sense, try earnestly to give us instruction about the concept, the types, and the solutions of sophisms.

They say that a sophism is an argument that plausibly but treacherously induces one to accept its conclusion, which is false, or looks false, or is nonevident or in some other way unacceptable. For example, the conclusion is false in the case of this sophism:

> Nobody offers you a predicate to drink.
> "Drinks absinthe" is a predicate.
> Therefore, nobody offers you absinthe to drink.

and it looks false in this case:

> What neither was nor is possible, is not nonsensical.
> It neither was nor is possible for the doctor, qua doctor, to commit murder.
> Therefore, that the doctor, qua doctor, should commit murder is not nonsensical.

231  Again, it is non-evident in a case such at this:

> Not both: I have already asserted something, and the stars are not even in number.
> I have already asserted something.
> Therefore, the stars are even in number.

And again, it is unacceptable for other reasons in the so-called "solecistic" arguments, as, for example,

> What you look like, exists.
> You look like a delirious person.
> Therefore, a delirious person exists.

or

> What you see exists.
> You see an inflamed spot.
> Therefore, an inflamed spot exists.

232  Furthermore, they also try to provide solutions of the sophisms, saying in the case of the first one that one thing has been agreed upon by means of the premises and another has been concluded. For it has been agreed upon that a predicate is not drunk and that "drinks absinthe" is a predicate, but not that "absinthe" by itself is such. Hence, whereas one ought to conclude "Therefore, nobody drinks 'drinks absinthe'," which indeed is true, it has been concluded that "Therefore, nobody drinks absinthe" which is false and does not follow
233  from the premises agreed upon. In the case of the second sophism they say that while it seems to be leading to a false conclusion, so as to make the unwary hang back from giving their assent to it, the conclusion is in fact true, namely, "Therefore, that the doctor, qua doctor, should commit murder is not nonsense." For no proposition is nonsense, and "The doctor, qua doctor, commits

murder" is a proposition; therefore, this is not nonsense. And the sophism 234 inferring the nonevident, they say, is a member of the class of fallacies involving a shift of meaning. For when, by hypothesis, nothing has been asserted beforehand, the negated conjunction is true since the conjunction itself contains the false conjunct "I have already asserted something." But after the negated conjunction has been asserted, when the second premise, "I have already asserted something," has become true owing to the fact that the negated conjunction has been asserted before the second premise, the premise that is a negated conjunction becomes false since the false conjunct in the conjunction becomes true; so that it is never possible to draw the conclusion because the negated conjunction and the second premise do not hold simultaneously. And 235 some say that the last group, that is, the solecistic arguments, are absurdly introduced contrary to linguistic usage.

Such things are what some of the logicians have to say about sophisms (others say other things); perhaps their comments can tickle the ears of less thoughtful people, but they are superfluous and worked out in vain. I suppose that this can be seen from what we have observed already; for we have shown that, on the basis of what the logicians say, the true and the false cannot be apprehended; and we have shown it by a variety of arguments but in particular by refuting their evidence for syllogistic force, namely proof and the undemon- strated arguments. It is possible to say much more relating specifically to the 236 topic before us, but now, in our outline, the following point should be made.

In the case of those sophisms that logic seems particularly capable of refuting, the explanation is useless; while as regards those for which explana- tion is useful, it is not the logician who would explain them away but rather those in each art [*technē*] who have got an understanding of the facts. For 237 example, to mention one or two cases, if such a sophism as this were propounded to a doctor:

> In the abatement stage of disease, a varied diet and wine are
>     to be approved.
> In every type of disease, abatement occurs before the first
>     three days are up.
> Therefore, it is necessary for the most part to take a varied
>     diet and wine before the first three days are up.

the logician would have nothing to say toward explaining the argument away, useful though such an explanation would be; but the doctor will do so, 238 knowing that "abatement" is ambiguous and refers either to that of the entire disease, or to the tendency to betterment, after crisis, of each particular attack; and knowing also that the abatement of the particular attack occurs for the most part before the first three days are up but that it is not in this abatement but in the abatement of the whole disease that we recommend the varied diet. Whence he will say that the premises of the argument are incoherent, with one kind of abatement — of the whole disease — taken in the first premise, and another kind — of the particular attack — taken in the second.

239    Again, when someone suffers from a fever related to an attack of cramping and such an argument as the following is propounded,

> Opposites are remedies for opposites.
> Cold is opposite to this feverish condition.
> Therefore, cold is the corresponding remedy for this feverish condition;

240 the logician will have nothing to say, but the doctor, knowing what are the principally relevant *pathē* and what are the symptoms of these, will say that the argument does not apply to the symptoms (indeed, the result of applying cold is that the fever increases) but rather to the relevant *pathē*, and that what is relevant is the constipation, which calls for a relaxing mode of treatment, rather than a cramping one; whereas the consequent fever is not principally relevant, nor, therefore, is what seems to be the remedy corresponding to it.

241    And thus, in the case of the sophisms that can be usefully explained away, the logician will have nothing to say, but instead he will propound to us such arguments as these:

> If you don't have beautiful horns and have horns, you have
>     horns.
> You don't have beautiful horns and have horns.
> Therefore, you have horns.

242

> If something moves, either it moves in the location where it
>     is, or in the location where it isn't.
> But it neither moves in the location where it is (for it is at rest)
>     nor in the location where it isn't (for how could a thing do
>     anything in a location where it has no presence?).
> Therefore, nothing moves.

243

> Either what comes into existence is at that time existent, or it
>     is nonexistent.
> But the existent does not come into existence, for it already
>     exists.
> Nor does the nonexistent, for when a thing is coming into
>     existence something is happening to it, but nothing hap-
>     pens to the non-existent.
> Therefore, nothing comes into existence.

244

> Snow is frozen water.
> But water is dark in color.
> Therefore, snow is dark in color.

    And, when he has gathered together a collection of such nonsense, he knits his brow and takes logic to hand, trying very solemnly to establish for us by means of syllogistic proofs that something does come into existence and something does move and snow is white and we do not have horns — even though it is sufficient, perhaps, to set obviousness over against these and to demolish their conclusion, firmly maintained though it may be, by means of the equipollent contradictory evidence derived from the appearances. Thus, in fact, when the argument about motion was propounded to a certain philosopher, he just silently walked around, and in daily life people make trips by land and by sea, and build ships and houses and beget children, paying no attention to the arguments about motion and genesis.

An amusing tale is told of the physician Herophilus; he was a contemporary of Diodorus who, exhibiting with logic his foolishness, was wont to rehearse sophistical arguments about many things and especially about motion. So when Diodorus had dislocated his shoulder and went to Herophilus for treatment, the latter said jokingly to him:    245

> While the shoulder was going out, it was either in the place
>     where it was or in a place where it wasn't.
> But it was neither in the place where it was, nor in a place
>     where it wasn't.
> Therefore, it has not gone out.

The sophist begged him to skip such arguments and just give him the medical treatment suited to his case.

At any rate I think it sufficient to live, empirically and undogmatically, in accord with the common observances and notions, suspending judgment about the things that are said as a result of dogmatic subtlety and are very far from the usage of daily life.    246

If, then, logic fails to explain away such sophisms as might usefully be solved, while in the case of those that somebody might suppose that it does explain, the explanation is useless, then logic is simply of no use in the solution of sophisms.

And even on the basis of what is said by the logicians one could show    247
concisely that their technical treatment of the sophisms is useless. The logicians assert that they are motivated toward the art or craft of logic not only in order to ascertain what is implied by what, but mainly in order to know how to distinguish the true and the false by means of demonstrative arguments; thus they say that logic is the science of things true, false, and neither. Since, then,    248
they tell us that a true argument is one that validly infers a true conclusion by means of true premises, when an argument with a false conclusion is propounded we shall know immediately that it is false and we shall not assent to it. For the argument itself must either be unsound or not have true premises.    249
And this is evident from the following: Either the argument's false conclusion follows from the conjunction of the premises, or it does not. Now if, on the one hand, it does not so follow, then the argument will not be sound; for they say that an argument is sound when its conclusion follows from the conjunction of its premises. But if, on the other hand, it does follow, then, according to their own principles of logic, the conjunction of the premises must also be false; for

250 they say that the false follows from the false, but never from the true. And from what has been said above it is evident that, according to them, an argument that is not sound or not true is not demonstrative either.

If, therefore, when an argument is propounded in which the conclusion is false we know at once that because of having the false conclusion it is not true and sound, we shall not give our assent to it even though we may not know where the fallacy lies. For just as we do not give our assent to the truth of what the sleight-of-hand artists do, and we know that they are deceiving us even though we cannot tell how they are doing it, so likewise we do not give credence to the false but seemingly plausible arguments even though we cannot tell in what way they are going wrong.

251 Further, since the Dogmatists say that sophisms lead not only to falsehood but also to other paradoxical results, we need to discuss them more generally. Any propounded argument either leads us to an unacceptable conclusion or to one which is such that we ought to accept it. In the latter case there will be nothing paradoxical in our assenting to it; but if the argument leads us to something unacceptable, it is not we who should give precipitate assent to the paradoxical result because of the plausibility of the argument, but it is the Dogmatists who should desist from an argument that forces them to assent to paradoxes, if indeed they have chosen, as they profess, to seek the truth and not indulge in silly talk like little children.

252 For just as, if there is a road leading to a precipice, we do not push ourselves over the edge just because there is a road leading up to it, but we avoid the road on account of the precipice, so also if an argument is leading us to something generally considered paradoxical we shall not assent to the paradox because of the argument, but we shall avoid the argument because of 253 the paradox. So whenever this sort of argument is propounded to us, we shall suspend judgment on each premise, and then, when the whole argument is propounded, we shall conclude whatever seems to be the case.

And if the Chrysippean Dogmatists say that when the heap argument is being propounded one ought to stop and suspend judgment while it is going on, in order not to fall into paradox, all the more would it be appropriate for us as Skeptics, when we suspect paradox, not to give precipitate approval when the premises are propounded, but to suspend judgment about each of them 254 until the whole argument has been presented. And whereas we, taking our start undogmatically from the conventions of daily life, thus avoid the fallacious arguments, the Dogmatists will find it impossible to distinguish a sophism from an argument that seems to be correctly propounded, for they have to determine dogmatically whether or not the schema of the argument is sound and the 255 premises are true. But we have shown above that they are neither able to apprehend the sound arguments nor to determine that something is true, having no agreed-upon criterion or proof, as we have shown on the basis of what they themselves say.

In view of these points, then, the logical treatment of sophisms that is so much boasted about by the logicians is useless.

We say similar things about the distinguishing of amphibolies. For if an   256
amphiboly is a linguistic expression having two or more meanings, and if
linguistic expressions have meaning by convention, then those amphibolies that
are worth resolving—such as occur in some practical situation—will be
resolved, not by the logician but by the people practiced in each particular art,
who themselves have the experience of how they have created the conventional
usage of the terms to denote the things signified, as, for example, in the case of   257
the amphiboly "In periods of abatement one should prescribe a varied diet and
wine." Further, in daily life we see that even children distinguish amphibolies
when such distinction seems to them to be of use. Thus certainly, if someone
who has different servants with the same name were to direct a boy called, say,
Manes (supposing that this is the name the servants have in common), to be
summoned to him, the child will ask, "Which one?" And if someone having a
number of different wines should say to his boy, "Pour me the wine to drink,"
the boy will ask, similarly, "Which?" Thus, the experience of what is useful in   258
each particular case produces the distinction.

Concerning all the amphibolies, however, that are not involved in some
practical matter of daily life but reside instead in dogmatic principles and are
probably useless for living undogmatically, the logician, with his own particular point of view about these, will be similarly forced by the Skeptic attacks to
suspend judgment concerning them, insofar as they are probably connected
with objects or states of affairs that are nonevident, nonapprehensible, and even
nonexistent. We shall discuss these matters again another time. But if some   259
Dogmatist tries to refute any of these points he will strengthen the Skeptic
argument, himself lending support, because of the argumentation from both
sides and the unresolved controversy, to suspension of judgment about the
matters in question.

Having said thus much about amphibolies, we here conclude the second
book of the Outlines.

# Outlines of Pyrrhonism

## *Book 3 of Three*

**Contents of Book 3**

As regards the logic part of what is called "philosophy", the foregoing account 1 may be sufficient by way of outline.

# 1. Physics

Coming now to the physics part of it, we shall follow the same mode of exposition and shall not refute each of the things the Dogmatists say, topic by topic, but instead we shall undertake to deal with the more general aspects, which encompass the rest.

# 2. Productive Sources [*Archai*] of Things

And since it is agreed by most people that some sources of things are material and others are productive, we shall begin our account with the productive ones, for these, they say, are more important than the material.

# 3. God

In view of the fact that the majority assert that god is a maximally productive 2 cause, let us first give consideration to god, noting in advance that, on the one hand, we follow without doctrinal belief the common course of life and we say that there are gods, and we reverence gods and ascribe to them foreknowledge, but, on the other hand, that we have the following points to make against the precipitancy of the Dogmatists.

When we conceive of objects or states of affairs, we are bound to conceive of their substances as well, for example, whether they are corporeal or incorporeal. And also of their forms; for nobody could conceive of a horse without first comprehending the form of the horse. Also, the object conceived of must be conceived of as being somewhere. Since, then, some of the 3 Dogmatists say that god is corporeal and some that he is incorporeal, and some say that he is anthropomorphic and some that he is not, and some that he is located somewhere and others that he is not, while of those saying that he is located somewhere, some say that he is inside the cosmos and others that he is outside — how shall we be able to form a concept of god when we have no agreed-upon substance nor form of him, nor location where he is? Let the Dogmatists first agree and concur with one another that god is such and such, and only then, when they have sketched this out for us, let them expect us to form a concept of god. But as long as they do not settle their disagreements we cannot tell what agreed-upon conception we are supposed to get from them.

But, they say, when you have conceived of something immortal and 4 blessed, consider that to be god. This, however, is silly, for just as whoever does not know Dion cannot conceive of accidents as belonging to Dion, so, since we do not know what god is, we are not able to learn about or even conceive of his accidents. And aside from these points, let the Dogmatists tell us what a 5 "blessed" thing is, whether it is something that acts upon its subordinates in accord with virtue and forethought, or it is something inactive, neither having any business of its own nor providing any for someone else; for, disagreeing without resolution about this, too, they have made the blessed, and consequently also god, inconceivable for us.

6     Furthermore, if we go by what the Dogmatists say, even if we form a conception of god it is necessary to suspend judgment concerning whether he exists or does not exist. For it is not pre-evident that god exists. If he affected us just of and by himself, the Dogmatists would agree about who, of what sort, and where he is; but their unresolved disagreement has made him seem
7 non-evident to us and in need of proof. Now, anyone who proves that a god exists either does this by means of something pre-evident or by means of something non-evident. But certainly not by means of something pre-evident, for if what proves a god to exist were pre-evident, then in view of the fact that the thing proved is thought of relatively to what proves it and therefore is apprehended along with it, as we have established, the existence of a god will also be pre-evident, being apprehended along with the pre-evident fact that proves it. But it is not pre-evident, as we have shown. Therefore, it is not
8 proved by means of something pre-evident. Nor is it proved by something non-evident. For if the non-evident proposition that is to prove that a god exists, and which itself needs proof, is said to be proved by means of something pre-evident, it will no longer be nonevident but rather pre-evident. But neither is it proved by means of something non-evident, for anyone who says that will fall into an infinite regress, since we shall always be asking for a proof of the non-evident proposition that is offered as proving the last one propounded.
9 Therefore, that a god exists cannot be proved from any other proposition. And so, if it is not of itself pre-evident nor provable from something else, whether a god exists will not be apprehensible.

Further, this too should be said. Anyone who asserts that god exists either says that god takes care of the things in the cosmos or that he does not, and, if he does take care, that it is either of all things or of some. Now if he takes care of everything, there would be no particular evil thing and no evil in general in the cosmos; but the Dogmatists say that everything is full of evil; therefore god shall not be said to take care of everything. On the other hand, if he takes care of only some things, why does he take care of these and not of
10 those? For either he wishes but is not able, or he is able but does not wish, or he neither wishes nor is able. If he both wished and was able, he would have taken care of everything; but, for the reasons stated above, he does not take care of everything; therefore, it is not the case that he both wishes and is able to take care of everything. But if he wishes and is not able, he is weaker than the cause on account of which he is not able to take care of the things of which
11 he does not take care; but it is contrary to the concept of god that he should be weaker than anything. Again, if he is able to take care of everything but does not wish to do so, he will be considered malevolent, and if he neither wishes nor is able, he is both malevolent and weak; but to say that about god is impious. Therefore, god does not take care of the things in the cosmos.

Further, if god does not take care of anything and there is no work or product of his, nobody will be able to say from whence he apprehends that god exists, if indeed god neither appears of himself nor is apprehended through his products. And thus, whether god exists is not apprehensible. From these 12 considerations we conclude that most likely those who firmly maintain that god exists will be forced into impiety; for if they say that he takes care of everything, they will be saying that god is the cause of evils, while if they say that he takes care of some things only or even of nothing, they will be forced to say that he is either malevolent or weak, and manifestly these are impious conclusions.

## 4. Cause

In order to keep the Dogmatists from attempting to defame us, too, seeing that 13 they are at a loss as to how to refute us with facts, we shall consider the active cause more generally, after first trying to understand the concept of cause. Now, if we go by what the Dogmatists say, nobody could have a conception of cause, since in addition to offering conflicting and strange notions of cause, by their disagreement about it they have also made the existence of it undiscoverable. For some say that causes are corporeal, and others say that 14 they are incorporeal. It would seem that according to them a cause, in the wider sense, would be that by the action of which the effect comes about; for example, the sun or the sun's heat is the cause of the wax being melted or of the melting of the wax. But they have even disagreed about this, with some using appellatives— for example, "the melting"—for what the cause is the cause of, and others using predicates—for example, "is melted." Anyhow, in the wider sense, as I was saying, the cause would be that by the action of which the effect comes about.

Most of the Dogmatists hold that of these causes some are conclusive, 15 some are associates, and others are synergistic. Causes are conclusive when the effect is present when they are present, absent when they are absent, and diminished when they are diminished; it is thus, they say, that fastening the halter is the cause of the choking. And a cause is associate if it contributes a force equal to that of its fellow cause toward the existence of the effect; thus, they say, each of the oxen that pull the plow is a cause of the pulling of the plow. And a cause is synergistic if it contributes a small force toward the easy occurrence of the effect, as when two people are lifting something heavy and a third helps to lift it.

Some people, however, have asserted also that present things are causes of 16 things future, as, for example, the proximate causes. For instance, extended exposure to the sun is the cause of fever. But others reject this view, on the ground that, since the cause is relative—that is, relative to the effect—it cannot precede the effect as its cause.

In our state of *aporia* about these matters, we have the following to say.

## 5. Is Anything a Cause of Anything?

That there are causes, is plausible; for how else could growth occur, and 17 diminution, generation, destruction, change in general, and each of the physical

and psychological effects, the disposition of the whole cosmos, and all the rest,
18  if not because of some cause? And if there were no causes, everything would
come from everything, and by chance. For example, perhaps horses would
come from mice, and elephants from ants; and in Egyptian Thebes there would
have been rainstorms and snow and the south would have had no rain, if there
had not been a cause on account of which the south is stormy in winter and
19  the east is dry. Further, anyone who says there are no causes is refuted; for if
he claims to make this statement simply and without any cause he will not be
worthy of belief, while if he says that it makes it because of some cause, he is
positing a cause while wishing to deny it, in granting a cause why causes do
not exist.

20      For these reasons it is plausible that there are causes. But that it is also
plausible, on the other hand, to say that nothing is the cause of anything will
be plain when we have set forth a few of the many arguments to show this.
Thus, for instance, it is impossible to conceive of a cause before apprehending
its effect as *its* effect. For only then do we recognize that it is a cause of the
21  effect, when we apprehend the latter as an effect. But we are not able to
apprehend the effect of the cause as *its* effect if we do not apprehend the cause
of the effect as *its* cause. For only then do we suppose ourselves to recognize
that the effect is an effect of it, when we apprehend the cause as the cause of
22  that effect. If, then, in order to conceive the cause it is necessary to have prior
recognition of the effect, and in order to recognize the effect, as I said, it is
necessary to have prior acquaintance with the cause, the circularity type of
*aporia* shows that both are inconceivable, it being impossible to conceive the
cause as a cause or the effect as an effect; for, since each of them needs
credibility from the other, we do not know with which of them to begin the
conceiving. Hence we shall not be able to assert that anything is the cause of
anything.

23      Further, even if someone should grant that it is possible to form a concept
of cause, because of the disagreement it would be considered not to be
apprehensible. For some say that there are examples of causation, some say
that there are not, and some suspend judgment. Now anyone who says that
something is the cause of something will either admit that he just says this,
without being motivated by any rational cause, or else he will say that he has
arrived at his assent due to some causes. If, on the one hand, he admits that
he just says it, he will be no more worthy of belief than the person who just
says that nothing is the cause of anything; while if, on the other had, he speaks
of causes because of which he thinks that something is the cause of something,
he will be trying to establish what is in question by means of what is in
question; for while we are calling into question whether anything is the cause
of anything, he asserts that, since there exists a cause of there being a cause,
24  there is a cause. And besides, as we are questioning the very existence of causes,
it will of course be necessary for him to supply a cause of the cause of there
being a cause, and a cause of that, and so on ad infinitum. But it is impossible
to supply an infinite number of causes; therefore, it is impossible to assert with
firm assurance that anything is the cause of anything.

Furthermore, a cause produces an effect either at a time when it already 25 exists and exists as a cause, or when it is not a cause. Now it certainly does not do so when it is not a cause; but if it does so when it is a cause, it must have existed and have become a cause beforehand, and then, this done, it must bring about the effect, which is said to be produced by it at a time when it is already a cause. But since the cause is relative, that is, relative to the effect, clearly it cannot, as a cause, exist before the effect; therefore it is not possible for the cause, at the time when it is the cause, to produce that of which it is the cause. And if it cannot produce anything either when it is a cause or when 26 it is not, then it cannot produce anything. Wherefore, it will not be a cause, for apart from producing something a cause cannot be conceived as a cause.

Whence some people say also the following: The cause must either exist at the same time as the effect, or before it, or come into being after it. But to say that the cause is brought into existence after the genesis of its effect would be ridiculous. But neither can it exist before it, for it is said to be conceived 27 relatively to it, and the Dogmatists hold that relatives, qua relative, coexist and are conceived together with one another. Nor can it exist at the same time as the effect; for if it is productive of the effect, and if what comes into being must come into being through the agency of what exists, it is necessary that the cause first become a cause, and then, this done, produce the effect. Consequently, if the cause exists neither before nor at the same time as the effect, and the effect does not come into being before it, it does not, I suppose, have any existence at all. It is also clear, I think, that by these considerations, too, the concept of 28 cause is once again destroyed. For if the cause, as a relative thing, cannot be conceived as existing before the existence of its effect, but yet, in order to be conceived as the cause of its effect, it must indeed be conceived as existing before its effect, then since it is impossible to conceive of anything as existing before something before the existence of which it cannot be conceived as existing, it is in consequence impossible for the cause to be conceived.

From these points we conclude further that if the arguments by which we 29 show the existence of causes are plausible, and if those, too, are plausible which prove that it is incorrect to assert the existence of a cause, and if there is no way to give preference to any of these over others—since we have no agreed-upon sign, criterion, or proof, as has been pointed out earlier—then, if we go by the statements of the Dogmatists, it is necessary to suspend judgment about the existence of causes, too, saying that they are "no more" existent than nonexistent.

## 6. Material Sources

Concerning the productive sources, then, it will suffice for the present to have 30 said this much; and now we should briefly discuss the so-called "material" sources. That these are not apprehensible may be seen easily and at once from the disagreement about them that has grown up among the Dogmatists. For Pherecydes of Syros said that the earth was the source of everything, and

Thales of Miletus, that the source was water; Anaximander, his student, the infinite; Anaximenes and Diogenes of Apollonia, air; Hippasus of Metapontum, fire; Xenophanes of Colophon, earth and water; Oenopides of Chios, fire and air; Hippo of Rhegium, fire and water; Onomacritus in his Orphics, fire, water,

31  and earth; the followers of Empedocles, as well as the Stoics, fire, air, water, earth — and is there any need even to mention the mystical "matter devoid of quality" that some of them talk about, when even they themselves do not firmly maintain that they apprehend it? The followers of Aristotle the Peripatetic take

32  as their sources fire, air, water, earth, and the "revolving body"; Democritus and Epicurus, atoms; Anaxagoras of Clazomenae, homogeneous things; Diodorus, surnamed Cronus, minimal bodies having no parts; Heracleides Ponticus and Asclepiades Bithynus, continuous masses; the followers of Pythagoras, the numbers; the mathematicians, the boundaries of bodies; Strato the Physicist, the qualities.

33      With so much (and even more) disagreement existing among the Dogmatists concerning material sources, we shall, if we give our assent, either assent to all the positions stated and the others as well, or to some of them. But it is not possible to assent to all; for we shall not be able, I presume, to assent both to the followers of Asclepiades, who say that the elements are frangible and have qualities, and also to the followers of Democritus, who claim that the elements are indivisible and devoid of quality, not to mention the followers of Anaxagoras, who ascribe every sensible quality to the homo-

34  geneous things. And if we give preference to one position over the others, either we simply do so, that is, without proof, or we do so with proof. But we shall not give assent without proof, and if with proof, the proof must be true. However, it would not be conceded to be true unless it had been determined by a true criterion to be such, and a criterion is shown to be true by a proof

35  that has been determined to be correct. If, then, in order to show that the proof giving preference to some position is true, it is necessary for its criterion to have been proved, and in order that the criterion have been proved, it is necessary for its proof first to have been determined to be correct, we have circularity, which does not let the argument go forward, since the proof is always in need of a proven criterion and the criterion is in need of a proof that has been

36  determined correct. And if anyone should wish to determine the criterion by a criterion and to prove the proof by a proof, he will be headed for infinity. If, then, we are neither able to assent to all the positions about the elements nor to some of them, it is appropriate to suspend judgment about them.

37      It is possible, I think, to show by means of these arguments alone that the elements, that is, the material sources, are not apprehensible. But in order that we may be able to refute the Dogmatists more fully, we shall linger upon the topic for such time as is required. However, since the doctrines about the elements are, as we have shown, numerous and indeed almost infinite, we shall, in view of the character of our treatise, beg off from arguing against each one specifically, but shall instead oppose all of them by implication. For since any position one might take concerning the elements will involve regarding them either as corporeal or incorporeal, we think that it will be sufficient if we show

that both corporeal and incorporeal things are not apprehensible; for thus it will be clear that the elements, too, are not apprehensible.

## 7. Are Bodies Apprehensible?

Now some people say that a body is that which is capable of acting or being 38 acted upon. But if we go by this conception, bodies are not apprehensible. For, as we have shown, causes are not apprehensible; and when we cannot say whether there is such a thing as a cause, we are also not able to say whether there is any such thing as something acted upon, for what is acted upon is always acted upon by a cause. And if both the cause and what is acted upon are not apprehensible, it follows that bodies are not apprehensible, either. But 39 some say that a body is what is extended in three directions and is solid. They say that a point is that which has no parts, a line is length without breadth, a surface is length with breadth; when depth and solidity are added to this, there is a body, that is, the object of our present discussion, composed of length, breadth, depth and solidity. But arguing against these people is easy. For they 40 will say either that the body is nothing over and above these things or that it is something other than the combination of them. Now, apart from the length, breadth, depth, and solidity, there would be no body; and if the body is these, then anyone who showed that they do not exist would also abolish bodies, for wholes are abolished when all their parts are abolished.

It is of course possible to disprove the existence of these in various ways, but for the present it will suffice to say that if boundaries exist, they are lines or surfaces or bodies. Now, if someone should say that a surface or line exists, 41 it will also be said that each of the four features mentioned above either can exist by itself or is found only in connection with the so-called "bodies." But it is silly, I think, to fancy a line or surface existing by itself. And if it should be said that each of these is found only in connection with the bodies and does not exist by itself, then, first of all, it will thereby be granted that bodies have not been generated from them (for it would have been necessary, presumably, for them to have acquired existence by themselves beforehand, and then to have combined to produce the bodies); and second, they do not exist even in 42 the so-called "bodies."

And it is possible to show this by means of a number of arguments, but for the present it will suffice to mention the *aporiai* having to do with touch. For if juxtaposed bodies touch one another, they contact one another with their boundaries—for instance, with their surfaces. But the surfaces will not be unified as a whole with one another because of the touching, for otherwise the touching would be a fusion and separating the things touching would be a tearing apart, which we do not find to be the case. But if the surface touches 43 the surface of the juxtaposed body with some of its parts only, and with others of the parts is united with the body of which it is a boundary, ⟨then it will not be without depth, its parts being understood to be different in respect to depth, with one part touching the juxtaposed body, and the other being that by which it is joined to the body of which it is a boundary⟩. Therefore, not even in connection with a body can one find length and breadth without depth, nor, consequently, a surface.

And likewise when, by hypothesis, two surfaces are juxtaposed to one another along the boundaries where they terminate—that is, edgewise, that is to say, along lines—then these lines, by means of which the surfaces are said to touch each other, will not be unified with one another for they would fuse; but if any one of these lines touches the juxtaposed line with some of its parts and with others is united to the surface of which it is a boundary, it will not be without breadth and hence will not be a line. And if no line or surface is in a body, neither will length, breadth, or depth be in it.

44    If someone should say that boundaries are bodies, the answer to him will be brief. For if length is a body, it will have to be partitioned into its three dimensions, each of which, being a body, will again be partitioned into another three, which will be bodies, and these, likewise, into others, and so on ad infinitum; so that the body becomes infinite in size, having infinitely many parts; which is absurd. Therefore, the aforementioned dimensions are not bodies. And if they are neither bodies nor lines nor surfaces, they will not be considered to exist.

45    Solidity, too, is not apprehensible. For if it were apprehended, it would be apprehended by touching. If, therefore, we show that touch is not apprehensible, it will be clear that solidity, too, cannot be apprehended. But by means of the following considerations we conclude that touch is not apprehensible. Things that touch one another either touch parts to parts or whole to whole. But certainly not whole to whole, for that way they will be unified and not touching one another. But not parts to parts, either. For their parts are parts

46    relative to the whole, but relative to their own parts they are wholes. Now these wholes, which are parts of other things, will not, in view of what has been said above, touch each other whole to whole, but also not parts to parts; for the parts of these, too, as being wholes relative to their own parts, will not touch one another whole to whole nor parts to parts. But if we apprehend touch neither as occurring with respect to wholeness nor with respect to parts, it will not be apprehensible. And for this reason solidity, too, will not be apprehensible. Whence the same holds of bodies, for if these are nothing other than the three dimensions together with solidity, and we have shown that each of those is not apprehensible, bodies too will not be apprehensible.

Thus, insofar as this depends on the concept of body, it will not be apprehensible whether there is any such thing as a body. And the following

47    also needs to be said about the topic at hand. The Dogmatists assert that, of things that exist, some are objects of sense perception and others are objects of thought, and that the latter are apprehended with the intellect and the former with the senses, and further that the senses are simply passive, while the intellect proceeds from the apprehension of the objects of sense perception to that of the objects of thought. So if there is such a thing as a body, it is either an object of sense perception, for it seems to be apprehended as an assemblage of length and depth and breadth and solidity and color and some other things together with which it is experienced, whereas the senses are said by them to

be single receptive. Yet if bodies are said to be objects of thought, then in the 48 nature of things there must certainly exist some objects of sense perception from which the thought of the bodies thought about will be derived. But nothing exists besides bodies and the incorporeal, and of these the incorporeal is unquestionably an object of thought, while bodies are not objects of sense perception, as we have shown. Since, then, there is in the nature of things no object of sense perception from which the thought of a body will be derived, bodies will not be objects of thought. And if they are neither objects of sense perception nor objects of thought, and besides these there is not anything else, it must be said that if we go by the Dogmatists' account there are not any bodies, either. For these reasons, by opposing the arguments about bodies to 49 the apparent existence of bodies, we are brought to suspension of judgment about them.

The non-apprehensibility of bodies brings with it the non-apprehensibility of the incorporeal. For privations are thought of as privations of positive states; for example, blindness is a privation of sight, deafness of hearing, and similarly in the other cases. Wherefore, in order that we may apprehend a privation it is necessary that we have apprehended beforehand the state of which it is said to be the privation; for someone who had no concept of sight would not be able to say that this person does not have it, that is, is blind. If, therefore, the 50 incorporeal is the privation of the corporeal, and if when states are not apprehended it is not possible for the privations of them to be apprehended, and if further it has been shown that bodies are not apprehensible, then the incorporeal too will not be apprehensible. Furthermore, either the incorporeal is an object of sense perception or an object of thought. And if it is an object of sense perception it will not be apprehensible, by reason of the difference of animals and of human beings and of the senses and of the circumstances and owing to the admixtures and the rest of what we have said before in our remarks on the ten modes; and if it is an object of thought, then since we do not have direct apprehension of the sensible objects, starting from which we are supposed to move to the objects of thought, we will not have direct apprehension of the objects of thought, nor, consequently, apprehension of the incorporeal.

Also, anyone claiming to apprehend the incorporeal will assert that he 51 apprehends it either by sense or by means of argument. But certainly not by sense, since the senses seem to perceive their objects by a kind of impacting or "stinging." Take sight, for instance, whether it occurs by the presence of a cone or with emissions and admissions of images or with effusions of rays and colors, and take also hearing, whether it is impelled air or the parts of the sound that come around the ears and strike the acoustic gas so as to produce the perception of the sound. Also, smells impinge on the nose and tastes on the tongue, and the objects affecting the sense of touch impinge on the sense of touch. But incorporeal things cannot admit of such impacting, so that they 52 would not be apprehensible by sense.

But not by means of an argument, either. For if an argument is a *lekton* and incorporeal, as the Stoics say, anyone who asserts that incorporeal things are apprehensible by means of an argument is begging the question. For while we are questioning whether it is possible to apprehend something incorporeal, he, taking up an incorporeal object, proposes to produce, just by means of this,

53　the apprehension of incorporeal things. Yet the argument itself, since it is incorporeal, is one of the things in question. How, then, will anyone prove that this incorporeal thing—I mean, the argument—is previously apprehended? If by means of another incorporeal thing, we shall question the proof of the apprehension of that, and so on ad infinitum; but if by means of a body, the apprehension of bodies is also in question. By what means, then, shall we show that the body is apprehended that is taken up in order to prove the incorporeal argument? If by means of a body, we are thrown into an infinite regress, and if by means of something incorporeal, we fall into circularity. So, with the argument thus remaining inapprehensible, if indeed it is incorporeal, nobody would be in a position to say that the incorporeal is apprehensible by means of it.

54　　　But if the argument is a body, then, as there is disagreement about bodies too as to whether or not they are apprehended (because of what is called their "continual flux," so that they are thought neither to admit of the demonstrative "this" nor to exist, wherefore Plato calls them "things that are coming into being" and never "things that are"), I am at a loss as to how this disagreement about bodies will be settled, since because of the difficulties stated just above it cannot be settled either by means of a body or by means of something incorporeal. Therefore, it is not possible to apprehend incorporeal things by

55　means of an argument. And if they neither fall within the scope of the senses nor are apprehended by means of an argument, they will not be apprehended at all.

　　　If, then, it is impossible to take a firm stand about the existence of bodies or about incorporeal things, one must also suspend judgment about the elements and perhaps even about what are derivative from the elements, seeing that of these, some are bodies and some are incorporeal, and there are *aporiai* about both. In any case, with judgment suspended for these reasons on both the productive and material sources, the whole story about sources is aporetic.

## 8. Blending

56　Next, leaving also these matters aside, how do the Dogmatists say that the compounds arise from the primary elements, when neither contact nor touch nor blending nor mixture has any existence at all? For there is no such thing as touch, as I showed a bit earlier when I was discussing the existence of bodies; and I shall now briefly show that, if we go by what the Dogmatists say, the way of blending, too, is impossible. For much is said about blending, and the Dogmatists' positions on the problem at hand are almost endless; hence from the unresolved disagreement one might conclude at once that the matter is not apprehensible. And for the moment, in view of the plan of the treatise, we shall beg off from opposing each of their points individually and shall consider it sufficient at present to say the following.

They state that blended things are composed of substances and qualities. 57 So, one will say either that the substances are mixed but the qualities are not, or that the qualities are mixed but not their substances any longer, or that neither is mixed with the other, or that the two are unified with one another. But if neither the qualities nor the substances are mixed with one another, a blending cannot be conceived; for how will a single sensation arise from the things that are blended if the things blended are not mixed in accord with any of the aforementioned ways? And if the qualities are said to be simply 58 juxtaposed but the substances are mixed, then in this way, too, the account would be absurd, for we do not perceive the qualities in the blended materials as separate, but as completely unified, derived from the mixing. And if somebody should say that the qualities are mixed but the substances are not, he will be asserting the impossible. For the qualities subsist in the substances, wherefore it would be ridiculous to say that the qualities, separated from the substances, are somehow privately mixed with one another, and the substances, devoid of qualities, are left apart.

It remains to say that both the qualities and the substances of the things 59 blended permeate one another and by mixing produce the blend. But this is more absurd than the preceding possibilities; for such a blend is impossible. For example, if a cup of hemlock juice is mixed with ten cups of water, it would be said that the hemlock is blended together with all the water, for certainly if someone took even the smallest portion of the mixture he would find it full of the power of the hemlock. But if the hemlock is mixed into every part of the 60 water and is distributed as a whole through the whole of it by the mutual penetration of the substances as well as their qualities, thus giving rise to the blend, and if, further, the things distributed over one another occupy in every part equal space, so that they are equal to each other, then the cup of hemlock will be equal to the ten cups of water, so that the mixture ought to be either twenty cups or only two, if we are to go by the present hypothesis about how blending occurs. And if, again, a cup of water is poured into the twenty cups, the quantity ought to be forty cups, if we go by the hypothesized theory, since it is both possible to consider the one cup to be the twenty over which it is distributed, and also possible to consider the twenty cups to be the one, to which they are made equal. And thus it is possible, pouring in one cup at a 61 time and reasoning in like manner, to conclude that the original twenty cups of the mixture must be twenty thousand and more, as well as only two, going by the hypothesis of how the blending occurs — a conclusion that reaches the ultimate of absurdity.

But if it is not possible for blending to occur when either the substances 62 alone are mixed together, or the qualities alone, or both, or neither, and if no other possibilities can be conceived, the way in which blending, as well as mixing in general, takes place is inconceivable. Wherefore, on this account of blending, too, if the so-called "elements" are not capable of forming compounds either by being placed in contact with one another by way of juxtaposition or by being blended or mixed, the natural philosophy of the Dogmatists is unintelligible.

## 9. Motion

63 In addition to the things said above, we could have based our case on the argument about types of motion, since on this basis, too, the natural philosophy of the Dogmatists could be held impossible. For certainly the compounds must come about as a result of some motion in the elements and the productive source. If, then, we show that no type of motion is agreed upon, it will be clear that even granting hypothetically all the assumptions mentioned above, the so-called "physical theory" has been elaborated by the Dogmatists in vain.

## 10. Transitional Motion

64 Those who are supposed to have given the most complete accounts say that there are six kinds of motion: local transition, natural change, increase, diminution, generation, and destruction. We shall consider each of these forms of motion separately, beginning with local transition. This, according to the Dogmatists, is that by which the thing in motion goes from one location to another, either as a whole or in part — as a whole in the case of people walking around, in part in the case of a sphere moved around its center, for while as a whole it stays in the same location, the parts exchange their locations.

65 The principal views about motion are three, I think. The common people and some of the philosophers assume that motion exists, but Parmenides and Melissus and some others think that it does not. The Skeptics said that motion "no more" exists than not, for if we go by the appearances motion seems to exist, but if we go by the philosophic account it seems not to exist. So when we have set out the opposition between those who assume that motion exists and those who assert that it does not, and when we find the disagreement equally balanced, we shall be forced to conclude that, if we go by what people

66 say, motion "no more" exists than not. We shall begin with those who say that it exists. These rely most of all on "obviousness." If motion does not exist, they say, how does the sun go from east to west, and how does it make the seasons of the year, seeing that these come about by its approaches to us and its recessions from us? Or how do ships set sail from harbors and put in at other harbors very far away? And how does the person who denies motion manage to go forth from his house and return to it again? They say that these facts are completely irrefutable. Thus, when one of the Cynics heard an argument against motion he did not reply but simply stood up and walked around, showing by deed and "obviousness" that motion exists.

These people, then, undertake in this way to discomfit those who hold a

67 position opposite to theirs, whereas those who deny the existence of motion venture such arguments as the following. If something is moved, it is moved either by itself or by something else. But if it is moved by something else, then (since what moves is active and what is active moves) that too will need another moving thing, and the second thing a third, and so on ad infinitum, so that the motion has no beginning; which is absurd. Therefore, it is not the case that what is moved is always moved by something else. But neither is it

moved by itself. For that which is said to be moved by itself will be moved 68 either without a cause or on account of some cause. But they say that nothing comes to pass without a cause; and if it is moved on account of some cause, the cause on account of which it is moved will be what moves it, whence, in accord with the consideration stated a moment ago, the process goes on to infinity. And furthermore, since everything that moves moves either by pushing or pulling or lifting or pressing down, that which moves itself will have to move itself in one of these ways. But if it moves itself by pushing, it will have to be 69 in back of itself; if by pulling, in front of itself; if by lifting, underneath itself; and if by pressing down, above itself. But it is impossible for anything to be above or in front of or underneath or in back of itself. And if nothing is moved either by itself or by something else, then nothing is moved.

If somebody takes refuge in the notions of motive and choice, it is 70 necessary to remind him of the controversy about "what is in our power" and that the controversy remains unresolved since up to now we have not found a criterion of truth.

Moreover, there is also this to be said. If something is moved, either it is 71 moved in a location where it is or in a location where it is not. But it cannot be moved in the location where it is, for if it is there, that is where it rests; nor can it be moved in the location where it is not, for where something is not, there it cannot act or be acted upon. This argument is that of Diodorus Cronus, and it has had many refutations, of which, on account of the character of our treatise, we shall set out only the more striking ones, together with a judgment about them, as it appears to us.

Some, then, say that it is possible for something to be moved in the 72 location where it is, for example, that spheres revolving around their centers are moved while remaining in the same location. Against these people one must transfer the argument to each of the parts of the sphere, and, noting that if we go by their account it is not even moved part by part, conclude that nothing is moved in the location where it is. We shall make the same point also against 73 those who say that what is moved has two locations, that in which it is and that to which it is going. For we shall ask them *when* the thing moved is going from the location in which it is to the other one — whether while it is in the first location or in the second. But when it is in the first location it does not go over to the second, for it is still in the first; and when it is not in this location, it is not departing from it. And besides, the question is being begged; 74 since where a thing is not, there it cannot act; for certainly nobody is going to agree that what he does not grant to move at all nevertheless goes to some location.

Some, however, say that "location" is used ambiguously: in a broad sense 75 to denote, for example, my house, and in an exact sense to denote, say, the air enveloping the surface of my body. Then what is moved is said to be moved in a location, not in the exact sense but in the broad sense. Against these people it is possible to say, dividing up the broad-sense location, that in one part of it the body said to be moved is properly located (i.e., in the exact-sense location), but that it is not in the other part (i.e., in the remaining parts of the broad-sense location); and then, arguing that nothing can be moved in the location where it is or in a location where it is not, to conclude that it is not even possible for a thing to be moved in what is called, in the broad but not strictly correct sense, a "location," for the latter is composed of the exact location where the thing is and the exact locations where it is not, and it is been shown that a thing cannot move in any of these.

76     The following argument needs to be brought up, too. If something moves, either it moves step by step or over a divisible distance all at once; but it is not possible for something to move step by step, nor over a divisible distance all at once, as we shall show; therefore, nothing moves.

That it is not possible for something to move step by step is immediately apparent. For if the bodies and the locations and times in which they are said to move are divided to infinity, motion will not occur, as it is impossible to find among an infinite number any first thing, from where the thing said to be
77 moved will initially be moved. And if the division of the aforesaid things (bodies, locations and times) ends in indivisible parts, and each of the things moved traverses in like manner the first indivisible portion of the location in the corresponding first indivisible portion of the time, then all things in motion will go at equal velocity — for example, the fastest horse and the tortoise; which is even more absurd than the former case. Therefore, motion does not take place step by step.

78     But neither does it occur over a divisible distance all at once. For if, as they say, non-evident things ought to be evidenced by the appearances, then, since in order for someone to travel over the distance of a stade he must first travel over the first part of the stade, and secondly over the second part, and the other parts likewise, so also everything that moves ought to move step by step; for certainly if that which moves were said to go through at once all the parts of the location in which it is said to move, it will be in all parts of that location at once, and if one part of the location through which it moves is cold and one part is hot, or one part, say, is black and one part is white in such a way as to color the things that happen to be there, the object in motion will be
79 simultaneously cold and hot or black and white; which is absurd. Next, let them say how much of a given location the moving thing goes through all at once. For if they are going to say that it is an indefinite amount, they will be admitting the possibility of something moving through the whole earth at once; but if they avoid this, let them define for us the amount of the location. But trying to define accurately the location beyond which it will not be possible for the object in motion to proceed even the slightest distance all at once is, I think, not only arbitrary and rash or even ridiculous, but it throws us again into the original *aporia*; for all things will have equal velocity if indeed each of them makes its transitional movements in like manner through accurately defined
80 locations. And if they are going to say that the thing in motion moves all at once through a small but not accurately defined location, it will be possible for us, in accord with the Sorites *aporia*, always to add a tiny amount to the given amount of location. If, then, they will take a stand anywhere when we are making such an argument, they will fall again into that humbug about accurately defined location; and if they accept the process of addition, we shall force them to agree that it is possible for something to move all at once over

the whole earth. So that the things said to move do not move through a divisible location all at once. And if something moves through a divisible 81 location neither all at once nor step by step, it does not move at all.

Those who deny transitional motion make these points and still more. But we, being unable to dismiss either these arguments or the appearance on the basis of which people assert the existence of motion, suspend judgment (in view of the antithesis of the appearances and the arguments) concerning whether motion exists or does not exist.

## 11. Increase and Diminution

Using the same reasoning we also suspend judgment about both increase and 82 diminution, for "obviousness" seems to support their existence, while arguments seem to refute it. For consider: The growth in size of that which increases must occur while it is existing as a substance, presumably, so that it will be false for anyone to say that a thing increases when something else is added to it. Since, then, substances are never stable but are always in flux, with parts supplanting parts, the thing that is said to have increased does not possess both its previous substance and, together with this, the added substance, but a wholly different one. Just as if, for example, when there is a three-cubit pole 83 somebody should bring a ten-cubit pole and say that the three-cubit pole had increased, what he said would be false because the one is wholly different from the other, so also in every case of so-called "increase," where the former material is flowing away and the other is supplanting it, if the so-called "addition" is really added, one would not say that such a condition is increase but rather that it is complete alteration.

The same argument applies also to diminution; for how would something 84 be said to diminish if it did not as a whole maintain its substance? Besides, if diminution takes place by the subtraction of something, and increase by addition, and there is no such thing as addition or subtraction, there will not be any such thing as diminution or increase.

## 12. Subtraction and Addition

That there is no such thing as subtraction, they argue as follows. When 85 something is subtracted from something, either the equal is subtracted from the equal, or the greater from the lesser, or the lesser from the greater. But subtraction does not take place in any of these ways, as we shall show; therefore, subtraction is impossible.

That subtraction does not take place in any of the aforementioned ways is evident from the following. What is subtracted from something must, before the subtraction, be included in that from which it is subtracted. But the equal 86 is not included in the equal, for example, six in six; for that which includes must be greater than what is included, and that from which something is subtracted must be greater than what is subtracted, in order that something be left over after the subtraction; for just in this respect does subtraction seem to differ from complete abolition. Nor is the greater included in the lesser, for example, six

87 in five, for that is absurd. And for the following reason the lesser is not included in the greater, either. For if five were included in six, as less in more, then also four is going to be included in five, three in four, two in three, and one in two. So six will contain five, four, three, two, and one, and these when taken together come to 15, which, on the supposition that the lesser is included in the greater, has to be included in six. And similarly, 35 is included in 15, which is included in six — and so on, step by step, to infinity. But it is absurd to say that infinitely many numbers are included in the number six. Therefore, it is

88 also absurd to say that the lesser is included in the greater. So if what is subtracted from something must be included in that from which it is going to be subtracted, and the equal is not included in the equal, nor the greater in the lesser nor the lesser in the greater, then nothing is subtracted from anything.

Moreover, if something is subtracted from something, either a whole is subtracted from a whole, or a part from a part, or a whole from a part or a

89 part from a whole. But it is plainly absurd from the start to say that a whole is subtracted either from a whole or from a part; and so the remaining possibilities are to say either that a part is subtracted from a whole or from a part; which again is absurd. For example (basing the argument on the case of numbers, for clarity), consider ten and let a unit be said to be subtracted from it. Now this unit cannot be subtracted from the whole ten nor from the part of ten left over, that is, nine, as I shall show; therefore, it is not subtracted at all.

90 For if the unit is taken from the whole ten, then, since the ten is neither something other than the ten units nor one of the units, but the aggregate of the units, the given unit ought to be subtracted from each of the units in order to be subtracted from the whole ten. But certainly nothing can be subtracted from a unit. For the units are indivisible; and hence the given unit will not be

91 subtracted in this way from the ten. And even if somebody should grant that the unit was subtracted from each of the units, the unit will have ten parts and having ten parts will be ten. But also, since ten other parts have been left over, after the subtraction of the ten parts of the unit just mentioned the ten will be twenty. But it is absurd to say that one is ten and ten is twenty, and that the indivisible is divisible, as they claim. Therefore, it is absurd to say that the unit is subtracted from the whole ten.

92 Nor is the unit subtracted from the remaining nine; for that from which something is subtracted does not remain complete and entire, while the nine does remain complete and entire after the subtraction of that unit. And besides, since the nine is nothing other than the nine units, if it should be said that the unit is subtracted from all nine, there will be a subtraction of nine; and if from a part of the nine — say, eight — the same absurdities will follow, and if from the ultimate unit, they will be saying that the unit is divisible, which is absurd.

93 So, then, the unit is not subtracted from the nine, either. But if it is subtracted neither from the whole ten nor from a part of it, it is not possible for a part to be subtracted from a whole or a part. If, then, nothing is subtracted as a whole

or a part from a whole or a whole from a part or a part from a part, nothing is subtracted from anything.

Furthermore, they consider addition, too, to be impossible. For what is 94 added, they say, is either added to itself or to what existed beforehand, or to the combination of both; but none of these alternatives holds; therefore, nothing is added to anything. For example, suppose that there are four cups of something, and let a cup be added. To what, I ask, is it added? For it cannot be added to itself, since what is added is other than that to which it is added, and nothing is other than itself. Nor is it added to the combination of itself 95 and what subsisted beforehand, that is, of the four cups and the cup. For how could something be added to what does not yet exist? Besides, if the added cup is mixed with the four cups and the one cup, a six-cup quantity will result from the four cups and the one cup and the added cup. But if the cup is added to 96 the four cups alone, then, since that which is spread out over something is equal in extent to that over which it is spread out, the cup spread out over the four-cup quantity will double it, so that the whole quantity will be eight cups—which is contrary to what is observed. If, then, what is said to be added is added neither to itself nor to what existed beforehand nor to the combination of both, and there is no alternative besides these, then nothing is ever added to anything.

## 13. Exchange

Exchange, too, is covered along with the existence of addition, subtraction, and 97 local motion, for it is the subtracting of something and the addition of something, in a shift.

## 14. Whole and Part

And both whole and part are covered. For the whole seems to come into being 98 by the aggregation and addition of the parts, and to cease from being the whole by the subtraction of one or more of them. Furthermore, if there is such a thing as a whole, either it is other than its parts or else the parts themselves are the whole. But the whole appears to be nothing other than the parts, for surely 99 when the parts are taken away nothing is left that would permit us to reckon the whole as something other than these parts. But if the parts themselves are the whole, "the whole" will be a mere name, that is, an empty appellative, and the whole will have no individual existence, just as there is no such thing as separation apart from the things separated or a roof apart from the components that have been made into the roof. Therefore, there is no such thing as a whole.

Nor are there any such things as parts, either. For if there are parts, either 100 they are parts of the whole or of one another or each of itself. But they are not parts of the whole, since it is nothing else than the parts (and besides, on this basis the parts will be parts of themselves, since each of the parts allegedly serves to complete the whole), nor of one another, since a part seems to be included in that of which it is a part, and it is absurd to say that the hand, for

101  example, is included in the foot. But neither will each be a part of itself; for because of the inclusion something will be both greater and less than itself. If, then, the things said to be parts are parts neither of the whole nor of themselves nor of one another, they are not parts of anything. And if they are not parts of anything, they are not parts; for relative things stand or fall together.

Let this much be said, just by way of digression, since we have considered whole and part once before.

## 15. Natural Change

102  And some, using arguments such as the following, say that so-called "natural change" too does not exist. If something changes, what changes is either a body or incorporeal; but each of these alternatives leads to *aporia*; therefore, the

103  account of change is aporetic. If something changes, it changes by some action of a cause and by being a thing that is acted upon. But it does not change by being a thing that is acted upon, for the existence of causes has been refuted, whereby the existence of what is acted upon is also refuted, as there is nothing

104  by which it is acted upon. Therefore, nothing changes at all. Again, if something changes, either what is changes or what is not. But what is not does not exist and thus cannot be acted upon or act, and so it does not allow of change. But if what is changes, either it changes insofar as it is in being, or

105  insofar as it is not in being. But insofar as it is not in being, it does not change, for, not being, it is not. But if it changes insofar as it is in being, it will be other than being in being, that is, it will not be in being. And it is absurd to say that what is is not in being; therefore, what is does not change, either. And if neither what is nor what is not changes, and there is nothing else, it only remains to say that nothing changes.

106  Some people say also the following things. Whatever changes has to change in some time, but nothing changes in the past nor in the future nor yet in the present, as we shall show; therefore, nothing changes. Now nothing changes in the past or future, for neither of these is present, and it is impossible to do anything or to be acted upon at a time that does not exist, that is, is not

107  present. But it does not change in the present, either. For the present time, I think, is also nonexistent, and, even if we set this aside for now, it is indivisible; and it is impossible to suppose that a piece of iron, for instance, changes in an indivisible time from hard to soft, or that any of the other changes takes place, for they appear to require some continuation of time. If, therefore, nothing changes either in the past time or in the future or in the present, it must be said that nothing changes.

108  In addition to these points, if there is change it is either sensible or intelligible. But it is not sensible, for the senses are simply passive, while change seems to involve simultaneous awareness of both that from which it changes and that into which it is said to change. And if it is intelligible, then, since there is an unresolved controversy among the ancients concerning the existence of intelligibles, as we have already pointed out many times, we shall be unable to make any assertion about the existence of change.

## 16. Generation and Destruction

Both generation (coming into being) and destruction are eliminated together   109
with addition and subtraction and natural change. For apart from these
nothing would be generated or destroyed. For example, it is by the destruction
of the ten that a nine is generated, as they say, when a unit is taken away, and
conversely, by the addition of the unit the ten is generated from the destruction
of the nine; and by natural change the rust is generated as the bronze is
destroyed. So that when the aforementioned changes are eliminated it is
necessary, I think, that generation and destruction are eliminated, too.

But nevertheless some people say also the following. If Socrates came into   110
being, either he came into being at a time when he did not exist or at a time
when he already existed. But if he were said to have come into being when he
already existed, he would have come into being twice; while if he came into
being when he did not exist, then simultaneously he existed and did not exist —
by his having come into being he existed, but by hypothesis he did not. And if   111
Socrates died, he either died when he was living or when he was dead. But
when he was living he did not die, since he would have been both living and
dead, nor did he die when he was dead, since he would have died twice.
Therefore, Socrates did not die. By applying this argument to each case of
something said to come into being or to be destroyed, it is possible to eliminate
generation and destruction.

Moreover, some reason thus: If something comes into being, either what is   112
comes into being, or what is not. But what is not does not come into being.
For nothing, including coming into being, happens to what is not. Nor does
what is come into being. For if what is comes into being, either it comes into
being insofar as it is in being or insofar as it is not in being. But insofar as it
is not in being, it does not come into being. And if it comes into being insofar
as it is in being, then, since they say that what comes into being becomes one
thing from being another, what comes into being will be other than what is in
being, that is, will not be in being. Therefore, what comes into being will not
be in being, which is nonsense. If, then, neither what is nor what is not comes   113
into being, nothing at all comes into being.

For the same reasons, nothing is destroyed. For if something is destroyed,
either what is or what is not is destroyed. But what is not is not destroyed, for
it is necessary that what is destroyed be acted upon. What is is not destroyed,
either. For either it is destroyed while it remains in a state of being, or while it
does not so remain. And if it is destroyed while it remains in a state of being,
the same thing will simultaneously be in a state of being and in a state of
nonbeing. For since it is not destroyed insofar as it is in a state of nonbeing   114
but rather insofar as it is in a state of being, it follows that, on the one hand,
insofar as it is said to have been destroyed it will be other than what is and
therefore in a state of nonbeing, while on the other hand, insofar as it is said
to be destroyed while remaining in a state of being, it will be in a state of being.
But it is absurd to say that the same thing is both in a state of being and in a
state of nonbeing; therefore, what is is not destroyed while it remains in a state
of being. And if what is is destroyed while it does not remain in a state of being,

but at first passes into nonbeing and then in this way is destroyed, it will no longer be what is that is destroyed, but rather what is not—which we have shown to be impossible. If, then, neither what is is destroyed nor what is not, and besides these there is nothing else, nothing is destroyed.

It will suffice in an outline to have made these points about the changes—points from which it follows that the physical theory of the Dogmatists is not factual and is even unintelligible.

## 17. Rest

115 On the same basis some have been perplexed about permanence in nature, saying that what is in motion is not at rest. But every body is continually in motion, according to the assumptions of the Dogmatists, who say that everything is in flux and is always undergoing divisions and additions—thus, Plato does not even call bodies "beings," but only "things that are coming into being," and Heraclitus likens the mobility of our everyday matter to the swift

116 flow of a river. Therefore, no body is at rest. What is said to be at rest is thought to be constrained by the things around it, and what is constrained is acted upon; but nothing is acted upon, since causes do not exist, as we have shown. Therefore, nothing is at rest.

And some people also propound the following argument. What is at rest is being acted upon, and what is acted upon is moved; therefore, what is said

117 to be at rest is in motion; but if it is in motion it is not at rest. From these considerations it is plain that not even the incorporeal is at rest. For if what is at rest is being acted upon, and being acted upon is a property of bodies, if anything, and not of incorporeal things, nothing incorporeal can be acted upon or be at rest. Therefore, nothing is at rest.

118 So much for the subject of rest. And since each of the aforementioned items cannot be conceived without location and time, we must pass to a consideration of these. For if we show that these are nonexistent, then through them each of the others, too, will be nonexistent. Let us begin with location.

## 18. Location

119 The word "location" is used in two ways, strictly and loosely—loosely in a broad sense (e.g., my location is the city), and strictly for what exactly contains us and by which we are enclosed. We are now inquiring about the exact type of location. Some people have affirmed and others have denied the existence of

120 this, and some have suspended judgment about it. Of all these, those who say that it exists take refuge in "the obvious." For, they say, who will assert that there is no such thing as a location when he sees its parts, such as right and left, up and down, before and behind, and when he is here at one time and there at another, and sees that where my teacher was conversing, there I am conversing now, and when he apprehends that things naturally light have a different location from those that are naturally heavy, and, further, when he

hears the ancients [Hesiod] saying "For verily, first of all chaos came into being"? For they say that the totality of locations is called chaos from its  121 capacity to contains the things that come to be in it. And if there is such a thing as a body, they say, there will also be a location. For without this there would be no body. And if there is the "by which" and the "from which," there is also the "in which," which is a location. But the antecedents of both of the aforementioned conditionals hold; therefore, the consequents of both of them hold, too.

Those who abolish locations do not grant that the parts of locations exist;  122 for a location, they say, is nothing other than its parts, and whoever tries to infer that locations exist by assuming that their parts exist is seeking to establish the point at issue by means of itself. Similarly foolish, they claim, are those who say that something is or has been in some location, when location in general has not been granted. Such people, they say, assume also the existence of bodies, which has not been granted without question; besides which, the "from which" and the "by which," like locations, have been shown not to exist. They claim also that Hesiod is not a trustworthy judge of  123 philosophical matters. And while thus disposing of the considerations tending to support the existence of locations, they also establish in a more complex way that these do not exist, by using in addition what seem to be the most weighty views of the Dogmatists about locations, namely those of the Stoics and Peripatetics, in the following way.

The Stoics say that a void is that which is capable of being occupied by an  124 existent thing, but is not so occupied, or that it is an interval empty of body, or an interval not occupied by a body, and that a location is an interval occupied by an existent thing and equal in extent to what occupies it (here meaning by "existent thing" the body), and that a space is an extension partly occupied by a body and partly unoccupied, though a few say that a space is the location of a large body, so that the difference between location and space is in size. Then it is argued as follows. When the Stoics tell us that a location  125 is an interval occupied by a body, in what sense do they say that it is an interval? Is it the length of the body or the width or the depth only, or the three dimensions together? For if it is only one dimension, the location will not be equal in extent to that of which it is the location; besides, that which includes will be part of what is included, which is wholly nonsensical. And if the three  126 dimensions together, then, since in the so-called "location" there exists neither a void nor some other body having dimension, but only the body said to be in the location, which body is composed of the dimensions (for it is length and breadth and depth and hardness, the last of which is said to be an accident of the first three), the body itself will be its own location, and the same thing will be containing and contained, which is absurd. Therefore, there exists no dimension of an existing location. For this reason, there is no such thing as a location.

And the following argument, too, is put forward. Seeing that the dimen-  127 sions are not found to be twofold in each of the things said to be in a location, but there is one length and one width and one depth, are these dimensions of the body only or of the location only or of both? If they are of the location

only, the body will not have any particular length, breadth or depth, so that
128 the body will not be a body, which is absurd. And if of both, then, since the
void has no subsistence aside from the dimensions, if the dimensions of the void
exist in the body and serve to compose the body itself, what composes the void
will also be what composes the body. For concerning the existence of solidity
nothing can be firmly maintained, as we have shown above; and since as
regards the so-called "body" only those dimensions appear which are of the
void and are identical with the void, the body will be a void; which is absurd.
And if the dimensions are of the body only, there will be no dimension of the
location, whence there will be no location. If, then, no dimension of location is
found in any of the aforementioned ways, there is no such thing as a location.

129      In addition to these points it is said that when the body enters the void
and a location comes into being, either the void remains or withdraws or is
destroyed. But if it remains, the same thing will be both full and empty, and if
it withdraws by a transitional movement or is destroyed by change, the void
will be a body, for these *pathē* are characteristic of a body. And it is absurd to
say that the same thing is both empty and full, or that the void is a body.
Therefore, it is absurd to say that the void can be occupied by a body and
130 become a location. For these reasons, the void too is found to be nonexistent,
if indeed it is impossible for it to be occupied by a body and to become a
location; for it was said that a void is what is capable of being occupied by a
body. And space is eliminated together with these; for if it is a large location it
is dealt with along with location, and if it is a dimension that is partly occupied
by a body and partly empty, it is eliminated together with both of those.

      These arguments, then, and still more, are directed against the views held
131 by the Stoics as regards location. Now the Peripatetics define location as the
boundary of what encloses, insofar as it encloses, so that my location is the
surface of the air that forms a mold of my body. But if this is what location is,
the same thing will both be and not be. For when the body is about to come
to be in some location, it is necessary that the location exist beforehand so that
the body can come to be in it, since nothing can come to be in that which does
not exist; thus, the location will exist before the body comes to be in it. But
insofar as the location is brought about when the surface of the enclosing
material forms a mold of what is enclosed, it is not possible for the location to
subsist before the body's coming to be in it, and for this reason it will not exist
at that time. But it is absurd to say that the same thing both does and does
not exist; therefore, a location is not "the boundary of what encloses, insofar
as it encloses."

132      Furthermore, if there is such a thing as a location, either it is created or it
is non-created. But it is certainly not non-created, for, they say, it is brought
about by being molded around the body in it. But neither is it created, for if it
is created, then either the location in which the body-in-location is already said
to be comes into existence when the body is in the location, or when the body
133 is not in the location. But it cannot be when the body is in the location (for
the location of the body in it already exists), nor when the body is not in the
location, since, as they say, what encloses is molded around what is enclosed,

and in that way the location comes into existence, and nothing can be molded around what is not in it. And if a location does not come into existence either when the body is in the location or when it is not, and besides these no other alternative is conceivable, the location is not created. And if it is neither created nor non-created, it does not exist.

It is also possible to state these points in a more familiar way. If there is    134
such a thing as a location, either it is a body or it is incorporeal. But each of these alternatives is aporetic. So too, therefore, is the concept of location. Again, a location is conceived in relation to the body of which it is the location; but the account of the existence of bodies is aporetic; and therefore so is the account about locations. The location of each thing is not eternal, but since there is no such thing as generation, if the location is said to come into being, it turns out to be nonexistent.

It is possible to give still more arguments, but in order not to lengthen our    135
account, let it just be added that while the arguments give pause to the Skeptics, "obviousness," too, makes them uncomfortable. Consequently, insofar as it is a matter of what is said by the Dogmatists, we join neither side but instead suspend judgment about location.


## 19. Time

We feel the same way about the question of time, too, for insofar as we go by    136
the appearances there seems to be such a thing as time, while if we go by the things said about it, it appears not to exist. Some people define time as the dimension of the motion of the whole (and by "the whole" I mean the cosmos), and others as that motion itself; Aristotle, or as some say, Plato, defines it as the amount of before and after in motion; Strato, or as some say, Aristotle,    137
defines it as the measure of motion and rest; and Epicurus, according to Demetrius the Laconian, as an event made up of events, accompanying days and nights, seasons, *pathē* and the opposite, motions and rests. As regards    138
substance, some—for example, the followers of Aenesidemus—have said that time is a body (claiming that it does not differ from Being and Primary Body), and some have said that it is incorporeal. Either all these positions are true, or all are false, or some are true and some are false; but they cannot all be true (for they are mostly inconsistent), nor will the Dogmatists admit that they are all false. And besides, if it were granted false that time is a body, and also false    139
that it is incorporeal, it will automatically be granted that time does not exist; for besides these alternatives there is no other possibility. Nor, in view of the equipollent disagreement and the *aporia* concerning Criterion and Proof, is it possible to apprehend which positions are true and which are false. For these    140
reasons, therefore, we shall be unable to maintain anything firmly about time.

Moreover, since time seems not to exist without motion and rest, time is abolished when motion and rest are eliminated. But nevertheless some people make also the following points concerning time. If time exists, either it is finite or infinite. But if it is finite, it began at some time and will come to an end at    141 some time, and for that reason there was once a time when time did not exist, namely, before it began, and there will be a time when time will not exist, namely, after it comes to an end; which is absurd. Therefore, time is not finite.

142  But if it is infinite, then, seeing that part of it is said to be past, part present, and part future, either the past and future exist or they do not. But if they do not exist, and only the present, which is momentary, remains, time will be finite and the original *aporiai* will follow. On the other hand, if the past and future do exist, each of them will be present. But it is absurd to call past and future time "present." Therefore, time is not infinite, either. And so, if it is neither infinite nor finite, it does not exist at all.

143      In addition, if time exists, it is either divisible or indivisible. But it is not indivisible. For, according to the Dogmatists, it is divided into the present and the past and the future. Nor is it divisible, for anything divisible is measured by some part of itself, the measuring part being put alongside what is being measured, part by part, as when we measure a cubit with a finger. But time cannot be measured by any of its parts. For if, say, the present measures the past, it will be put alongside the past and for this reason will be past; and, similarly, in the case of the future it will be future. And if the future should measure the others, it will be present and past; and so, likewise, the past will be future and present; which is nonsense. Therefore, time is not divisible, either. But if it is neither indivisible nor divisible, it does not exist.

144      Also, time is said to be tripartite, that is, partly past, partly present, and partly future. Of these, the past and the future do not exist. For if past and future time exist now, each will be present. Nor does the present time exist, either. For if it does exist, either it is indivisible or divisible. But it is not indivisible, since things that change are said to change in the present time and nothing changes—like iron becoming soft, etc.—in an indivisible time. Thus

145  the present time is not indivisible. But neither is it divisible. For it would not be divided into presents, as the present is said to change into the past imperceptibly because of the swift flux of things in the cosmos. Nor would it be divided into past and future; for that way it will be nonexistent, with one

146  part of it no longer existent and the other part not yet existent. Whence, too, the present cannot even be the termination of the past and the beginning of the future, since then it will both exist and not exist. For it will exist since it is present, but it will not exist since its parts do not exist. Therefore, it is not divisible, either. But if the present is neither indivisible nor divisible, it does not even exist. And if neither the present nor the past nor the future exists, there is no such thing as time, since a composite of nonexistents is nonexistent.

147      The following argument, too, is given against time. If time exists, either it is liable to generation and destruction or it is immune to these. But it is not immune to generation and destruction, since part of it is said to be past and no longer to exist, while part of it is said to be future and not yet to exist. Nor,

148  on the other hand, is it liable to generation and destruction. For, according to the hypotheses of the Dogmatists themselves, things that come into being must come into being from something that exists, and things that are destroyed must be destroyed into something that exists. So, if time is destroyed into the past, it is destroyed into a nonexistent, and if it comes into being from the future, it

also comes into being from a nonexistent, for neither of these exists. But it is absurd to say that something comes to be out of a nonexistent or is destroyed into what does not exist. Therefore, time is not liable to generation and destruction. And if it is neither immune nor liable to generation and destruction, it does not exist at all.

On top of this, since everything that comes into being seems to come into 149 being in time, if time comes into being, it comes into being in time. Now either it comes into being in itself or in another time. But if in itself, the same thing will both exist and not exist. For since that in which something comes into being must exist before that which comes into being in it, the time that is coming into being in itself, insofar as it is coming into being, does not yet exist, but insofar as it is coming into being in itself, does already exist. Therefore, it does not come into being in itself. But neither does it come into being in 150 another time. For if the present time comes into being in the future time, the present time will be future, and if in the past time, it will be past. And the same must also be said concerning the other times. So that one time does not come into being in another time. But if it neither comes into being in itself nor in another time, time is not liable to generation. And it has been shown that it is not immune to generation, either. Therefore, being neither liable nor immune to generation, it does not exist at all; for everything that exists is bound to be either liable or immune to generation.

## 20. Number

Since time seems not to be found apart from number, it will not be out of place 151 to give a brief discussion of number, too. Now as a matter of custom we speak (in a manner free of doctrine) of numbering something, and we hear that there is such a thing as number; but the sophistry of the Dogmatists has provoked arguments against this, too. For example, the Pythagoreans even claim that 152 numbers are elements in the cosmos. They say, in fact, that the appearances are composite but that the elements must be simple; therefore, the elements are non-evident. But of things non-evident, some, such as atoms and aggregates, are bodies, while others, such as figures and forms and numbers, are incorporeal. Of these, the bodies are composite, being combinations of length, breadth, depth and resistance, or perhaps weight. Thus the elements are not only non-evident but also incorporeal. But of the incorporeal things, each has a 153 number that is intuited along with it; for it is either one or two or more. On this basis it is concluded that the elements of what exists are non-evident and incorporeal numbers that are intuited along with everything whatever. And not only these, but also the Monad and the Indefinite Dyad that comes into being by the addition of the Monad, and by participation in which the particular dyads become dyads. For they say that it is from these that the other numbers, 154 which are intuited along with the things enumerated, arise, and that the cosmos is established. And they say that the point involves the notion of the Monad, and the line that of the Dyad (for it is considered as lying between two points), and the surface that of the Triad (for they say that it is the sideways flowing

of the line to another point lying outside of it), and the body that of the Tetrad, for a body arises through the ascension of the surface up to a point lying above
155  it. And thus they model bodies and the whole cosmos, which they say is ordered in accord with harmonic ratios, namely that of "by fours," which is the interval of a fourth, as eight is to six, and that of "by fives," which is the interval of a fifth, as nine is to six; and that of "by alls," which is the octave, as twelve is to six.

156      These are their dreams. And they also claim that a number is something other than the things enumerated, arguing that if by definition an animal were, say, one, then a plant, since it is not an animal, will not be one; but a plant is one; therefore, the animal is not one just by being an animal but only in virtue of something that is intuited with it, external to it, and in which each animal participates with the result that it becomes one. Also, if the number is the things enumerated, then since the things enumerated are, say, human beings, cattle and horses, the number will also be human beings, cattle, and horses, and it will be white and black and bearded if the things counted should happen
157  to be such. But all this is absurd; therefore, the number is not the things enumerated, but it has a special existence apart from these, whereby it is intuited along with the things enumerated and is an element.

But when the Pythagoreans had thus concluded that a number is not the things enumerated, the *aporia* about number came in as a corollary. For it is argued that if there is such a thing as a number, either it is the enumerated things themselves or it is something else external to these; but the number is not the enumerated things themselves, as the Pythagoreans have proved, nor is it something other than these, as we shall show. Therefore, there is no such thing as a number.

158      That a number is not anything external to the things enumerated, we shall establish, for the sake of clarity, by giving the argument for the case of the Monad [i.e., the abstract number One]. If, then, there is any such thing as the Monad-in-itself, by participation in which each of the participants becomes one, either this Monad will be one or it will be as numerous as its participants. But if it is one, does each of the things said to participate in it participate in all of it, or only in a part of it? For if one human being, say, has all of the Monad, there will no longer be a monad for the one horse to participate in, or
159  the one dog or any of the other things we call "one," just as, supposing that there are a number of naked people and that there is only one cloak, which has been donned by one of the people, the others will remain naked and without a cloak. But if each thing participates in a part of it, then, in the first place, the Monad will have a part—indeed, it will have infinitely many parts, into which it will be divided, which is absurd. And in the second place, just as a part of the Decad, for example, the Dyad, is not a group of ten, so neither will a part of the Monad be a unit, and for this reason nothing at all will participate in the Monad. So the Monad in which the particulars are said to participate will not be one.

160      But if the monads, by participation in which each of the particulars is said to be one, are equal in number to the enumerated things that are called "one," the monads participated in will be infinitely many. And either these participate

in a "basic" monad or in monads equal in number to themselves, and are monads for that reason, or else they do nor participate but are monads without any participation. For if they can be monads without participation, then every 161 perceptible thing can be unitary without participation in a monad, and so the monad said to be perceived "in itself" is straightway eliminated. But if those monads, too, are monads by participation, either they all participate in one thing or each participates in its own particular thing. And if all in one, each will be said to participate either in a part or in the whole, and the original *aporiai* will remain; but if each in its own, then a monad will have to be intuited 162 along with each of those monads, and others along with the intuited ones, and so on ad infinitum. If, then, in order to apprehend that there are such things as "monads in themselves," by participation in which each existent thing is one, it is necessary to have apprehended an infinite infinity of intelligible monads, and if it is impossible to apprehend an infinite infinity of intelligible monads, then it is impossible to show that there are any such things as intelligible monads and that each existent thing is one, becoming one by participation in its own monad.

Therefore, it is absurd to say that there are just as many monads as there 163 are things participating in them. But if the so-called Monad-in-itself is neither one nor as many as the things participating in it, then it does not exist at all. Likewise, none of the other numbers will exist "in itself," for in the case of every number it is possible to use the argument here presented paradigmatically for the case of the monad. But if the number does not exist in itself, as we have shown, nor is it the things enumerated, as the Pythagoreans have proved, and besides these there is no other alternative, it must be said that there is no such thing as a number.

Further, how do those who think that a number is something other than 164 the things enumerated say that the Dyad arises from the Monad? For when we combine a monad with another monad, either something is added to these monads from outside, or something is subtracted from them, or nothing is either added or subtracted. But if nothing is either added or subtracted, there will not be a dyad. For neither when they were apart from one another did the monads have the Dyad intuited along with them, in accord with their own definition, nor has anything been added to them from outside, just as, by hypothesis, nothing as been subtracted. So that the combination of the monad 165 with the monad will not be a dyad, since no subtraction or addition has taken place. But if a subtraction does take place, not only will there not be a dyad, but the monads will even be diminished. And if the dyad is added to them from outside, in order that a dyad may come to be from the monads, the things seeming to be two will be four; for to start with there exists a monad and another monad, and when a dyad from outside is added, the number four will result. The same argument applies also in the case of the other numbers said 166 to result from combination.

If, then, the numbers said to be combinations of the basic ones arise neither by subtraction nor by addition nor without subtraction or addition, the genesis of the number said to be in itself and apart from the things enumerated is impossible. But the Dogmatists themselves make it evident that the numbers

formed by combination are not really ungenerated, when they say that they are compounded and generated from the basic numbers, for example, from the
167 Monad and the Infinite Dyad. Thus, numbers do not exist of themselves. And if the numbers are neither found to exist of themselves nor have their existence in the things enumerated, then, if we go by the subtleties introduced by the Dogmatists, there will be no such thing as a number.

Let it suffice to have said thus much in outline about the so-called Physics part of philosophy.

## 21. The Ethics Part of Philosophy

168 There remains the Ethics part, which is supposed to concern itself with things good, bad, and indifferent. So in order that we may treat this subject, too, in a summary way, we shall inquire into the existence of things good, bad, and indifferent, first setting forth the concept of each.

## 22. Things Good, Bad, and Indifferent

169 Accordingly, the Stoics say that the good is "beneficial activity or what is not alien to beneficial activity," meaning by "beneficial activity" virtue and worthwhile action, and by "what is not alien to beneficial activity" the worthwhile person and the friend. For virtue, which is "the ruling part of the soul in a certain state," together with worthwhile action, which is "an activity in accord with virtue," are precisely beneficial activity, and the worthwhile person and
170 the friend are not alien to beneficial activity. And beneficial activity, being the ruling part of the soul, is a part of the worthwhile person. But they say that wholes are not the same as their parts, for a human being is not a hand, nor are they other than the parts, for without the parts they do not exist. Thus they say that wholes are "not alien" to the parts. Hence, since the worthwhile person is a whole in relation to his ruling part, with which they have identified beneficial activity, they say that he is "not alien" to beneficial activity.
171 They also declare that "good" has three senses. In one sense, they say, good is that by which it is possible to be benefited, this being the primary good, that is, virtue; in another sense it is that of which being benefited is an accidental result, for example, virtue and virtuous actions; and in a third sense it is that which is capable of benefiting, and such are virtue and also virtuous actions and the worthwhile person and the friend, and gods and worthwhile subordinate deities — so that the second signification of "good" includes the first, and
172 the third includes the second and the first. But some define "good" as "that which is choiceworthy for its own sake," and others as "that which assists happiness or supplements it"; where the happy life is, as the Stoics say, "the serene life."

Such things as these are what they say concerning the concept of good.
173 But he who asserts that the good is "what benefits" or "what is choiceworthy

for its own sake" or "what contributes to happiness" is not setting before the mind what the good is, but only mentioning one of its accidents, which is to no effect. For either the aforesaid accidents pertain only to the good, or also to other things as well. But if also to other things as well, then these accidents are not, thus extended, definitive of the good; and if only to the good, we cannot get from them a concept of the good. For just as the person who has 174 no concept of horse will not know what neighing is, and cannot acquire the concept of horse by means of this (provided that he has not previously encountered a neighing horse), so also anyone who, because he lacks knowledge of the good, is asking what it is, will not be able to recognize the attribute that belongs properly to it and only to it, so as to be able to form therefrom a concept of the good itself. For one must first learn the nature of the good itself, and then find that it benefits and that it is choiceworthy for its own sake and that it is productive of happiness. And that the aforementioned accidents 175 do not suffice to reveal the concept and nature of the good the Dogmatists make evident by what they do. That the good is beneficial and choiceworthy (wherefore the good is said to be, as it were, revered) and that it is productive of happiness, all, I suppose, will agree; but when they are asked to what these accidents pertain, they plunge into implacable combat, with some saying virtue, some saying pleasure, others absence of pain, and still others something else. But if from the aforementioned definitions it had been brought to light what the good itself is, they would not have been in conflict as though its nature were unknown.

So, those of the Dogmatists who appear to be most esteemed differ in this 176 way about the concept of the good; and they have also differed similarly about the bad, with some saying that the bad is "hurtful activity or what is not alien to hurtful activity," and others that it is "what is to be avoided for its own sake," and others that it is "what is productive of unhappiness." But in setting forth by means of these phrases, not the substance of the bad but only some of its supposed accidents, they fall into the previously mentioned *aporia.*

They also say that the word "indifferent" is used in three senses — in one, 177 it is applied to that which is the object of neither inclination nor disinclination, such as its being the case that the stars, or the hairs on the head, are even in number. And in another sense, to that which is indeed an object of inclination or disinclination but of inclination or disinclination directed no more to one thing than to another, such as in the case of two indistinguishable four-drachma pieces, when it is necessary to choose one of them, for there is an inclination to choose one of them, but no more this one than that one. In a third sense they say that the indifferent is that which contributes neither to happiness nor to unhappiness, for example, health and wealth; for they say that what can be used sometimes well and sometimes ill is indifferent. They claim to discuss this most of all in their ethics. However, what one ought to think 178 about this concept too is evident from what we have said about things good and bad.

So it is clear that they have not brought us to a conception of any of the aforementioned items; but there is nothing surprising about their failing in this way when they are dealing with matters that, perhaps, do not exist. Indeed, there are some people who argue on this basis that nothing is by nature good, bad, or indifferent.

## 23. Is Anything by Nature Good, Bad, or Indifferent?

179 Fire, which heats by nature, appears to everyone to be productive of heat, and snow, which cools by nature, appears to everyone to be productive of coolness, and all things that are affective by nature affect in the same way those who are, as the Dogmatists put it, "in a natural condition." But, as we shall show, none of the so-called "goods" affects everyone as being good; therefore, there does not exist anything that is good by nature. That none of the so-called "goods"
180 affects everyone in the same way is, the Dogmatists agree, evident. For, not to mention the common people — some of whom consider physical fitness to be good, others sexual intercourse, others gluttony, others drunkenness, others gambling, others greed, and still others certain things even worse than those — some of the philosophers themselves, for example, the Peripatetics, say that there are three kinds of good, and of these some concern the soul, e.g., the virtues, and some concern the body, e.g., health and similar things, and others are external, e.g., friends, wealth, and the like. The Stoics themselves, too,
181 say that there are three types of goods; and of these some, e.g., the virtues, concern the soul, and some, e.g., the worthwhile person and the friend, are external, and some, e.g., the person who is worthwhile in relation to himself, neither concern the soul nor are external; but the Stoics claim that those which concern the body and which are said by the Peripatetics to be goods are not goods. And some have welcomed pleasure as a good, whereas some say that it is downright bad, so that one philosopher actually proclaimed: "I had rather be demented than delighted."
182      Hence, if things that move us by nature move everybody in the same way, and we are not all moved in the same way by the things called "good"; nothing is good by nature. Furthermore, in view of their inconsistency it is impossible to give credence to all the positions that have been propounded, or even to any one of them. For anyone who says that we ought to give credence to this position and not to that becomes a party to the controversy, since opposed to him he has the arguments of those who believe oppositely; and so for this reason he himself, along with the rest, will have need of an adjudicator instead of making determinations for the others. And since there is no agreed-upon criterion or proof, he will arrive at *epochē* because of the unresolved dispute about these things, and thus he will not be able to maintain any firm position as to what the good by nature is.
183      Again, some say this: The good is either the act of choosing or that which we choose. Now the act of choosing, in its ordinary meaning, is not good; for otherwise we would be in no hurry to get that which we are choosing, in order not to lose the power of continuing to choose it; for example, if seeking after something to drink were good, we would not hasten to obtain it; for when we have enjoyed it we are freed of the seeking. And likewise in the case of hunger

and love and the rest. The act of choosing, therefore, is not choiceworthy in itself, if indeed it is not actually disagreeable; for the hungry person hastens to obtain food, so as to get rid of the discomfort of the hunger; and similarly with the lover and the person who is thirsty.

But neither is the good the choiceworthy. For this is either external to us 184 or in us. But if it is external to us, either it produces in us a comfortable feeling and a welcome condition and a delightful *pathos*, or it does not affect us at all. And if, on the one hand, it is not delightful to us, neither will it be good nor will it attract us to choosing it nor will it be choiceworthy at all. But if, on the other hand, there arises in us, from the external object, a gentle condition and an agreeable *pathos*, the external object will not be choiceworthy for its own sake but for the sake of the condition that arises in us from it; so that what is 185 choiceworthy for the sake of itself cannot be external. But neither is it in us. For it is said to be either in the body only or in the soul only or in both. But if it is in the body only, it will elude our *gnōsis* [i.e., our ability to recognize things as being what they are]. For this ability is said to belong to the soul, and the Dogmatists claim that the body by itself is *alogos* [languageless, incapable of language] . But if the good is said to extend to the soul, too, it would seem to be choiceworthy via the soul's perception and its *pathos* of delight, for, according to them, what is determined to be choiceworthy is determined to be such by the intellect and not by the languageless body.

There remains the alternative that the good is in the soul only. And, from 186 what the Dogmatists say, this too is impossible. On the one hand, the soul perhaps does not even exist. On the other, even if it does exist, and we go by what they say, it is not apprehended, as I have shown in the section on the Criterion. How, then, would anyone make bold to claim that something takes place in something that he does not apprehend? But, leaving these points to 187 one side, in what way, then, do they say that the good comes into existence in the soul? For surely, if Epicurus posits that the goal is pleasure and says that the soul, like everything else, consists of atoms, there is no way of explaining how in a heap of atoms there can arise pleasure or assent, or a determination that this is choiceworthy and good while that is to be avoided and bad.

## 24. What Is the So-called "Art of Living"?

Again, the Stoics say that the goods in the soul are certain arts, namely, the 188 virtues. And they say that an art [*technē*] is "a system of jointly exercised apprehensions," and that apprehensions come into existence in the ruling part of the soul. But how a store of apprehensions, that is, an aggregation of enough of them to produce an art, can come into existence in the ruling part (which, according to them, is breath) is impossible to understand, since breath is fluid and is supposed to be moved as a whole by each impression. And it is humbug 189 to say that the soul as imaged by Plato is capable of receiving the good — and here I am referring to the blend of indivisible and divisible being and that of the nature of the other and the same, or the numbers. Hence, the good cannot

190     be in the soul, either. But if the good is not the act of choosing, and what is choiceworthy for its own sake does not exist externally and is neither in the body nor in the soul, as I have shown, then nothing at all is good by nature.

Nor, for the reasons stated above, is there anything that is bad by nature. For things that seem to some people to be bad are pursued as goods by others, for example, intemperance, injustice, money grubbing, incontinence, and the like. Hence, if the things that are what they are by nature naturally affect everybody in the same way, whereas the things said to be bad do not affect everybody in the same way, nothing is bad by nature.

191     Likewise, in view of the controversy about indifferent things, nothing is indifferent by nature. For instance, the Stoics say that of indifferent things some are preferred, some rejected, and some neither preferred nor rejected; preferred are the things having sufficient value, like health and wealth; rejected are the things having insufficient value, like poverty and disease; and neither preferred

192     nor rejected are, for example, extending or bending the finger. But some say that none of the things indifferent by nature are simply preferred or rejected; for every indifferent thing appears, in differing circumstances, sometimes preferred and sometimes rejected. For surely, they say, if the wealthy are being plotted against by a tyrant while the poor are being left in peace, everyone would choose to be poor rather than wealthy, so that wealth becomes a thing

193     rejected. Consequently, since every so-called "indifferent" thing is called "good" by some people and "bad" by others, whereas all alike would consider it indifferent if it were indifferent by nature, nothing is indifferent by nature.

So also, if someone should say that courage is by nature choiceworthy, because lions seem to be naturally bold and courageous, and also bulls, perhaps, and roosters and some human beings, then we reply that on this basis cowardice, too, is one of the things choiceworthy by nature, since deer and hares and many other animals are naturally inclined to it. Furthermore, most human beings are found to be cowardly; for rarely does anyone give himself up to death for the sake of his country . . . but the great mass of mankind are averse to all actions of that kind.

194     Along the same lines the Epicureans, too, think they have shown that pleasure is by nature choiceworthy; for the animals, they say, right from birth

195     and when still untrained, are inclined to pleasure and averse to pains. But against these people one can argue that what is productive of the bad is not by nature good. And pleasure is indeed productive of bad things; for pain, which according to them is bad by nature, is bound up with every pleasure. Thus, for example, the drunkard feels pleasure when filling himself up with wine; and the glutton, with food; and the lecher when having immoderate sexual intercourse; but these are productive of poverty and disease, which, as

196     the Epicureans admit, are painful and bad. Therefore, pleasure is not by nature good. And, similarly, that which produces good things is not by nature bad, and pains produce pleasures; for we gain knowledge by hard work, and in this way, too, a person acquires wealth and a loved one, and pains produce health as a by-product. Therefore, hard work is not by nature bad. And if pleasure were by nature good and hard work bad, everybody would be similarly

disposed to these, as we have said; but we see many philosophers choosing hard work and temperance while disdaining pleasure.

Similarly, those who say that the virtuous life is good by nature could be 197 refuted by the fact that some wise people choose a life with pleasure, so that the claim that a thing is by nature of this or that sort is parried by the disagreement among the Dogmatists themselves.

And, in addition to these points, perhaps it may not be out of place briefly 198 to give more specific attention to the assumptions concerning things shameful and not shameful, prohibited and not prohibited, laws and customs, reverence toward the gods, piety as concerns the departed, and the like. For in this way, too, we shall find great anomaly concerning what ought or ought not to be done.

For example, among us sodomy is regarded as shameful, and moreover 199 even illegal, whereas by the Germani, they say, it is not considered shameful but just a customary thing. And it is said that also among the Thebans, in the past, this was not believed to be shameful, and they say that Meriones the Cretan got his name by reference to the Cretans' custom, and some people refer to this the burning affection of Achilles for Patroclus. But is there anything 200 surprising about this, when not only the followers of the Cynic philosophy but also those of Zeno of Citium, namely Cleanthes and Chrysippus, say that this practice is indifferent? Further, to have intercourse with a woman in public seems to us to be shameful, but it is not considered so by some of the people in India; indeed, they are completely indifferent about having intercourse in public, as we have also heard about the philosopher Crates. Moreover, to make 201 prostitutes of women is for us shameful and most reprehensible, but it is emphatically approved by many of the Egyptians; in fact, they say that those women who have the most lovers wear an ornamental anklet as a sign of something they are proud of. And among some of them the young women, before marriage, gather together a dowry by means of prostitution. We also find the Stoics saying that there is nothing wrong with cohabiting with a prostitute or living off her work.

Again, tattooing seems to us to be shameful and degrading, but many of 202 the Egyptians and Sarmatians tattoo their children. Moreover, for us it is 203 shameful for men to have earrings but for some of the barbarians, for example, the Syrians, it is a sign of high birth. And some, to add further signs of high birth, pierce the nostrils of their children and hang silver or gold rings from them, which nobody among us would do, just as no man here would put on a 204 flowery, floor-length dress, which we consider shameful though the Persians deem it very becoming. And when, at the court of the Sicilian tyrant Dionysius, a dress of that kind was offered to the philosophers Plato and Aristippus, Plato refused it, saying "Since I am male by nature, I could never put on a woman's dress," but Aristippus accepted it, saying, "Even in the Bacchanalia a prudent woman will not be defiled." Thus, even in the case of these wise men, this seemed shameful to one of them and not to the other. And with us it is 205 prohibited to marry one's mother or one's own sister. But the Persians, and especially those of them who are supposed to be wise, namely, the Magi, marry their mothers; and the Egyptians take their sisters in marriage; and, as the poet says,

> Zeus spoke to Hera, his sister and wife.
>
> Iliad 18.356

Further, Zeno of Citium says that there is nothing wrong with a man's rubbing his mother's private parts with his own, just as nobody would say that it is wicked for him to rub any other part of her body with his hand. And Chrysippus, also, in his *Politics*, decrees that a father may produce children by his daughter, and a mother by her son, and a brother by his sister. Plato, more
206  generally, said that women should be held in common. And Zeno does not disapprove masturbation, though to us it is abominable; and we are informed that others, too, practice this evil as though it were a good.

207      Furthermore, for us it is prohibited to eat human flesh, but for entire barbarian tribes it is indifferent. Indeed, why should we speak of the barbarians, when even Tydeus is said to have eaten the brain of his enemy, and the Stoics say that there is nothing wrong with eating the flesh of other people or
208  of oneself? And with us it is prohibited to the general public to defile an altar of a god with human blood, but the Laconians whip themselves fiercely on the altar of Orthosian Artemis in order that there be a great flow of blood on the altar of that goddess. Also, some people sacrifice a human being to Cronus, just as the Scythians sacrifice strangers to Artemis; but we think that holy
209  places are polluted when a human being is killed. And among us the law punishes paramours, but for some people having intercourse with the wives of others is an indifferent matter; even some philosophers, too, say that intercourse with another's wife is indifferent.

210      With us, the law decrees that parents should receive care from their children; but the Scythians kill them when they become more than 60 years old. And what is remarkable about that?—seeing that Cronus cut off his father's genitals with a sickle, and Zeus hurled Cronus down to Tartarus, and Athena, together with Hera and Poseidon, tried to put their father in chains.
211  Moreover, Cronus decided to do away with his own children, and Solon gave the Athenians the law concerning extralegal matters, by which he turned over to each individual the decision whether to kill his own children. But with us the laws prohibit the killing of children. The Roman lawgivers also decree that children are servants and slaves of their parents, and that the parents, not the children, have control over the property of the children until the children have bought their freedom; but among other people this has been rejected as
212  tyrannical. Also, it is the law that killers be punished, but often when gladiators kill they are honored. Furthermore, the laws forbid striking free men, but when athletes strike free men, often even killing them, they are thought to deserve
213  honors and crowns. And with us the law decrees that each man shall have one wife, but among the Thracians and Gaetulians (this is a Libyan tribe) each man
214  has many wives. Again, for us piracy is illegal and unjust, but for many of the barbarians there is nothing wrong with it. In fact, people say that the Cilicians considered it a fine thing, so much so that they deemed those who died in

piracy to be worthy of honor. And Nestor, according to the poet, after greeting Telemachus and his comrades, said to them,

> Can it be that you are wandering aimlessly, like pirates?
>
> Odyssey 3.73

and yet if there were something wrong with piracy, he would not have greeted them in that friendly way, since he suspected that they were that kind of people.

Further, stealing is unjust and illegal for us; yet those who say that Hermes 215 is the most thievish god cause it not to be considered unjust, for how could a god be bad? And some say that the Laconians punished thieves, not for having stolen but for having gotten caught. Also, among many peoples the coward and 216 the man who throws away his shield are punished by law; which is why the Laconian mother, giving the shield to her child as he was going out to war, said, "Either come back *with* this shield, my son, or *on* it." But Archilochus, as though praising himself to us for throwing away his shield and fleeing, says,

> Some Saïan is gloating over the shield, which I unwillingly
> Left in the bush, but I, on the other hand,
> Did escape the finality of death.
>
> Frag. 6 Diehl

And the Amazons used to maim their male offspring so as to make them 217 incapable of any manly action, while they themselves kept charge of war; whereas with us the opposite has been regarded as right. Besides, the mother of the gods is favorably disposed toward effeminate people, and the goddess would not have made this judgment if not being manly were by nature bad. 218 Thus, there is a great deal of anomaly as regards both matters of justice and injustice and the excellence of manliness.

There is also a full supply of controversy regarding religion and the gods. For the majority say that gods do exist, but some, like the followers of Diagoras of Melos and Theodorus and Critias the Athenian, say that they do not. And of those asserting that gods exist, some believe in the traditional gods, and others in those invented by the Dogmatic systems—for example, Aristotle said that God is incorporeal and "the boundary of the heavens"; the Stoics, that he is a breath that pervades even ugly things; Epicurus, that he is anthropomorphic; and Xenophanes, that he is a sphere having no *pathē*. And 219 some say that he cares about our affairs, and others that he does not; for Epicurus; says that what is blessed and incapable of being destroyed has no concerns of its own nor provides any to others. Whence some of the common people, too, say that there is one god, others that there are many and of various shapes; and they descend even to the suppositions of the Egyptians, who believe in gods that are dog-faced or hawk-shaped, as well as cows, crocodiles, or what have you.

Whence, too, there is a great deal of anomaly as concerns the sacrificial 220 practices and worship of the gods in general; for things that are holy in some rites are considered unholy in others. But this would not have been the case if the holy and the unholy were such by nature. Thus, for instance, nobody would

sacrifice a pig to Sarapis, but people do sacrifice pigs to Heracles and Asclepius. The sacrificing of sheep to Isis is prohibited, but they are offered up with
221 favorable omens to the so-called Mother of the Gods and to other gods. And some people sacrifice human beings to Cronus, but most think that this is wicked. In Alexandria they sacrifice a cat to Horus and a beetle to Thetis, which none of us would do. To Poseidon they sacrifice the horse, with good omens, but to Apollo, especially the Apollo of Didymus, that animal is odious.
222 It is an act of piety to sacrifice goats to Artemis, but not to Asclepius. I could mention a whole lot of other instances similar to these, but I am omitting them since my aim is brevity. But certainly, if a sacrifice were holy or unholy by nature, it would have been considered so by all alike.

It is also possible to find instances similar to these in the religious
223 observances having to do with the human diet. A Jew or an Egyptian priest would rather die than eat pork; for the Libyan it is completely prohibited to taste the flesh of the sheep; for some of the Syrians, that of the dove; for others, that of sacrificial victims. And in some rites eating fish is sanctioned; in others, it is sacrilegious. And, of the Egyptians considered to be wise, some think it impious to eat an animal's head, others the shoulder, others the foot, and
224 others some other part. And nobody would bring forward an onion as something to be dedicated to Zeus Casius at Pelusium, just as no priest of the Libyan Aphrodite would take a taste of garlic. In some rites they avoid mint, in some catnip, and in others parsley. And there are people who say that they
225 would sooner eat their fathers' heads than eat beans. But for still others these things are indifferent. Further, eating dog meat seems to us impious, but some of the Thracians are reported to do this. And perhaps there was such a custom even among the Greeks; thus Diocles, too, prompted by the practices of the Asclepiads, prescribed that puppy meat be given to some of his patients. And some people, as I was saying, eat with indifference even the flesh of human
226 beings, a thing that has been considered by us to be sinful. Yet if religious usages and prohibitions were valid by nature, they would be recognized by everybody alike.

It is possible to make similar observations about reverence toward those who have passed away. Some people, after wrapping the dead up completely, bury them in the ground, considering it sacrilegious to expose them to the light of day; but the Egyptians, removing the entrails, embalm them and keep them
227 above ground with themselves. And the fish-eaters among the Ethiopians throw the dead into the lakes, to be consumed by the fish; but the Hyrcanians put them out as food for the dogs, and some of the Indians do likewise for the vultures. And they say that the Troglodytes take the dead person to some hilly place and then, tying him head to foot, laughingly throw stones at him; and
228 when they have covered him with these, they go away. And some of the barbarians sacrifice and eat those who are over sixty years of age, but bury in the ground those who die in their youth. Some peoples burn the dead; of these, some retrieve and bury the bones, while others carelessly leave them strewn about. And it is said that the Persians impale the dead and embalm them with sodium nitrate, and then they bind them up with strips of cloth. And so we see how much trouble other people undergo as concerns the dead.

Also, some people regard death itself as something to be feared and 229 avoided, but others do not. Indeed, Euripides says,

> Who knows whether to be alive is really to be dead,
> While to be dead is considered, down below, to be alive?
>
> Frag. 638 Nauck

And Epicurus says,

> Death is nothing to us; for what is dissolved is insensible, and what is insensible is nothing to us. (Ed. Usener, pp. 61.6, 71.6)

They say, too, that if indeed we are composed of soul and body, and death is a dissolution of soul and body, then when we exist death does not (for we are not dissolved), but when death exists we do not (for when the composite of soul and body no longer exists, we do not exist either). And Heraclitus says 230 that both living and dying exist in both our state of life and our state of death; for when we are alive our souls are dead, that is, entombed within us, and when we die the souls revive and live. Further, some people suppose that dying is better for us than living. Thus Euripides says,

> For the newborn child, headed for so many evils,
> We ought to get together and sing a dirge;
> But the dead man, who is done with evil,
> We should haul off with rejoicing and shouts of triumph.
>
> Frag. 449 Nauck

The following lines, too, were said from the same point of view. 231

> For mortals the best thing is not to have been born at all,
> Nor to have looked upon the rays of the fiery sun,
> But, if born, to reach the gates of Hades as quickly as possible
> And lie buried deep in the earth.
>
> Theognis 425ff.

We know, too, the facts about Cleobis and Biton, which Herodotus relates in the story about the Argive priestess. Also, some of the Thracians are reported 232 to sit around the newborn child and sing a dirge. So, then, death should not be considered something terrible by nature, any more than life should be considered something good by nature. Nor are any of the aforementioned things of this character or that by nature, but all are conventional and relative.

The same type of treatment can be carried over to each of the other 233 customs, which, because of the brevity of our account, we have not here described. And if we are not able immediately to point out the anomaly concerning them, it should be noted that there may well be disagreement concerning them among various peoples that are unknown to us. For just as, 234 even if we did not happen to know of the Egyptians' custom of marrying their sisters, we would not be right in maintaining it to be universally agreed that people should not marry their sisters, so also it is not right to maintain that there is no disagreement about those customs concerning which the anomaly has not been noticed by us, since it is possible, as I was saying, that there is disagreement about them among peoples that are unknown to us.

235    Thus the Skeptic, seeing so much anomaly in the matters at hand, suspends judgment as to whether by nature something is good or bad or, generally, ought or ought not be done, and he thereby avoids the Dogmatists' precipitancy, and he follows, without any belief, the ordinary course of life; for this reason he has no *pathos* one way or the other as regards matters of belief, while his *pathē* in regard to things forced upon him are moderate. As a human being he has sensory *pathē*, but since he does not add to these the belief that what he experiences is by nature bad, his *pathē* are moderate. For having in addition a belief like this is worse than the actual experience itself, just as sometimes people undergoing surgery or some other such experience bear up under it while bystanders faint because of their belief that what is going on is
236    bad. Indeed, he who supposes that something is by nature good or bad or, in general, ought or ought not be done, is upset in all sorts of ways. When things he considers bad by nature happen to him he thinks himself pursued by the torments of the Furies, and when he gets possession of things that appear to him to be good, then, because of vanity and the fear of losing them, not to mention concern lest he should land back among the things he considers to be
237    bad by nature, he sinks into a state of extraordinary disquietude. And as for those who say that goods cannot be lost, we shall hold them in check by the *aporia* having to do with the controversy about that. From all this we reason that if what is productive of the bad is bad and to be avoided, and if confidence that certain things are by nature good and others bad produces disquietude, then assuming confidently that something is naturally good or evil is bad and to be avoided.

    It will suffice for the present to have made these points about the good, the bad, and the indifferent.

## 25. Whether There Is an Art [*Technē*] of Living

238    From what has been said it is evident that there can be no such thing as an art of living. For if there is such an art, it involves the experience of things good, bad, and indifferent; consequently, since these do not exist, there is no art of living, either. Furthermore, since the Dogmatists do not all with one voice specify a particular art of living, but some postulate one art and others another, they land in controversy and in the argument about controversy that
239    I gave in our discussion concerning the good. Yet even if all of them should postulate one art of living—such as the celebrated "prudence" [*phronēsis*] dreamed of by the Stoics and seemingly more convincing that the rest—even so, no less absurdity will follow. For since prudence is a virtue, and only the wise possess virtue, the Stoics, who are not wise, will not possess the art of
240    living. And in general, since according to them it is impossible that there exist an art or skill at all, there will not exist any art of living if we go by what they have to say.

    Thus, for example, they say that an art is a system of apprehensions, and that an apprehension is an assent to an apprehensive *phantasia*. But the apprehensive *phantasia* cannot be made out. For not every *phantasia* is apprehensive, nor is it possible to determine which *phantasiai* are apprehensive, since we cannot decide simply by means of just any *phantasia* which *phantasia* is apprehensive and which is not, and if we need an apprehensive *phantasia* in order to determine which *phantasia* is apprehensive we fall into an infinite regress, always requiring another apprehensive *phantasia* in order to determine whether the *phantasia* taken to be apprehensive is indeed apprehensive. And 241 also in the following respects the Stoics do not reason correctly in their exposition of the concept of apprehensive *phantasia*, for when they say that an apprehensive *phantasia* is one that arises from what exists, and that the existent is what is such as to produce an apprehensive *phantasiai*, they fall into the circularity type of *aporia*. So if, in order for there to be an art of living, there must first be an art, and in order for there to be an art there must be an apprehension beforehand, and in order that there be apprehension it is necessary that assent to an apprehensive *phantasia* be apprehended, but the apprehensive *phantasia* cannot be made out, then the art of living cannot be made out, either.

Additionally, the following is argued. Every art seems to be apprehended 242 by means of its own special activity, but there is no activity special to the art of living; for whatever activity somebody might ascribe to it is found to be common to ordinary people as well — for example, honoring parents, returning deposits, and all the rest. Therefore, there exists no art of living. We shall not determine, just on the basis of something said or done by a prudent person, apparently from a prudent condition, that the art of living is "the activity of prudence," as some assert. For the prudent condition itself is not apprehensible, 243 being apparent neither from itself directly nor from its activities; for these latter are common to ordinary people as well. And the claim that by means of the consistency of his actions we apprehend the one who possesses the art of living is the claim of those who overestimate human nature and are wishful thinkers rather than truth-tellers.

> For the mood of mortal man
> Is like the day, which the father of gods and men brings on.
>
> *Odyssey* 18, 136–7

There remains the claim that the art of living is apprehended from those 244 activities that the Stoics describe in their books; as these are numerous and similar to one another, I shall set forth just a few as typical examples. Thus, for instance, Zeno, the leader of the sect, in his essays says various things about the treatment of children, and in particular the following: "Have carnal knowledge no more and no less of a favorite child than of a non-favorite, of a female than of a male; for the same things befit and are befitting to favorite and non-favorite, female and male." And as concerns piety to parents 245 the same man says, referring to the story of Jocasta and Oedipus, that there was nothing shocking about his rubbing his mother. "And if, when some part of her body was ailing, he had been helpful by rubbing it with his hands, that would not have been shameful; was it shameful, then, if by rubbing other parts he cheered her up and stopped her grief, and produced noble children by his mother?" With these comments Chrysippus, too, agrees. For instance, in his

*Politics* he says, "I approve of living in accord with what is, quite rightly, customary among many peoples these days, that is, that the mother has children by her son, the father by his daughter, and brothers by sisters of the
246 same mother." And in the same treatises he introduces cannibalism to us; he actually says "If from the living some part is cut off that is good for food, we should not bury it or get rid of it in some other way, but should eat it in order
247 that from our parts another part may be produced." And in his writings on propriety he says expressly, concerning the burial of parents, "When one's parents pass away, one should use the simplest burials, treating the body, like nails or teeth or hair, as being nothing to us, and we need bestow no care or attention on such a thing as that. Hence, also, if the flesh is good, people should use it for food, just as when one of their own parts, such as a foot, is cut off, it would be appropriate to use it and similar things; but if the flesh is not good, they should either bury it deep and leave it, or burn it up and abandon the ashes, or throw it away and have no concern for it, just as with nails and hair."
248      Most of the philosophers' statements are of such a sort, but they would not dare to put them into practice unless they lived under a government by the Cyclopes or Laestrygonians. And if they are in every way incapable of carrying out these ideas, and what they do do is common to ordinary people, there is no activity that is special to those who are supposed to possess the art of living. If, then, the arts do require to be apprehended through their special activities, and no activity is seen that is special to the so-called "art of living," this art is not apprehended. Consequently, nobody can firmly maintain that it exists.

## 26. Whether People Acquire the Art of Living

249 And if the art of living comes to be in people, either it comes to be in them by nature or by means of learning and teaching. But if by nature, then either the art of living arises in them insofar as they are human, or insofar as they are not human. But certainly not insofar as they are not human. And if insofar as they are human, *phronēsis* would belong to all human beings, so that all would be prudent and virtuous and wise. But the Stoics say that most people are bad.
250 Hence, the art of living would not belong to them insofar as they are human. Therefore, it does not belong to them by nature.
     Furthermore, since the Stoics claim than an art is a system of apprehensions that are exercised together, they imply that both the other arts and the one under discussion are to be acquired by some kind of experience and learning.

## 27. Whether the Art of Living Can Be Taught?

251 But it is not acquired by teaching or learning. For in order that these should exist, three things must first be agreed to exist, namely, the subject taught, the teacher and the learner, and the method of learning. But there is no such thing as any of these. Neither, therefore, is there any such thing as teaching.

## 28. Whether Anything Is Ever Taught

Now what is taught is either true or false; and if false, it could not be taught; 252
for they say that the false is the nonexistent, and the nonexistent could not be
an object of teaching. But neither would it be taught if it were claimed to be
true; for in our discussion of the criterion we pointed out that the true does
not exist. If, then, neither the false nor the true is taught, and aside from these
there is nothing that can be taught (for nobody will claim that while these
cannot be taught, he teaches things that are objects of *aporiai*), then nothing
can be taught. And the matter taught is either an appearance or is nonevident. 253
But if it is an appearance, it will not need to be taught. For appearances appear
to everybody alike. But if it is nonevident, then since nonevident things are also
not apprehensible because of the unresolved controversy about them, as we
have shown many times, it will not be capable of being taught. For how could
a person teach or learn something he does not apprehend? But if neither
appearances nor nonevident things are taught, nothing is taught.

Again, what is taught is either corporeal or incorporeal. But, according to 254
our argument of a moment ago, neither of these, whether it is an appearance
or a nonevident thing, can be taught. Therefore, nothing is taught.

Moreover, either an existent state of affairs is taught, or a nonexistent state 256
of affairs. But a nonexistent state of affairs is not taught, for if it was taught,
then, since teaching is considered to be of truths, a nonexistent state of affairs
will be true. And, being true, it will exist, for they say that the true is what
exists and is opposed to something. But it is absurd to say that a nonexistent
state of affairs exists; therefore, a nonexistent state of affairs is not taught. But 257
neither is an existent state of affairs. For if an existent state of affairs is taught,
either it is taught insofar as it is existent or insofar as it is something else. But
if it is to be taught insofar as it is existent, it will be one of the things that exist,
and because of this will not be a thing to be taught; for teaching should proceed
from certain things that are agreed upon and are not to be taught. Therefore,
an existent state of affairs, insofar as it is existent, is not a thing to be taught.
But neither is it a thing to be taught insofar as it is something else. For what 258
exists does not have any accident that does not exist, so that if what exists is
not taught insofar as it exists, it will not be taught insofar as it is something
else, for whatever is an accident of it exists. And besides, whether the existent
state of affairs that they will say is taught is an appearance or something
nonevident, since it is subject to the aforementioned *aporiai* it will not be a
thing to be taught. And if neither what exists nor what does not exist is taught,
then there is nothing that is taught.

## 29. Whether There Is Any Such Thing as a Teacher or Learner?

The foregoing takes care also of the teacher and the learner, although they are 259
no less objects of *aporiai* in their own right. For either the skilled [*technitēs*,
artist] teaches the skilled, or the unskilled the unskilled, or the unskilled the
skilled, or the skilled the unskilled. But the skilled does not teach the skilled,

for neither of them, insofar as he is skilled, needs learning. But neither does the unskilled teach the unskilled, just as the blind cannot lead the blind. Nor does
260 the unskilled teach the skilled, for that would be ridiculous. It remains to consider the possibility that the skilled teaches the unskilled. But this, too, cannot happen. For it is declared to be wholly impossible that there should even exist such a thing as a skilled person, since nobody is observed to be skilled by nature and right from birth, nor to become skilled from previously being unskilled. For either a single principle, that is, one apprehension, can
261 make the unskilled person skilled, or there is no way. But if one apprehension makes the unskilled person skilled, we can say, in the first place, that an art or skill is not a system of apprehensions; for the person who knows nothing at all would be termed skilled if only he had been taught a single principle of the art in question. And in the second place, even if somebody should say, of a person who has already mastered certain principles but is unskilled for lack of one more, that if he got that one he would change from unskilled to skilled by a
262 single apprehension, he will be making a capricious assertion. For it is not possible to point out any individual person who is still unskilled but will become skilled by the addition of one principle; nobody knows how to enumerate the principles of a skill so as to be able to say, by counting off the principles already known, how many are left to make up the total number of its principles. Accordingly, knowledge of one principle will not make the
263 unskilled person skilled. And if this is true, then, in view of the fact that nobody acquires all the principles of an art at once but only one by one, if at all (but let us grant that as an assumption), the person said to acquire the principles of the art one by one would not become skilled; for we recall that the knowledge of just one principle cannot make the unskilled skilled. Hence, nobody can become skilled from being unskilled. So that for these reasons there appears to be no such thing as a skilled person or artist. And because of that, no such thing as a teacher, either.
264      Nor is it possible for the alleged learner to learn and apprehend the principles of an art he does not possess. For just as he who is blind from birth would not, insofar as he is blind, have any perception of color, nor, likewise, he who is deaf from birth a perception of sound, so the unskilled person would not apprehend the principles of the art he does not possess. For if he did, he would be skilled and unskilled in the same things — unskilled, since that is what he is by hypothesis, and skilled, since he apprehends the principles of the
265 art. So that the skilled does not teach the unskilled. And if the skilled does not teach the unskilled, nor the unskilled the unskilled, nor the unskilled the skilled, nor the skilled the unskilled, and besides these there are no other possibilities, then there is no such thing as a teacher or a person who is taught.

## 30. Whether There Is Any Such Thing as a Method of Learning

And if there is no such thing as a teacher or learner, the "method of teaching"
266 disappears, too. It is equally subject to *aporiai* for the following reasons as well. A method of teaching will proceed either by appeal to obviousness or by

discourse. But it will not proceed either by appeal to obviousness or by discourse, as we shall show; therefore, the "method of learning" is not free of *aporiai*, either.

For teaching cannot occur by appeal to obviousness, since the obviousness is of things displayed. And what is displayed is apparent to everybody; and what is apparent, in that it is apparent, is grasped by everybody; and what is grasped by everybody in common is not a thing to be taught; therefore, nothing is taught by appeal to obviousness.

Nor is anything taught by discourse. For this discourse either signifies 267 something or it does not. But if it does not signify anything, it cannot serve to teach anything, either. And if it does signify something, either it signifies by nature or by convention. But it does not signify by nature, because not everybody understands everything he hears; for example, Greeks hearing barbarians and barbarians hearing Greeks. And if it signifies by convention, 268 clearly those who have apprehended in advance the objects with which the several words are associated will be aware of those objects, not by being taught by the words things of which they were ignorant, but by remembering and calling to mind things they already know; but those who need to learn things they do not know and who do not know with which objects the words are associated, will not grasp anything. Consequently there cannot be any such 269 thing as a method of learning. For the teacher needs to produce in the learner the apprehension of the principles of the art that is being taught, in order that thus the learner, apprehending the system of these, may become skilled. But there is no such thing as apprehension, as we have shown previously; therefore, there cannot be any such thing as a method of teaching. And if there is no such thing as a matter taught, nor a teacher nor a learner, nor a method of learning, there is no such thing as learning or teaching.

These, then, are the points typically raised concerning learning and 270 teaching. And one can be similarly aporetic about the so-called "art of living." Thus, for example, we have shown previously that there is no such thing as the matter taught, for example, in this case, prudence; and there is no such thing as a teacher or learner. For either the prudent person will teach the prudent person, or the imprudent will teach the imprudent, or the imprudent the prudent, or the prudent the imprudent; but none of these teaches the other; therefore, the so-called "art of living" is not taught. It is superfluous, I suppose, 271 to speak about the other cases; but if the prudent person teaches prudence to the imprudent, and prudence is the knowledge of things good, bad, and neither, then the imprudent person is ignorant of things good, bad, and neither, and, as he is ignorant of these, he will merely hear what is said when the prudent person is teaching him about these but he will not recognize them for what they are. For if he should grasp them while he is in the state of imprudence, then imprudence, too, will be capable of observing what things are good, bad, or neither. But, according to the Dogmatists, imprudence is certainly not a 272 state conducive to observing these things, since, if it were, the imprudent person would be prudent. Therefore, according to the definition of prudence, the person without it does not grasp the things said or done by the person with it. And not grasping, he would not be taught by him, especially since, as we have shown above, he cannot be taught either by appeal to obviousness or by discourse. But if one cannot come to possess the so-called "art of living" either by learning and teaching or by nature, that art so much vaunted by the philosophers cannot be discovered.

273     But even if, giving good measure, someone were to go ahead and grant that this dreamed up art of living is present in somebody, it will appear to be hurtful and the cause of disquietude, rather than beneficial, to those possessing it.


## 31. Whether the Art of Living Benefits Its Possessor

Thus, to take by way of example a few arguments out of many, it might seem that the art of living would benefit the possessor by providing him self control

274 in his impulses toward the good and away from the bad. The person who they say is a wise man with self control is said to have self control either insofar as he has no impulse toward the bad and away from the good, or insofar as he does have evil impulses toward and from, but masters them with reason.

275 But as regards making bad decisions he would not have self control, for he will not control what he does not possess. And just as one would not say that a eunuch has self-control with respect to sexual pleasures, nor that a person with a bad stomach has self control with respect to the enjoyment of food (since for such things they have no craving that they can combat by means of self-control), in the same way one ought not say that the wise man has self-control

276 if he has no natural *pathos* to restrain by his self-control. And if they are going to say that he has self-control insofar as he makes bad decisions but overcomes them with reason, then first of all they will be granting that prudence was of no benefit to him just when he was perturbed and in need of help, and secondly he turns out to be even more unfortunate than those who are called "wicked." For if he has an impulse toward something, he is certainly perturbed, and if he controls it with reason, he still has the bad in himself, and because of this he is more perturbed than the "wicked" person who no longer has this feeling; for

277 if the latter has an impulse, he is perturbed, but when he gets what he desires, the perturbation ceases.

        Thus, insofar as it is up to his prudence, the wise man does not acquire self-control, or if he does, he is the most unfortunate of all, so that the art of living has brought him no benefit but the greatest perturbation. And we have shown previously that the person who supposes that he possesses the art of living and that through it he can recognize which things are good by nature and which evil, is very much perturbed both when he has good things and

278 when evil. It must be said, then, that if the existence of things good, bad, and indifferent is not agreed upon, and perhaps the art of life, too, is nonexistent, and that even if it should provisionally be granted to exist, it will provide no benefit to those possessing it, but on the contrary will cause them very great perturbations, the Dogmatists would seem to be idly pretentious in what is termed the "ethics" part of their so-called "philosophy."

On the subject of ethics, too, we have now gone over as many points as is 279
appropriate in an outline, and here we terminate both the third book and the
whole work, *The Outlines of Pyrrhonism*, adding only the following.

## 32. Why the Skeptic Sometimes Purposely Puts Forward Arguments Weak in Persuasiveness

Because of his love of humanity the Skeptic wishes to cure by argument, so far 280
as he can, the conceit and precipitancy of the Dogmatists. Accordingly, just as
the doctors who treat physical symptoms have remedies that differ in strength,
and prescribe the severe ones for people with severe symptoms and milder ones
for those mildly affected, so too the Skeptic sets forth arguments differing in
strength. And in the case of those who are severely afflicted with precipitancy 281
he employs arguments that are weighty and capable of vigorously disposing of
the Dogmatists' symptom of conceit, but in the case of those who have this
symptom in a superficial and easily curable way, and are capable of being
restored to health by milder persuasion, he uses the milder arguments. Hence
the person motivated by Skepticism does not hesitate to advance at one time
arguments that are weighty in persuasiveness and at another time such as even
appear weak — he does this purposely, on the assumption that many times the
latter suffice for accomplishing his task.

# Commentary

# About the Translation

Except as otherwise noted, the translation follows the Greek text of H. Mutschmann and J. Mau, in *Sexti Empirici Opera*, vol. 1, (1958). Professor Mau's revision incorporates a number of emendations proposed in Heintz (1932) and Mates (1949b). The Mutschmann/Mau text is based on that of Bekker (1842). Bekker omitted both the tables of contents prefixed to the three books in the MSS. and also the corresponding chapter headings; Bury, in the translation cited below, kept the chapter headings but omitted the tables of contents as a superfluous duplication (although the correspondence between the two is not quite exact); Mutschmann/Mau keep both, and in this translation I have followed suit.

As of this writing, the only available English translation of the *Outlines* as a whole is that of Bury (1933–49), vol. 1, although one by Annas and Barnes is forthcoming. Portions are translated in Annas and Barnes (1985), in Long and Sedley (1987), in Hallie and Etheridge (1964), and, most recently, in Inwood and Gerson (1992). Hossenfelder (1968) contains an excellent German translation and a companion essay.

The Bury translation has its virtues, which I have come to appreciate all the more during my efforts to improve upon it. There are quite a few places, however, where it completely misses the sense. The most prominent of these are in the middle sections of Book 2, where Sextus refers to various principles of Stoic logic, and in the main they are due to a failure to respect the Stoic distinction between an argument (*logos*), which is defined as a system of propositions (*axiōmata*), and a conditional (*sunēmmenon*), which is a single proposition of "if–then" form. In section 137, for example, where Sextus states the Stoic principle that an argument is valid if the conditional whose antecedent is the conjunction of the premises and whose consequent is the conclusion is sound, Bury's translation becomes unintelligible.

But the main reason why I considered that I should produce a translation of my own is that the Bury version hides several of the philosophically most important features of Pyrrhonism, features that serve to distinguish it from post-Cartesian forms of skepticism and that render it immune to many of the "standard" responses to the latter. Thus, to mention a few examples, the reader of the Bury translation would never guess that Pyrrhonism does not, in the first instance at least, concern knowledge, or that doubt is not the characteristic attitude of the Pyrrhonist, or that the propositions from which he withholds assent are only such as purport to describe an external world, or that, far from believing in the existence of an external world, he is not even convinced that there is a concept corresponding to the term.

Another problem with the Bury translation is that some of the philosophically central terms are rendered in such a way as to make Pyrrhonism seem more like modern skepticism than it is. For instance, the word *pragma*, which for Sextus stands for whatever we purport to be talking about when we use language, is rendered simply as "object"; the reader would naturally take this to refer only to individual things, like the books, tables, and other "moderate-sized specimens of dry goods" which predominate in modern epistemologists' examples, whereas in fact the word is used by Sextus to denote also what some people call "states of affairs," expressed by full declarative sentences or "that" clauses. Hence, I have chosen to translate it as "object or state of affairs." There is a similar drawback to translating *phantasia* as "impression." In epistemological contexts, and against the background of Hume, one is likely at first to think of such "impressions" as the appearance of a sunset or the look of a bent stick, and not to think of the kind of impressions that Sextus has in mind, for instance, the impression that the bad fare well and the good fare ill, or the dog's alleged impression (when he is chasing an animal) that "if this is its footprint, then the animal went in that direction." Another example of the effect of "back pressure" from modern skepticism on the translator's choice of words is Bury's rendering the Greek verb *aporō* (which expresses the characteristic attitude of the Pyrrhonean skeptic) as "to doubt." But the verb *aporō* means "to be at a loss," and, for reasons that I have set forth in the Introduction, the difference is important.

There are also various philosophically important terms that Sextus uses almost technically but that Bury, doubtless in the interest of producing smooth prose, translates differently in different places. An example is the verb *diabebaiousthai*, which for Sextus means "to maintain firmly, over time and against objections," and which denotes which precisely what the Pyrrhonean skeptic characteristically does *not* do. Its frequent occurrences, which should not be hidden by using a variety of alternative translations, remind us that the Pyrrhonist assents only to propositions of the form

It seems to me now that *P*

and never to *P* itself if *P* is non-modal; he only reports a present *pathos* of his soul and maintains no firm thesis about the external world; he makes no suggestion that things will seem the same to him tomorrow, or that they do or should seem the same to other people at the present or any other time.

To all these complaints about Bury's translation it must be added that he was by no means the first to blur the distinctions I have been emphasizing. Thus even Henri Estienne's Latin translation, the publication of which in 1572 started Renaissance skepticism going in earnest, renders *aporō* as *dubito*, and the early English translation by Thomas Stanley (in vol. 4 of his *History of*

*Philosophy*, London, H. Mosely & T. Dring, 1669) represents it everywhere as "to doubt." The other crucial terms are treated with similar inexactitude.

I should also repeat my earlier remark that Bury's translation has its very considerable merits; time and again I have found his choice of word or phrase more appropriate than any alternative I could think of, and in such cases I have not hesitated to follow his lead. I wish also to acknowledge that I have profited (I think) from the Annas and Barnes, Long and Sedley, and Hossenfelder translations, and especially from various exegetical remarks in the writings of M. Frede and M. Burnyeat.

# Who Was Sextus Empiricus?

Alas, the answer to this question is that almost the only thing we know about him is that he is the author of the *Outlines of Pyrrhonism* and of *Against the Mathematicians*.

Most scholars have placed him late in the second century *A.D.* There is a brief mention of him at Diogenes Laertius 9.116:

> Antiochus of Laodicea...was the teacher of Menodotus of Nicomedia, an empiric physician, and of Theiodas of Laodicea; and Menodotus was the teacher of Herodotus of Tarsus, son of Arieus and Herodotus was the teacher of Sextus Empiricus, author of ten books on skepticism and other very fine works [κάλλιστα]. And Saturninus, who was also an empiric, was a student of Sextus.

But Diogenes's dates are no less uncertain than those of Sextus. House (1980), who thoroughly examines the whole matter, concludes (p. 281) that the evidence is such that one cannot do more than limit the possible dates of Sextus to between A.D. 100 and the first part of the third century.

Sextus was apparently a physician. But whether he was correctly called "Empiricus" is open to question. At PH 1.236–41 he argues that the Methodic school of medicine was closer to the Skeptic Way than the Empiric school was; and throughout the *Outlines* and *Against the Mathematicians* he speaks of the Skeptics as "we." Also at M 8.327–8 he appears to distinguish himself from the Empirics, though M 8.191 leans the other way. According to House (1980, p. 237), "the only conclusion which one can come to from all this is that if Sextus belonged to the Empirical sect he did so contrary to his position as a Pyrrhonean." For a less skeptical conclusion, see Frede (1987, p. 252). See also my note on PH 1.236–41 below.

It is also not known where Sextus lived and worked. Rome, Athens, Alexandria, and "some unknown city in the East" have all been conjectured, each on equally flimsy evidence.

As House points out, the multifarious conjectures about Sextus's life are harmless enough until by repetition they gradually become treated as fact and in turn are taken to throw light on the philosophical content of Sextus's thought.

# Outlines of Pyrrhonism, Book 1

### Sections 1–4. The Main Difference Between the Philosophies

If Sextus himself is a typical Pyrrhonist, it appears that the principal way in which Pyrrhonists "search for the truth" is to raise questions about assertions purporting to be true. So the verb ζητέω, translated in the present chapter as "to search," is usually better rendered as "to question." Other translators use "to investigate" (defined by Webster as "to observe or study by close examination and systematic inquiry"), but that does not seem to fit the typical activity of the Pyrrhonist.

As noted in the Introduction, I attach great importance to the caveat at the end of section 4, with its use of διαβεβαιούμεθα, τὸ νῦν φαινόμενον ἡμῖν, and ἀπαγγέλλομεν, all of them quasi-technical terms that Sextus generally employs when he describes what the Pyrrhonist characteristically does or does not do. It has seemed to at least one reader that if the caveat is taken as seriously as I suggest, the Pyrrhonist is precluded from describing Pyrrhonism, and, indeed, from saying or describing anything at all. But I think that here we must guard against building into our semantic theory an assumption that there must be elements of an external world to serve as denotations of our linguistic expressions, and thus against begging one of the very questions the Pyrrhonist raises. The verbs "to say" and "to describe," as I hear them, are not loaded with any presupposition that the utterance in question must be intended as referring to some sort of external reality, the existence and attributes of which are independent of the soul and its πάθη. And thus, so far as I can see, there is no barrier to using language successfully while intending all one's utterances to be nothing more than expressions of what seems to one at the moment to be the case. Indeed, for all we know, some of the people (especially philosophers) with whom we converse may actually be doing this.

Observe that although the common man is not included in the list of examples of Dogmatists "properly so called," he, like the Dogmatists, suffers from the beliefs that the Skeptic is challenging (PH 1.30, 3.180; cf. M 11.44). Therefore, we cannot interpret the Skeptic's message (insofar as he has a message) as directed to or against philosophers alone.

Regarding ἴσως ("I think"), see p. 10.

224

Photius (a ninth-century patriarch of Constantinople) points out the essential difference between Pyrrhonism and Academic skepticism:

> I read Aenesidemus' eight *Pyrrhonist Discourses.* The overall aim of the book is to establish that there is no firm basis for apprehension, either through sense perception or indeed through thought. ... The followers of Pyrrho, in determining nothing, remain absolutely above reproach, whereas the Academics, he [Aenesidemus] says, incur a scrutiny similar to that faced by the other philosophers. Above all, the Pyrrhonists, by being at a loss about everything, maintain consistency and do not conflict with themselves, whereas the Academics are unaware that they are conflicting with themselves. For to make unambiguous assertions and denials, at the same time as stating, as a generalization, that nothing is apprehensible, introduces an undeniable conflict: how is it possible to recognize that this is true, this false, yet still be at a loss and in doubt, and not be clearly choosing the one and rejecting the other? (*Bibl.* 170, as translated by Long; and Sedley (1987), pp. 468–9, but with a few terminological changes)

### 5–6. The Accounts of Skepticism

With these sections cf. M 7.1.

Skepticism is treated by Sextus as "a philosophy," competing with other philosophies such as Stoicism and Epicureanism. However, in the apparently deprecatory phrase ἡ καλουμένη φιλοσοφία ("what is called 'philosophy'" or "so-called 'philosophy'"), which appears here and in many other places in the text, φιλοσοφία is used in a somewhat different sense; we are told, for example, that what is called philosophy is supposed by some to consist of three parts: logic, physics, and ethics. In this sense, philosophy is something of which the Skeptic plainly disapproves.

"Withholding of assent" is a better translation than "suspension of judgment" for ἐποχή, because there is no suggestion in ἐποχή that eventually a decision or judgment will be made. See the definition of ἐποχή in section 10 and that of the corresponding verb ἐπέχω in section 196. That what is "withheld" is assent, is shown by M 7.157, where ἐπέχειν is said to be equivalent to ἀσυγκαταθετεῖν.

The "specific account" referred to in section 5 is the content of Books 2 and 3.

### 7. The Nomenclature of the Skeptic Way

Pyrrhonean skepticism is not a doctrine but an ἀγωγή ("way," "method," "mode of life"). The word comes from the verb ἄγω ("to lead"), and its core meaning, which probably infects all of its various senses, is "a leading." Annas and Barnes suggest "lifestyle" (cf. 1.145). But this does not seem to me to be quite right, because, as Sextus explains in several places, the Skeptic's overt behavior will on the whole resemble that of the common man; it is largely in the domain of thought that he will be different. Hence I have chosen the relatively noncommittal word "way."

The Skeptic is said to be at a loss as to whether or not to assent (συγκατατίθημι) to assertions purporting to do more than express a *pathos* of the speaker's soul. The verb is another quasi-technical term for Sextus. Frede (1984) has carefully studied its use in this connection; see 13 below. Cf. also Diogenes Laertius, 9.69–70.

Janacek (1992, pp. 28–9) thinks that the explanation of "Ephectic" in this section implies that the Skeptic does not, after all, "continue to search" as is stated in sections 2 and 3, and that he stops searching when he reaches *epoche*. But sections 2, 3, and 7 are consistent if the phrase μετὰ τὴν ζήτησιν in 7 means in effect "after some searching"; certainly some searching is required to bring the Skeptic into a state of *aporia* and from there to *epoche*, but there seems to be no reason why, just because he is withholding assent, he must close his mind to all further consideration of the matter in question.

As regards "aporetic": see section 6 of the Introduction.

## 8–10. What Skepticism Is

The Skeptic Way is a δύναμις. Here δύναμις seems to mean more than what is meant by such terms as "capacity," "ability," "power," "faculty," and "potentiality," by which it is usually translated in Greek philosophical discourse. Clearly, the point is not just that the Skeptic *could* note the various oppositions if he chose, but, as the rest of Sextus's account shows, that he *does* note them, and it is this practice, rather than the bare ability to do it, that constitutes the ἀγωγή.

It seems that in these sections Sextus is quoting traditional formulations and considering what they might mean. At any rate, it is clear that here and in section 31 he is using τὸ φαινόμενον (which I have translated as "appearance" almost everywhere else) in a restricted sense, in which τὰ φαινόμενα are the (presumably direct) objects of sensory perception, to be contrasted with τὰ νούμενα, thoughts or thought objects. To preserve the contrast I have rendered φαινόμενον and νούμενον simply as "phenomenon" and "noumenon." But in general τὰ φαινόμενα include everything that appears to one to be the case, including what are here called τὰ νούμενα. I suspect that, lurking in the background, there is a basic confusion as to whether φαινόμενα and νούμενα are to be taken as propositions (as indicated in section 12) or as corresponding states of affairs in the external world.

## 11. The Skeptic

The Pyrrhonist is again included among philosophers. Perhaps we should not make too much of this, but prima facie it seems to be a bit of further evidence against interpreting Pyrrhonism as a defense of common sense, that is, the views of the common man, against all forms of philosophy.

## 12. The Origins of Skepticism

The ἀρχαί are obviously origins or sources, not principles (in the modern sense of the latter term). Cf. the note on PH 3.1 below.

It seems a bit odd that the Pyrrhonists (or the Pyrrhonists and the Dogmatists, if that is what is meant) are described as οἱ μεγαλοφυεῖς τῶν ἀνθρώπων ("the better-quality people", *die bessere Leute*—which I have watered down to "talented"), and I have not found a good explanation of this.

I am using "the facts" (in quotes) for τὰ πράγματα here, for want of a better alternative. The term is very general, denoting loosely anything whatever that we talk about or are concerned about. Often "thing" is the best translation, but "to assent to things" sounds odd to me (though "to assent to something" seems all right). The addition of quotes to "the facts" is meant to signal that some of these so-called "facts" may be false, that is, may not exist.

## 13–15. Does the Skeptic Dogmatize?

Regarding "dogma," see section 11 of the Introduction. Frede (1984) tries to explain how the Skeptic can assent to a *pathos* "in accord with" a *phantasia* that P without assenting to the claim that (or having the thought that) P is true. He says, "It might be the case that action does not, in addition to the impression [*phantasia*] that P, require a positive act of assent or the further thought that P" (p. 208). But it seems to me that the explanation is simply that the predicate "true" is restricted to propositions about the external world, as Burnyeat and others have pointed out (see section 9 of the Introduction).

Section 13 is discussed at length in Frede (1987), especially as concerns the verb εὐδοκεῖν and the phrase οἷον οὐκ ἂν εἴποι θερμαινόμενος ἢ ψυχόμενος ὅτι δοκῶ μὴ θερμαίνεσθαι ἢ ψύχεσθαι. In my opinion, Frede is right in taking εὐδοκεῖν to mean a weak form of assent—"to be content with," "to raise no objection to"—but I do not understand his puzzlement about the phrase, which only serves to assure us that in reporting his *pathē* the Skeptic will not lie. If he feels warm, he will not report "It seems to me that I am not warm," etc. (Here, I think, δοκῶ = δοκῶ μοι = δοκεῖ μοι). Thus, if it seems to the Skeptic that the honey is sweet, and you ask him, "Does it seem to you that the honey is sweet?" he will say "Yes," or at least will not say "No"; whereas if you ask him "Is the honey sweet?" he will not give a "yes" or "no" answer, for he is at a loss.

"Slogans." The Greek is φωναί ("sounds"), and Sextus's choice of this word for the Skeptic formulae may be significant. See the note on 1.187 below.

14. Note that the slogans are described as concerned with the ἄδηλα, the "non-evident" components of the external world.

15. In putting forward his slogans, the Skeptic is saying what appears to him (τὸ ἑαυτῷ φαινόμενον) and is reporting (ἀπαγγέλλει) his *pathos* without belief (ἀδοξάστως), not firmly maintaining anything (μηδὲν διαβεβαιούμενος) about the external objects (περὶ τῶν ἔξωθεν ὑποκειμένων). All this terminology

is quasi-technical for Sextus in his description of Pyrrhonism. Cf. Janacek (1972, p. 61). On "external objects", see section 4 of the Introduction.

## 16–17. Does the Skeptic Have a System?

The word αἵρεσις often means "sect," but we see from the context that here it must be translated in some other way, perhaps as "system" or "line." Cf. 1.34, where it seems to mean "system," as also at 1.145, 185, 212, 236, 237, 241; 2.6; 3.218; M 7.27. Bury uses "doctrinal rule."

Note that a "dogma" is defined as an "assent to something nonevident"; "the nonevident" is another description of the external world. Cf. 13 above, and the last paragraph of section 11 of the Introduction.

17. The Skeptic ἀγωγή follows a certain λόγος. Some commentators have inferred from this that the Skeptic *believes* the λόγος. But what is meant, I think, is only that the Skeptic's way of life is not haphazard or erratic but follows a pattern, which is described in sections 23–4. The Skeptic is not maintaining that we ought to join him in following this ἀγωγή if we want to be happy; he is only reporting, "like a chronicler," what seems to him now to be the case.

"A more ordinary sense" (ἀφαλέστερον): Ἀφαλής, as regards language, means "simple," "not intricate or involved"; and I think that the point is that "rightly" is not to be understood here as a term of philosophical art, but in an ordinary sense in which it implies, not righteousness, but only conformity to the relevant laws and customs.

## 19–20. Do the Skeptics Deny the Appearances?

This passage, though difficult in certain respects, is very important. Its general tenor is clear enough, but there is a question as to the sense of the clause ὅσον ἐπὶ τῷ λόγῳ, which I have translated as "insofar as this has to do with the [philosophic] theory." Sextus makes very frequent use of phrases of this rather unusual form (i.e., ὅσον ἐπὶ followed by a dative). They occur, for example, at PH 1.20, 93, 215, 229, 235; 2.22, 26, 80, 104, 166; 3.13, 29, 48, 65, 81, 135–6, 167, 186, 241; M 7.87, 283; 8.3; 9.49; 10.49; 11.165. In general they seem to mean "insofar as concerns...," "insofar as relates to...," "insofar as it is a matter of ...," "if we go by... ." They are thoroughly and instructively discussed in chapter 2 of Janacek (1972).

In the present instance there is the problem of determining to what τῷ λόγῳ refers. Bury renders it as "essence"; others have suggested "reason." But the relative clause, ὃ οὐκ ἔστι τὸ φαινόμενον ἀλλὰ περὶ τοῦ φαινομένου λεγόμενον ("which is not the appearance but something said about the appearance"), shows that, as would be expected, the λόγος is some portion of discourse—"something said."

In his note on the passage, Estienne (Stephanus) proposes that the λόγος is the statement "the honey is sweet." That proposal has at least the merit of making sense of the passage, but I think that a much more likely hypothesis is that the λόγος in question is what Sextus elsewhere (e.g., at M 7.112) calls ὅ φιλόσοφος λόγος ("the philosophic theory" or "the philosophic account"). Janacek (1972, 14 ff.), cites a number of passages supporting this interpretation. The "theory" or "account," as I have suggested in the Introduction (p. 13), would include the claim, common to most of the Dogmatists, that in making a statement like "The honey is sweet" we are saying that there is an external object, the honey, which has the attribute of sweetness and which is causing us to experience the *phantasia* in accord with which we make the statement. Perhaps neither "theory" nor "account" is the best translation; other possibilities are "story," "explanation," "doctrine."

Passages that are relevant to the question of how the ὅσον ἐπὶ τῷ λόγῳ phrase should be understood include the following: 3.65: ὅσον μὲν γὰρ ἐπὶ τοῖς φαινομένοις δοκεῖν εἶναι κίνησιν, ὅσον δὲ ἐπὶ τῷ φιλοσόφῳ λόγῳ μὴ ὑπάρχειν ("for if we go by the appearances motion seems to exist, but if we go by the philosophic account it seems not to exist"). This is repeated almost verbatim at M 10.49. M 11.165: ταῦτα δὴ λέγοντες οὐ συνιᾶσιν ὅτι κατὰ μὲν τὸν φιλόσοφον λόγον οὐ βιοῖ ὁ σκεπτικός (ἀνενέργητος γάρ ἐστιν ὅσον ἐπὶ τούτῳ) ("In saying these things they do not understand that the Skeptic does not conduct his life according to the philosophic theory (for insofar as this is concerned he is inactive). 1.215: εἶτα ἡμεῖς μὲν ἐπέχομεν ὅσον ἐπὶ τῷ λόγῳ περὶ τῶν ἐκτὸς ὑποκειμένων... ("Further, we suspend judgment as regards the [philosophic] theory about the external objects . . ."). These passages, together with those at 2.22, 26, 104 and several others, clearly imply that Janacek (1972) is right in considering the philosophic theory to be τὰ λεγόμενα ὑπὸ τῶν δογματικῶν. Similarly, at M 7.283 we have, "If we go by the conceptions [ἐννοίαις] of the Dogmatists," and at M 8.3, "if we go by the λόγοι of the Dogmatists." At M 9.49 we are told that "The Skeptic, I suppose, will be found in a safer position as compared with other philosophers, since in conformity with the laws and customs of his country he says that gods exist and he does everything that contributes to their worship and veneration, but, when it is a matter of philosophic investigation [ὅσον ἐπὶ τῇ φιλοσόφῳ ζητήσει] he makes no rash judgments."

All of this makes it likely, I think, that in the present passage as well as in 1.215 and 229, τῷ λόγῳ is in effect short for τῷ φιλοσόφῳ λόγῳ, as the latter appears at 3.65, M 10.49, and M 11.165, and that the reference is to the Dogmatists' doctrine about how knowledge of the external world is acquired.

There remains the further question of what Sextus could mean by saying, at the end of section 20, that "the philosophic theory [ὁ λόγος] is so deceptive as to all but snatch away the appearances from under our very eyes." My guess is the following. Most of us, I suppose, would agree with the portion of "the philosophic theory" that treats ordinary discourse as being about the external world, for the most part, and not about appearances. After all, what the conventions of language encourage us to say, when it appears to us that the honey is sweet, is not "It appears to me that the honey is sweet," but rather the categorical sentence, "The honey *is* sweet." If we are reminded of the distinction between appearance and reality, we may acknowledge that what we are directly aware of is only the appearance, but the philosophic theory reassures us that appearances are transparent, as it were, and we can look right through them at the real world that causes them. Thus, like the person who does not keep in mind that his visual perception is affected by the glasses he is wearing, and who forgets that he *is* wearing his glasses, we, misled by the philosophic story about appearance and reality, forget about the appearances and imagine ourselves to be dealing directly with reality.

At any rate, it is clear that categorical assertions like "the honey is sweet," when they are put forward as descriptions of things in the external world, are what Sextus questions. This is apparent at M 7.365f. There he offers some argumentation to show that the Dogmatists' views are incoherent. He expects them to agree that:

> When honey is presented and I sense the sweetness, I conjecture [στοχάζομαι]
> that the externally existing honey is sweet, and when fire is brought close and
> I feel warm, I take my condition as a sign that the external object is warm,
> and the same applies to the other cases.

Then he adds, again presumably with the expectation that the Dogmatists will agree, that of course it is possible for the fire to warm without being itself warm, and for the honey to produce the sensation of sweetness without itself being sweet. From these premises he draws the conclusion, with which the Dogmatists will certainly *not* agree, that it is impossible in general to get knowledge of external objects through our sensory experience. However, he himself is not assenting to either the premises or the conclusion of this "argument"; rather, as I read him, he is at a loss as to how much, if any, of the Dogmatists' story about our way of establishing such propositions as "The honey is sweet" is acceptable. But his discussion shows that he will question any categorical assertion that is offered as more than a report of the state of the speaker's soul and thus is supposed to be a description of an independently existing real world.

20. The phrase ἐρωτῶμεν λόγους has bothered translators (see Stephanus's note to this passage in Fabricius [1718]), since the usual meaning of ἐρωτάω is to "question." Here the phrase means to propound arguments (in dialectical form). See my note on 2.231 below.

The προπέτεια ("rashness," "precipitancy," "impetuousness") of the Dogmatists, which is mentioned time and again in the *Outlines* (e.g., at 1.177, 186, 205, 212, 235, 237; 2.21, 94; 3.2, 235, 280) is their tendency to jump to a conclusion about the way things really are (e.g., "Motion does not really exist") without giving due attention to the arguments on the other side—arguments that, according to the Skeptics, seem always to be available.

## 21–24. The Criterion of the Skeptic Way

21. Note that the first kind of criterion, later to be called "the criterion of truth" (2.14f.), has to do with belief in existence or nonexistence, that is, with belief about the external world.

22. Line 28. I am following Fabricius, Bekker, and Bury in reading αὐτοῦ ("here"), because I do not know of any other text in which *phantasiai* are explicitly identified with appearances, even "in effect." At the same time, I have to confess that, not really understanding either of the terms *phantasia* or "appearance" as these are used by Sextus and/or the Dogmatists, I am in no position to decide whether these terms denote the same things. Sextus often attacks *phantasiai* (PH 2.70: "the first thing to say on this topic is that it is impossible to form a concept of *phantasia*"); by contrast, he never says anything negative about appearances. But clearly his attacks are directed against *phantasiai as these are described by the Dogmatists*. At PH 1.19 the Skeptic himself is said to be "led by appearances to assent in accord with a passively received *phantasia*," and at 2.10 we are told that the Skeptic "assents to whatever things affect him in accord with a passively received *phantasia*, insofar as that *phantasia* appears to him." Clearly, some or all *phantasiai* are closely associated with appearances, but the exact relationship is unclear.

"In feeling [πεῖσις] and involuntary *pathos*": the "and" may be explicative.

The last sentence in section 22 may throw light on the meaning of ἀζήτητος as used by Sextus. Perhaps statements of the form "It seems to me now that *P*" are ἀζήτητος in that they are taken for granted in disputes. Thus perhaps it is not that they cannot be questioned, but only that they are in fact not questioned. Much of Sextus's argumentation is framed in what might be called the debate mode: "If they say…, then we shall say…, but…" and "If we grant for the sake of argument that…, then…," and so on.

On the question of whether we can make other than language mistakes when we honestly report what appears to us, cf. Ayer (1956, pp. 53ff.) regarding "basic statements."

23–4. How the Skeptic lives. Sextus echoes this passage at 1.226, 237–8, 2.246, 254, 3.235; cf. M 11.165. In most cases he emphasizes that the Skeptic follows the ordinary regimen of life (ἡ βιωτικὴ τήρησις), free of belief (ἀδοξάστως).

The four items are described at 1.237 as four "parts" or "aspects" of the everyday life in which the Skeptic shares. So the first item seems to be that the Skeptic, like everybody else, naturally experiences a sequence of sensations and thoughts. The meaning of the other three items is more clear.

## 25–30. What Is the Goal of Skepticism?

This is supposed to explain, at least in part, what is bad about having beliefs. Note the limitation, frequently repeated elsewhere, of ἀταραξία to "matters of belief," that is, to questions and assertions about how things stand in the external world.

27–8. Cf. M 11.127ff. and section 15 of the Introduction. Apelles is supposed to have been a court painter to Alexander the Great. Note that the painter got results when he gave up trying; but the Skeptic is supposed to "continue to seek." How can he have peace of mind when he is continuing, presumably without success, to seek for the truth? The answer has to be, I suppose, that this "seeking" consists only in raising questions about assertions purporting to be true. Cf. the note on PH 1.4 above.

With 25–6 cf. 3.235–7; with 27–8 cf. M 11.116–7, 127ff., 146, and section 15 of the Introduction.

30. According to Diogenes Laertius, 9.107, the "notable Skeptics" would include Timon and Aenesidemus.

## 31–5. The General Modes of *Epochē*

The phenomenon that the tower is square is opposed to the phenomenon that it is round. The phenomenon that snow is white is opposed to the noumenon that snow is frozen water and water is dark in color, so that snow is dark in color. And the noumenon that since the heavenly bodies move in orderly paths, divine providence exists, is opposed to the noumenon that since the good fare ill and the bad fare well, divine providence does not exist.

Thus, here, as in sections 8–10 above, $\phi\alpha\iota\nu\acute{o}\mu\epsilon\nu o\nu$ is contrasted with $\nu o\acute{u}\mu\epsilon\nu o\nu$ and hence cannot have the broad sense it usually has for Sextus.

31. "Everything" must mean everything that purports to describe the external world and is not merely an expression of the speaker's *pathē*. For the Skeptic does not withhold assent from the appearances.

32. Note that he says "the *same* tower..."; at 1.101 and 118 this is repeated, and we have also "the same water...," "the same boat...," "the same honey...," "the same Stoa...," and "the same things...." And the conclusions to several of the Modes are framed in like manner; for example, that of the first Mode (59) is:

> But if the same things do appear differently because of the difference of animals, then we shall be in a position to say how the external object looks to us, but we shall withhold assent as to how it is in nature.

All of this has led Burnyeat (1982) understandably to conclude that the Pyrrhonist is a kind of frustrated realist. He says, "It is one and the same external thing, honey or the tower, which appears thus and so and which has a real nature that the Skeptic is unable to determine."

This point, if valid, would be strong evidence for the view, held by Annas and Barnes as well as by Burnyeat, that the Pyrrhonist accepts the existence of an external world. And it would be valid, I think, if Sextus's usage were sharp enough to preserve a distinction between, for instance,

> It appears to me that the tower is round

and

> The tower appears to me to be round,

where "the tower" might be considered as occurring obliquely in the first sentence and directly in the second. But it seems to me that Sextus uses these forms interchangeably and that the sense of both of them is determined by the fact that the Pyrrhonist intends all his "seems that" and "appears that" statements to be mere reports of his own *pathē*, and to imply nothing about the existence or nature of an external world. In my opinion, therefore, the occurrences of "the tower" in both of the above sentences are oblique and hence are not subject to existential generalization. For more on this point see Mates (1992b, p. 223).

Still, in that case what sense can be made of Sextus's use here of the word "same," when the possibility is left open that there is nothing that is literally the same? Here we must keep in mind that it is the Dogmatist, not Sextus, who asserts all these propositions about "the same thing." It is not Sextus's problem, but the Dogmatist's, to explain how the relevant *phantasiai* must be related, whether by similarity or other more complicated relations, if, when from afar it appears to him that the tower is round and from close up it appears to him that the tower is square, he is to be justified in saying that it is the *same* thing that appears round at one time and square at another.

33. I agree with Mau that Mutschmann's addition of κατασκευάζοντι in line 4 is unnecessary.

34. It is obvious, I trust, that the argument in this section is just a dialectical ploy by Sextus and that he is not agreeing that the argument supporting the Dogmatist's system really was sound.


## 36–163 The Ten Modes

The Modes or Tropes are sets of considerations from which *epochē seems* to result. Though they are also called *logoi*, they are clearly not arguments in any relatively strict sense of that term. Sextus gives groups of ten, five, and two Modes, together with some Modes "for refuting people who give causal explanations." Of these, the ten have been by far the most influential; they are generally ascribed to Aenesidemus (see M 7.345), a first-century B.C. philosopher who was originally an Academic but later rejected the Academy as too dogmatic. Several ancient accounts of the ten are preserved; that of Sextus is the most lucid and complete.

This is the place to recommend, once and for all, the excellent exposition and commentary by Annas and Barnes on the Modes of *Epochē*. It is filled with

interesting and useful information about the sources; it includes exemplary
translations of the relevant passages in Sextus, Diogenes Laertius, and Philo;
and, more important from my point of view, it subjects the argumentation to
a philosophical critique. I shall not try to equal it in these notes; indeed, I could
not do so if I tried. The few places where my interpretation differs significantly
from theirs will be indicated.

## 40–78. The First Mode

Different animals get different *phantasiai* from the same objects. The "conclusion," at section 59, seems to be: there is no more reason to suppose that
the external world is the way it appears to us (i.e., is in accord with our
*phantasiai*) than that it is the way it appears to other animals; and there are
plenty of indications that their *phantasiai* are quite different from ours.
Awareness of this puts us in a state of *aporia*; we are at a loss as to whose
*phantasiai*, if any, should be trusted to give us information about the external
world. Thus, we withhold assent from claims like "The honey is sweet," if these
are taken as more than the speaker's report of his own *pathē*. The evidence
cited for the thesis that the various animals receive different *phantasiai* from the
same things is that their bodies differ in structure and that from our own case
it appears that such structural differences give rise to different *phantasiai*. But
none of this is asserted by Sextus as his own view.

41. Of all the conjectures for filling the lacuna, I like Kochalsky's ὡς ἔντερα
γῆς ("earthworms").

48–9. Although several of the assertions seem to be in error, the point is
clear enough: the quality of the visual field experienced by an animal depends
upon the shape of the eye and its various parts; so that if the shape of *A*'s eye
is unlike that of *B*'s eye, *A*'s visual field may be expected to be qualitatively
unlike that of *B*.

60–2. What is non-rational about the so-called "non-rational" (ἄλογοι)
animals is that they do not have language or speech, internal or external. (Thus
Bury's translation of ἄλογος as "irrational" is perhaps misleading). Hence they
cannot carry on that "discourse of the soul with itself" that we call "thinking,"
and, what is most relevant in the present connection, they are in no position
to "apprehend" things, that is, to recognize them as being what they are.

In Sextus's ironic discussion (63f.) of the dog and other animals, note the
emphasis on the claim that they can and do talk, after all. To be sure, we do
not understand what they are saying, but then we do not understand certain
other human beings, the barbarians, either. Thus, Sextus is saying to the
Dogmatists, don't be so sure that these lower animals lack λόγος.

63–4. The eulogy of the dog. (The dog story is found in other sources, e.g.,
in Philo of Alexandria, *On Animals*, 45–6.) Cf. Plato's *Theaetetus* 154A:
"Would you maintain that each color appears to a dog, or any other animal
you please, just as it does to you? No, by Zeus, I wouldn't."

65–7. "Reason" (ὁ λόγος), as here spoken of, is not so much a capacity to form deductive or inductive arguments, with premises and conclusion, as a capacity to think, to carry on internal and external discourse.

68. Note that an "apprehensive *phantasia*" is supposed to be the sort of thing that can be retained over time.

69. διὰ πλειόνων in line eleven means "by multiple applications." According to Chrysippus, the dog reasons according to the schema:

> *P* or *Q* or *R*
> Not *P*
> Not *Q*
> Therefore, *R*.

The fifth undemonstrated argument schema (see 2.158) is:

> *P* or *Q*
> Not *P*
> Therefore, *Q*.

Thus it is obvious that the dog's schema can be derived, as Chrysippus claimed, by repeated application of the fifth schema:

> *P* or *Q* or *R*
> Not *P*
> Therefore, *Q* or *R*
> Not *Q*
> Therefore, *R*.

We may wonder whether Sextus is telling us that it does seem to him that different animals get different *phantasiai* from the same objects, or whether he is only borrowing this hypothesis from the Dogmatists in order to show them that on their own views there is no basis for asserting that such and such really is the case. Annas and Barnes say (p. 41) "In general, the items of information and misinformation with which each of the ten Modes is illustrated are all pillaged from the writings of the Dogmatists," and they give some details to support this (e.g., some of the examples of spontaneous generation Sextus lists in 41 can be found in Aristotle's *History of Animals*). Except for the general statement at the end of section 4 of the *Outlines*, there are few, if any, places in Sextus's writings where he explicitly tells us what seems to *him* to be the case; and at all events it is clear that his main purpose is not to report how things, for example, the half-immersed oar or the pigeon's neck, look to *him*, but to exhibit incoherence in the Dogmatists' story.

69. Line 8. I agree with Annas and Barnes that the received text, with πολεμοῦντα, makes good sense, and thus that the various proposed emendations, including Mutschmann's συμπολεμοῦντα, are unnecessary.

Other statements of the first Mode may be found at Diogenes Laertius 9.79–80 and Philo of Alexandria, *On Drunkenness*, 171–5.

## 79–90. The Second Mode

Here the argument is as follows. Suppose that, contrary to the considerations put forward in the first Mode, we have somehow established that the *phantasiai* of human beings are more to be trusted than those of the non-rational animals when it comes to giving an accurate picture of the external world. Even under that supposition we are led to *aporiai* and *epochē*. For human beings are said to consist of body and soul; but we find that people differ greatly in their physical attributes, and consequently, as the body is a kind of image of the soul, it is likely that they will also differ among themselves as regards the soul. An even stronger indication of such psychological differences is the fact, recognized by the Dogmatists and often pointed out by the poets, that the very things that some people regard as pleasant and choiceworthy are regarded by others as painful and to be avoided. The conclusion, says Sextus, is that these people are not affected alike by the same things.

Thus, when it is granted that different persons will probably receive different *phantasiai* from the same things, we are left with the question: Whose *phantasiai* shall we trust? The suggestion that we go by the views of the majority is impracticable and silly, and any Dogmatist who proposes to give preference to his own *phantasiai* is begging the question (since he is in effect reporting his *phantasia* that preference should be given to his *phantasiai*). In sum, even if we, as human beings, are self-centered enough to suppose that the *phantasiai* of human beings are more trustworthy than those of the other animals, we are left with essentially the same *aporia* as appeared in the first Mode, for human beings differ in their *phantasiai* and there appears to be no more reason to trust the *phantasiai* of one person than to trust those of another. The Skeptic therefore withholds assent when, on the basis of their *phantasiai*, people make statements about the external world.

It is perhaps worth noting that we are already on the slippery slope when we accept the conceptual framework behind the provisional supposition that the *phantasiai* of human beings picture the external world more accurately than do those of the other animals. We are saying that when the apple looks red to us but gray to the dog and the crocodile, so much the worse for the dog and the crocodile: for the apple really *is* red, the way it looks to *us*, no matter how it may look to those handicapped animals. If they see only various shades of gray where we see colors, that may be an interesting fact of zoology, but it does not require a revision of our picture of what the external world is really like. We want to say that the apple *is* red, but it *looks* gray to them.

Once again, it is reasonably clear that Sextus is not subscribing to any part of this "argument" but is only exploring the interconnections of views apparently espoused by the Dogmatists. The "data" he cites are expressly taken from the Dogmatists; note the "they say" in section 80 and the parenthetical remark in the first sentence of section 85. Later Sextus makes another point with which he plainly expects the Dogmatists to agree, namely, that nobody, man or beast, can compare his *phantasiai* with the external objects and states of affairs to see if there is a good fit; we can only compare our various *phantasiai* with one another. Thus even the hypothesis that human beings and animals (or different human beings) have different *phantasiai* from the same external things cannot be checked and may not even make sense.

When Sextus, considering the suggestion that if there is disagreement we should adopt the view of the majority, instead of observing that the majority is often wrong makes the surprisingly weak reply that we cannot determine what the majority thinks because we cannot interview the whole human race, Annas and Barnes (p. 65) come to his defense: "Sextus, however, was writing seventeen hundred years ago, when the notions of statistical sampling and of probability had not been elaborated" and "Anybody in Sextus' time who ventured the opinion that a majority of mankind were subject to such-and-such experiences would have been making an unwarrantably rash judgment." But is Sextus not, once again, simply bringing up a consideration with which he could expect the Dogmatist to agree? He surely is not himself conceding that if only you could interview the whole human race, you could find out what was pleasing to the majority (cf. M 7.196–8).

90. This is the only place I have found where Sextus says ἐπιστάμεθα, and on the basis of the context I think it means "we understand" and not "we know."

Other statements of the second Mode may be found at Diogenes Laertius, 9.80–1 and Philo 175ff.


## 91–9. The Third Mode

But suppose that, despite the foregoing considerations, we could somehow pick out one "expert" or "wise man" whose *phantasiai* were to be trusted above those of all other human beings and animals. Alas, that will get us nowhere. For the different senses give rise to different *phantasiai* from the same thing, and consequently even a single individual can be led to different conclusions as to whether an object is smooth or rough, pleasant or unpleasant, and so forth. Much worse than this, however, is another puzzle. Each thing that appears to us in sensation seems to affect us as complex; for instance, we perceive the apple as smooth, fragrant, sweet, yellow. But does this imply that the apple really has just the qualities that we perceive? There are equipollent arguments pro and con. It is a given that the nature of the *phantasiai* obtained by means of a particular sense organ depends upon the structure of that sense organ, so perhaps the real apple has just one quality, which nevertheless produces in us a variety of *phantasiai* because of the structural differences in our various sense organs. Or maybe, on the other hand, the real apple has a large number of qualities, the majority of which go unperceived by us because we have only the five senses. Thus, no matter how good the sense organs of our alleged expert may be, his testimony will throw no light on the nature of the real apple, or on that of the real world in general.

But what if somebody claims that nature, that is, the external world, has caused our senses to be exactly appropriate to the qualities of the objects of sense? In other words, what if nature has arranged that, since the external objects make sounds, have colors, smells, and so on, a natural adaptation has resulted in our bodies' having ears, eyes, noses, and the other sense organs with which to perceive them. According to this hypothesis it is no accident that the external world has just the kinds of qualities we take it to have, for its having those qualities has resulted in our having the corresponding sense organs. Annas and Barnes cite Epictetus (1.6.3–6) to the same effect:

> If God had made colors, but had not made the faculty of seeing them, of what good had it been? — None at all. — But, conversely, if He had made the faculty of seeing them, but in making objects, had made them incapable of falling under the faculty of vision, in that case also of what good had it been? — None at all. — What then, if He had even made both of these, but had not made light? — Even thus it would have been of no use. — Who is it, then, that has fitted this to that and that to this? And who is it that has fitted the sword to the scabbard, and the scabbard to the sword? (Loeb translation by W. A. Oldfather)

To this notion, that nature has made the senses exactly proportional to the objects of sense, Sextus responds:

> But what is this "nature," seeing that there is so much unresolved controversy among the Dogmatists concerning its very existence? For anyone who decides this question, that is, whether nature exists, will have no credibility with them if he is an ordinary person, while if he is a philosopher he will be part of the controversy and instead of being a judge will be subject to judgment himself.

Thus the Dogmatists, who cannot even agree as to whether the external world exists, let alone about what it is like, are in no position to advance the proportionality hypothesis. And although Sextus's reply is typically dialectical and ad hominem, I think that we can justifiably take it as indicating that he himself is not convinced of the existence of the external world; after all, he is at least as skeptical as any Dogmatist.

The idea that the objects of which the real world consists do not themselves have colors, smells, tastes, and so on, but instead produce in us (by a very complex process involving also the particles constituting the medium and our sense organs) the experienced qualities that we customarily ascribe to the macroscopic objects around us, should not seem strange to the modern reader. For it is, and has been for a long time, the received view.

Annas and Barnes (pp. 66–79) give an especially useful discussion of this Mode, identifying previous formulations and possible sources of many of Sextus's examples. Regarding section 92, however, they make the surprising assertion that "Sextus means in fact that honey is unpleasant when it is smeared on or dripped into the eyes," and they seem to have forgotten Plato when they say (p. 77), apropos of section 99, that empiricism "is an almost universal feature of Greek philosophy: dogmatists of every persuasion held that all our concepts, and all our knowledge of the external world, derive ultimately from sense-perception."

99. Line 29. Reading εἰ ἐγχωρεῖ, with Heintz.

Another statement of the third Mode may be found at Diogenes Laertius 9.81.


## 100–17. The Fourth Mode

As I read it, the argument of this Mode consists of two parts. The first begins with the observation that the *phantasiai* experienced by a person depend upon the condition that the person is in. Thus, things affect us in dissimilar ways depending on whether we are awake or asleep, drunk or sober, sick or healthy, in motion or at rest, distressed or cheerful, wanting or satisfied, courageous or fearful, and so forth. Also one's age, prior experiences, predispositions, and other such factors produce differences in the *phantasiai*. In general, the same thing will appear one way to a person who is in one condition, and another, incompatible, way to a person who is in another condition. From this it is concluded that:

> Since, therefore, there is so much anomaly depending on conditions, and human beings are in one condition at one time and another at another, how each external object appears to each person is easy to say, I suppose, but not how it is, since the anomaly is unresolved. (112)

The remainder of the argument is to the effect that anybody who tries to resolve the various anomalies will be in some condition himself and thus will be unable to avoid begging the question. For instance, we are told at section 110 that the same wine that appears sour to people who have previously eaten dates or figs seems sweet to those who have eaten nuts or chickpeas, the obvious point being that how the wine tastes to a person depends on what that person has eaten beforehand. Consequently, if, by tasting the wine, you try to referee a dispute as to whether it is sour or sweet, the question will arise: what have you eaten beforehand? Furthermore, if you just ignore this question and issue an unsupported pronouncement, nobody will give any credence to that (since the disputants will be making their own pronouncements and you will have no claim to authority); but if you try to give an argument for your conclusion, you will end up in a "circularity" *aporia*. For to show that the purported proof is indeed a proof, you will need a criterion for correctness of proof, and to establish that the criterion is a good one, you will need a proof. The final "conclusion," as stated at 117, is:

> Therefore, if nobody, with or without a proof and criterion, is able to give one *phantasia* preference over another, then the differing *phantasiai* that arise depending on the different conditions will be undecidable; so that this mode, too, leads to suspension of judgment [*epochē*] concerning the nature of the external objects.

In connection with this Mode Annas and Barnes endeavor to distinguish skepticism from relativism. They say (pp. 97–8):

> Suppose that your coat appears white to me today, but that tomorrow I get a black eye and your coat appears orange (PH 1.101). A *sceptic* is led to suspend judgment about the color of the cloak. That is to say, he holds *first* that the coat really is in itself white or orange (or some other color); and *secondly* that he cannot tell what color it is. His scepticism consists precisely in the fact that there is something there to be known which he is not in a position to know. A *relativist* does not suspend judgment. He holds, *first*, that your coat is not in itself white or orange (or any other color) but rather that it is white relative to those with normal eyes, orange relative to those with black eyes, and so on. And he holds *secondly* that he can tell all there is to tell about colors: he can tell that the coat is, say, orange relative to those with black eyes—and there is nothing else to tell about its color.

It is clear from Sextus's discussion of Protagoras's doctrine, at 1.216–9 and M 7.61–4, that Sextus is no relativist. But on the proposed definition of "skeptic" he would be no skeptic, either. He does not agree that the coat really is in itself white or orange or some other color but that he cannot tell what it is, nor does he agree that in general "there is something there to be known which he is not in a position to know." Instead, he keeps an open mind on the matter, allowing it possible that sense can be made of the issue and that one side or the other may prevail. I confess, however, that although this is his official position, he gives no example to convince us that such a possibility is a real one.

Regarding section 104 and the question: How do I know that I am not now dreaming? See Aristotle *Metaphysics* 1010b8–11 and 1011a7; Plato *Theaetetus* 158B–C, Galen *Commentary on Hippocrates' On Diet in Acute Diseases* 15. 449K; and of course Descartes *First Meditation*.

There seems to be something wrong with the text at section 101, where the jaundiced person, instead of seeing everything yellow, finds the taste of honey bitter (cf. also section 211), and the person with the bloodshot eyes, instead of seeing things blood-colored, as at sections 44 and 126, sees the coat as orange (cf. M 7.192). Sextus's sudden references to himself are also odd.

104. Line 10. Apelt and Mutschmann have αὐταῖς; the MSS. and Bekker have αὐτοῖς. The former would refer to *phantasiai*; for a *phantasia* to "exist" is for it to be "true," that is, to be the case or to be of an existent object. The latter alternative would perhaps refer to the external objects (τὰ ἐκτὸς ὑποκείμενα), which, however, were most recently mentioned only in section 102 above; or it could refer indefinitely to the things, whatever they may be, that are under discussion in this section.

Other statements of the fourth Mode are found at Diogenes Laertius 9.82 and Philo 178ff.

## 118–23. The Fifth Mode

The fifth Mode has to do with "positions, distances, and locations", that is, the position or posture of the observed object, the distance or other spatial relation of the observer to the object, and the location or place where the object is when it is observed. (Annas and Barnes correctly point out that διαστήματα, which generally means distances, must have a wider sense here, as is shown by the Stoa example.) The claim—not asserted by Sextus himself but taken from the Dogmatists' epistemologies—is that the *phantasiai* an observer experiences from a given object are affected or in part determined by each of these three factors. Many familiar examples, including the broken (not bent; see the note on section 119 below) oar, are given to illustrate the point. So the Dogmatist should not be telling us, on the basis of his *phantasiai* of a particular object, how that object is in fact; he should recognize that the most he can say is how that object appears to him when it is in such and such a posture, in such and such a spatial location, and at such and such a distance from him. In short:

> Therefore, since everything apparent is viewed as being in some location and from some distance and in some position, each of which produces a great deal of variation in the *phantasiai*,... we shall be forced also by this mode to have recourse to suspension of judgment. (121)

To this, Sextus adds the same kind of metatheoretic argument he included in the fourth Mode. If the Dogmatist tries to give preference to some of the *phantasiai* over others—saying, for instance, that when the tower looks round from afar and square from close up, the close-up view is to be preferred and the tower deemed to be square—he falls into a logical *aporia*. This time the difficulty is infinite regress, whereas in the fourth Mode it was circularity. If the Dogmatist just declares, without supporting argument, that certain of his conflicting *phantasiai* are more to be trusted than the others, nobody will be impressed by that. But if he offers an argument, the question will arise as to whether it is a good argument, and if he tries to establish this by an argument, he is on the way to an infinite regress.

It will be noticed that Sextus, following his adversaries, predicates "true" and "false" of arguments as well as of propositions. An argument is true, according to the Stoics, if it is valid and has true premises (and hence also has a true conclusion). We might be inclined to hold that the predicate "true" is being used here in two different senses, but I suppose that a Stoic would reply that in both cases it is being used for a relation of correspondence between a body of discourse and the external world, and that the discourse is "true" if and only if the world is as the discourse says it is. Thus, just as we are supposed to have:

> "The oar is broken" is true if and only if the oar is broken,

we would have something like:

> "It is day, and if it is day it is light; therefore it is light" is true if and only if the fact that it is light is contained in the fact that it is day and if it is day it is light.

In this connection we should keep in mind that, despite the almost exclusive concern of these Modes with objects of sense perception, *phantasiai* are not limited to *phantasiai* of such objects. They include also those stemming from the intellect, such as the *phantasiai* that 50 is a few and that 10,000 is a few (M 7.418) and the *phantasia* that no *phantasia* is worthy of credence (PH 2.76). The dog cannot have the *phantasia* that "If this is its footprint, the animal went that way," but only because he does not possess the use of language (M 8.269f.).

Consequently, when, as in the present Modes, the question is how we can determine from our *phantasiai* the truth about the external world, the truth of arguments is as relevant as the truth of propositions like "The honey is sweet." For at bottom we are concerned with how to infer reality from appearance, and the gap between "The argument appears to be a good one" and "The argument is a good one" is exactly similar to the gap between "The honey appears to be sweet" and "The honey is sweet."

119. Throughout history the oar has been described as looking "bent," not "broken." But of course oars do not bend; they break, at least if they are made of wood; and the line of the shaft of our partially immersed oar appears κεκλασμένη, as changing direction abruptly, not gradually. In any case, the basic meaning of the verb κλάω is "to break"; even in geometry, a κεκλασμένη γραμμή is a broken line, that is, a line that changes direction at a point, not gradually through a curve (cf. *Euclid's Elements*, trans. T. L. Heath, New York, Dover, 1956, vol. 1, p. 159).

Concerning the examples generally, cf. Plato *Republic* 602CD and Euripides *Ion* 586–7. The ship: Cicero *Academics* 2.25.81, and Plotinus *Enneads* 2.8. The square tower: PH 1.32; M 7.208, 414; Lucretius 4.353–63, Proclus *Commentary on Euclid* 40 and Descartes *Meditations*. Other statements of the fifth Mode are found at Diogenes Laertius 9.85–6 and Philo 181ff.

## 124–8. The Sixth Mode

According to the Dogmatists' account of how perception takes place, none of the external objects affects us by itself but always in combination with something else. Thus we see, hear, and smell objects through the medium of air, and our visual, auditory, and olfactory *phantasiai* vary depending on the condition of that medium. The same point holds, mutatis mutandis, for the other senses. Furthermore, not all the media are external to our bodies. For example, our eyes contain liquids and membranes, which make their own contributions, depending on the condition they are in, to the quality of our visual *phantasiai*. Thus, when we look at the tower, the qualities of the *phantasia* are determined not only by the attributes of the tower but also by those of the intervening air, the lens of the eye, the vitreous humor, and so on. All of this is part and parcel of the Dogmatists' epistemology, though it is not, of course, believed by the Skeptic. But it seems to follow that in no case do we perceive the external object just as it is, but only, at most, as it is in an environment that includes not only itself but also the air and other intervening material, and even the sense organs of the perceiver. Yet the Dogmatist, neglecting these filters through which, on his own account, he observes the tower, uses his *phantasia* as a basis for assertions and beliefs, not just about how the tower *looks* when observed through these complex media, but about how it *is* in fact.

Annas and Barnes (p. 116) quote Hume (1902) sect. 117, where Hume, in connection with the broken oar, says that the evidence of sense must be corrected by reason. And at first glance it seems that Hume is right: we do not always accept the present testimony of the senses, but often reject some of it on the basis of theory and other information. But Sextus gives two brief arguments against this idea.

One is that if we cannot trust the senses, we cannot trust the intellect either, for the senses are the "guides" of the intellect. This, as Annas and Barnes note, seems to be a summary statement of epistemological empiricism. The classic, if clumsy, formula was "There is nothing in the intellect that was not previously in the senses." We do not know how Sextus would elaborate this skimpy "argument." But to the claim that we do after all figure out that, for example, the "broken" appearance of the oar is not representative of the oar's real shape, we may conjecture that he would reply along the following lines: Any figuring out that we do in such a case will be based ultimately on other *phantasiai* derived from the senses, and no matter how complicated and involved the procedure may be, the fact remains that what we are trying to do is to determine the features of reality when given those of appearances. But, as Berkeley said, it is granted on all sides that the appearances could be as they are even if there were no such "reality" of independently existing objects:

> In short, if there were external bodies, it is impossible we should ever come to know it; and if there were not, we might have the very same reasons to think there were that we have now. (*Principles of Human Knowledge*, sect. 20)

In other words, according to this empiricism the intellect has nothing to go on other than the *phantasiai* furnished it by the senses, and if the general credibility of the senses is called into question, the intellect is helpless. For, from any set of propositions that only express the *pathē* of a perceiver, the intellect cannot derive any single categorical proposition about the external world; that is the essence of the matter.

Sextus's other argument is in effect the observation that if you track the process of perception further back, to the seat of the intellect — whether that abode is the brain, the heart, or whatever part of the body (cf. M 7.313) — you find that it, no less than the eye, is supposed to have a physical structure and environment that will to some extent determine the *phantasiai* received. Does any dogmatist nowadays doubt that the quality of a person's experience is greatly affected by the structure and condition of his brain and the rest of his central nervous system? So do not expect the intellect, any more than the senses, to give us the unvarnished truth about the external world.

All of this reminds us, of course, of Gilbert Ryle's strictures (1949) against treating perception as a process in which a ghostlike soul, located inside our bodies, looks out through the eyes and reports what it sees. That picture of perception may be as absurd as Ryle thought it was, but it can hardly be denied that the nature of the "media" mentioned by Sextus does in part determine what is directly perceived, and that it is easy to overlook what these media contribute. Indeed, the usual move of epistemologists is not to deny this, but to put conditions (which Sextus would question) on the various co-determining factors. We will be told, for example, that the tower *is* round if it *looks* round when observed from close up, in clear air, by a perceiver with eyes free of astigmatism, floaters, and other abnormalities, and with a central nervous system in similarly "normal" condition. To this move, Sextus always replies by raising the question: *Why* should we suppose that things in the external world really are as they appear to a so-called "normal" observer?

The upshot is that since we never perceive an object by itself but only in and through a complex environment, we are able at most to say how the object appears in such and such a combination, but not how it is *simpliciter*.

125. Line 20. MS. Ac omits τῇ φύσει, so that the sentence would read "and so we cannot say how our complexion is, but only how it looks together with each of the two kinds of air." From my point of view, the two versions are equivalent.

Other statements of this Mode are at Diogenes Laertius 9.84–5 and Philo 189ff.

## 129–34. The Seventh Mode

Whereas the sixth Mode dealt with the effect that an object's environment makes on how that object appears to us, the seventh Mode considers how different *phantasiai* are produced depending on the quantity and arrangements of the objects or their parts. Particles of a given material appear to have one color or texture when they are viewed separately, and another when they are viewed together; substances like wine or certain medicines produce one kind of *phantasia* in us when taken in the "right" amount, and a quite different *phantasia* when "too much" or "too little" is taken. Therefore we are never in a position to make simple categorical assertions like "Taenarean marble is yellow" or "This medicine is beneficial," but only "The medicine appears beneficial when used in such and such quantity" or "These bits of Taenarean marble appear yellow when combined in the whole stone."

In section 132 Sextus may seem to be agreeing that individual bits of silver not only look black but are black when they are separate from one another, and that they not only look white but are white when they are combined into a single piece. But the concluding clause of that section shows that he is still talking about *phantasiai* and appearances, and is still making his customary point, namely, that according to the Dogmatists' own picture of how we acquire knowledge or justifiable beliefs about the external world, the quality of our *phantasiai* depends to some extent on variable factors other than the attributes of the objects in question, and that consequently, when we seek to answer such a question as "What color is silver?" we are stumped by the anomaly of these *phantasiai*. Thus, not only is Sextus not asserting that lumps of silver are in fact white, he is not even asserting that they appear white; rather, he is only trying to show the Dogmatists that, on their own premises, they have no good reason to believe one way or the other.

Contrary to this, Annas and Barnes (p. 123ff.) read Sextus as "conceding" that silver not only appears white in large lumps but that it is white in large lumps. They add that he is not merely being careless. I do not know whether in this connection we should invoke Sextus's repeated admonitions that precision in language is not to be expected from the Pyrrhonist, though I agree with Burnyeat that the admonitions should be taken seriously. But, as noted above, the last clause of section 132 shows that Sextus's point in this Mode is that "combinations" produce anomaly in the *phantasiai*, in the appearances, and that therefore we seem not to be justified when, on the basis of such *phantasiai*, we make unqualified assertions about the things in question. And, as I have suggested perhaps too many times already, the Pyrrhonists' general refusal to believe or assert anything at all about the external world requires us to take the argumentation in these Modes dialectically, as exercises in drawing out discomforting consequences from premises that the opponent will admit.

I would interpret section 133 along the same lines. If the Dogmatist will admit that a drug is beneficial in small quantities but harmful in large, he will presumably also admit, a fortiori, that in small quantities it appears beneficial while in large quantities it appears harmful. So if he tries to determine, on the basis of these appearances, whether the drug is beneficial or harmful, he will once again be stultified by the anomaly of the *phantasiai*. Or perhaps, in the context of medical treatment, to be "beneficial" simply *is* to replace the patient's unpleasant and painful *phantasiai* with some that are at least neutral. In any case, the text does not seem to me to require us to suppose that in this Mode Sextus is making "concessions" or departing in any way from his project of showing that the Dogmatists' own account of gaining knowledge or justified belief through *phantasiai* is incoherent.

Annas and Barnes comment (p. 125) that Sextus's example of silver filings (and also the example of the goat's horn) was used by Asclepiades, a first century B.C. physician (Caelius Aurelianus, *On Acute Diseases* 1.106) and that a recently published papyrus suggests that the example may be even older (Oxyrhynchus papyrus 3659). They also refer appropriately to Locke's *Essay* 2.3.20, where Locke gives the example of almonds as objects that look and taste one way when they are whole but another way when they are reduced to powder. But when they conclude (p. 129): "The seventh Mode does establish something. It establishes, for example, that silver is not white," I cannot agree.

134. I read συνέχει ("blocks") instead of συγχεῖ ("confuses").

Other statements of this Mode may be found at Diogenes Laertius 9.86 (where it is called the eighth Mode) and at Philo 184–5.


## 135–40. The Eighth Mode

The argumentation in this Mode is contaminated to a considerable extent by an ancient confusion, one of several introduced by Aristotle and afflicting philosophy ever since. This one stems in part from his odd use of the prepositional phrase πρός τι ("in relation to something") as though it were an adjective, like καλός ("beautiful"), from which Greek syntax permits us to form a noun phrase by adding the definite article. Thus he obtains, analogous to τὰ καλά ("the beautiful things") the curious phrase τὰ πρός τι. Because "the in relation to something things" would be too weird an expression even for philosophy, translators have had to make up a quasi-technical term to represent it. Nowadays the most common translation is "the relatives."

These so-called "relatives" constitute one of the Aristotelian categories. Literally, they are "things that are in relation to something." At first hearing, therefore, one might suppose that the category in question includes everything, for, after all, everything is related to something since it is identical with itself and different from everything else. But obviously Aristotle did not intend that everything should be a relative.

Unfortunately, it is very difficult to know what his intentions actually were. At *Categories* 6a36–7 (see Ackrill, 1963) he first defines relatives as "things that are called [λέγεται] what they are in relation to something" (Πρός τι δὲ τὰ τοιαῦτα λέγεται, ὅσα αὐτὰ ἅπερ ἐστὶν ἑτέρων εἶναι λέγεται), and he follows this with a number of examples and with some conditions that he thinks relatives must satisfy. The examples include the double, the large, and the similar, as well as virtue, perception, knowledge, and some other items. The most important of the conditions is "reciprocity"; for example, "the slave is called slave of a master and the master is called master of a slave" (6b29–30).

Let me parenthetically assure the careful reader that I, too, have noticed that the entire discussion is saturated with use-mention confusion.

Two pages later, however, Aristotle rejects his first definition, on the ground that it would allow some substances to be relatives. His new definition, found also at *Topics* 142a29 and 146b3, is "relatives are those things for which being is the same as being somehow related to something" (ἔστι τὰ πρός τι οἷς τὸ εἶναι ταὐτόν ἐστι τῷ πρός τί πως ἔχειν) (8a31–2), and he comments that "The previous definition does, indeed, apply to all relatives, yet this—their being called what they are, of other things—is not what their being relatives is." Thus the first definition refers to what is said (λέγεται) and what things are called; the second does not. Sextus, however, seems to be using the first definition, since at section 137 he argues that whatever differs from anything is a relative, "for it is called or spoken of [λέγεται] in relation to that from which it differs."

The second definition and the various examples given by Aristotle and Sextus show that the major source of trouble here is in effect the hidden use of a very strong form of modality. A slave is a relative, for it is impossible to be a slave without being a slave of someone. Indeed, to be a slave *is* to be a slave of someone. Similarly, a thing on the right is a relative since it is impossible to be a thing on the right without being on the right of something that is on the left. And so on. On the other hand, Callias, an individual human being, is not a relative, for he is an Aristotelian primary substance, which implies that his existence does not require that of anything else. Thus, while in order for something to be on the right, there must be something on the left, it is not the case that in order for something to be Callias, that is, for Callias to exist, there must be something else.

Thus a slave is a relative but Callias is not. But what if the slave is Callias? This brings us to the bankruptcy of the whole notion. The root of the trouble is failure to recognize that words occurring with the scope of modal operators occur obliquely, that is, are words that do not have their ordinary denotations and hence are not available for existential generalization or class abstraction. What Aristotle and his followers were attempting to do was to classify things on the basis of abstraction into an oblique context, and the attempt was bound to lead to paradox and confusion.

The point was clearly and classically made by Quine many years ago (see, for example, Quine, 1961, pp. 143–4). One of his oft-cited examples has to do with the four sentences:

1. Necessarily, nine is greater than seven,
2. Nine is the number of the planets,
3. Necessarily, the number of the planets is greater than seven,
4. There is a number $n$ such that necessarily, $n$ is greater than seven.

It would seem that (3) follows from (1) and (2) by Leibniz's Law, but (3) is false while (1) and (2) are true. The explanation is that the occurrence of "nine" in (1) is not direct, or, in Quine's related terminology, it is not "purely designative," while Leibniz's law applies only to occurrences that are direct or purely designative. Similarly, it would seem that (4) follows from (1) by the rule of inference usually called "existential generalization," but from (2) we can see that (4) not only does not follow from (1); it is devoid of sense. For, Quine asks, what is this number, that is necessarily greater than seven? Is it nine, that is, the number of the planets? We see also that class abstraction on the occurrence of "nine" in (1) leads to similar nonsense, for suppose that we try to form the class of all numbers $n$ such that necessarily $n$ is greater than 7. Is the number nine a member of this class? If we designate it by the numeral "9," the answer will seem to be "Yes," but if we designate the very same number by the description "the number of the planets," the answer is apparently "No." Thus the class is not "well-defined," that is, there is no such class.

It will be seen that Aristotle's formation of the category of relatives involves the same kind of illegitimate class abstraction. Remember that a slave is a relative because it is impossible to be a slave without being a slave of somebody, and an object on the right is a relative because it is impossible to be an object on the right without being an object on the right of something and, in general, an $X$ is a relative if it is impossible to be an $X$ without being an $X$ of something. Thus the category of relatives is supposed to be the class of all those $X$'s such that it is impossible to be an $X$ without being an $X$ of something. But there is no such class. For consider again poor Callias, who happens to be a slave. Is he a member of the class, or isn't he? He is a member, because he is a slave, and it is not possible to be a slave without being a slave of somebody. He is not a member, because he is a human being and it is perfectly possible to be a human being without being somebody's human being.

The upshot is that in forming his category of relatives Aristotle constructs a grotesque name (τὰ πρός τι) by treating a prepositional phrase as though it were an adjective, and then he defines an extension for this odd expression by, in effect, employing class abstraction on an oblique context. The result is a conceptual mess.

(Incidentally, one cannot evade Quine's point, as some have attempted, by using locutions of the form "*X*, under the description *D*, is *Y*," for example, "Nine, under the description, 'the number of the planets,' is not necessarily greater than seven." These locutions introduce an unwelcome change of subject, as they, unlike the sentences they are supposed to interpret, refer to linguistic expressions as well as to what they may denote. As a result, the rules for their use [which we are never given explicitly] are far from obvious. For instance, it would seem that "Nine, under the description, 'the number of the planets,' is not necessarily identical with nine" is supposed to be true, but the existential generalization of it, namely, "There is something which, under some description, is not necessarily identical with itself" is supposed to be false. I have discussed this matter in the *Journal of Symbolic Logic* 27 [1962]: 216.)

In any case, it is disappointing that Aenesidemus, or whoever originated Sextus's version of the eighth Mode, took the category of relatives seriously enough to construct a separate Mode for it. The result is a Mode containing no clear content beyond what has already appeared in its seven predecessors. What we find in sections 135–40 are two sets of considerations. According to sections 135–6, previous Modes have noted that when something appears, it appears to someone and in relation to such and such circumstances; thus they have made their point, that the *phantasiai* purportedly coming from the thing in question vary with the perceiver and the circumstances. Then, in sections 137–9 we find an argument claiming to show that, despite the intentions of Aristotle and his followers, everything is relative. The argument is impossible to assess, in view of the aforementioned confusion infecting the notion of "relative." Finally, in section 140, the weak conclusion is drawn that "Now, when we have shown that all things are relative, the obvious result is that as concerns each external object we shall not be able to state how it is in its own nature and absolutely, but only how, in relation to something, it appears to be."

Regarding 137, cf. M 8.161f.:

Of existing things, some, the Skeptics say, exist absolutely [κατὰ διαφοράν] and some relatively. Existing absolutely are all such things as are conceived with a subsistence of their own and absolutely [ἀπολύτως], for example, white, black, sweet, bitter, and everything of a similar kind; for we think of these by themselves alone and separately and without conceiving them together with anything else.

(The context shows that in this passage "the Skeptics say" does not mean "the Skeptics assert" but only "the Skeptics put forward as a presumably acceptable proposition in the dialectic.") M 10.263 is similar:

Of existing things some, they [the Pythagoreans] say, are conceived absolutely (κατὰ διαφοράν), some by way of contrariety [κατ' ἐναντίωσιν], and some relatively [πρός τι]. Absolute [κατὰ διαφοράν], then, are those which exist of themselves and in complete independence, such as man, horse, plant, earth, water, air, fire, for each of these is regarded absolutely [ἀπολύτως] and not in respect of its relation to something else.

In view of these passages, the question and its following sentence in section 137 could just as well have been translated as:

> Do the things that exist absolutely differ from the relative things, or not? If they do not differ, then they too are relative; if they do differ, then, since whatever differs is relative (for it is spoken of in relation to that from which it differs), the things that exist absolutely are relative.

Whether this makes better sense than the other, I leave to the reader's judgment.

138. One might wonder what the difference is between things that are "pre-evident" (πρόδηλα) and things that are merely "evident" (δῆλα). The answer is: there is no difference. Evident things are called "pre-evident" in the context of an epistemology that holds that the process of acquiring knowledge about the non-evident begins with intuiting the evident.

139. I follow Pappenheim's addition of μὴ in line 29.

Finally, note Sextus's comment at 135 that he uses "are" for "appears to be" (cf. 198).

## 141–4. The Ninth Mode

The skeptical force, if any, of the ninth Mode is not very apparent; indeed, Annas and Barnes (p. 149) find that "the examples which the skeptics adduce do nothing towards establishing a skeptical conclusion or inducing a state of suspension of judgment." But this may be a bit too strong.

Let us look first at the sun-and-comet example. Sextus begins with the statement, "The sun is certainly a much more marvelous thing than a comet," a premise with which he presumably expects the Dogmatist to agree. Consequently, in this statement the word "marvelous" has to mean, not just "marveled at," but something like "worthy of being marveled at." Otherwise we shall have Sextus saying in this sentence that the sun is more marvelous than the comet, and in the next sentence that, because we see the sun frequently but the comet infrequently, we marvel at the comet more than the sun. Thus, "the sun is certainly a much more marvelous thing than a comet" is taken here as a purported truth about the external world, and the point is the usual one about appearance and reality: the Dogmatist will have to admit that the sun *is* more marvelous but *appears* less marvelous, from which it seems to follow that he cannot determine, as he thinks he can, how a thing *is* from how it *appears*.

Annas and Barnes are surely right (p. 148) in considering such questions as "Are earthquakes really striking or not?" and "Is the sun really marvelous or not?" to be, in their words, misconceived and silly. But I suppose that a certain amount of sense can be given to the question whether something is worthy of being marveled at. For instance, at a magician's performance one might want to say that a few of his tricks were worthy of being marveled at, while most of them were not, and intend this remark as more than an autobiographical comment about one's own feelings of wonder or amazement.

Similarly in the example about gold, it seems that "precious" has to mean something like "in itself worthy of being prized" rather than simply "prized", and I think that once again we must understand Sextus to be working with statements that he finds the Dogmatists making, but for the sense of which he takes no responsibility himself. The Dogmatists think that gold is really precious in itself, and they base this judgment on their *phantasia* that it is precious, overlooking another part of their own doctrine, namely, that the quality of the *phantasia* is determined not only by the intrinsic properties of gold but also by its rarity. I do not know whether any of the Dogmatists were actually that stupid, but whoever originated the ninth Mode seems to have thought that some were.

As for the general point of the Mode, the best that I can do for it is the following. The Dogmatists think that some things (like the sun) are in themselves really worthy of being marveled at, and that some things (like gold) are in themselves really precious, that is, worthy of being prized. They of course base these judgments on their own *phantasiai*. But they concede that the quality of these *phantasiai* is a function not only of the attributes of the sun and the gold, but also of (among other things) the relative frequency or rarity with which they occur. Thus the Skeptic onlooker finds the Dogmatists' story incoherent, and he takes no position as to whether their assertions are true, false, or neither, that is, devoid of sense.

There is a brief and confused version of the ninth Mode at Diogenes Laertius 9.87; Philo omits it altogether.


## 145–63. The Tenth Mode

The tenth Mode is announced as being primarily concerned with ethics (τὰ ἠθικά). The very broad scope given to ethics in this context is apparent from the topics that Sextus lists as belonging to it: ways of life, customs, laws, mythic beliefs, and dogmatic suppositions. At PH 3.168 and M 11.2–3 it is explained that the subject matter of ethics is "things good, bad, and indifferent"; thus, as Annas and Barnes point out (p. 157), it is concerned with value in general and not only with moral value. Nevertheless, the mythic beliefs and dogmatic suppositions seem somewhat out of place. But the particular mythic beliefs considered—for instance, the one to the effect that Cronus, instead of taking care of his children, ate them—have a conspicuous value-theoretic aspect. And the justification for including the so-called "dogmatic suppositions," which comprehend not only such propositions as "The divinity does not care about us," or "Glory is an evil thing," but also such as "The elements of things are atoms," is apparently that some of them seem to collide with items included in the four other categories mentioned.

For each of the various ways in which the five categories can be opposed to one another, Sextus gives examples. The examples are typical of Greek anthropological lore, and for the most part they are plainly designed to shock the reader into an awareness that much of what we consider to be wicked or even obviously outrageous behavior actually meets with approval in certain other societies. It seems unlikely that much of what Sextus recites in these sections even *seems* to him to be the case, but the point he is making is clear enough. Thus his "conclusion," in 163, is that

> At any rate, since by this mode, too, so much anomaly in "the facts" [τὰ πράγματα] has been shown, we shall not be in a position to say how any external object or state of affairs [τὸ ὑποκείμενον] is in its nature [κατὰ τὴν φύσιν], but only how it appears [φαίνεται] in relation to a given way of life or law or custom, and so forth. And so, by reason of this mode, too, we must suspend judgement [or withhold assent] about the nature of the external "facts" [περὶ πῆς φύσεως τῶν ἐκτὸς ὑποκειμένων πραγμάτων].

Thus the tenth Mode is taken by Sextus to be on a par with the other nine as regards its point: we cannot, on the basis of the appearances, determine what is the case in the external world.

The use in this passage of τὰ ἐκτὸς ὑποκείμενα, as well as that of the elliptic τὸ ὑποκείμενον shows clearly that this phrase covers not only "objects" in the external world, but also states of affairs. (Of course one might redefine the word "object" so as to make it apply not only to towers, oars, and the like, but also to counterparts of full sentences, like "The bad fare well and the good fare ill".) Bury translates τὰ ἐκτὸς ὑποκείμενα πράγματα as "external objects," and this results in a very odd rendition of the passage in question:

> Only, since by means of this Mode also so much divergence is shown to exist in objects, we shall not be able to state what character belongs to the object in respect of its real essence, but only what belongs to it in respect of this particular rule of conduct, or law, or habit, and so on with each of the rest. So because of this Mode also we are compelled to suspend judgment regarding the real nature of external objects.

Such a translation leaves us to wonder which "objects" Sextus could be talking about, in view of the fact that what "appear" (φαίνεται) in his examples are not denoted by names such as "the tower" but by entire sentences, such as "Glory is good." Thus once again we see that, for Sextus and the rest of the Pyrrhonists, the world of τὰ ἐκτὸς ὑποκείμενα is not to be thought of as merely a collection of things that exist independently of us and our *pathē*, but includes, in the words of Wittgenstein, "everything that is the case," that is, the objective counterparts of all true sentences.

It is important to keep in mind that consideration of the kinds of matters presented in this Mode will not lead the Skeptic to a state of intellectual or behavioral paralysis as regards the issues concerned. His way of life involves "going by the appearances"; if it appears to him that, for example, tattooing babies is wrong, he will act accordingly regardless of the alleged fact that to the Egyptians it appears that such tattooing is a fine thing to do.

Other statements of the tenth Mode will be found at Diogenes Laertius
9.83–4, where it is called the fifth Mode, and at Philo 193–202.
    154. Line 20. I keep the ὡς.


## 164–77. The Five Modes

The five Modes, said by Sextus to have been handed down by the "more recent
Skeptics," are usually ascribed to a person named "Agrippa," about whom
nothing is known beyond what can be inferred from his alleged authorship of
these Modes.

    The five Modes are neither clear in themselves nor clearly distinct from one
another. They are offered as five ways in which one is led to *epochē*, and, as we
are told in section 177, "they are not put forward by way of throwing out the
ten modes, but in order to combat the precipitancy of the Dogmatists in
greater detail by means of both together."

    The first of the five, described as "based on disagreement," is "that
according to which we find that, both in ordinary life and among philosophers,
with regard to a given topic there has been reached an unresolvable impasse
on account of which we are unable to reach a verdict one way or the other
[αἱρεῖσθαι ἤ ἀποδοκιμάζειν], and we end up with suspension of judgment
[*epochē*]." Presumably this does not mean that whenever there is a disagreement we are at a loss as to which side is to be preferred, but that sometimes
this occurs and leads to *epochē*. The second Mode has to do with arguments
to infinite regress; we sometimes find that the support offered for an assertion
needs the same kind of support it tries to give, and so on, ad infinitum. The
third Mode is based on our old friend, relativity (τὰ πρός τι), and refers to what
has already been considered in sections 135–6.

    As regards section 170ff., I have with reluctance followed Bury in translat-
ing τὰ αἰσθητά and τὰ νοητά as "sense objects" and "thought objects," because
I cannot find any better expressions that are reasonably short. Now, what are
these αἰσθητά and νοητά? They are supposed to be objects or states of affairs
that exist in the external world. Thus, at 1.94, the apple is given as an example
of an αἰσθητόν, and at M 7.141 Platonic Ideas are νοητά. One might have
surmised that τὰ αἰσθητά are sense data, on the internal side of the internal-external division, but the argument at 2.74–75 shows that they are
definitely components of the external world:

> Nor again can one say that the soul apprehends the external objects by means
> of the sensory *pathē* because the *pathē* of the senses are similar to the external
> objects. For from whence will the intellect know whether the *pathē* of the
> senses are similar to the objects of sense [τοῖς αἰσθητοῖς], when it has not itself
> met with these external objects, and when the senses do not reveal to it the
> nature of those objects, but only their own *pathē* (as I have argued from the
> Modes of *Epochē*)? For just as the person who does not know Socrates but
> has seen a picture of him does not know whether the picture is like [or

resembles] Socrates, so also the intellect, looking at the *pathē* of the senses but not having observed the external objects, will not know whether the *pathē* of the senses resemble the external objects.

Thus here an αἰσθητόν is a "sensible" thing or state of affairs, that is, a thing or state of affairs the qualities of which (see 3.33) are supposed to be directly apprehensible by means of the senses, and, correspondingly, a νοητόν is a theoretical entity or state of affairs, the attributes of which are determined by the intellect.

The argument of sections 170–2 therefore begins as follows. Any object or state of affairs that is claimed to exist in the external world will be either the kind of thing that is supposed to be directly apprehended by the senses (e.g., an apple) or the kind of thing the existence and nature of which is figured out by the intellect (e.g., a number or other mathematical entity). Some people, Epicurus for example, think that only the former kind of thing exists; others, for instance Plato, hold that only the latter really exist; and still others, such as the Stoics, believe that some of the former and some of the latter exist.

That "are true" in section 170 means "exist and are such as they appear" is evident from the related passage at M 8.184–5:

For Democritus asserts that none of the sense objects [τῶν αἰσθητῶν] exists, but our perceptions of them are certain empty affections of the senses, and that among the external objects there exists nothing sweet or bitter or hot or cold or white or black or any other of the things that are apparent to everybody; for these are names for our *pathē*. But Epicurus said that all sense objects exist such as they appear and affect us in sensation, as sense perception never lies although we think that it does. And the Stoics and Peripatetics, pursuing a middle course, said that some of the sense objects exist as true and some do not, when sensation lies about them.

Coming back to the argument of sections 170–2: The Skeptic now asks, can this issue be decided? If the opponent replies that it cannot, the Skeptic concludes that we must suspend judgment about the matter. If the opponent replies that the issue can be decided, the Skeptic asks: how? Will the existence of a given sense object be supported by that of another sense object? But since we are questioning the existence of sense objects, the existence of the new sense object will require similar support. But if the existence of the given sense object is to be supported by that of a thought object, then, since we are also questioning the existence of thought objects, it too will need support. Hence we shall have either an infinite series of sense objects or of thought objects, or a series containing circles in which sense objects support thought objects and thought objects support sense objects. In short, when the Skeptic is questioning whether there are any "facts" at all about the external world, it is futile to try to establish one such "fact" for him by citing others.

At first glance it may seem that the argument in these sections is pure sophistry and that actual scientific inquiry succeeds all the time in doing precisely what is here depicted as impossible. A physical theory is confirmed by observations, and if an observation is challenged, the support offered for it typically involves citing other observations and other theories, and so on. Thus the astronomer may cite laws of optics in backing up an observational report which is itself used to back up a theory about the gravitational bending of light rays. But Sextus is not denying that this sort of activity will assist us in constructing theories that enable us to predict what will appear at what time and under what circumstances. In other words, he is not denying that we can achieve useful organization within the domain of appearances. His challenge is rather to the notion that somehow, on the basis of the appearances, we can figure out what is the case in an independently existing "real" world.

He is aware, of course, that people sometimes try, in effect, to define "reality" in terms of appearance — so that, for example, the "real" color of the sweater is to be the color it appears to have when observed by a "normal" observer in "normal" circumstances. But that attempt founders because the real properties of a thing are supposed to be properties it does have *and would have no matter how (or whether) it appeared to anybody*. Thus the physical universe is thought of as an immense assembly of objects, with only a very small proportion of it observed by us, and we suppose that even that tiny bit would be as it is if it were never observed at all. It is this notion, I think, that Sextus challenges.

Sections 173–4 add the consideration that if the Skeptic's opponent seeks to avoid the infinite regress of "reasons" by simply taking a stand somewhere and asserting something without attempting to support it, the Skeptic can with equal legitimacy simply assert the opposite. The remark may have some force as an observation about debates, but it seems to have no philosophical validity.

Sections 175–7 merely repeat, with minor variations, what has gone before.

The five modes are also found at Diogenes Laertius 9.88–9, where they are ascribed to Agrippa and his associates.


## 178–9. The Two Modes

The two additional Modes said to be handed down by the more recent Skeptics amount to nothing new, and the arguments they contain are in effect those of sections 170–73, with "*X* is supported by *Y*" replaced by "*X* is apprehended through *Y*."


## 180–6. Some Modes for Refuting People who Give Causal Explanations

From the "more recent" Skeptics we return to Aenesidemus for eight modes by which *aporia* about causal explanations may be produced.

It is important to remember that although the word αἰτία and its variants are traditionally translated as "cause," many things are αἰτίαι that we would not ordinarily regard as causes. Aristotle makes this apparent with the examples he gives for his four causes. See the note on 3.19 below.

Note the ἴσως in section 185; it is translated by Bury as "probably," but I think that it means "maybe" and merely serves, as usual, to signal that Sextus does not want to be caught asserting confidently that something is the case.

## 187. The Skeptic Slogans

Sextus uses the term φωναί for such Skeptic catchwords and phrases as οὐ μᾶλλον ("not more"), ἀφασία ("non-assertion"), ἐπέχω ("I withhold assent"), οὐδὲν ὁρίζω ("I do not determine anything"), παντὶ λόγῳ λόγος ἴσος ἀντίκειται ("To every argument an equal argument is opposed"). Aristotle, at *De anima* 420b5 and elsewhere, defines a φωνή as a sound, properly the sound of the voice, whether of a human being or any animal with a larynx and lungs. Thus Sextus's use of this label for the Skeptic formulae has a somewhat deprecatory air, and I think that it reflects his defensiveness against the possible criticism that the words and phrases in question are in effect dogmatic assertions by the Skeptic. To convey something of this deprecatory air, I have translated φωναί as "slogans."

Sextus's explications of the various slogans are of some interest as such, but they also contain a number of comments that throw light on the more general question of how a Skeptic's own utterances are to be understood, given that, as is clearly the case, they are not meant to be "true."

## 188–91. The "Not More" Slogan

As would be expected, the οὐ μᾶλλον slogan is explained as elliptical for something like "not more this than that, up than down." The "up than down" (ἄνω κάτω) part is puzzling; as Jonathan Barnes has suggested to me (private communication), it probably should be excised. In Photius's summary of Aenesidemus's *Pyrrhonean Arguments* (*Bibliotheca* 212), "this or that" is expanded into a whole list of contrasts, including "at this time or at that time," "to this person or that person," "of this sort or of that sort," and the like.

In any case, sections 190–1 make the important point that when the Skeptic utters this slogan with reference to some proposition, he is not claiming that the proposition is neither true nor false, nor even that there is no more reason to affirm it than to deny it rather, he is merely expressing a *pathos* of his soul to the effect that he just does not know to which, if any, of the alternatives he should assent. Thus (191):

> Even if the slogan "nothing more" exhibits the character of assent or denial, we do not use it in that way, but rather we take it in an imprecise and not strictly correct sense [ἀδιαφόρως καὶ καταχρηστικῶς], either in place of a question or of saying "I don't know to which of these I ought to assent and to which I ought not to assent." For our goal is to make evident what appears to us, and we do not care with what expression we do it. And this also should be noticed: that in uttering the "nothing more" slogan we are not maintaining

[οὐ διαβεβαιούμενοι] that it is entirely true and firm [ἀληθῆ καὶ βεβαίαν], but in its case, too, we are speaking in accord with what appears to us [ἀλλὰ κατὰ τὸ φαινόμενον ἡμῖν καὶ περὶ αὐτῆς λέγοντες].

I think that this attitude of the Pyrrhonist applies not only to his utterance of the slogans but to everything he says. He makes no claim that what he says is true; he does not suggest that it is lasting and secure (βέβαιος), that is to say, that he will not give a contrary report tomorrow; he is only making evident what appears to him to be the case, that is, he is reporting one of his *pathē*.

### 192–3. "Non-assertion"

On any given occasion when the Skeptic utters the "non-assertion" catchword, he is not saying anything about how things are in the external world, but is only revealing the *pathos* of his soul that makes him unwilling to affirm or deny any such statement.

The last sentence in section 193 reminds us that the Skeptic *epochē* applies only to statements about non-evident things (τὰ ἄδηλα), that is, objects and states of affairs that are external.

### 194–5. "Perhaps," "It Is Possible," "Maybe"

Presumably what Sextus says here about τάχα applies also to his use of ἴσως, namely, that "the person who says 'perhaps it is the case,' by not firmly maintaining [τῷ μὴ διαβεβαιοῦσθαι] that it *is* the case, is in effect also asserting the seemingly inconsistent "perhaps it is not the case."

Again, as in sections 191 and 207, we are told that the Skeptic does not fight over words but uses them loosely. This means, I think, that the Skeptic, unlike the other philosophers, does not try to provide exact definitions or concepts for his terms (for "man," "motion," "location," etc.), but uses them for the imprecise "pre-concepts" (προλήψεις) they represent in ordinary speech.

### 196. "I Withhold Assent"

What we Skeptics will say, *at the time when the appearance affects us* (ὅτε ἡμῖν ὑπόκειται), is what appears to us to be the case about them (τὸ φαινόμενον ἡμῖν περὶ αὐτῶν). Temporary assent is contrasted with διαβεβαιούμεθα.

### 197. "I Determine Nothing"

This slogan, which at section 187 is also given in the form "Nothing is to be determined," means "I do not determine (i.e., settle upon) the truth value of any proposition." One might suppose that it meant "I do not define anything," for Plato and Aristotle regularly use ὁρίζω for "to define," and in this sense, too, the slogan would fit very well the Skeptic point of view. Thus at 2.207–12 Sextus explicitly attacks definitions as worse than useless; he thinks that misguided attempts to replace the common man's loose προλήψεις with precise concepts lead to inconsistency and *aporia*. And he does occasionally use ὁρίζω for "to define" (cf. 2.101, 207–8; M 7.281, 426). But in most of its occurrences he gives it the broader sense described in this section. However, we should recognize that the difference between defining a word or concept, on the one hand, and ascertaining what is the case in the external world of non-evident things, on the other, was probably below the level of his definiteness of intention (see Naess, 1968, p. 10). This can be seen at 3.79 for instance, where either "define" or "determine" will do for ὁρίζω.

Bury translates τάχα in this section as "no doubt," which is all the more remarkable because Sextus has just finished explaining (194–5) that it is a Skeptic catchword meaning "perhaps." This is one of the passages that convince me that Sextus inserts τάχα, ἴσως, and similar expressions to block critics from claiming that they have caught him dogmatizing. No doubt Bury thought that τάχα cannot mean "perhaps" here, because the proposition asserted, namely, "the Skeptic will be found not to be determining anything," is a central item in Sextus's characterization of the Skeptic. But it is just in such cases, when an opponent may think that he has at last come upon something that the Skeptic maintains firmly, that Sextus is most likely to throw in a "perhaps" or a "maybe" to counter that impression.

Note that here again the role of the Skeptic slogan is just to express a present *pathos* of the Skeptic's soul, in this case "such a state of mind as neither dogmatically to affirm nor deny any of the matters in question."

## 198–9. "Everything Is Indeterminate"

Indeterminateness is the *pathos* mentioned in the preceding paragraph.

Once again, as in sections 135, 200, 202, and elsewhere, the Skeptic is said to use the verb "is" as short for "appears to me to be."

The "matters of dogmatic inquiry," that is, the questionable beliefs of the Dogmatist, are regularly specified as those which concern the non-evident.

Because in Greek, as in Latin, the verb endings by themselves show the person and number, Greek syntax allows the omission of the subject nominative in many cases; thus "I am walking around" can be said with or without the pronoun ἐγώ (I).

## 200. "Everything Is Non-apprehensible"

Concerning apprehension, see section 8 of the Introduction.

This section is full of the quasi-technical terminology of Pyrrhonism. The Skeptic is not *firmly maintaining* anything; he is only *reporting* a *pathos* of his to the effect that up to now, because of the *equipollence of the opposites*, he has not established by apprehension any of the Dogmatists' beliefs about *non-evident things*, and that therefore nothing that is brought forward by way of refutation is relevant to what he is *reporting* (i.e., his own *pathos*).

### 201. "I Am Non-apprehensive" and "I Do Not Apprehend"

The two slogans are synonymous.

### 202–4. "To Every Argument an Equal Argument Is Opposed"

As Sextus stated in section 13, a dogma is an assent to something non-evident, and here, correspondingly, "dogmatically" is glossed as "concerning the non-evident."

This section shows that the "arguments" Sextus has in mind are not only deductive arguments, with premises and a conclusion that follows logically from the premises, but any considerations whatever that are brought forward in support of a statement about the external world. So the slogan does not mean merely that, for any such statement, the deductive arguments for it appear to be no more effective than those against it; it covers also considerations purporting to establish that the statement in question is more probable (or more "worthy of belief") than its negation.

Thus, to say *P* dogmatically (δογματικῶς) is to put forward *P* as true of the external world, and it is contrasted with saying *P* as a report (ἀπαγγελτικῶς). Likewise, to establish *P* dogmatically is to establish it as true of the external world. Here, the verb "to establish" (κατασκευάζω) is no stronger than "to support."

In section 205 I follow Heintz's suggested αὐτοὺς instead of Mutschmann and Mau's αὐτοῦ.

### 206–9. More about the Skeptic Slogans

206. The cathartic drug simile occurs again at 2.188. And at M 8.480–1 we read:

> For there are many things that do to themselves what they do to other things. For example, just as fire, after consuming the fuel, destroys also itself, and as cathartic drugs, after driving out the fluids from bodies expel themselves as well, so too it is possible for an argument against proof, besides refuting every proof, to apply also to itself. And again, just as it is not impossible for the person who has climbed to a high place with the help of a ladder, to kick over the ladder after the ascent, so there is no reason why the Skeptic, after having achieved — using a ladder as it were — the establishment of his thesis by an argument showing that there is no such thing as a proof, should not then refute that very argument.

With this compare the famous section 5.54 of Wittgenstein's *Tractatus:*

> My propositions serve as elucidations in the following way: anyone who understands me eventually recognizes them as nonsensical, when he has used them—as steps—to climb up beyond them. (He must, so to speak, throw away the ladder after he has climbed up it.)
>
> He must transcend these propositions, and then he will see the world aright.

## 210–14. Differences between Skepticism and the Heraclitean and Democritean Philosophies

Sextus is concerned to refute a suggestion that Pyrrhonism is a step on the way either to the philosophy of Heraclitus or to that of Democritus. The Skeptic says that opposites *appear* to be the case about the same thing; it is suggested that Heraclitus simply went a bit farther down the road and declared that opposites *are* the case about the same thing, while Democritus took the other fork in the road and concluded that the external objects are neither sweet nor bitter, hot nor cold, white nor black, nor any of the other apparent opposites (see M 7.135, 8.184).

Note that Sextus does not criticize Heraclitus for apparently violating the counterpart, for opposites, of the law of contradiction, nor does he object to Democritus's seeming violation of the counterpart of the law of excluded middle. Instead, he contents himself with pointing out various dogmas that the two of them hold. And he asks, somewhat plaintively: why blame these philosophies on us, when all they share with us is the observation that opposites appear to be the case about the same thing—an observation which we also share with all the other philosophers and with the plain man as well?

## 215. Wherein Skepticism Differs from the Cyrenaic Way

With this section compare M 7.190–200, where the Cyrenaic view is set forth at some length. In section 4 of the Introduction I suggested that Sextus's account of the Cyrenaics is quite sympathetic, though he points out certain things that they accept as fact while presumably the Skeptic would only acknowledge them as apparent. One of these is the claim that none of us has any way of discovering whether on any given occasion his neighbor is having the same sort of *pathē* as he is, for he would have to have his neighbor's *pathē* in order to make the comparison. On this basis, the external world, for a given person at a given time, would include not only a physical world "out there" but also the *pathē* of his neighbor and even his own *pathē* at other times.

"Some people say that the Cyrenaic Way is the same as the Skeptic Way, since it too says that only *pathē* are apprehensible." The text here is uncertain, but Sextus seems to be agreeing that *pathē*, or only *pathē*, are apprehensible.

Yet, from what he says later about apprehension, one might conclude that he does not accept *anything* as apprehensible.

There is of course a question as to what it *means* to say that *pathē* are apprehensible. As I pointed out in section 8 of the Introduction, in most of its occurrences "to apprehend" is used in such a way that, for example, "to apprehend a man" means "to apprehend something as being a man." But in the present connection the phrase "to apprehend a *pathos*" presumably does not mean "to apprehend something as being a *pathos*," but rather, "to apprehend a *pathos* as being something." For example, a person might apprehend his present *pathos* as being painful, or sweet tasting, or green in color, or whatever, but not (unless he is a philosopher, with a concept of *pathos*), as being a *pathos*.


## 216–9. Wherein Skepticism Differs from the Protagorean Way

Sextus seems unsure how he should characterize the doctrine of Protagoras. In section 216 he says that Protagoras thinks (βούλεται) that human beings are the measure (μέτρον) of all things (πάντῶν χρημάτων), and that by "measure" Protagoras means the criterion and by "things" he means objects or states of affairs (τὰ πράγματα). Thus in this section Sextus seems to be ranging Protagoras on the side of those who regard human beings, in contrast with the "non-rational" animals, as the "by whom" criterion of truth (cf. 2.22ff.)

In M 7, however, we first read (at section 48) that Protagoras rejected the existence of a criterion. This seems to be confirmed when (at section 60) we are told that "some have counted Protagoras of Abdera among the company of those philosophers who reject the criterion." But, oddly, that remark is immediately followed by an argument to the effect that if a human being says that human beings are not the criterion, he will be reinforcing the view he is combating, since he, a human being, is affirming what appears to him. Thus, the argument seems designed to suggest that no human being, Protagoras included, is in a position to reject human beings as the criterion of truth.

At M 7.388ff. Protagoras is again described as one who accepts the existence of a criterion; this time the criterion is the *phantasia*, and Protagoras is supposed to have said that every *phantasia* is true. Here the kind of criterion in question is presumably what is discussed at 2.70ff. as the "according to which" (καθ' ὅ) criterion. Protagoras's view would seem to be a limiting case, as it were, of the view that we can use our *phantasiai* to determine what is true and what is not; every *phantasia* would give us truth.

I suspect that the root of the vacillation is that Protagoras has put forward a doctrine that simply does not fit the usual categories. On one common interpretation of his doctrine, he holds that it makes no sense to say that something just *is* the case or just *is not* the case. Thus he has sidestepped the question of how, from what appears to be the case, we can determine what is the case. In place of the verb "to be," as it occurs in sentences of the form "*X* is *Y*," he in effect substitutes a whole family of relativized expressions of the form "is, for person *P*." He holds that if the honey appears sweet to you, it is sweet for you; and if it appears bitter to me, it is bitter for me; the question whether it is sweet or it is bitter is dropped. So in one sense Protagoras denies the existence of a criterion of truth, when a criterion is understood as something by which we can determine what is the case from what appears to be the case; but in another sense he accepts such a criterion, for he (trivially) infers what is the case for person *P* from what appears to *P* to be the case.

It is interesting that in establishing that Protagoras was no Pyrrhonean Skeptic, Sextus bypasses "man is the measure" altogether and simply lists a number of dogmas that he thinks Protagoras held.

In these sections I have, for the sake of tradition, translated ἄνθρωπος as "man" instead of as "human being."

## 220–35. Wherein Skepticism Differs from the Academic Philosophy

Of course, Sextus should have no difficulty in showing that Plato was no Skeptic, for the independent existence of the Ideas, which constitute Plato's external world, is the central tenet of Platonism.

More interesting is his criticism of the New Academy. The members of the New Academy, he says, differ (ἴσως, "perhaps") from the Skeptics in that they firmly maintain (διαβεβαιοῦνται) that all things are non-apprehensible, while it seems to the Skeptics to be possible for some things to be apprehended. In view of the difficulties that Sextus raises elsewhere about the very concept of apprehension, one wonders how the Skeptic can even accept it as possible for something to be apprehended. But maybe the Skeptic is simply not ruling out the possibility that, unbeknownst to him, there is a coherent concept of apprehension and something falls under that concept.

I am resisting the usual translation of πιθανός as "probable," since only subjective probability — that is, plausibility, persuasiveness — is involved here.

Something is surely wrong with the text in section 228, for the Alcestis story, as given in this passage, evidently does not illustrate a *phantasia* that is plausible, tested, and stable. Sextus does not tell us here what a "stable" (ἀπερίσπαστος) *phantasia* is, but in the corresponding passage at M 7.176–7 we learn that a *phantasia* is stable if it is part of a coherent chain or concurrence of plausible *phantasiai*. We are given an example to illustrate this:

> Anyone experiencing a *phantasia* of a man must necessarily have a *phantasia* both of his personal qualities, such as color, size, shape, motion, speech, dress, and footgear, and of things external to him, such as air, light, daytime, sky, earth, friends, and all the rest. And whenever none of these *phantasiai* disconcerts us by appearing false, but all with one accord appear true, we are the more inclined to have belief.

In mythology Alcestis was the wife of Admetus, king of Pherae in Thessaly, and a curious set of circumstances had resulted in her giving up her own life in order that her husband might continue to live. Heracles, who had previously been done a favor by Admetus, went down to Hades, fought successfully with the god of the underworld, and brought Alcestis back. As Sextus tells the story, upon her return Admetus got a plausible and tested *phantasia* of her, but then, since he knew she had died, he ceased to believe in it. Thus his *phantasia* can hardly be considered "stable," as claimed. Hossenfelder (1968) thinks that a sentence is missing from our text at this point, though it is hard to imagine what it would be. For plausible, tested, and stable *phantasiai*, see the Introduction, pp. 38–9.

224. "He ridiculed the deceit of Homer" (τὴν παρ' Ὁμήρῳ ἀπάτην διέρυσεν). According to Diogenes Laertius 9.18, what Xenophanes ridiculed were Homer's stories about the gods.

226–7. When the Skeptic says that something is good or evil, not only does he not assert this as *true*, he does not even assert it as *plausible* (πιθανόν), as the Academic does. Instead, he says it without belief (ἀδοξάστως), "following the common course of life in order not to be incapable of action." In other words, he does not put forward such a statement as even plausible of the external world, but only as an expression of his own *pathos*. The contrast between relying on the plausible (or probable) and living without belief is emphasized again in section 231.

## 236–41. Whether Medical Empiricism Is the Same as Skepticism

The passage seems to show that Sextus Empiricus regarded himself, not as a "medical empiricist," but more like a practitioner of the "methodic way."

Galen and other writers on the medicine of later antiquity distinguish three schools: the so-called Rational, Empiric, and Methodic schools. Frede (1987, chaps. 12–15), gives a full account of these and their relation to philosophy. He describes their main differences as follows (pp. 161–2):

> In medicine the issue came to take the form of the question "How does the doctor, in a particular case, know how the patient is to be treated?" And one particular way this question was formulated was the following: "Which is the correct method of treatment?"... Obviously "method of treatment" here does not mean the way one treats a patient, but rather the way in which one arrives at the conclusion that a certain treatment is the right treatment.... Accordingly, one talked of a rational method and an empirical method. For the Empiricists claimed that it is all a matter of experience, that it is by experience that we have the general knowledge we have, and that it is from experience that we know what to do in a particular case. The Rationalists, on the other hand, claimed that it is, at least in part, by reason that we have the general knowledge we have and hence know what to do in a particular case. In part they thought so because they assumed that professional medical practice had to be based on scientific theory and that a scientific theory had to account for the phenomena in terms of the underlying reality and that this reality included hidden natures, causes, and actions, not open to observation, but only accessible to reason, e.g., atoms, invisible pores, functions of organs, or

essences. Thus the rational method involves the knowledge of truths about nonobservable items which can be obtained only by reason....

Medicine, according to the Methodists, amounts to no more than a "knowledge of manifest generalities"..., i.e., of certain general, recurrent features whose presence or absence can be determined by inspection.

Thus, as Bury notes, the Rational school theorized about "non-evident" causes of disease; the Empiric school regarded these alleged causes as not discoverable; and the Methodic school refused either to affirm or deny the existence of such causes. Hence it is not surprising that, as a Pyrrhonist, Sextus finds the Methodic school more congenial.

Note that although the Skeptic and the Methodic physician are said to be alike in that both are led to action by the *pathē*, the Skeptic is led by his own *pathē*, whereas the Methodic physician is led by the *pathē* of his patient.

# Outlines of Pyrrhonism, Book 2

Book 1 having given the "general account" of Skepticism, "stating its basic idea, its origins, definitions, criterion and goal, as well as the modes of *epochē*, and how we take the Skeptic statements, and the distinction between Skepticism and the competing philosophies," Sextus proceeds in Books 2 and 3 to give the "specific account," in which he raises questions about various specific doctrines of the Dogmatists. Taking their division of philosophy into logic, physics, and ethics, he devotes Book 2 to matters classified as belonging to logic, and Book 3 to those belonging to physics and ethics.

### 1–12. Can the Skeptic Question What Is Said by the Dogmatists?

These sections are interesting for the light they throw on the meaning of "apprehension." Sextus takes up an old puzzle: how is it possible to look for (seek, inquire into, investigate, question, *zētein*) something of which one has no conception? Here the puzzle is phrased as follows: how can the Skeptic raise questions about that which he does not apprehend? At M 8.337ff. it is presented in a somewhat different way. I have discussed the matter on pp. 24–5 of the Introduction.

In sections 1–12 Sextus uses the puzzle as the occasion for distinguishing two senses of "apprehend." In one sense, he tells us, to apprehend something is just to conceive of it, without also maintaining the existence of what one is talking about; in the other sense, to apprehend something involves not only conceiving of it but also grasping that it exists. Thus, in one sense "*A* apprehends an *X*" does not imply "An *X* exists," and in the other sense it does. Now since, as the Dogmatists say, we conceive not only of things and states of affairs that exist, but also of those that do not (section 10), Sextus argues that there is no problem with raising questions about the existence of something we apprehend in the first of the two senses. "For I suppose," he says, "the Skeptic is not precluded from a conception that arises during the discussion itself from clear appearances affecting him passively, and which does not at all imply the existence of its objects." On the other hand, Sextus conjectures that not even the Stoics themselves will want to claim that one cannot raise questions about things that one has not apprehended in the second of the two senses. There is no trace elsewhere of the "first" sense of "to apprehend," in which it just means "to conceive of"; this is surely not surprising, for in the Dogmatists' epistemologies the role of apprehension is to give us knowledge or justifiable beliefs about a world of objects that exist independently of our souls and all their *pathē* and parts (including the *dianoia* or intellect). But the present passage does show that Sextus understands the Dogmatists' use of "apprehend" to be such that having a concept of *X* is a minimal condition for apprehending *X*. You could see a wombat without knowing what a wombat is (i.e., without having a concept of wombat), but under that condition you could not apprehend one.     For a general discussion of apprehension, see section 8 of the Introduction.

3. The "by means of two conditionals theorem" (τὸ διὰ δύο τροπικῶν θεώρημα) is the following inference schema:

If *P*, then *Q*
If *P*, then not *Q*
Therefore, not *P*.

Or perhaps it is the metatheoretic assertion that all instances of the schema are sound. In any case, we are indebted to Origen for preserving a Stoic example of this sort of argument (cf. Mates 1953, pp. 80–1):

If you know that you are dead, you are dead.
If you know that you are dead, you are not dead.
Therefore, you do not know that you are dead.

Presumably, this would qualify not only as a sound argument, but as a proof.

No one has satisfactorily explained what the so-called "reduced with respect to" theorem is. Manuscript T, which is a Latin translation, gives the theorem as "omnis triangulus habet tres angulos equales duobus rectis," which is half of theorem 32 of Book 1 of Euclid's *Elements*. But Euclid's statement and proof make no mention of anything being "reduced with respect to" anything.

With 5 cf. 3.219; with 8 cf. 1.178–9.

## 13. Where the Criticism of the Dogmatists Should Begin

The division of philosophy into three parts is taken up at greater length at M 7.2ff., where it is ascribed principally to Xenocrates (the successor in the Academy to Speusippus, who was the successor to Plato) and to the Peripatetics and the Stoics.

> They plausibly compare philosophy to a garden with every kind of fruit, likening the physics part [of philosophy] to the height of the plants, the ethics part to the ripeness of the fruit, and the logic part to the security of the walls. And others claim that it is like an egg, with ethics like the yolk, which some say is the chick, and physics like the white, which is food for the yolk, and logic like the hard external shell. But since the parts of philosophy are

inseparable from one another, while plants are seen as quite other than fruits, and walls are separated from plants, Posidonius [Stoic philosopher, c. 135–50 B.C.] preferred to compare philosophy to an animal — physics to the blood and flesh, logic to the bones and nerves, and ethics to the soul. (M 7.17–9)

Of course, the terms "logic," "ethics," and "physics" are used here in a much wider sense than we are accustomed to give them. "Physics" refers to all speculation about the physical world, and thus it includes theology insofar as the gods were supposed to affect what happens here below. "Ethics," as indicated at 1.145, covers "ways of life, customs, laws, mythic beliefs, and dogmatic assumptions." What is here called "logic" includes epistemology and rhetoric; the closest Greek term for what we call "logic" was "dialectic" (ἡ διαλεκτική).

## 14–17. The Criterion

Sextus now returns to the first of the two senses of "criterion" he distinguished in 1.21. Note that "the criterion by which we decide questions of existence and nonexistence" is described as "what is called the criterion of truth." Thus truth has to do with what exists and what is the case in the external world, as distinct from the *pathē* of the soul.

M 7.29–37 corresponds to these sections of the *Outlines*. M 7 in its entirety is devoted to the criterion of truth.

In distinguishing the various senses of "criterion" and narrowing his discussion to the "logical" or "most specific" sense, Sextus shows that at this point he is not interested in the kinds of criteria by which we ordinarily take ourselves to be distinguishing veridical from non-veridical appearances. Thus, he will find it irrelevant if he is told that the way to discover whether one's "broken-oar" *phantasia* is veridical is simply to look more closely, or to observe the oar out of the water, or to touch the section where it looks broken, or anything like that. Nor is it relevant to his concerns here that in order to find out whether we are dreaming we need only to wait and see whether we wake up, or else to make the decision directly from the quality of the experience (since, after all, dreamed experience is not exactly like waking experience but has that dreamlike quality with which we are all well acquainted). In other words, he is not asking how in practice we go about making such determinations, for what we actually do amounts to nothing more than determining whether or not our various *phantasiai* stand in certain regular though fairly complex relationships to one another. The problem here is not how our *phantasiai* are related to one another; rather it is to determine whether, or to what extent, they correspond to an external world that exists and goes its way independently of what may appear to us or anyone else to be the case.

With section 16 cf. M 7.35ff.:

It is also possible to subdivide the logical criterion, calling one part of it the "by whom" criterion, another the "by means of which" criterion, and another that of the "application" and "use." The "by whom," for instance, would be a human being, the "by means of which" might be sense perception, and the third might be the application [πρόσβολή] *of the phantasia.* For just as in the examination of heavy and light things there are three criteria, the weigher and the balance beam and the placement of the balance beam, and of these the weigher is the "by whom" criterion, the balance beam is the "by means of which," and the placement of the balance beam is the "use"; and again, just as for the determination of things straight and crooked there is need of the technician [ὁ τεχνίτης] and the rule and the application of the rule, so in the same way in philosophy, for the determination of things true and false we have need of the aforementioned three criteria, and the human being corresponds to the weigher and the technician, "by whom" the decision is made, and sense perception and intelligence correspond to the balance beam and the rule, "by means of which" the decision is made, and the application of the *phantasia* corresponds to the "use" of the implements mentioned above.

It thus appears that in this discussion the word "criterion" is used, with reference to a given decision-making process, for those factors that most significantly affect the outcome.

## 18–21. Does There Exist a Criterion of Truth?

Xeniades of Corinth is also mentioned at M 7.53, 388, and Xenophanes of Colophon at M 7.48, 110.

Note that Sextus says we need an "agreed-upon" criterion, and not just a criterion. This is an indication of what I am describing as his debate-mode approach.

When Sextus keeps saying that there is no "agreed upon" criterion, it might be replied: "So what? It doesn't follow that there is no criterion." The criterion sought is a criterion for determining from our *phantasiai*— "the evident"— the attributes of external objects— the "non-evident"— and he seems to think that the criterion must be something evident. But surely it is one thing for the criterion to be something evident (e.g., the taste of the honey under normal conditions) and quite something else for it to be evident that this is the criterion.

## 22–47. The "By Whom" Criterion

The structure of this chapter is as follows. The question is: by whom shall determinations be made as to which *phantasiai* are veridical and which are not? The only answer considered is: by human beings. In sections 22–8 it is argued that "human beings are inconceivable," that is, that there is no satisfactory concept of human being. Sections 29–33 argue that even if there were such a concept, human beings would not be apprehensible, that is, that there is no way of determining that something is a human being. In sections 34–6 Sextus says that, even granting that human beings are apprehensible, we cannot show that the sought-after determinations should be made by them.

And, finally, in sections 37–46 he argues that even if it is further granted that the determinations should be made by human beings, the difficult question remains: by *which* human beings? Various possible answers are eliminated, and in section 46 the conclusion is drawn that "we cannot find anyone by whom things and issues [*ta pragmata*] are to be determined, despite our having granted so much for the sake of argument."

22–28. The Dogmatists tell us that the determinations should be made by human beings, but they cannot even agree on what a human being is. Socrates, lacking a good definition of human being, had a problem with responding to the Delphic oracle's command to "Know thyself!" for he could not even decide whether he was a human being or a monster (cf. M 7.264). Democritus (cf. M 7.265), attempting to set forth the concept, could only come up with the trivial remark, "We all know what human beings are." But that does not tell us what a human being is, says Sextus, for we all know what dogs are, too, and presumably dogs are not human beings. Epicurus (cf. M 7.267–8) tried an ostensive definition: "A human being is something that possesses a soul and is shaped like *that*" (pointing). But if he pointed at a woman, a man will not be a human being, and if he pointed at a man, a woman will not be a human being. Another definition offered by some of the Dogmatists is "a human being is a rational mortal animal, capable of thought and knowledge," but we have already seen, in the first Mode of *epochē*, that other animals are rational and capable of thought and knowledge. What Sextus gives as Plato's definition (which, not surprisingly, we do not find in the extant works) is "a human being is a wingless biped with flat nails, capable of political knowledge;" but he says that Plato does not put this forward as something he firmly maintains, and anyway, the attributes listed are accidental, not essential, and thus do not tell us what a human being really is (M 7.281–2).

Now, as for Socrates not knowing whether he is a human being, perhaps the reference is to *Theaetetus* 174B, where in describing the typical philosopher he says:

> For really such a man pays no attention to his next door neighbor; he is not only ignorant of what he is doing, but he hardly knows whether he is a human being or some other kind of creature; but what a human being is and what is proper for such a nature to do or bear different from any other, this he inquires and exerts himself to find out.

Bury also refers in this connection to *Phaedrus* 229E ff., where Socrates, speaking of myths about centaurs, gorgons, the Chimera, and the like, says:

> But I have no leisure for them at all; and the reason, my friend, is this: I am not yet able, as the Delphic inscription has it, to know myself; so it seems to me ridiculous, when I do not yet know that, to investigate irrelevant things. And so I dismiss these matters and, accepting the customary belief about them, as I was saying just now, I investigate myself and not these things, to know whether I am a monster more complicated and more furious than Typhon or a gentler and simpler creature to whom a divine and quiet lot is given by nature.

The "definition" attributed to Democritus (ἄνθρωπός ἐστιν ὅ πάντες ἴσμεν) is unclear, since, among other reasons, ἴσμεν ("we know") is ambiguous between *kennen* and *wissen*. Thus the statement might mean "human beings are what we all are acquainted with" or "human beings are what we all have knowledge of." Or, I suppose, it might be intended as nothing more than "Everybody knows what a human being is" — an impatient dismissal of the question. Greek sometimes makes the *kennen-wissen* distinction with γιγνώσκω and εἴδω, but in this passage the two verbs are apparently used interchangeably. A comment in the corresponding passage at M 7.265–6 suggests that Sextus takes Democritus's statement to mean or imply "we all know what sort of thing a human being is" (τὸν ἄνθρωπον ὁποῖός ἐστιν).

Sextus's argument against Democritus's definition is even less clear than the definition itself, as it is beset by another ambiguity besides the one concerning "know." For the expression ὁ ἄνθρωπος ("the human being") can denote the concept (or class) human being (ἡ ἐπίνοια τοῦ ἀνθρώπου), or human beings in general, or a particular human being who has been under discussion, or it can be used in quantifications like "If a dog and a human being have different *phantasiai* of the same thing, the human being will give preference to his own." The same applies, of course, to the term ὁ κύων ("the dog"). Thus it is possible that Democritus was saying that the concept of human being is a (or the) concept with which we are all acquainted.

How can Sextus, Skeptic that he is, assert in section 26 that all animals are capable of thought and knowledge? He says that this is shown in the first Mode of *Epochē*. What we find there, especially at 1.62ff., is a kind of joke with a serious point. It is humorously argued that even a dog has reason, knowledge, and virtue, and clearly the serious point is that if we go by the Dogmatists' definitions of the relevant terms, we are led to this absurd conclusion. So I take section 26 as another dialectical jibe at the Dogmatists: "You define a human being as a rational, mortal animal, capable of thought and knowledge, but on your own definitions of 'rational,' 'thought,' and 'knowledge' it will follow that all animals are human beings."

Note the conclusion at the end of section 27: the concept of human being is ἀσύστατος, incapable of holding or hanging together.

Regarding what is ascribed to Plato in section 28: at *Theaetetus* 152D Socrates says that all the philosophers except Parmenides agree that "nothing ever is, but is always becoming."

31–3. It seems to be hinted that the Pyrrhonist has suspended judgment as to whether or not there is any such thing as a soul. The scenario in the latter part of this passage is apparently this: Sextus says to the Dogmatist, "By what are you going to decide the question whether souls exist?" The Dogmatist replies, "By the intellect." Sextus responds, "But the intellect is supposed to be the most non-evident part of the soul, so you are proposing to establish the less questionable by the more questionable." The point, I suppose, is: Don't tell me you are using the intellect to establish the existence of souls, for if there are no souls, there are no intellects either.

34. As a translation of κρίνειν I am using "to make a determination about" instead of Bury's "to judge," in order to reflect the "separating the wheat from the chaff" aspect of its sense. When claims about the external world are inconsistent with one another, we try to determine which of them, if any, is true. The phrase, "to make determinations about the senses and the intellect" therefore means to determine which of them, if any, is telling the truth; and "to make determinations about τὰ πράγματα" means to determine which statements about the external objects and states of affairs are true.

34–36. Note that a "true" proof is a sound argument with true premises. We are trying to decide by whom determinations about things and issues should be made. The Dogmatist says, "By human beings." If he gives no proof of this, we will not be convinced. If he gives a proof, we say, "By whom has this been determined to be a true proof?" If he says, "By a human being," we have circularity. If he says, for example, "By a dog," we have an infinite regress. It is a peculiar argument.

37. The "saying" is part of the inscription on the tomb of Midas, as quoted by Plato, *Phaedrus* 264D.

46. The "conclusion" Sextus draws is that the "by whom" criterion is not apprehensible, whereas it looks as though the most he has shown is that *the Dogmatist will not be able to establish in a satisfactory way*, that is, without circularity or an infinite regress, that any particular thing is the "by whom" criterion.

47. We really do not need to consider the "by means of which" and "according to which" criteria, for what the Dogmatists have proposed under these headings are, by definition, either parts or *pathē* or actions of human beings, and since it has been shown that human beings are not apprehensible (if we go by what the Dogmatists say), these are not apprehensible either. That is to say, if you cannot recognize things as human beings, you cannot recognize anything as a part, *pathē*, or action of a human being. However, in order to avoid appearing evasive, Sextus will say a few things about the "by means of which" and "according to which" criteria, "for good measure."

## 48–69. The "By Means of Which" Criterion

In this chapter it is argued that if human beings are the "by whom" criterion, then, since they have only the senses and the intellect by means of which to decide conflicting claims about the external world, one or both of these will have to be the "by means of which" criterion. But neither the senses alone (section 56), nor the intellect alone (section 61), nor both of them together (section 63) suffice. And there are further difficulties. Whose senses and whose intellects are to be trusted? And will it be the senses or the intellect by means of which we are to get an answer to that question? In general, the testimony of the senses as well as that of the intellect will have to be determined by the senses or the intellect to be reliable; but, bearing in mind that the question before us is whether it is possible for a human being to make the requisite determinations about any subject by means of either the senses or the intellect or both, we see that every proposed way of evaluating this testimony will involve begging the question. In sum, going by what the Dogmatists say, there is no "by means of which" criterion (section 69).

48. Cf. M 7.243.

49. In other words: Some people say that the senses by themselves give us no answers to questions about the external world. (Cf. Santayana's "nothing given exists.") Others say that every sensory experience is the effect of, or a sign of, the existence of something in the external world; and still others say that some sensations give us information about the external world and some do not. Obviously we cannot determine by means of the senses which of these conflicting claims is true.

At M 7.126ff. the first of these views ("none") is associated with Heraclitus and Democritus; at M 7.369 the second ("all") is associated with Epicurus and Protagoras.

(Notice that the issue raised in this section, that is, the question which of the three views is correct, is itself treated as one that concerns τὰ ὑποκείμενα, the objects and states of affairs that constitute the external world, and hence it is considered self-applicable. Thus a statement about the reliability of the speaker's senses may, for him as well as for anyone else, be a statement about his external world.)

51. "For example, taste perceives the same honey sometimes as bitter and sometimes as sweet, and to sight the same color seems sometimes blood red and sometimes white." (A "color" [χρῶμα], for the ancients, is the colored surface of the thing, not the color of the thing.) Despite Sextus's use of γοῦν ("of course") in the quoted sentence, I do not regard this statement or others like it as showing that Sextus accepts the existence of the external world (see my note on 1.32). Thus, at the beginning of this section he grants, but only for the sake of argument, that the senses are fit to perceive things, and the subsequent statements are further premises which he takes from the Dogmatist without committing himself to their truth or falsity, or even to their meaningfulness. It is not excluded, of course, that he might assent to some of them as expressions of his own *pathē*.

57. This section corresponds to M 7.348ff.

63. This section corresponds to M 7.354ff.

64. Concerning "determinations," see the note on 2.34.

69. Sextus concludes that "for these reasons" there would be no such criterion as the "by means of which" criterion. But all the considerations he raises seem designed to show, not that no such criterion exists, but that the Dogmatist cannot support in a satisfactory way any claim that this or that is the criterion.

## 70–9. The "According to Which" Criterion

The general Dogmatic position under scrutiny is evidently the claim that human beings, using the senses or the intellect or both, can somehow "read off" truths about the external world from their *phantasiai*. In the present chapter Sextus attacks this claim from several standpoints. His first and most serious objection is that the Dogmatists have not even given us an intelligible definition of *phantasia*. The following way of putting the matter might illustrate the point he has in mind:

> You are looking at the half-immersed oar, and it looks broken. You wonder: is it really broken, or does it just look that way? The Stoic advises: examine your *phantasia* and see whether it is apprehensive. But, with no intelligible definition of *phantasia* you are unable even to get started on following this advice; for if you should ever meet with a *phantasia*, you will not recognize it as such.

Of course, one might respond that there are many terms — "green," "heavy," "anger" — that we understand well enough although we have never been given definitions of them. But I suppose that no one would expect to learn a technical term like *phantasia* in the way that we have learned those (although I must acknowledge that G. E. Moore and others have attempted to introduce the related term "sense datum" by indicating purported examples and adding "and things like those").

In any case, Sextus goes on to argue that even if the Dogmatists had given us a satisfactory concept of *phantasia*, *phantasiai* would not be apprehensible (section 70). For a *phantasia* is a *pathos* of the ruling part of the soul, and the ruling part is not apprehensible (section 71). Clearly, Sextus is taking the Dogmatists' statement that "a *phantasia* is a *pathos* of the ruling part" as analytic and hence as expressing a relation between the *concepts* of *phantasia, pathos, and ruling part*; and his inference here seems to presuppose that if the concept "$X$ is composed of the concepts $Y, Z, \ldots$, then $X$ is apprehensible if and only if $Y, Z, \ldots$, are apprehensible"; see pp. 48–9 above.

Next, even if *phantasiai* could be apprehended, that is to say, if they could be recognized as being *phantasiai*, it would not be possible to make determinations about the external world "according to" or "in accord with" them. For the Dogmatists say (first) that the intellect does not of itself contact the external objects and receive *phantasiai*, but does so only by means of the senses, and (second) that the senses do not apprehend the external objects but only their own *pathē*, which of course are not identical with those objects. Thus the *phantasiai* will not be *phantasiai* of the external objects but only of the perceiver's *pathē*. Hence, determinations made "in accord with" our *phantasiai* will not characterize the external objects but only, if anything, our own *pathē* (section 73). But even waiving all these difficulties, there would remain the question of which *phantasiai* to trust, and, on the Dogmatists' theory, the only way of finding that out would be by means of one or more trustworthy *phantasiai*. Thus *phantasiai*, if there are any, will in any case have no utility as criteria for making determinations about the external world (section 78).

With this chapter compare M 7.34–7, 370ff.

70. Note that it is here said that an art (*technē*) is constituted by *theōrēmata*, principles.

72. Here and in section 74 it is asserted that the senses apprehend only their own *pathē*, "if anything." Sextus ascribes this view explicitly only to the Cyrenaics (at 1.215 and M 7.191), but probably he has in mind mainly the Epicureans, who identified *phantasiai* with certain *pathē* of the soul (M 7.203).

74. The claim that the soul can apprehend the external objects by means of its sensory *pathē* because these *pathē* are in some sense similar to the objects is dismissed on the familiar ground that the alleged similarity (or even abstract isomorphism) cannot be determined.

79. Compare M 7.443.

## 80–84. The True and Truth

We are going to consider "the true"; it is defined in section 81 as an *axiōma* and ergo a *lekton*. Presumably this is only the Stoic definition, for the Epicureans regard the *phōnē* as the bearer of truth and say (107) that *lekta* do not exist. Already in section 84 "the true" seems used in a wider sense. But in most of what follows Sextus is attacking the Stoics and seems to be using the principal terminology in their way.

83. I read γνώςεων, in accord with the Latin translation T.

## 85–96. Is There Anything True by Nature?

The point of this chapter is surely that if there is no such thing as a true proposition, there will be no (nontrivial) criterion for distinguishing true propositions from false, or, what comes to the same thing, for distinguishing true *phantasiai* from false.

85. To understand the circularity charge, one must understand that "true" is used both of propositions and of arguments (and, a fortiori, of proofs). Cf. 2.143: a proof is an argument that is valid and true and has a nonevident conclusion disclosed by means of the force of the premises. Also 2.135–8: an argument is a system of propositions consisting of premises and a conclusion; an argument is valid if the corresponding conditional is sound; an argument is true if it is valid and has true premises.

86–7. "*X* is something," which is equivalent to "*X* exists," is treated as analogous to "*X* is a man," "*X* is an animal," or "*X* is a living thing," and hence as amounting to "*X* belongs to a huge class named 'something.'"

88–94. If we bear in mind that "the true" are propositions (*axiōmata*), the alternatives given at the beginning of section 88 seem to be: either all true propositions are appearances, or all are non-evident, or some are appearances and some are non-evident. I think that this means: either all true propositions express appearances (i.e., are of the form "it appears that..."), or they all purport to describe the non-evident, that is, the independently existing external world, or some express appearances and some purport to describe the non-evident.

90. Reading, with Heintz, καὶ for ἤ in line 18.

95. Remember that we are talking about the criterion of truth (see also section 80), and the criterion of truth "is that by which we decide questions of existence and non-existence" (section 14), which, in view of the wide sense of "to be," will include deciding questions about what is or is not the case, that is, the truth or falsity of propositions.

## 97–103. Signs

This topic would seem to be of essential importance to the Dogmatists' epistemologies, for they all hold that in one way or another we justify assertions about reality (the "non-evident by nature") on the basis of what appears to us to be the case. But how is this possible, we ask, granting that in principle we cannot compare appearance with reality in order to see whether there is any similarity or even isomorphism between the two. The Dogmatists' answer is that the appearances are indicative signs of the reality, in the way that the motion and certain other attributes of the body are signs of the soul. In effect, therefore, to the question, "How do you know that there is an external world?" the Dogmatist is replying, "The same way that you know that there are other minds."

The Pyrrhonist is unconvinced by this; indeed, as I interpret him, he is unconvinced that there is any truth or even meaning in the whole Dogmatic story to the effect that by means of the appearances we get information about an independently existing external world.

It can be argued that, in view of the pre-evident–non-evident distinction and the examples we are given of indicative signs (sweat–invisible pores; bodily motions–souls), we must suppose that in the present connection the Dogmatists are not talking about a relation between appearances (considered as things to which the Skeptics will assent) and external objects, but rather about a relation between two sorts of external objects. We have seen (p. 14–15) that the expression τὸ φαινόμενον is ambiguous in an epistemologically significant way. Literally it means "what appears," and the question is: what's *that*? When the oar appears broken, is τὸ φαινόμενον the oar or the proposition that the oar is broken (i.e., what appears to be the case), or something else? If the Dogmatists are only claiming that one kind of external object—for example, sweat—can be a sign of another kind of external object—for example, invisible pores in the skin—it is hard to see how this is in any way relevant to the problem question before the house, namely, how knowledge of the external objects can be obtained from the appearances (τὰ φαινόμενα) to which the Skeptic gives his assent.

100. Note the definitions of mnemonic and indicative signs. The Skeptic does not question the existence of mnemonic signs, where the terms of the sign-significate relation are both appearances or types of appearances; perhaps he is granting that when it seems to him that there is smoke, it seems to him that there is fire (section 102). But he challenges the existence of indicative signs; they have been invented by the Dogmatists, he says, and obviously they are at the root of the Dogmatists' epistemologies. However, as I have indicated in section 4 of the Introduction, I suspect that, if pushed, Sextus would have to follow Hume and consider anything other than a person's *pathē* at a given time to be part of that person's "external world" at that time, so that inferences from our present *pathē* to other people's *pathē* or to our own *pathē* of the past and future would be on the same weak footing as inferences from our *pathē* to independently existing material objects.

At M 8.157, where Sextus discusses the two kinds of signs, he again uses the example of smoke as a mnemonic sign of fire. He says, οὕτω καὶ αὐτοὶ ἔγνωμεν, ἐκ μὲν καπνοῦ πῦρ, ἐκ δὲ οὐλῆς προηγησάμενον ἕλκος... λαμβάνοντες ("but as it is, we ourselves think along the same lines [as the common man], inferring fire from smoke, a previous wound from a scar"). The use of ἔγνωμεν and λαμβάνοντες has been taken to support the view that the Skeptic in many instances does think of himself as knowing something. In my opinion, however, there is no knowledge claim here. As this passage of the *Outlines* confirms, all Sextus has in mind is association: after smoke-*pathē* are repeatedly conjoined with fire-*pathē*, the next smoke-*pathos* brings with it a fire-*pathos*; that is, when it seems that there is smoke, it seems that there is fire. Note that living in accord with the προλήψεις of the common man does not even require *belief* (PH 2.246), let alone knowledge.

101. Mau, following Heintz and Natorp, deletes the last sentence of this section, on the ground that it roughly interrupts the course of the argument. But the sentence does not seem to me to be especially incongruous. The "whence" is at first puzzling, until one realizes that it relates particularly to the last clause of the Stoic definition.

## 104–33. Is There Such a Thing as an Indicative Sign?

The answer to this question, reached at section 133, is that "with such plausible arguments presented both for and against the existence of [indicative] signs, it must be said that it is 'not more' the case that they exist than that they do not."

Sextus tells us that the Stoics characterize the indicative sign (σημεῖον ἐνδεικτικόν) as "a proposition that is the true antecedent in a true conditional and serves to disclose the consequent." On this basis, both the indicative sign and what is signified are *lekta*, since each is a proposition (ἀξίωμα). But if not only the sign but also the object signified is a *lekton* and hence not part of the external world, it is hard to see why *this* notion of sign would be of any use to the epistemologist in his task of explaining how appearances give us a clue to reality.

On the other hand, when in chapter 10 the Stoics distinguish indicative signs from mnemonic, they do so on the basis of a distinction between things that are "pre-evident" (πρόδηλα) and those that are "non-evident" (ἄδηλα) and the indicative signs are supposed to be pre-evident things that are signs of non-evident things. Therefore, since "the non-evident" (τὰ ἄδηλα) usually denotes the external world of objects and states of affairs, this seems to be the kind of sign needed for the explanation sought. But how can the significate be at once a *lekton* and an externally existing object? After all, in the well-known passage at M 8.11–3 *lekta* are said to exist in the intellect and are contrasted with externally existing objects. The answer, I fear, is that we have here another example of the fundamental confusion of sense and denotation: propositions about the external world are being confused with the states of affairs they denote, both being called indifferently τὰ ἄδηλα.

Sextus does not seize upon on this ambiguity of τὰ ἄδηλα, but instead raises the question whether there is any such thing as a *lekton*. He observes that while some of the Dogmatists hold that *lekta* do exist, others claim that they do not. And he points out that the Stoics are in a poor position to offer any doubter a proof that *lekta* exist, for a proof is defined as a system of *lekta*. Next, he argues that even if some *lekta* exist, propositions (which the Stoics consider to be composite *lekta*) do not, since a composite object cannot exist unless its parts exist simultaneously, and the parts of a proposition would only exist seriatim as the corresponding sounds were being uttered (cf. section 144). Then, leaving this too aside, he argues that in any case the Stoic definition cannot be applied, as there is no agreement among the Dogmatists on the truth conditions for conditional propositions.

The most that would seem to follow from this is something we already know, namely, that we shall not find a definition of "sign" that is satisfactory to all the Dogmatists. But again Sextus contents himself with showing that the Stoics are in no position to prove to the Dogmatists or anyone else that one or another of the alternative criteria for the truth of conditionals is correct, for the proof would have to be a sound argument, and the Stoic criterion for the soundness of an argument is that the conditional corresponding to the argument is true.

Next, Sextus argues that the sign is relative to what is signified, and hence they are apprehended together with one another (see also section 125). But the sign must be apprehended before what is signified, in order to reveal it. Therefore, it is impossible to conceive of the sign. The argument is bad; things are not "relative"; one might say that a thing is relative "under a given description", but it is better to say that "relative" is at most a predicate of concepts, not the things that fall under them. See my note on 1.135–40.

He goes on to argue that there is no use offering us a proof that signs exist, as a proof is supposed to be a special case of a sign. Again, it seems that we have to think of this "argument" in a dialectical context. The Dogmatist says to the Skeptic, "Here is a proof that signs exist." The Skeptic says, "What do you mean by 'proof'?" The Dogmatist replies that a proof is a certain sequence of signs. The Skeptic then says, "I am not convinced that what you have given me is a proof, for I am not convinced that there are any signs."

At this point (section 124) Sextus's arguments cease to be directed specifically against the Stoics. Presupposing the internal-external, or appearance-reality, distinction, which of course is nowadays suspected of being the source of the entire quagmire, he raises the crucial question of the status of signs in this regard. Either all of them are appearances or all are non-evident—parts of the external world—or some are appearances and some are non-evident. If all the signs are external, then, since the Dogmatists hold that an external object can only be apprehended via something that is not external, we have the conclusion that, on their theory, signs are not apprehensible. For the case in which all the signs are internal, that is, appearances, Sextus offers (sections 125–6) a purely sophistical argument based on the notion of "relatives" (see my note on 1.135–40) and involving the claim that since the sign and the significate are "relatives," one is an appearance if and only if the other is an appearance as well. But "if the significatum is an appearance, it will not be a significatum, since it will not need anything to signify and disclose it" (section 126). The case in which some signs are appearances and some are not is in effect reduced to the first two cases. Thus, this portion of the chapter is especially disappointing; for the case we should have liked Sextus to analyze seriously is precisely the case in which the sign is an appearance and the object signified is an object or state of affairs in the external world. He could have argued that, on the Dogmatists' theory, we are never able to discover that this case exists, for to determine that an appearance is a sign of an external object we would need to apprehend the external object by means of some other appearance; otherwise we would be assuming what we were trying to discover.

Finally, Sextus tips his hat to the "not more" slogan by adding a few equally spurious arguments to support the thesis that signs do exist after all.

106. I am translating προκαθηγούμενον as "guiding proposition"; it denotes the true antecedent of a true conditional, but I need another expression for it in order that the definition in this section and in section 115 not have the form "*A* is *A*."

110–2. This passage is important for the history of logic. Four different interpretations of the "if-then" connective are given, in order of increasing "strength." The passage is cleverly crafted: for each of the first three cases an example is provided that is true under that interpretation but false under the next. Part of the content of the passage is presented in greater detail at M 8.112–7.

The dispute over the truth conditions for conditionals was notorious in antiquity. Callimachus reports (M 1.309–10) that "Even the crows on the rooftops are cawing about the question which conditionals are true," and Cicero says (*Academica* 2.143):

> Even on this matter that is among the very rudiments taught by the logicians, that is, the proper mode of determining the truth or falsity of such a conditional as "If it is day, it is light," what a controversy goes on! One view suits Diodorus, another Philo, another Chrysippus.

The condition proposed by Philo of Megara seems to define what is now called "material implication" (cf. M 8.113ff. for what amounts to the truth table for material "if-then"). It is not quite clear, however, whether Philo's notion of truth is relativized to time—whether, for instance, he means that "If it is day, then I am conversing" is true *at any time when* it is day and I am conversing, or he means that the conditional is true *on the assumption that* it is day and I am conversing. Diodorus, Philo's teacher, laid the foundation for so-called "temporal logic" by (in effect) defining a conditional as true if and only if it holds *at all times* in the Philonean sense. (It appears also that he defined a proposition as necessarily true if and only if it holds at all times; this, incidentally, impressed Leibniz, who often cites Diodorus as the first of a long line of philosophers who confuse hypothetical necessity with absolute.)

The third definition, where of course "inconsistent" propositions are such as not only *are* not both true but *cannot* be both true, is commonly thought to be that of Chrysippus (see Mates 1958, p. 48). This relatively strong interpretation of the "if-then" connective seems required if sense is to be made of the Stoic version of the so-called "conditionalization" principle, that an argument is sound if and only if the corresponding conditional (i.e., the conditional whose antecedent is the conjunction of the premises of the argument and whose consequent is the argument's conclusion) is true.

The usage of the two adjectives ὑγιής ("sound") and ἀληθής ("true") is less than neat and clear. As applied to propositions they are for the most part used interchangeably to denote truth, but as applied to arguments there is a difference. A true argument is defined as an argument that is not only sound but also has true premises.

113. See the note on section 137 below. Also, there is some unclarity here as to what proof and what circularity Sextus has in mind. He may only be arguing, with respect to an argument

$$A_1, A_2, \ldots, A_n; \text{ therefore, } B.$$

and its corresponding conditional

$$\text{If } A_1 \text{ and } A_2 \text{ and} \ldots \text{ and } A_n, \text{ then } B,$$

(where $B$ is a statement to the effect that one of the four views in section 112 is correct), that in order to prove that the argument is a proof we have to prove that the conditional is true, and, in order to do that, we have to prove that its consequent follows from its antecedent, which in effect is no different from proving that the original argument is valid and hence is a proof. (Sextus apparently considers it obvious that both *B* and the statement that the argument is a proof are "non-evident"—see the definition of "proof" in section 135.)

Or, his point may be that any argument we offer as a proof that the original argument is a proof will itself have to be established as being a proof, which will involve proving its corresponding conditional. So that the "circle" would be that to establish that an argument is a proof you have to give a proof of the corresponding conditional, but then you have to establish that what you have given is in fact a proof, and this requires proving a corresponding conditional (though not the same one as before).

## 134–43. Proof

This chapter is of interest principally for the definitions and examples it gives for terms in Stoic logic. From here and elsewhere we learn that:

An argument (λόγος) is a system of propositions consisting of premises (λήμματα) and conclusion ἐπιφορά or συμπέρασμα).

The premises of an argument are the propositions agreed upon for the establishment of the conclusion.

The conclusion of an argument is the proposition established from the premises.

An argument is valid (συνακτικός) if the conditional (συνήμμενον) whose antecedent (ἀρχόμενον or ἡγούμενον) is the conjunction (συμπεπλεγμένον or συμπλοκή) of the premises and whose consequent (λῆγον) is the conclusion of the argument is sound (ὑγιές), that is, true.

An argument is true if it is valid and the conjunction of the premises is true.

A proof (ἀπόδειξις) is an argument that is true and has a non-evident conclusion disclosed by the force of the premises.

Elsewhere we have definitions for the other technical terms employed here:

A conditional is a proposition that is formed from two occurrences of a single proposition or from different propositions by means of the connective "if-then" (M 8.101ff.).

The antecedent of a conditional is the proposition that immediately follows "if," even if the whole proposition is expressed in reverse order, "*Q* if *P*"; the other part is the consequent (M 8.110).

A conjunction is a proposition compounded by means of "and" (Diogenes Laertius 7.72).

Propositions are inconsistent (μαχόμενα) if it is impossible that all be true (Diogenes Laertius 7. 73, 77).

137. Here, and at every other place in Sextus's writings where a so-called "corresponding conditional" occurs, the texts—as found in most of the MSS. and as presented by all the editors before Mau—are garbled. However, there

are two circumstances that make it quite easy to see what the original text must have been. One is that in most cases Sextus gives us a description of the conditional before he formulates it. The other is that the conditionals have been garbled in different ways in different occurrences and in different MSS., so that by laying the garbled versions over one another, as it were, we can "look through" them to the original text.

Thus, instead of the conditional in this section, Bekker has "If it is day, and if it is day it is light," which is not even a proposition, let alone a conditional. No doubt in this case the erroneous text arose when somebody deleted the final "It is light" from the conditional, supposing that it was a scribe's repetition. Similarly, for the conditional in section 139 Bekker gives "If it is night, and if it is night, therefore [ἄρα] it is dark," which is not a conditional (because of the "therefore") and which in any case does not have a conjunction as an antecedent as the text specifies. Here again, somewhere along the line the final "It is dark" has been cut off, presumably as a supposed repetition, and a "therefore" has been inserted.

Elsewhere, as in section 113 above, where the premises of the argument are conjoined in the opposite order, the corresponding conditional has to begin with two consecutive occurrences of "if"; needless to say, somebody dropped one of them as superfluous, and the result is nonsense.

For details, see Mates (1949b).

## 144–92. Are There Proofs?

The official answer to this question, as stated in sections 180 and 192, is that proof "no more" exists than not. But most of the present strung-out and repetitive chapter is devoted to arguing that, if we go by what the Dogmatists say, there is no such thing as a proof. Most of the argumentation does not challenge the concept of proof, but at section 171ff. Sextus offers to make plain that not only does proof not exist, it is not even conceivable.

Like its predecessor, this chapter is noteworthy as one of the principal sources of information about the Stoic propositional calculus.

144. If you go by the Dogmatists' definition of "proof," there is no such thing as a proof. For a composite thing cannot exist unless its parts exist simultaneously, but a proof, as defined by the Dogmatists, would be a composite thing with parts that existed seriatim. Cf. section 109.

145. On the Dogmatists' definition of validity we cannot determine whether an argument is valid, for this depends on whether or not the corresponding conditional is sound, and we have seen in sections 113–5 that there is no way to determine whether a given conditional is sound.

146–50. Sextus now considers four ways in which the Dogmatists say that an argument may be invalid, namely, it may be (1) incoherent, (2) deficient, (3) in an unsound schema, or (4) redundant. After arguing in the succeeding sections that we cannot determine that an argument is invalid in any of the four ways, he concludes in section 167 that it is not possible to determine whether an argument is valid, which presumably is a corollary of the unstated conclusion that we cannot determine whether an argument is invalid.

152–3. We cannot determine that an argument is invalid by incoherence, for this requires determining that the corresponding conditional is not sound, which we cannot do.

154. To establish that a given argument is invalid by being in an unsound schema, a valid argument to that effect is needed, which, in turn, requires us to determine that the corresponding conditional is sound.

155. For the same reason, we cannot establish that a given argument is invalid by deficiency.

156–8. The Stoic propositional calculus consisted of five basic (or "unde-monstrated") valid inference patterns, from which other valid inference patterns were derived in accord with four metarules ($\theta\acute{\epsilon}\mu\alpha\tau\alpha$), of which we possess only the first and the third. The five undemonstrated patterns were very well known in antiquity, and in addition to the present statement of them there are many others, often giving the same examples (see Mates 1953, p. 66).

Sextus says that we cannot distinguish a redundant argument from a (Stoic) proof, for all five of the postulated ("undemonstrated") valid inference patterns of the Stoics are redundant, and hence so are all the complex inference patterns that the Stoics reduce to chains of these simples. (He implies that the Stoics thought that *all* valid inference patterns are reducible to their five basic ones.)

159–62. In support of the aforementioned claim that each of the five basic types of inference is redundant, Sextus considers them seriatim. In each case, the argument given is a version of what used to be included in logic books under the heading, "Is the syllogism a petitio principii?" For example, it is claimed that if

If it is day, then it is light.
It is day.
Therefore, it is light,

is a proof of "It is light," the conditional "If it is day, then it is light" would be superfluous, for anyone for whom this proposition could serve as a premise, that is, to whom its truth is evident, would be willing to infer "It is light" directly from "It is day" alone.

163–6. Like the arguments of the Stoics, the categorical syllogisms of the Peripatetics are redundant when offered as proofs. For example, if the second premise of the argument at section 164 is not evident to a person, the argument will not be a proof for him; but if it is evident, he will infer the conclusion from the first premise alone. The modern (and equally bad) variant of this is, I think, the following. Nobody will be convinced by this argument that Socrates is an animal, for in establishing the second premise he will already have considered the case of Socrates along with all the other human beings. In other words, anybody who grants the premises will not need the argument in order to grant the conclusion; or, "nothing new" will be learned from the conclusion.

It seems that if Sextus is following the pattern of sections 146–55 he should be showing that we cannot establish that a given argument is invalid by redundancy. Instead, he tries to show that according to the doctrines of the Stoics and Peripatetics *all* valid arguments are redundant and hence invalid. From this it would appear to follow that all arguments, redundant or not, are invalid; but whether from that it follows in turn that we cannot establish that a given argument is invalid by redundancy, I leave to the reader.

167–8. After inferring from sections 146–66 that, going by what the Dogmatists say, it is not possible to determine whether an argument is valid, Sextus briefly argues that true arguments are indeterminate (i.e., cannot be determined to be such) not only because they must be valid but also because the conclusion must be true and non-evident. His discussion is puzzling. First, although in the definition of "true argument" at sections 138–9 there is no indication that the conclusion need be anything more than a true consequence of true premises, here he seems to assume that, like the conclusion of a proof, it must also be "disclosed" by means of the premises. There is also a problem about the inference from the "dispute" to non-apprehensibility. The clause, "as we have pointed out previously," seems to refer to section 116, where the dispute in question is described as a dispute as to which, if any, of the non-evident things are true and which are false. But if that is what the dispute is about (rather than about the concept of non-apprehensibility itself), it is difficult to see how it follows that the Dogmatist will be unable to apprehend a non-evident thing.

169–70. After another application of the confused principle that "relatives must be apprehended together with one another," Sextus draws a major conclusion: "It is plain that there is no such thing as a proof."

171–6. But not only that; proof is not even conceivable. The argument in these sections involves confusion compounded. First, there is a supposed distinction (M 8.382) between the generic proof (ἡ γενική ἀπόδειξις) and the particular proofs (αἱ ἐπὶ μέρους ἀποδείξεις):

> Now if we propose to object to the particular proofs and those belonging to each art, we shall be making our objection in an unmethodical way, as there are an infinite number of such proofs. But if we abolish [i.e., refute the existence of] the generic proof, which is thought to include all the particular proofs, it is evident that we shall have thereby abolished all included in it. For just as if animal does not exist, neither does human being, and if human being does not exist, neither does Socrates—the particulars being abolished along with the genera—so if generic proof does not exist, particular proof wholly disappears as well. (M 8.337aff.)

One source of confusion is that the term ἀπόδειξις γενική ("generic proof," or "proof in general") is treated as though it denoted a certain kind of proof, whereas in such of its uses as are unobjectionable it is clearly syncategorematic. Thus presumably the phrase "to abolish generic proof" should mean "to show generally that there is no such thing as a proof," to be contrasted with showing that, for example, there is no such thing as a proof that the number of the stars is even. But Sextus treats that phrase as if it meant that there is no such thing as a certain very special kind of proof, namely, a "generic" proof. A second source of confusion making this passage practically untranslatable is a problem that we have mentioned elsewhere, namely, that due in part to the fact that Greek has no indefinite article and uses the definite article in ways that do not completely match the use of English "the," the expression ἡ ἀπόδειξις can refer either to the concept of proof or to a particular proof that is under discussion, or it can be used to express generality ("the proof," like "the tiger" in "The tiger is a mammal"). And here Sextus uses it to refer to what he calls "generic proof."

Thus he can argue that if the so-called "generic" proof does not have premises and a conclusion, it is not a proof (since every proof, by definition, has premises and a conclusion), whereas if it does have these, it is a particular proof (since only particular propositions qualify as premises and conclusion).

In any case, he is surely right in his conclusion, that there is no such thing as a generic proof. Cf. M 7.222, where he describes the generic man (γενικὸς ἄνθρωπος) as a φάντασμα, (something imaginary), and M 7.246 where he explains that although every man is a Greek or a barbarian, the generic man is neither.

177–9. Four cases are distinguished, of which only the fourth (in which something non-evident is to be inferred from evident premises) is relevant to the central epistemological problem of inferring reality from appearances. Alas, the only argument Sextus offers to eliminate this case rests on the confused "relatives must be apprehended together" principle.

180-2. Whether a given system of propositions is a proof of its conclusion is in general a non-evident matter and hence needs to be proved. This, unlike many of the other difficulties Sextus raises, is a serious problem; indeed, it has been one of the primary motivating factors in the development of modern logic. It lies behind the demand that mathematical proofs be formalized in such a way that whether a given sequence of formulas is a proof can be determined by their shape and independently of their meaning. Thus, to avoid the problems that obviously result when a proof is considered to be just any series of statements sufficient to convince a "reasonable person" of the truth of the conclusion, it was proposed to define a proof as a finite sequence of formalized sentences such that every term or "step" of the sequence is either an assumption or follows from predecessors by certain formal rules of inference. For a formalized theory the task of deciding whether a given sequence of formulas is a proof of $X$ can be accomplished "mechanically" and may therefore be quite different from the task of finding a proof of $X$.

182–92. In a perfunctory way, Sextus gives and discusses purported proofs that there are proofs; obviously he feels he must do this in order to support the "conclusion" in section 192 that "If, on the one hand, the arguments on behalf of proof are plausible (and let them be so), while, on the other hand, the attacks made against proof are also plausible, it is necessary to suspend judgment about proof, saying that it 'no more' exists than not."

183–4. It is unclear exactly what Sextus has in mind, but one possibility would be something like the following. Suppose that I claim that there is a proof of $X$. You doubt that there is, so I offer to write it out (i.e., to produce a "sign" of it) for you. But then you question whether what I have written really signifies a system of propositions constituting a proof of $X$. So I need to give a proof that it does. And so on.

188. Cf. 1.206, M 8.480.


## 193–203. Syllogisms        204. Induction

Sextus now turns his attention to Peripatetic logic. As in the case of Stoic logic, he claims (section 194) that if the "undemonstrated syllogisms" are abolished, "all the remaining arguments are overthrown, since the proof of their validity is based on these." This time he takes as "undemonstrated" the syllogisms in the modes Barbara and Celarent. (In the *Prior Analytics* Aristotle reduces all the valid modes to those of the first figure, and then he shows, first, that the first figure modes Darii and Ferio can be reduced to the modes of the second figure, while second, all modes of the second figure can be reduced to Barbara and Celarent of the first figure.)

195–7. This is the kind of argument with which generations of philosophers have claimed to show that "the syllogism is a petitio principii."

196. I follow Bury's text, which inserts the words ἐπαγωικῶς βεβαιοῦντες, τὴν δὲ κατὰ μέρος, in the lacuna indicated by Bekker.

198ff. Sextus now attempts to transfer the circularity argument from Peripatetic logic to that of the Stoics. His account seems garbled, but the point appears to be that if we take the conditional,

> If it is day, it is light

in the sense of

> Whenever it is day, it is light,

we find that in order to establish the conditional we must already have examined the present day and found it accompanied by light.


## 205–12. Definitions

In order to check whether a proposed definition correctly defines $X$'s, you must be able to recognize an $X$ when you meet one, that is, you must be able to apprehend things as being $X$'s. Thus, to one who cannot apprehend $X$'s it is of no help to be furnished with a purported definition of $X$.

Further evidence of this lack of utility, says Sextus, is the fact that in practice we reject a proposed definition if it does not fit the already established extension of the term; hence the extension cannot have been established on the basis of the definition.

## 213–8. Division [διαίρεσις]

Sextus next takes up the topic of "division" or "classification," which, from its prominent role in Plato's *Sophist* and Aristotle's *Organon*, was traditionally regarded as a part of logic. In line with his goal of showing that logic, as presented by the Dogmatists, is at best useless and at worst unintelligible, Sextus raises questions about four kinds of classification or division that logicians have postulated.

214. I think that the rather odd phrase, "to divide a term into its meanings," just means "to give the meanings that the term has." Thus the point here is that there can be no such science as lexicography, which seeks to do this for each term in the language. For scientific knowledge (ἐπιστήμη) aims at being—"wants to be"—something firm and unchanging (βέβαιον τι καὶ ἀμετάπτωτον πρᾶγμα) and thus is supposed to consist of information about the external world, that is, about what is the case independently of our thoughts, feelings, and other *pathē* (cf. 1.13). From this, Sextus infers that there can be no scientific knowledge of what words mean, since that is a matter of convention, that is, it is "in our power" ("when *I* use a word, it means what I want it to mean, neither more nor less"). No doubt there is a fallacy here, but there will be little agreement on exactly where it lies.

215–8. Cf. 3.98ff. The modern reader will notice that Sextus is here confusing the aggregate or heap (such as a herd of sheep or a bunch of grapes) with a set whose elements are parts of the aggregate, and correspondingly that he is also confusing the whole-part relation with the set-element relation. Frege pointed out long ago that numerical predicates, such as "eight," "nine," or "ten" apply to sets and not to aggregates. When Sextus speaks of "the eight," "the nine," and so on, ambiguity and confusion threaten because the same aggregate or heap can be the "fusion" of many different sets—for instance, the same pyramidal stack of 14 cannon balls is not only the fusion of the set of the 14 cannon balls but also that of the much larger set of all molecules in the stack as well as that of the still larger set of all atoms in the stack.

Consider, for example, the twelve Apostles. "Twelve" is a predicate of the set, not the aggregate, even though we say, "The Apostles were twelve." Hence such a phrase as "the twelve" is misleading in that it seems simply to denote the aggregate when in fact it contains a reference to a set whose fusion is the aggregate.

The matter is further complicated by the fact that in Greek a numeral with the article, for example, τὰ δώδεκα ("the twelve"), may denote not only a 12-part aggregate like the Apostles, but also the number 12 itself. So the present passage is also ambiguous as to whether it concerns the division of numbers into factors or the division of aggregates into subaggregates.

## 219–27. Genera and Species

219. As Bury notes in connection with the remark "we shall treat it at greater length elsewhere," no such discussion is to be found in the extant works of Sextus.

220 ff. The argumentation in these sections, though unintelligible to me, is nevertheless reminiscent of that in the *Parmenides* and involves what Gilbert Ryle used to call "category mistakes." This is especially clear in section 220, where "human being" and "animal" refer ambiguously to the concepts and to objects that fall under the concepts. Thus, just as the "Third Man" argument in the *Parmenides* takes the Idea of Largeness to be one of the large things, so here we find a reductio ad absurdum argument resting on the implication that the concept of human being is an animal and hence is animate and sensitive.

224. Between γένος and πέρας in line 26 Mutschmann conjectures a lacuna, to be filled with the words ἔστιν, εἰ δὲ μηδὲ τὸ γένος. This would make the sentence read: "But if Something, that is, the genus, is absolutely none of these, the genus does not exist, and if not even the genus exists, the inquiry is terminated."

225. I follow Pappenheim's suggestion and place ζῷον after ἄλογον.

226. Adding τό τι in line 19, with Heintz.

227. The predicate ἄνθρωπος cannot have the same meaning when applied to Dion that it has when applied to Theon, for otherwise the proposition "a man is walking" (ἄνθρωπος περιπατεῖ) would have the same truth value when applied to the two of them, even though Dion were sitting down and Theon were walking. The argument clearly confuses the sense of ἄνθρωπος with its denotation.

Note the word-for-word example of what was later called "Leibniz's Law."

## 228. Common Accidents

As treated in this section, accidents (συμβεβηκότα) are not to be confused with attributes or concepts. The accidents of individuals are peculiar to those individuals, whereas attributes may be shared by different individuals. Thus Ajax and Milo both have the attribute "strong," or fall under the concept Strong, but the strength of Ajax is one thing and that of Milo is another; and it is by virtue of those individual accidents that they share the attribute.

Incidentally, this distinction plays an important role in the metaphysics of Leibniz. We know that he read and wrote out comments on the *Outlines*, and the present section is very Leibnizian.

The same matter is also involved in a well-known scholarly dispute concerning the proper interpretation of Plato's metaphysics, as to whether for Plato there are just two kinds of entities, namely, the Ideas (e.g., Justice) and the things that participate in the Ideas (e.g., just acts), or there are in addition entities of a third kind, denoted by such phrases as "the justice in us." Thus Gregory Vlastos sought to disarm the "Third Man" argument by distinguishing the Idea of Largeness from the largeness in us (cf. Vlastos, 1973, pp. 344ff.).

## 229–59. Sophisms

The point of this chapter is stated in section 236: "In the case of those sophisms that logic seems particularly capable of refuting, the explanation is useless; while as regards those for which explanation is useful, it is not the logician who would explain them away but rather those in each art who have got an understanding of the facts." This is echoed in sections 246 and 255.

However, most of the sophisms depend upon violations of Greek syntax and are practically impossible to translate into English. (They are not very good in Greek, either.) In a number of places the text is obviously corrupt.

230. Even in the Greek, the absinthe case looks like a plain mistake. As suggested by Sextus's explanation in section 233, the point of the doctor/murder example seems to be that ἄτοπον ("nonsense") is used in the premise and the conclusion as a predicate of propositions, and propositions, being senses of sentences, are never nonsense. Thus the conclusion follows from the presumably true premises and accordingly is true. But the unwary reader, now taking ἄτοπον in its common meaning of "odd," will feel that the conclusion is false.

231. The verb ἐρωτάω, when used by Sextus in reference to the steps of a dialectical argument, does not have its ordinary meaning, "to question," but instead means "to put forward as a matter to be debated." Thus, as Sextus explains in section 234, the puzzle, such as it is, is the result of the fact that "I have already asserted something" changes from false to true during the presentation of the argument.

The solecistic "look" and "see" examples are untranslatable into English, as they depend on the accusative case being improperly used in place of the nominative in the conclusions — as if, for example, the argument were

What you see exists.
You see him.
Therefore, him exists.

241. The "horn fallacy" (ὁ κερατίνης) is usually stated as follows (Diogenes Laertius 7.187):

What you have not lost, you still have.
You have not lost horns.
Therefore, you still have horns.

In the version given here, Mau, following Oskar Bekker, deletes the initial καὶ from the antecedent of the first premise and supposes that the fallacy arises from taking the second premise in the sense of "You don't both have beautiful horns and have horns." This seems to be the only way to given even a modicum of plausibility to the second premise.

242. It is interesting that when this argument, which is described in section 244 as "nonsense," reappears at 3.71, it is characterized (at section 3.81) as an argument that "we are unable to dismiss" and is thus by implication at least strong enough to keep the Skeptic from agreeing that motion exists.

According to 3.71 and M 1.311 the argument was due to Diodorus Cronus.

243. Cf. 3.110 and M 7.71; in the latter passage the argument is ascribed to Gorgias.

244. At 1.33 the "snow" argument is ascribed to Anaxagoras.

The "certain philosopher" is identified by Diogenes Laertius (6.39) as Diogenes the Cynic. Cf. 3.66.

246. The Skeptic Way is succinctly described: ἀρκεῖ γάρ, οἶμαι, τὸ ἐμπείρως τε καὶ ἀδοξάστως κατὰ τὰς κοινὰς τηρήσεις τε καὶ προλήψεις βιοῦν, περὶ τῶν ἐκ δογματικῆς περιεργίας καὶ μάλιστα ἔξω τῆς βιωτικῆς χρείας λεγομένων ἐπέχοντας. The βιωτικὴ τήρησις is described at 1.23, and the προλήψεις are the imprecise and "pre-philosophical" notions that function as meanings of our words in ordinary discourse.

250. Reading οὐδὲ in line 25.

252. There is a possibly apocryphal story that A. M. Turing, apropos the question whether Russell's Antinomy rendered "naïve" set theory useless (since everything follows from a contradiction), remarked that "We don't have to fall over cliffs just because they are there."

259. As Bury notes, no such discussion is to be found in the extant works of Sextus.

# Outlines of Pyrrhonism, Book 3

## 1. Physics    2. Productive Sources of Things

We see from M 9.4 and 12 that the ἀρχαὶ δραστικαί are the ἀρχαὶ ποιητικαί ("productive sources.") The discussion of causes, in sections 13ff., shows that in this context the words ἀρχή and αἴτιον are practically synonymous. I am avoiding the customary translation of ἀρχαί as "principles" because that word nowadays usually refers to propositions, not things or events.

## 3–12. God

It must be borne in mind here that the primary subject is "physics," not religion, and the question is whether the Dogmatists' account of the role of gods in the origin of the physical world is acceptable or even intelligible. Gods enter the discussion, not as beings deserving of worship, but as purported "productive sources" of physical things.

The Pyrrhonist will say that there are gods. This comment is repeated at M 9.50. So the Pyrrhonist will say this although he does not believe it. It is possible that he makes the statement merely as a report of his own present *pathos*, as short for "It seems to me now that there are gods." But from the tenor of the discussion here and elsewhere I suspect that it does not even *seem* to him that there are gods, and that he only says such things in order to avoid trouble.

There is nothing in the text to justify Bury's translation of ὁ θεός everywhere as "God" with a capital "G," instead of as, for example, "the god" or "god." When the plural οἱ θεοί occurs, Bury goes so far as to render it as "Gods," again with a capital "G," thus not risking giving offense to polytheists as well as monotheists. In any case, it is clear that Sextus intends his remarks to apply to any and all gods that may be cited as sources of anything physical; he is not speaking to monotheists only. In the review at 3.218ff. he reports that not only the philosophers but also the common people differ on whether there is one god or many.

Note that the same considerations that are offered in sections 3–5 to substantiate the conclusion that, if we go by what the Dogmatists say, there is no concept of god, apply equally well to the common man's πρόληψις of god, as this is set forth at M 9.33:

All people have a common πρόληψις of god, according to which he is a kind of blessed living being [μακάριόν τί ἐστι ζῶον], immortal, completely happy, and not accepting of anything evil.

4. If you cannot understand "Dion," you cannot understand "the birth of Dion," "the wisdom of Dion," and so forth Cf. 2.228, 3.228.

6–8. If we go by what the Dogmatists say (ὅσον ἐπὶ τοῖς δογματικοῖς), the existence of a god or gods, which is non-evident, is not provable and not apprehensible.

9–12. In these sections we have the essentials of the so-called "problem of evil." It is sometimes formulated as follows:

> Evil exists. If God knows about it and wants to remove it, he must be unable to do so. If he knows about it and is able to remove it, he must be unwilling. If he is willing and able to remove the evil, he must be ignorant of its existence. But God is omniscient, omnipotent, and completely benevolent. Therefore, God does not exist.

Sextus concludes only that god has no πρόνοια for things in the universe. Προνοέω: to provide for, take care of, take thought for. Πρόνοια: providence (in the corresponding sense).

## 13–16. Cause

Sextus seems to be identifying the ἀρχαὶ δραστικαί ("productive sources") with αἴτια ἐνεργητικά ("active causes"). See the beginning of section 30.

13. In line 13, I prefer Bekker's suggested ἀποδιδόναι to Mutschmann/Mau's ἀποδίδοσθαι.

## 17–29. Is Anything a Cause of Anything?

17. Cf. M 9.200–7.

19. ".... granting a cause why causes do not." The argument here shows that Greek αἴτιον (or αἰτία) covers reasons as well as what we call "causes". Gregory Vlastos, in his paper "Reasons and Causes in the Phaedo" (chapter 4 of Vlastos, 1973), gives a clear explanation of the use of αἰτία and related terms by Plato and Aristotle. He has us consider the following "why" questions:

1. Why did the Persians invade Attica? Because the Athenians had raided Sardis. The αἰτία is the Athenian raid.
2. Why is this statue so heavy? Because it is made of bronze. The αἰτία is the bronze.
3. Why is he taking after-dinner walks? Because of his health. The αἰτία is his health.
4. Why is the angle *A* inscribed in a semicircle a right angle? Because it is equal to an angle *B* that is half of a straight angle. The αἰτία is the angle *B*.

(Examples 1, 3, and 4 are from *Posterior Analytics* 2.11; 2 and 3 are from *Physics* 2.3, with 2 slightly altered). Note that our word "cause" does not apply comfortably in cases 2–4. We would say that, properly speaking, the cause of the statue's being so heavy is not the bronze but the statue's having been made of bronze, which is an event occurring over a certain span of time. Similarly, the cause of the man's taking after-dinner walks is not his health, which does not now (and may never) exist, but his wishing to be healthy, which again occurs over a certain time span. And "cause," which for us involves a temporal sequence, does not apply at all in geometry. Incidentally, the αἰτία in this case is not even the proposition that the angle *A* is equal to the angle *B* that is half of a straight angle, which would be a reason and not a cause; perhaps surprisingly, it is the angle *B* itself.

On the basis of these examples, it seems that in general *Y* will be called an αἰτία of *X*'s being in such and such a condition if *Y* must be prominently mentioned in an appropriate answer to a question as to why *X* is in that condition. Note that Greek uses διὰ τί ("on account of what?") for "why?" Thus αἰτίαι include not only what we call "reasons" and "causes" but other things as well.

Plato's use of the word fits this generalization. See, for example, *Phaedo* 98C–E, where the usual English translations, using "cause" for αἰτία, have Socrates ridiculing the suggestion that the cause of his sitting there in prison is that his sinews, by relaxing and contracting, have brought his bodily components into that configuration. "What is really the cause," he says, "is that the Athenians decided to condemn me and that I, for my part, have thought it best to sit here." He does concede, "If anyone were to say that without having bones and sinews, and so on, I could not have done what I had in mind, he would be right." And it would seem that such a *conditio sine qua non* would deserve to be called a "cause." But Socrates declares that "to call such things αἴτια [a synonym for αἰτίαι] is absurd." It is thus apparent that in order to qualify as giving the αἰτία, an answer to the question "Why are you sitting there?" must be not only true but in some sense appropriate.

There is, however, a puzzling feature of the use of αἰτία and αἴτιον in the present passage. It seems that for Sextus these two words are in general synonyms. But we see that here, in sections 19 and 23–4, αἴτιον is systematically used for "cause" in the thesis "there are no causes," while αἰτία is used for the reason that might be given for that thesis. However, if this pattern were meant to mark a distinction between reason and cause, the circularity suggested at the end of section 19 would disappear, the initial question in section 17 would lack sense, and the conclusion of section 23 would be a plain non sequitur.

Frede (1987, pp. 129 ff.) points out that some Greek authors do distinguish αἴτιον and αἰτία in such a way than an αἴτιον is an entity that is "responsible" for the effect — the τί in the διὰ τί — while the αἰτία is the λόγος ("account") of the αἴτιον. Thus the αἰτία would be a proposition, while the αἴτιον would be whatever, according to that proposition, is "responsible" for the effect. But, as noted above, it is fairly clear that in the present sections Sextus cannot have this distinction in mind, for otherwise the argument would collapse altogether.

In translating τὸ αἴτιον I have had to pluralize because this chapter purports to be about whether anything is the cause of anything, and not about the existence of the concept of causation.

In line 23 of this section, I read ἀποδιδοὺς, with Pappenheim and Bury.

20–2. To apprehend a cause is to apprehend it as a cause of its effect. Thus, as we have seen in section 8 of the Introduction, the verb "to apprehend" generates an oblique context. From "The motion of the moon is the cause of the motion of the tides" and "I apprehend the motion of the moon" it does not follow that "I apprehend the cause of the motion of the tides."

What can Sextus mean by saying that in order to conceive of a cause it is necessary to apprehend it as the cause of its effect? Usually, as, for example, in the first sentence of section 23, τό αἴτιον ἐννοεῖσθαι means "to form a concept of Cause", that is, "to form a concept of causation," and Sextus indicates that having a concept of $X$ is a necessary but not a sufficient condition for apprehending an $X$. But here the phrase has to mean "to conceive of a (particular) cause," and it is unclear what this would amount to, or how it would differ from what is expressed by "to apprehend a cause." Of course, the verb ἐννοεῖσθαι could mean simply "to think of", but it would seem absurd to say that in order to think of Socrates (or of a cause) one must first apprehend him (or it). Perhaps the most plausible explanation is that Sextus is simply not attending to the ambiguity of τὸ αἴτιον between "causation" and "the cause (that we've been talking about)."

23–4. The argument starts out dealing with the cause of *somebody's saying that* there are causes, and then slides over onto the question of there being a cause that there are causes. The same confusion threatens in section 19.

25–8. Again, the Dogmatists' confused principle, "Relatives qua relatives coexist and are conceived together" is used to refute them. Cf. M 9.282ff.

26. Line 10. Mutschmann's expansion of the text to bring it in line with the Latin MS. T does not seem to affect the sense materially.

## 30–7. Material Sources

At first Sextus seems to be saying that since there is disagreement among the Dogmatists as to what the material sources are, the material sources are not apprehensible. This seems to be a plain non sequitur, and it is hard to believe that he is making a point so trivial as that nothing can be a material source if it must accord simultaneously with all the differing Dogmatic concepts of what the material sources are. But as the argument proceeds it appears that the point is rather that there is no rational way of deciding which, if any, of the Dogmatists is right, since we are always in the position of needing a proof that a purported proof is in fact a proof. The route from there to the conclusion, in section 37, that "the material sources are not apprehensible" is still pretty murky. But perhaps it is something like the following: to apprehend something as being a material source, you must know what it is to be a material source;

and if you know this, you know which, if any, of the Dogmatists is right; but there is no way of knowing which, if any, of the Dogmatists is right; ergo,.... With this chapter cf. M 9.359ff.

## 38–55. Are Bodies Apprehensible?

Here again the bothersome ambiguity in Sextus's use of the phrase, "to apprehend an *X*" is involved. In most instances this phrase seems equivalent with "to apprehend something as being an *X*" and implies an understanding of what it is to be an *X*, which is to say that it implies possession of a concept of *X*. There are passages in which the argument depends upon this implication. But we have seen that there are also cases in which Sextus uses "to apprehend an *X*" without any such implication. I have conjectured that in this use, to apprehend an *X* is to apprehend an *X* as being something, not to apprehend something as being an *X*. Thus, to apprehend a *pathos* would be to apprehend it as being, perhaps, a sweet taste, a pain, or green in color.

It is reasonably clear that in the topic question of this chapter the phrase "to apprehend a body" has the former of the two uses just described. What is being denied is that we can ever apprehend anything as being a body; we are never in a position to determine that something is in fact a body. Such questions as whether we can see, hear, or otherwise perceive a body are left open. The point here is in effect that even if we perceived a body we could not recognize it as such. The reason, of course, is that we have no coherent, agreed-upon, concept to associate with the term "body," as this term is used by the philosophers. And thus we cannot understand or apply the metaphysical and epistemological theories in which the term occurs.

Hence in these sections Sextus is not to be understood as making the Berkeleyan point that since the concept of "body" is inconsistent there cannot be any such thing as a body and therefore nobody can perceive one. His thesis is, rather, that since there is no agreed-upon concept of body and we have no reasonable way of deciding among the contending viewpoints, we are not in a position to apprehend anything as being a body—provided, as always, that "we go by what the Dogmatists say."

Sextus considers various proposals to define "body" by means of such terms as "cause," "point," "line," "surface," "length," "breadth," "depth," "solidity," and "boundary." The gist of his attack is that there is also no clear concept to be associated with any of these terms, at least when they are applied in connection with bodies, and that therefore they cannot figure in any acceptable definition of "body." Thus, for example, he raises the question of what exactly is meant by the "surface" of a body. Is it a part of the body? Does it have thickness? If, as may be thought, the juxtaposition (a "touching") of two bodies consists in their having a common surface, what is the difference between this situation and the situation in which there is only one body, which might be described as a "fusion" of the two? The notion of "surface" is obviously unclear when the bodies concerned are thought of as composites of particles that may have empty spaces between them, but even for "simple" bodies, which do not contain other bodies as parts, it threatens paradox.

We are accustomed to give an abstract sense to geometrical terms, even when they are applied to the physical world (as, e.g., in "the center of mass of the earth," "the surface of the sun," and "the distance between two bodies"), but Sextus has to consider the possibility of interpreting them as themselves standing for certain kinds of bodies. Thus when he considers the definition of a body as consisting of length, breadth, depth, and solidity, we may think at first that he is confusing the body with its concept, and the part-whole relation with the relation of concept-inclusion, as if one should consider rationality and animality to be parts of a human being. But even nowadays there is a use of these terms that does treat them as denoting parts of the bodies concerned, as is especially clear in the case of "surface." Thus, one might speak of "peeling off" the surface of an object. The argumentation in these sections will seem less bizarre if we keep in mind that the geometrical terms are being given a physical interpretation.

38–41. The burden of this part of the chapter is that you cannot satisfactorily define "body" by means of terms that are equally unclear. Cf. M 9.366–9, 434, 3.19–20, 83.

42–4. The details of this discussion are not very clear, but the main point seems to be the following. The naive notion that two bodies are in juxtaposition, or "touch" one another, if a vertex or edge or surface of one of them coincides at least in part with a vertex or edge or surface of the other, is incoherent. The argument presupposes that there is a distinction between a given amount of material constituting one body and its constituting two or more bodies that are in juxtaposition. And this in turn depends on somehow clearly distinguishing χωρισμός ("separation") and διασπασμός ("a tearing apart").

I suppose that the least that can be said is that at the common sense level our notion of what it is to be "one" body is insufficiently precise to permit us to decide certain frequently occurring borderline cases. For example, when what were formerly two bodies are now so fused that any attempt to tear them apart will fail, shall we call the result "one body"? Also, the considerations raised by Sextus seem to show that the notion of juxtaposition, which at first view appears to be merely a matter of spatial location, ultimately involves the historical and physical attributes of the things said to be juxtaposed.

The case in which the boundary (surface, edge, or vertex) is considered to be a sort of "rind" or "skin" of the body is treated somewhat more clearly at M 9.431:

> When a body is juxtaposed to a body, either the boundaries touch the boundaries, or the things bounded touch the things bounded, or the things bounded touch the things bounded and the boundaries touch the boundaries. Thus (for our meaning will be clear in an example), if we were to think of the external earthenware of the amphora as the boundary, and the wine in the amphora as the thing bounded, then when two jars are juxtaposed either the ware will touch the ware, or the wine the wine, or both the ware the ware and

the wine the wine. And if the boundaries touch the boundaries, the things
bounded, that is, the bodies, will not touch one another, which is absurd. But
if the things bounded touch the things bounded, that is, bodies touch bodies,
they will have to get outside their own boundaries, which again is absurd. And
if boundaries touch boundaries and the things bounded the things bounded,
the *aporiai* will be combined.

In section 43 the words in angle brackets are Bury's translation of what occurs
at this place in the Latin MS. T. The Greek MSS. have a lacuna here.
Mutschmann "reconstructed" the Greek from the Latin; Mau keeps this
addition.

45–8. I think that the argumentation here has to be considered in a
dialectical context. For example:

**Q.** How shall I recognize that something is a body?
**A.** Check to see if it has length, breadth, depth, solidity.
**Q.** How shall I know whether it is solid?
**A.** Touch it.
**Q.** But what does "touching it" mean?
And so on.

With these sections cf. M 9.259–61, 437–9.

49–55. Sextus argues that since bodies are not apprehensible, incorporeal
things cannot be apprehended, either. In his argument he seems to equate "to
apprehend" with "to conceive." Otherwise, the statement in section 49,

> In order that we may apprehend a privation it is necessary that we have
> apprehended beforehand the state of which it is said to be the privation for
> someone who had no concept of sight would not be able to say that this
> person does not have it, that is, is blind.

would be irrelevant. In the Introduction we have seen that, as "to apprehend"
is ordinarily used by Sextus, there are other reasons besides the inconceivability
of $X$ why one might not be able to apprehend an $X$. For example, there may
be no $X$'s to apprehend, or there may be $X$'s but, for a variety of reasons, they
may be inaccessible to us.

Again in this passage there is the troublesome vacillation we have often
noted between the two senses of "to apprehend." Consequently, we do not
know whether in these sections Sextus is arguing that it is impossible to
apprehend something as being an incorporeal object, or whether his point is
that it is impossible to apprehend an incorporeal object as being something,
for instance, a ghost. Thus, when in section 59 he speaks of apprehending
sensible objects and objects of thought, he can hardly mean apprehending them
*as such*, although in the privation argument back in section 49, apprehending
a blind person was obviously supposed to require having a concept of
blindness. Maybe the apparent vacillation just signifies lack of definiteness of
intention, or maybe it is only what might in any case be expected when an
author, disavowing any responsibility of his own for a given term, attempts to

use it in accord with the usage or usages of opponents whom he says he does not understand.

49. Line 11. In accord with Bury and the Latin translation T, I delete δοκεῖ.

51. Line 4. I keep the ἔνστασιν (*instantiam*) of the MSS. On this section Bury notes:

> The first of these theories of vision is that of Chrysippus (a cone of light connecting eye with object), the second that of Democritus and Epicurus, the third that of Empedocles, Pythagoreans, Plato (*Tim.* 45B) and Aristotle.

In sections 52–3 Sextus presents himself as showing that incorporeal things are not apprehensible by means of argument. Instead, what he actually shows is, at most, only that anyone who says that incorporeal things are apprehensible by means of arguments, and who also says that arguments are incorporeal things, is in effect telling us that incorporeal things can be apprehended by means of some of the things the apprehensibility of which we are questioning.

55. I agree with Hossenfelder's note 32, that τὰ μετὰ τὰ στοιχεῖα here denotes the things that arise from, or are composed of, the elements, and not, as Fabricius, Pappenheim, and Bury have taken it, things that are epistemologically "posterior" to the elements.

## 56–62. Blending

Liddell and Scott, in the "American edition" of 1860, give a relatively clear explanation of the difference between κρᾶσις and μῖξις:

> κρᾶσις—a mixture of two things so that they are quite blended and form a compound, as wine and water; whereas μῖξις is a mere mixing so that they can be separated again, as of two sorts of grain (or, we might say, κρᾶσις is chemical, μῖξις mechanical mixture).

Accordingly, I have translated κρᾶσις as "[a] blending" and μῖξις as "[a] mixture," reversing the terms as used by Bury. However, cf. also *Stoicorum Veterum Fragmenta* 2.471–2 and Aristotle's *Topics* 122b26.

## 63. Motion

Line 21. Bury's proposal of ᾧ καὶ seems to me to make better sense than the καὶ ὡς of the MSS. and Bekker, or even Mutschmann/Mau's suggestion of καὶ οὕτως.

## 64–81. Transitional Motion

The subject of κίνησις ("motion", in a very wide sense) is discussed at much greater length in M 10.37ff. Parallel to section 64 we have M 10.37–41, where the sixfold distinction is correctly ascribed to Aristotle:

> Aristotle said that there are six kinds of motion, of which one is change of
> location [τοπικὴ μετάβασις], another is change of nature [μεταβολή — cf.
> φυσικὴ μεταβολή in section 64], another is generation [γένεσις, coming into
> being], another is destruction [φθορά, the opposite of γένεσις], another is
> increase of amount [αὔξησις], and another is decrease of amount [μείωσις];
> but most people, including the followers of Aenesidemus, allow but two main
> kinds of motion, namely, motion of change [κ. μεταβλητική] and that of
> location [κ. μεταβατική]; and of these the motion of change is that by which
> the body, while remaining the same in substance [οὐσία], takes on different
> qualities at different times, shedding one quality and taking on another — the
> sort of thing that happens in the case of wine changing into vinegar and in the
> case of the grape when it changes from sour to sweet, or in that of the
> chameleon or octopus when it takes on different colors at different times.
> Whence it must be said that genesis and destruction and increase and decrease
> are particular kinds of change of nature [μεταβολή], which they also say are
> subordinate to the motion of change, unless somebody will say that increase
> belongs to the motion of location on the ground that it is the growth of bodies
> in length and breadth. And the motion of location is that in which the moving
> body passes from location to location, either as a whole or by parts.

With this we may compare Aristotle, *Categories* 15a13ff., as translated by
Ackrill:

> There are six kinds of change: generation, destruction, increase, diminution,
> alteration, change of place [κινήσεως δέ ἐστιν εἴδη ἕξ· γένεσις, φθορά, αὔξησις,
> μείωσις, ἀλλοίωσις, κατὰ τόπον μεταβολή]. That the rest are distinct from one
> another is obvious (for generation is not destruction, nor yet is increase or
> diminution, nor is change of place; and similarly with the others too), but there
> is a question about alteration — whether it is not perhaps necessary for what
> is altering to be altering in virtue of one of the other changes.

Sextus's terminology coincides with that of Aristotle, except that he uses
φυσικὴ μεταβολή ("natural change" or "change of nature") for Aristotle's term
ἀλλοίωσις ("alteration").

Thus Sextus's treatment of the subject in the *Outlines* is, for the most part,
in the framework of the Aristotelian sixfold distinction, with chapters on
transitional motion, increase and diminution, generation and destruction, and
change of nature; but in some passages he seems to be following the twofold
distinction ascribed to "most people, including the followers of Aenesidemus."
Thus some of the time we have to read κίνησις as practically synonymous with
"change," but elsewhere in these sections it has the ordinary sense of "motion."

The fundamental point of the chapters on κίνησις is stated succinctly in
section 65 (cf. M 10.49):

> The common people and some of the philosophers assume that motion exists,
> but Parmenides and Melissus and some others think that it does not. The
> Skeptics said that motion "no more" exists than not, for if we go by the
> appearances [ὅσον ἐπὶ τοῖς φαινομένοις] motion seems to exist, but if we go
> by the philosophic account [ὅσον ἐπὶ τῷ φιλοσόφῳ λόγῳ] it seems not to exist.

So when we have set out the opposition between those who assume that
motion exists and those who assert that it does not, and when we find the
disagreement equally balanced, we shall be forced to conclude that, if we go
by what people say [ὅσον ἐπὶ τοῖς λεγομένοις], motion "no more" exists than
not.

The ὅσον clauses are repeated almost verbatim at M 10.49.

Note the implication that in this matter the common people and some of
the Dogmatists go by the appearances, whereas the remaining Dogmatists go
by the so-called "philosophic account." This is reinforced in section 66, from
which we gather that "to go by the appearances" and "to rely on obviousness"
(ἐνάργεια) amount to the same thing.

63, line 21. I follow Bury in reading ᾧκαὶ in place of καὶ ὡς.

65. Cf. M 10.45–9.

66. Cf. M 10. 67–8.

67. Cf. M 10. 70–76.

68-9. Cf. M 10.83–4.

70. It is hard to see what this section has to do with the topic at hand. The
terms ὁρμή ("motive" or "inclination") and προαίρεσις ("choice") ordinarily
turn up only in discussions of ethics, as, for example, at 3.179.

71. Cf. 2.242 and M 10.87. The promised ἐπίκρισις seems only to be what
is given at the end of section 81 below, namely, that Sextus finds himself unable
to dismiss either the arguments pro or the arguments con, and thus withholds
assent.

72. Cf. M 10.93, 103–4.

73–4. Cf. M 10.94, 105–7. Not until the concept of a limit entered
mathematics did it become clear how an object that is located at a given point
in space at a given instant of time can nevertheless have non-zero velocity at
that point and time.

75. With this section compare section 119 below and also M 10.95, 108–10.

The location (τόπος, *locus*) of a body is what is mentioned in a true answer
to the question, "Where (ποῦ) is it?" I have decided to use "location" instead
of "place" for τόπος, and "space" instead of "room" or some other term for
χώρα. In section 124 below, Sextus explains the Stoic distinction of void
(κένον), location, and space.

Here and in the parallel passages mentioned above, Sextus takes notice of
two senses of "location," a "broad" (ἐν πλάτει) sense and an "exact" (πρὸς
ἀκρίβειαν) sense. Thus:

> For they [the Dogmatists] say that "being in a location" has two senses; in
> one, "location" is used broadly, as when we say that someone is in Alexandria;
> and in the other it is used exactly, as the air enveloping the surface of my body
> might be said to be my location. (M 10.95)

With reference to the same distinction Sextus also says that the term is used
"strictly" (κυρίως) and "loosely" (καραχρηστικῶς). Normally we would render
these two adverbs respectively as "correctly" and "incorrectly." But Sextus can
hardly mean that to use a term καταχρηστικῶς is to misuse it, for at ll.191 and

207 he congratulates the Skeptics on their practice of using words καταχρηστικῶς instead of fighting over them. And he obviously does not regard the term "location" as misused when we give Alexandria as somebody's present location. So in the present context καταχρηστικός has to mean something milder, like "not strictly correct." The only respect in which the broad sense of "location" might be thought "inferior" is that the exact sense is "prior" to it, in that things are in their broad sense locations only by virtue of being in their exact-sense locations.

The distinction goes back to Aristotle's discussion of "location" at *Physics* 208a27ff. There he comments:

> The physicist must have a knowledge of location as well as of the infinite — whether it exists or not, in what way it exists, and what it is. For everybody assumes that whatever exists exists somewhere (for what does not exist is not anywhere — where is the goat-stag or the sphinx?), and the most common and important kind of κίνησις is change of location, which we call "passage."
>
> But the question, what is location? presents many aporiai....
>
> That there is such a thing as location seems obvious from the fact of mutual replacement. Where water is now, there air is present when the water has gone out [from the vessel]...; the location is distinguished from the bodies that by turns come to be in it. Water was previously in the location in which air now is, so that it is obvious that the location or space [χώρα] into which and out of which they passed was something different from both. (208a27–b8)

> We distinguish between the location that is common, in which all bodies are, and that which is particular, in which each body is primarily. I mean, for example, that you are now in the universe because you are in the air and it is in the universe; and you are in the air because you are on the earth; and similarly on the earth because you are in this location which contains nothing more than you.
>
> And if the location of a body is its immediate envelope, then it would be a boundary, so that the location would be the form or shape of each body by which the magnitude or the amount of matter is determined; for this is the boundary of each body. (209a33–b6)

Thus Aristotle is saying in effect that the "exact" location of an object is a location such that the object is in it and nothing else is in it that is not part of the object.

As Bury observes, the point of making the distinction was to make "motion in a location" feasible. Sextus, of course, argues that the idea does not succeed.

76. Cf. M 10.139–41.

76–81. Again, we need the notion of limit in order to reconcile the existence of motion with the principle that a body cannot be in two locations at the same instant of time.

77. Cf. M 10.154.

78. Cf. M 10.124–6.

## 82–84. Increase and Diminution

This chapter, in which bodies are called οὐσίαι ("substances"), has no counterpart in M 9–10. Its point seems to be the usual one, that the concepts in
question are unclear. Thus, the "increase" or "growth" of a body is found to
be imperfectly distinguished from the "addition" to the body of one or more
other bodies, especially in view of the philosophic doctrine that all bodies are
in constant flux anyway, with parts continually added and subtracted .

## 85–96. Subtraction and Addition        97. Exchange

With these chapters cf. M 9.280–330.

What Sextus calls "subtraction" and "addition" are not among the six
types of κίνησις distinguished by Aristotle, and they seem to be discussed here
mainly because of the possibility (which Sextus has rejected in the preceding
sections) of explicating "increase" in terms of "addition" and of "decrease" in
terms of "subtraction." In any case, Sextus includes his discussion of them in
his comments on "the physics part of philosophy," and accordingly they must
be understood as having to do primarily with physical operations on aggregates of bodies, and not with arithmetic. If, for example, five bodies are
removed from an aggregate of six, the aggregate of five is said to have been
"subtracted" from the aggregate of six. The five are described as "less than"
and "(properly) included in" the six.

There is, nevertheless, some confusion with arithmetic, due to the previously noted fact that expressions like "the six" (τὰ ἕξ — note the plural article τά)
can stand either for the abstract number or for an aggregate of that number of
things. And the ambiguity carries over to the word ἀριθμός ("number") itself,
which likewise can refer to abstract numbers or to aggregates. (A somewhat
similar use of the word "number" occurs in English when we say, "a number
of people objected"; we of course mean that the people, not one of the positive
integers, did the objecting.)

Although it might seem utterly silly to identify a number with a collection
of that number of things, note that some set-theoretic definitions of the integers
are such that the non-negative integer $n$ is in every case a set having $n$ elements.
And further, when arithmetic is formulated as a theory of concatenation the
positive integers are treated as concatenations of, for example, strokes, so that
two is "‖", three is "‖‖", and five, i.e., "‖‖‖" is the result of concatenating (adding)
one and four, two and three, etc.

The point of these two chapters seems to be that the relational expressions
"$X$ is subtracted from $Y$" and "$X$ is added to $Y$" are used by the Dogmatists
in their physical theories in such a way as not to be satisfiable. But I am unable
to make much sense of Sextus's reasoning in support of this point. The
discussion of "blending" and "pervading" in Long and Sedley (1987, vol. 1, pp.
292–4, is helpful in showing that principles like "that which is spread out over
something is equal in extent to that over which it is spread out" (cited by

Sextus in section 96) were part of a general controversy set off by Aristotle's statement (*On Generation and Corruption*, 328a26–28) that a drop of wine cannot be blended with a very large quantity of water. Apparently this matter was of interest to the Stoics because of their doctrine that "breath" (τὸ πνεῦμα or ἡ πνευματικὴ οὐσία) blends with earth and water and pervades the entire universe.

87. When the number 35 pops up here, we may be puzzled, but at M 9.304–5 Sextus explains how he arrives at it:

> But if in six, according to the argument about it, 15 is contained, then necessarily four, three, two, and one, which make ten, will be contained in five. And just as ten is contained in five, so also three, two, and one, which make six, will be contained in four, and by analogy two and one, which make another three, will be contained in three, and in the remaining two, one. When the contents of the six numbers are added together—I mean 15, ten, six, three, and also one—the number six will contain the number 35.

So it seems to me that the text may just as well be left as Bekker has it.

90–1. συνελεύσις = ἀθροισμός ("aggregate"); cf. M 9.313. The idea, I suppose, is something like this: to paint an aggregate of things blue with blue paint is to paint each thing blue, with some of the paint going onto each; similarly, to diminish an aggregate of things by a unit would be to diminish each thing by a unit, with part of the unit diminishing each.

## 98–101. Whole and Part

This topic, which we have already met at 2.215–8, is treated extensively at M 9.331–58. Here, the unintelligibility of the part-whole relation is inferred from that of addition and subtraction, "For the whole seems to come into being by the aggregation and addition of the parts, and to cease from being a whole by the subtraction of one or more of them" (section 98). Alas, Sextus's argumentation in this chapter is no better than what one meets nowadays in connection with the curious question whether the whole is greater than the sum of its parts.

One possible source of confusion in these sections is the treatment of phrases of the form "all the *X*'s" or "all *X*'s" as though they denoted the aggregate of the *X*'s. Thus one might suppose that the whole herd or aggregate of Farmer Jones's sheep is what "all Farmer Jones's sheep" denotes. On this basis, if one of the sheep is a part of the herd, it will be a part of all Farmer Jones's sheep, including itself— which, as claimed in section 101, is absurd. Leibniz (Academy ed. 6.2.430–2), in commenting on Nizolius's *True Principles*, makes the similar point that by taking *omnis homo* ("every man") as standing for the aggregate of all men, Nizolius is stuck with the absurd consequence that to say "every man is an animal" is to say "the aggregate of all men is an animal."

Unfortunately, the more extended discussion at M 9.331ff. throws no additional light on the subject.

## 102–8. Natural Change

Of course, natural change (φυσικὴ μεταβολή) is not something to be contrasted
with "unnatural change," but rather a change in the nature, that is, the
qualities, of a thing.

I suppose that most of us share the perhaps naïve idea that when an object
undergoes a qualitative change something in or about it must remain the same,
as otherwise we could not distinguish such a change from a more or less rapid
replacement of that object by one or more other objects. When the apple turns
from green to red, we regard it as the same apple before and after the change.
But when a piece of wood is burned in the fireplace, or a building is demolished
by a blast, we do not say that the same piece of wood and the same building
have shed some of their former qualities, taken on new ones, and continue to
exist afterwards. Sextus seems to be making the point that the borders of this
distinction are indefinite.

Modern philosophers are right, I think, in regarding this whole matter as
more a question of how to talk than a deep issue in metaphysics, and perhaps
the peculiar arguments that Sextus rehearses in this chapter are best interpreted as attempts to show us that the conventions governing the use of the
terms "change," "same," and their various relatives and associates (like "cause"
and "quality") in the Dogmatists' physical theories are neither wholly consistent nor sufficiently precise to handle some of the frequently occurring borderline cases.

103. Line 10. Bury plausibly fills the lacuna with the words ἀλλ᾽ οὐχ ως
πάσχον μεταβάλλει ("but it does not change by being a thing that is acted
upon").

108. Line 7. I follow Bekker's conjecture for filling the lacuna with the
words αἰσθητή ἐστιν ἤ νοητή. καὶ αἰσθητὴ μὲν οὐκ ἐστιν· αἰ μὲν γὰρ ("…it is
either sensible or intelligible. But it is not sensible, for…").

## 109–14. Generation and Destruction

Sextus first argues that since the concepts of generation and destruction are
linked with those of addition, subtraction, and qualitative change, and as the
latter concepts are incoherent, so are the former.

But for good measure he throws in a few additional arguments. Thus (as
in section 111), it seems that at every instant of time between, say, 400 and 398
B.C. Socrates was alive or dead. Therefore, if he died at some time in that
interval, he died at a time when he was alive or he died at a time when he was
dead. But both of these alternatives are odd if not absurd. The point, I suppose,
is that in the case of what might be called "verbs of generation or destruction" — such as "die," "destroy," "dissolve," "extinguish," "produce," "construct," "create" — we think of them as denoting processes that span a period
of time, at the beginning of which they apply and at the end of which they do
not (or vice versa); but in general there is no instant of time *t* such that at all

times earlier than *t* they do apply and at all times later they do not (or, again, vice versa).

## 115–8. Rest

118. In this section we have a good example of a type of ambiguity that occurs frequently in Sextus's argumentation. When he speaks here of showing that space and time are ἀνυπόστατα ("nonexistent") we do not know whether he is speaking of the concepts themselves, saying that they are inconsistent or perhaps even nonexistent, or is allowing the concepts but denying the existence of anything falling under them. After all, it is one thing to deny the existence of centaurs, and another to deny that the concept is consistent. So in this case he might be arguing that (1) there is no such thing as time; (2) ergo, there is no such thing as a cause (for a cause is contiguous in time with its effect); (3) ergo, there is no such thing as a body at rest, for to be at rest is to be constricted and consequently acted upon causally by the surrounding bodies.

Or he might be arguing (1) that there are no coherent concepts of location and time; (2) ergo, there is no coherent concept of transitional motion; (3) ergo, there is no coherent concept of rest (defined, for bodies, as the absence of transitional motion).

## 119–35. Location

See my note on section 75 above, and cf. M 10.6–36.

Clearly the question whether there is any such thing as a location is essentially connected with the question whether there is any such thing as transitional motion, which has been discussed in the preceding chapters. Sextus here observes that on the one hand some people find it "obvious" that there are locations, while on the other we have the Dogmatists' arguments that there are not. He concludes that since the arguments give him pause and he is uncomfortable about so-called "obviousness" (cf. section 66), the Skeptic joins neither side but suspends judgment about location.

122. Cf. M 10.13–4.
124. Cf. M 10.3–4.
126. Line 9. Reading ὅ in place of οὐ, with Pappenheim.
129. Cf. M 10.21–23.
131. Cf. M 10.20.

## 136–49. Time

Compare the more full discussion of this topic at M 10.169–247.

The Skeptic suspends judgment about whether there is any such thing as time, and for the usual reason: "Insofar as we go by the appearances [ὅσον μὲν ἐπὶ τοῖς φαινομένοις] there seems to be such a thing as time, but if we go by the things said about it [ὅσον δὲ ἐπὶ τοῖς περὶ αὐτοῦ λεγομένοις] [presumably by the Dogmatists, but perhaps also by the common man], it appears not to exist."

140. "Time seems not to exist without κίνησις and μόνη." Recall that κίνησις is practically synonymous with "change." Leibniz, whose discussion of time shows unmistakable signs that he had read the relevant sections of the *Outlines*, held that to say that there is a time interval between states $s$ and $s'$ of the actual world is simply to say that $s$ is different from $s'$, that is, that the world has changed from $s$ to $s'$ or from $s'$ to $s$. For him, therefore, it is logically impossible that everything should remain unchanged over an interval of time. This is in direct conflict with the argument mentioned at M 10.171, namely, that it is possible to conceive that the world is not changing at a certain time (and hence time change cannot be identified with world change).

141. Sextus considers a number of puzzles. How could time begin or come to an end? How can time consist of past, present, and future, if the past does not exist any longer and the future is yet to be (and the present is regarded as some sort of "limit" between these nonexistent things)?

Most of the puzzles seem to arise from the fact that the paradigm use of the present tense of a Greek verb in simple declarative sentences is to describe what is occurring at the present time, that is, at the time of utterance. Thus "the past exists," as equivalent to "the past exists now," seems false. The solution requires recognizing that the present tense is also used in a "timeless" sense, so that, for example, "there does not exist a rational square root of two" does not mean merely that such a root does not exist *now*.

143. The most fundamental way of measuring the spatial extent of a body involves placing another body — for instance, a footrule — alongside it successively end-to-end. In this section it is suggested that time cannot be measured in an analogous way because there is no way of placing one period of time alongside another. But this seems to be a confusion. After all, in determining by means of the footrule that a person is, say, between five and six feet tall, we are comparing one body with another as to length. Similarly, in determining that the child has practiced on the piano for at least half an hour we compare two bodies, but in a different respect. This time the measuring body will be a clock; if it reads "03:15" when he begins, and he practices continuously and is still practicing when it reads "03:45", we conclude that he has done his half hour. It is a case of the clock looking like this when he looks like that. So while, as Sextus suggests, we cannot place one interval of time alongside another — for example, part of the past alongside part of the future — this is nothing to the point; for in measuring with the footrule we are not placing the *length* of the rule alongside the *height* of the person, but rather the rule alongside the person.

136. Cf. M 10.174, 176, 181, 219, 228.
138. Cf. M 10.216.
141. Cf. M 10.189–92.
143. Cf. M 10.193–5.

144. Cf. M 10.197–9.
146. Cf. M 10.200–22.
147. Cf. M 10.203–5.
149. Cf. M 10.206–11. I follow Heintz in reading $\tilde{\eta}\ldots\tilde{\eta}$ instead of $\varepsilon i \ldots \varepsilon i$ at lines 30–1.

## 151–67. Number

The principal *aporia* about number is this: Either the number of an aggregate of things is identical with the things enumerated or it is not. If it is identical with the things enumerated, we have the absurdity that the same number will be an aggregate of human beings and an aggregate of cattle and an aggregate of white things and an aggregate of black things, and the like. Sextus seems to identify the other alternative, in which numbers are held to be external to (i.e., to exist independently of) the things enumerated, with the Pythagorean doctrine that all numbers are generated from something called "the Monad-in-itself" of "the Unit-in-itself" ($\dot{\eta}$ $\kappa\alpha\theta$' $\dot{\epsilon}\alpha\upsilon\tau\dot{\eta}\nu$ $\dot{\eta}$ $\mu o\nu\dot{\alpha}\varsigma$). Against this notion, which is close to unintelligible anyway, he raises a variety of objections reminiscent of those brought against the Theory of Ideas at *Parmenides* 129ff. Is the Monad, that is, the One itself, one? Does each thing that is said to "participate in" ($\mu\epsilon\tau\acute{\epsilon}\chi\epsilon\iota\nu$, "have a share of") it participate in all of it, or only in a part of it?

In the present chapter I have translated $\dot{\eta}$ $\mu o\nu\acute{\alpha}\varsigma$ as "the Monad," $\dot{\eta}$ $\delta\upsilon\acute{\alpha}\varsigma$ as "the Dyad,"..., $\dot{\eta}$ $\delta\epsilon\kappa\acute{\alpha}\varsigma$ as "the Decad," in keeping with what has become customary in describing Pythagoreanism. The reader may wish to consult Aristotle's account of the subject, at *Metaphysics* 985b23ff.

As noted earlier, attempts to employ this terminology in rational discourse are beset by ambiguity in the Greek in addition to the inherent difficulty of the subject. The expression $\dot{\eta}$ $\mu o\nu\acute{\alpha}\varsigma$, for example, can mean "the [abstract] number one" or it can mean "the single thing," "the one thing," "the unit." Similarly, $\dot{\eta}$ $\delta\upsilon\acute{\alpha}\varsigma$ can mean "the number two" or "the pair of things." As a result, a sentence like $\dot{\eta}$ $\mu o\nu\grave{\alpha}\varsigma$ $\mu\acute{\iota}\alpha$ $\dot{\epsilon}\sigma\tau\iota$ ("the one thing is one") looks like a tautology and its negation looks absurd. But when the sentence is read as "the number one is one" it looks more like a category mistake than a tautology. Moreover, when this way of talking is applied to numbers greater than one, things become worse: apparent tautologies turn into sentences like "the number two is [are?] two" and "the number ten is [are?] ten."

Bertrand Russell argued long ago (Russell, 1945, p. 157) that questions like "Is the moon one?," together with their corresponding declarative sentences, are nonsense. We have to ask: One *what*? The moon is one satellite, many particles, no planet. It seems that the word "one" cannot intelligibly be predicated of individual things or aggregates of such, but only of sets or concepts of individual things. Russell says, "To say 'the earth has one satellite' is to give a property of the concept 'earth's satellite.'" As we noted earlier, this clarification was due to Frege.

152. Line 19. Pappenheim may be right in reading αἱ ἄτομοι ("atoms") instead of the manuscripts' οἱ ἀτμοί ("vapors").

153. Cf. M 7.104. See the note on 2.215–8.

154. Cf. M 7.99–100, 4.4–5.

155. Cf. M 7.95–7, 4.283.

156. Line 17. The various conjectures by Bury, Bekker, and Mutschmann do not seem to make any essential difference to the sense. Line 22. I omit ἀριθμὸς, with MS. M.

156-7. Cf. M 10.285–7, 4.11–3.

158. Cf. M 10.293–8.

164. Cf. M 4.21–2.

## 168. The Ethics Part of Philosophy

We come now to the third division of "so-called philosophy." Sextus devotes much less space to this division than to either of the other two, and his treatment of it seems relatively thin. The same is true of *Against the Mathematicians*, where he devotes books 7 and 8 to logic, 9 and 10 to physics, and only book 11 to ethics. His discussion consists for the most part of an extended rehearsal of odd customs and practices — which Sextus obviously expects his readers to find shocking — in support of the proposition that there is no universal agreement about what is good and what is bad, what is right and what is wrong. From this conclusion, which would hardly surprise anyone, he apparently moves to the further conclusion that nothing is really good, really bad, really right, really wrong. He does not mean by this, however, that there are no objective standards of value, but only that we do not have conclusive evidence for or against any value judgment that purports to be more than an expression of the present *pathē* of the speaker's soul. The Skeptic will not slip into asserting that there really is no basis for asserting that something is really good or really bad or really indifferent; instead he simply withholds assent from all such assertions.

In his argument Sextus does seem to be asserting that if these value judgments were true of the external world there would not be such great differences of opinion about them. I think that he himself did not accept this claim but regarded it as part and parcel of the Dogmatists' views. (Cf. section 179: "All things that are affective by nature affect in the same way those who are, as the Dogmatists put it, 'in a natural condition'" and section 182: "Things that move us by nature move everybody in the same way.")

It may be regretted that Sextus did not go as deeply into ethics as into epistemology and logic, for we would like to understand in much greater detail just how the Skeptic Way was supposed to result in *ataraxia*. The relative weakness of his treatment of ethics no doubt explains why his influence in that field was insignificant in comparison with the rest of philosophy.

## 169–78. Things Good, Bad, and Indifferent

169. ὠφέλεια, which I am rendering as "beneficial activity," could also (following Bury) be translated as "utility," but to my ear it sounds odd to say such things as that "utility is right or serious action." Cf. M 11.22–7.

σπουδαῖος: worthwhile, serious, weighty; thus ὁ σπουδαῖος: a person of character and importance, to be contrasted with ὁ φαῦλος: a disreputable person.

172. Cf. M 11.30. Line 19b: Either Bekker's συλλαμβανόμενον or Kayser's συμβαλλόμενον seems preferable to the συλλαμβάνον of the MSS.

173–4. The point is pretty clearly the following. Somebody might offer, as a definition of "horse," "A horse is an animal that neighs." But then a "neigh" is defined (cf. Webster) as "the loud and prolonged cry of the horse"; so the definition is useless to anyone who seeks to learn what a horse is. Similarly, it is argued here, "the good" is defined by the Dogmatist as, for example, "what is beneficial"; but to benefit a person is nothing more than to produce good for him. Thus, from such a definition nobody can find out what the good is. That such is the case, Sextus observes, is evidenced by the fact that the Dogmatists are in total disagreement about the extension of the term. Cf. M 11.35–9.

175. Cf. M 11.42–4.

176. Cf. M 11.40.

177. Cf. M 11.59–61.

178. This section makes it clear that it is the concepts (ἔννοιαι) of good, bad, and indifferent that are being called into question. Sextus considers the fact that the Dogmatists differ on the extension of these terms, and on their analytic relations to other terms such as "happiness" (εὐδαιμονία), "virtue" (ἀρετή), or "pleasure" (ἡδονή), as an indication that they do not share the same concepts.

## 179–87. Is Anything by Nature Good, Bad, or Indifferent?

179–82. See the note on 1.16. Section 179 shows that the principle, "All things that are affective by nature affect in the same way those who are in a natural condition," which Sextus occasionally cites, is considered by him to be one of the Dogmatists' principles. Cf. M 11.69–71.

180. Cf. M 11.44–7, 73.

181. According to Bury, the philosopher was Antisthenes the Cynic.

183. Cf. M 11.79–84.

185. Bury renders γνῶσις here as "perception." But the word is derived from γιγνώσκω, "to know," primarily in the sense of "to recognize," "to be acquainted with." Thus I think that in this passage γνῶσις denotes knowledge in the sense of an ability to recognize things as being what they are. To say that something is "in the body only" seems to mean that it depends for its

existence and nature (i.e., for its attributes) on the existence and nature of the body only. But the attribute "choiceworthy for its own sake" is an attribute that a thing would have by virtue of the existence and attributes of souls; things are not choiceworthy unless they are recognized as such, and only souls can do this "recognizing." Thus the particular point advanced seems to be that if the choiceworthy were in the body only, it would be unrecognized as choiceworthy, for the body by itself—like the so-called "non-rational" animals—is ἄλογος, ("speechless," "devoid of language"), and hence lacks the ability to recognize things as being of this or that kind. See the note on 1.60f. above. With this section compare M 11.87–9.

186. Note especially, "On the one hand, the soul perhaps does not even exist."


## 188–238. What Is the So-called "Art of Living"?

As is apparent, this chapter simply continues the argument of the previous chapter and has no special relevance to the so-called "art of living" (which is the topic of the chapter beginning with section 239). Thus, as Bury notes, the MSS. are mistaken in making a new chapter here.

188. Note that a τέχνη is defined by the Stoics as a system of apprehensions. Cf. M 1.75 and section 241 below. Bury cites Cicero *Academica* 4.7.22: "*ars...ex multis animi perceptionibus constat.*"

189. Cf. Plato's construction of the soul, at *Timaeus* 35A–36D.

191. Cf. M 11.62–6.

193. Cf. M 11.99. As regards lines 8 and 9, I agree with Mau that the words βλακευσάμενος ἢ ἄλλως θερμόν τι τυφωθεὶς ἔδοξέ τις διαπράττεσθαι ("spiritless, or otherwise seem foolishly to do something rash") do not make sense here. Finding no plausible reconstruction, I have left a gap in the translation where they occur.

194. Cf. M 11.96–8.

199. Germani. According to Bury, these are probably not Germans but rather a Persian tribe. Cf. 1.152. The name Μηριόνης is derived from μῆρος ("thigh"). Meriones the Cretan was the companion of Idomeneus (*Iliad* 2.651).

200. Bury draws our attention to section 249 below, reassuring us that the philosophers did not in practice carry out the "shocking theories" described in this and the following chapter.

201. Cf. Herodotus 4.176

204. Cf. 1.155. Diogenes Laertius, 2.78 gives the same story about Plato and Aristippus; the lines they are supposed to have quoted are from Euripides' *Bacchae*, 836 and 317.

209. Cf. Herodotus 4.180, Diogenes Laertius 6.72. Regarding Tydeus, cf. *Iliad* 14.114ff.

210. Cf. *Iliad* 14.204, 1.399.

214. In line 22, reading οὐκ ἂν ⟨ἦν⟩ οὕτως, with Bury.

216. Archilochus of Paros, iambic and elegiac poet. His dates are uncertain, but one of his fragments mentions an eclipse which is thought to be one that occurred on March 14, 711 B.C.

217. Cf. Herodotus 4.114.

218. Cf. Aristotle, *De caelo* 278b14; M 9.13ff.

219. Cf. Herodotus 2.41.

221. Line 10. I am filling the lacuna with τινὲς δὲ (And some people).

223. Cf. Herodotus 3.39, 47.

226. Cf. Diogenes Laertius 9.84; Cicero *Tusculan Disputations*, 1.45.

228. Cf. Herodotus 1.140.

231. Cf. Herodotus 1.30–1; Cicero *Tusculan Disputations*, 1.47. In the story of Cleobis and Biton, as told by Herodotus, Croesus was entertaining Solon in his palace, and, looking for flattery, he asked him who was the happiest man he had ever seen. To his consternation, Solon named Tellus, an Athenian. Croesus, expecting that he would at least be awarded second prize, then asked who was the next happiest man he had seen.

> "Two young men of Argos", was the reply; "Cleobis and Biton. They had enough to live on comfortably; and their physical strength is proved not merely by their success in athletics, but much more by the following incident. The Argives were celebrating the festival of Hera, and it was most important that the mother of the two young men should drive to the temple in her oxcart; but it so happened that the oxen were late in coming back from the fields. Her two sons therefore, as there was no time to lose, harnessed themselves to the cart and dragged it along, with their mother inside, for a distance of nearly six miles, until they reached the temple. After this exploit, which was witnessed by the assembled crowd, they had a most enviable death — a heaven-sent proof of how much better it is to be dead than alive. Men kept crowding round them and congratulating them on their strength, and women kept telling the mother how lucky she was to have such sons, when, in sheer pleasure at this public recognition of her sons' act, she prayed the goddess Hera, before whose shrine she stood, to grant Cleobis and Biton, who had brought her such honor, the greatest blessing that can fall to mortal man.
>
> "After her prayer came the ceremonies of sacrifice and feasting; and the two lads, when all was over, fell asleep in the temple — and that was the end of them, for they never woke again.
>
> "The Argives had statues made of them, which they sent to Delphi, as a mark of their particular respect." (Herodotus 1.30–1, trans. Aubrey de Selincourt, 1954)

232. Cf. Herodotus 5.4.

233. Cf. 2.40.

234. The argument of this section may have no other purpose than to shake up the Dogmatists' confidence about those matters, if any, about which there seems to be universal agreement. Or it may indicate that Sextus thought that the Dogmatists were assuming not only that *actual* differences of opinion among people who were in "a natural condition" imply that the proposition in question is not true "by nature," but also that even *possible* differences of

opinion would have that implication. In other words, a proposition true by nature would be such that anyone (in a "natural" condition, of course) who did not accept it would show thereby that he did not understand it.

235. Cf. 1.25–9 above, and my note on 1.20. Cf. also M 11.144ff., 158–61.

236. Line 22. Heintz's αἰσθητικῶς is plainly preferable to the αἰσθητικὸς of the MSS.

## 239–49. Whether There Is an Art of Living

239. In sections 169ff. Sextus has been arguing that the Dogmatists' concepts of good, bad, and indifferent are not consistent and coherent. It follows that nothing falls under these concepts, that is, nothing is good, bad, or indifferent. In this section he argues that on that basis there is no art of living, either, for such an art would involve θεωρία of things good, bad, and indifferent. Now θεωρία can mean the actual observation of such things or the consideration of them. The observation would be impossible because there are no such things; the consideration would be impossible because the concepts are inconsistent. Either way, the conclusion that there is no art of living would follow.

240. φρόνησις is defined by the Stoics as "the knowledge [ἐπιστήμη] of what ought and ought not be done and of what is neutral in this regard, or the knowledge of things that are good, bad, or neither" (*Stoicorum Veterum Fragmenta* 3.262).

243. The conclusion, "Therefore, there exists no art of living," is an obvious non sequitur here, unless "if we go by what the Dogmatists say" is understood. Cf. the following section.

249. Here the conclusion is not that the art of living does not exist, as was concluded in section 239, but rather that nobody is in a position to firmly maintain (διαβεβαιοῦσθαι) that it does exist. For it cannot be apprehended, and in order to firmly establish that something exists or is the case one must have apprehended it.

## 250–73. Chapters 26–30

The burden of these five chapters is to establish that the so-called "art of living," as described by its advocates, cannot be acquired. For either it is in us by nature, or we learn it. But it is not in us by nature, for not everyone has it. It cannot be taught, because nothing can be taught. Therefore, it cannot be acquired.

253. "Now what is taught is either true or false; and if false, it could not be taught; for they say that the false is the nonexistent, and the nonexistent could not be an object of teaching." This is a curious inference, apparently based on a confusion of sense and denotation. *P* occurs obliquely in

*A* teaches *B* that *P*

and thus denotes its ordinary sense. Hence the so-called "object of teaching" would be a sense or meaning. But it is not the meaning of *P* that does not exist if *P* is false; rather it is the state of affairs described by *P*.

At the corresponding place in *Against the Mathematicians*, (M 11.232), the above inference does not occur. Instead we have

> And again, if anything is taught, it is either true or false. But it is not false, as is immediately apparent.

This suggests, I think, that the verb "to teach" is understood to mean "to bring to know" or something like that, so that its very meaning involves the truth of what is taught. Cf. 3.256 and M 11.220.

254. "Appearances appear to everybody alike [ὁμοίως]." I do not know how to reconcile this remarkable statement with the general tenor of Sextus's argumentation, which usually takes it as obvious, and as certainly granted by the Dogmatists, that appearances vary with the perceiver, the time, the place, the circumstances, and so on.

The statement in question is conspicuously absent from the version of the argument that appears in the corresponding passage at M 11.227–8, where the premise that no sensible thing (αἰσθητόν) is taught or learned is simply supported by examples, such as "Nobody learns to see the white or to taste the sweet."

255. Cf. M 11.254ff.

256–8. This is a tough argument to make sense of. Consider the corresponding passage at M 11.219ff.:

> Now if anything is taught, either τὸ ὄν is taught or τὸ μὴ ὄν. But neither τὸ ὄν is taught, as we shall show, nor τὸ μὴ ὄν, as we shall explain. Therefore, nothing is taught. Now, τὸ μὴ ὄν is not taught; for it has no accident and thus it does not have the accident of being taught. And besides, if τὸ μὴ ὄν is taught, τὸ μὴ ὄν will be true; for learning is of things true. And if τὸ μὴ ὄν is going to be true, it will straightway become existent as well; for indeed the Stoics say that the true is what exists and is opposed to something. But for τὸ μὴ ὄν to exist is certainly absurd; therefore τὸ μὴ ὄν is not taught.... It remains to say that τὸ ὄν is taught; and this too we shall show impossible. For if τὸ ὄν is taught, either it is taught insofar as it is ὄν or insofar as it is something else. But if it is taught insofar as it is ὄν, nothing will be untaught, nor, indeed, will there be anything taught; for there must be something untaught in order that from it learning may come about. So that τὸ ὄν will not be taught insofar as it is ὄν. Nor yet insofar as it is something else, for τὸ ὄν does not have any accident that is not ὄν; every accident of it is ὄν. Thus if τὸ ὄν is not taught insofar as it is ὄν, neither will it be taught insofar as it is something else; for that other accident of it, whatever it be, is ὄν. If, therefore, neither τὸ ὄν is taught nor τὸ μὴ ὄν, and there is no alternative besides these, none of τὰ ὄντα is taught.

Keep in mind that the expression τὸ ὄν, which may be translated as "what is" or "what is the case," covers both existent objects and existent states of affairs. Now we read in section 257 that "teaching should proceed from certain things that are agreed upon and are not to be taught," and it is inferred from this that τὸ ὄν, insofar as it is ὄν, is not a thing to be taught. This shows, I think, that the locution, "to teach somebody *P* καθό ["insofar as it is a case of"] *Q*" means something like "to bring him to know *P* on the ground *Q*". So the reason why τὸ ὄν cannot be taught insofar as it is ὄν is that this would amount to getting him to know *P* by giving him *P* as the reason; but if teaching were that simple, nothing would go untaught.

Thus the argument seems to be the following: Anything that is taught is either an existent state of affairs or a nonexistent state of affairs. Now a nonexistent state of affairs is not taught, for what does not exist has no attributes (cf. the medieval principle, *non entis nulla attributa sunt*). If an existent state of affairs is taught, either it is taught by reference to its existence, that is, its truth, or by reference to something else. But in the former case (in which we give the learner no reason for our assertion, or we just respond to his "Why?" by saying "Because it's true!"), everything will be taught (for all the teacher has to do is to assert it). But if the existent state of affairs is taught by citing something else, that too will have to exist, that is, be true, since the accidents of what exists exist. In this case, therefore, we are headed for a regress.

On this interpretation the argument is one of Sextus's typical infinite regress arguments. First, because "to teach" is by definition "to make to know," you cannot teach somebody something false. If you try to teach him something true, you either just assert it (but that is not teaching) or you give reasons. But the reasons have to be good, that is, true, and will have to be taught him, and thus you will have either to just assert them, or to provide reasons for them. And so on.

The part of the argument that seeks to establish that τὸ ὄν cannot be taught insofar as it is something else is particularly obscure. To say of something (*A*) "that it is something else" (*B*), is just to say "*A* is *B*." The "something else" (*B*) is supposed to be an accident (συμβεβηκός) of the something (*A*). If we say "Achilles is strong" (as contrasted with "Achilles is Achilles"), the term "strong" refers to the strength of Achilles, which is one of his accidents. Sextus then cites the metaphysical principle that the accidents of what exists exist. This is more or less intelligible when we are dealing with objects, as contrasted with states of affairs. For example, the strength of Achilles (as contrasted with strength in general and with the amount of Achilles's strength) exists if and only if Achilles exists. But in the present connection we are dealing with teaching, which, at least in the ordinary sense of the term, is concerned with states of affairs rather than objects: we can be taught the facts about Achilles, but it is unclear what it would mean to be taught Achilles. Therefore, we need some interpretation of "*X* is an accident of *Y*" when *X* and *Y* are states of affairs, not things.

So we have to ask: how could one state of affairs be an accident of another? Consider the following: When it is inferred that this must be Belgium because today is Tuesday, perhaps the situation can be described in metaphysicalese by saying that today's being Tuesday is an accident of our being in Belgium today—that is, one of the features of the latter state of affairs is the former.

Hence somebody might try to teach us (make us know) that we are in Belgium by citing the fact that today is Tuesday. (Compare Leibniz, who regarded "*B* is an accident of *A*" as equivalent to "*A* is *B* and *B* is not *A*," and who suggested an equivalence of "If *C* is *D*, then *E* is *F*" and "*C*'s being *D* is *E*'s being *F*.")

### 259–65. Whether There Is Any Such Thing as a Teacher or Learner?

With this chapter cf. M 11.234–8.

Among the four cases meticulously distinguished, obviously the only interesting one is that in which the skilled is to teach the unskilled. Against this possibility Sextus offers us a version of the "heap" argument: To be an artist (τεχνίτης) is to know the principles of the art; these must be acquired one by one, but there is no point in the apprentice's learning process when, by acquiring just one more principle, from a non-artist he turns into an artist.

264. This argument, such as it is, depends upon the ambiguity of "apprehend" between mere understanding, on the one hand, and recognizing something as being the case, on the other. Cf. 2.4ff. The argument in the corresponding passage, M 11.238, is somewhat different but equally weak. It argues that the unskilled person, being incapacitated (insofar as he is unskilled — ἐφ' ὅσον ἐστὶν ἄτεχνως) for grasping the principles of the art, cannot possess the γνῶσις ("capacity to recognize") of them any more than a person blind from birth can acquire the concept of colors or a person deaf from birth can acquire that of sounds.

### 266–72. Whether Any Such Thing as a Method of Learning Exists

Cf. 1.36ff.; M 11.239–47.

### 273–9. Whether the Art of Living Benefits Its Possessor

Cf. M 11.210–5.

This chapter attacks the Stoic "sage" (σοφός), who, with his virtue of prudence (φρόνησις), is supposed to have self-control (ἐγκράτεια), which enables him to overcome by reason any bad impulses that afflict him. Sextus argues that if the sage has no bad impulses to restrain, he can hardly be described as exerting self-control, while if he does have such impulses and manages to get then under control with reason, the bad impulses will still be there and his inner state will not be one of ἀταραξία but more like a hostile stand-off between two antagonists.

The Skeptic, unlike the Stoic, does not propose to "master" by reason the *pathē* that are upsetting him; instead, he has found (cf. 1.163) that when he simply withholds assent from any and all claims as to what is really the case and relaxes into a life in accord with the appearances, he reaches ἀταραξία as a by-product of this.

### 280–1. Why the Skeptic Sometimes Purposely Puts Forward Arguments Weak in Persuasiveness

It seems to me quite obvious that these two final sections, with their odd and silly claim that weak arguments have been included for the benefit of those who do not need strong arguments, are not genuine but have been tacked on by someone during the long twelve centuries between Sextus and our earliest MSS.

# Glossary

ἀγωγή, way. ἡ σκεπτικὴ ἀγωγή, the Skeptic Way.

ἄδηλος, non-evident.

ἀδιάκριτος, indistinguishable.

ἀδιάφορος, indifferent.

ἀδοξάστως, undogmatically, without belief, without any doctrine (δόξα).

ἀζήτητος, not open to question.

αἵρεσις, a system, school.

αἴσθησις, sense, sensation, sense perception.

αἰσθητήριον, sense organ.

αἰσθητός, sensory. τὰ αἰσθητά, objects of sense perception.

ἀκατάληπτος, non-apprehensible, not apprehended.

ἀκολουθία, logical consequence.

ἀλήθεια, truth.

ἀληθής, true (of propositions, arguments, objects or states of affairs).

ἄλογος, non-rational.

ἀναιρέω, to abolish, deny.

ἀνάλυσις, reduction

ἀναπόδεικτος, undemonstrated.

ἀνασκευάζω, to tear down (opp. κατασκευάζω, to set up).

ἀνατρέπω, overturn.

ἀνεπίκριτος, undecided, unresolved.

ἀνεπινόητος, inconceivable.

ἀνεύρετος, not discoverable.

ἀντικείμενον, (the) contradictory of a proposition.

ἀντιλαμβάνω, to perceive.

ἀντίληψις, perception, awareness of, possession.

ἀνύπαρκτος, unreal, nonexistent.

ἀνυπαρξία, nonexistence.

ἀνυπόστατος, unreal, nonexistent.

ἀνωμαλία, anomaly.

ἀξιῶ, to claim.

ἀξίωμα, proposition.

ἀοριστία, indeterminacy.

ἀπέμφασις, nonsense.

ἀπέραντος, invalid.

ἀπερίσπαστος, stable.

ἄπιστος, not credible, not worthy of belief.

ἀποδεικτικός, probative, demonstrative.

ἀπόδειξις, proof, demonstration.

ἀπόλυτος, absolute.

ἀπορέω, ἀπορῶ, to be at a loss.

ἀπορητικός, aporetic, serving to put one in a state of ἀπορία.

ἀπορία, state of being at a loss.

ἀπόφαντος, declaratory.

ἀπόφασις, 1. declaration.   2. negation.

ἀποφατικόν, negative proposition.

ἄρνησις, denial (opp. συγκατάθεσις).

ἀρχή, origin, beginning.

ἀρχόμενον, (the) antecedent in a conditional.

ἀσύνακτος, invalid.

ἀταραξία, imperturbability, tranquillity, (intellectual) peace of mind.

ἄτοπος, absurd.


βέβαιος, firm.

βίος, ordinary life.


γιγνώσκω, to recognize.

γνῶσις, knowledge (recognition of a thing as being what it is).


δῆλος, evident.

διαβεβαιοῦμαι, to maintain firmly.

διάθεσις, condition, temper of mind.

διάκρισις, a deciding, a determination.

διαλεκτική, logic.

διάλληλος τρόπος, circular argument.

διάνοια, intellect.

διασπασμός, a tearing apart.

διάστασις, dimension.

διαφορά, difference.

διάφορος, different.

διαφωνία, dispute, controversy, disagreement.

διεζευγμένον, disjunction.

διεξωδεύμενος, tested.

δόγμα, belief.

δογματικῶς, with belief.

δοκεῖ, it seems.

δόξα, belief.

δοξαστής, believer.

δύναμις, capacity, ability, disposition, power. δυνάμει, in effect, implicitly.


ἐκβάλλω, to throw out.

ἐκκαλυπτικός, serving to disclose

ἐκτὸς ὑποκείμενα, externally existing objects and states of affairs.

ἐμπειρία, experience.

ἔμφασις, force (of an expression or *phantasia*).

ἐναλλάξ, alternando.

ἐνάργεια, obviousness.

ἐναργή, clear.

ἐνδεικτικός, indicative.

ἐνδιάθετος λόγος, internal speech or discourse.

ἔννοια, concept.

ἐξαλλαγή, variety.

ἐπαγωγή, induction.

ἐπέχω, to withhold assent

ἐπιγιγνώσκω, to determine, decide.

ἐπικρίνω, to determine, decide.

ἐπίκρισις, (a) determination, settling.

ἐπιλογίζομαι, to conclude, to reckon.

ἐπινοέω, to form a concept of, to conceive of.

ἐπινόησις, concept.

ἐπίνοια, concept.

ἐπιφορά, conclusion.

ἐποχή, withholding of assent, suspension of judgment, *epochē*.

ἐρωτάω, ἐρωτῶ, to put forward in a dialectical exchange.

ἑτεροίωσις, alteration.

εὐθέως, right off, at once.

εὑρίσκω, to find.

εὔροια (βίow), serene flow of life.

ἐφωδευτικῶς, as a guide leads


ζητέω, to question, seek, investigate.

ζήτησις, questioning.


ἡγεμονικόν, the ruling part of the soul.

ἡγούμενον, antecedent in a conditional.

θεωρεῖσθαι, to be observed.
θεώρημα, principle.
θεωρία, theory.

ἰσοσθένεια, equipollence.
ἴσως, maybe, perhaps, I guess.

καταλαμβάνω, to apprehend.
καταληπτικός, serving apprehension.
καταληπτός, apprehensible.
κατάληψις, apprehension.
κατασκευάζω, to set up, establish.
καταφατικόν, affirmative proposition.
καταχρηστικῶς, imprecisely, loosely, not strictly correct (opp. κυρίως).
κατηγόρημα, predicate.
κατηναγκασμένος, necessitated, unavoidable, inevitable.
κίνησις, motion, change.
κρᾶσις, blending.
κρίνω, to judge, to decide, to make a determination.
κρίσις, testing, deciding about.
κριτήριον, criterion, basis for decision.

λεκτόν, *lekton*, what is said, a meaning.
λέξις, speech.
λῆγον, consequent in a conditional.
λῆμμα, premise.
λόγος, argument, account, discourse, talk.

μάχομαι, to be inconsistent with.
μῖξις, mixture.
μοχθηρός, false, invalid (opp. ὑγιής).

νοέω, to think of.
νόησις, thought, concept.
νοῦς, thought.

ὀνειροπολέω, to imagine.
ὁρίζω, to determine, to make a determination.
ὅρος, definition.

πάθος, feeling, affect, state (of the soul), *pathos*, pl. *pathē*.
παράθεσις, juxtaposition.
παραστατικός, serving to set — before the mind.

παρίστημι, to set before the mind.

πείσμα, confidence.

περίεργος, overly subtle.

περιπίπτω, to fill into, to occur, to befall.

περιπτώσις, accident, opportunity, occurrence, what befalls you, experience.

περίστασις, circumstance.

περιτρέπω, to confute, refute, controvert, get rid of, get out of the way.

περιωδεύμενος, tested.

πιθανός, plausible.

πιθανότης, plausibility.

πίστις, credibility.

πιστός, credible, worthy of belief.

πρᾶγμα, thing, object, or state of affairs.

πρόδηλον, evident beforehand.

προκρίνω, to prefer.

πρόληψις, preconception, assumption, presupposition, intuitive concept.

προπετεία, precipitancy, tendency to rush to judgment.

προσβολή, application.

προσηγορία, term (class name), appellative.

προσπίπτω, to impress, affect, occur.

προφορικὸς λόγος, external discourse, speech.


σημεῖον, sign, point.

σκέψις, skepticism, the Skeptic Way.

συγκαταλαμβάνω, to apprehend together with.

συγκατάθεσις, assent (opp. ἄρνησις).

συγκατατίθημι, to give assent to.

σύγχυσις, fusion.

συμβεβηκός, accident, attribute.

συμπεπλεγμένον, conjunction.

συμπέρασμα, conclusion.

συμπλοκή, conjunction.

συνακτικός, conclusive, valid.

συνημμένον, a conditional (proposition).

σχῆμα, inference schema.


τεχνή, art, craft, skill.

τεχνίτης, artist, craftsman, skilled person.

τήρησις (βιωτική), ordinary regimen of life.

τόπος, location, point.

τρόπος, mode (of *epochē*), inference schema.

ὑγιής, true (of propositions), valid (of arguments).

ὕπαρξις, existence.

ὑπάρχω, to exist, to be the case (in the external world).

ὑποκείμενον, existent.

ὑπολαμβάνω, to assume.

ὑπομιμνήσκω, to remind, put in mind of, mention.

ὑποπίπτω, to affect, befall.

ὑπόστασις, existence, substance.

φαίνομαι, to appear.

φαινόμενον, τό, the appearance, what appears.

φαντάζομαι, to have a *phantasia*.

φαντασία, *phantasia*, impression.

φάντασμα, image.

φανταστόν, τό, the object of the *phantasia*, what produces the *phantasia*.

φωνή, utterance, (Skeptic) slogan.

χωρισμός, separation.

ψεῦδος, false.

# Select Bibliography

## Editions and Translations

Only editions of the Greek text and translations into English, German, French, or Italian are listed.

Annas, J., and J. Barnes. 1985, *The Modes of Scepticism*. Cambridge: Cambridge University Press. (Includes translations of portions of the *Outlines of Pyrrhonism*.)

Bekker, I. 1842. *Sextus Empiricus*. Berlin: Reimer.

Bissolati, S. 1917. *Sesto Empirico, Delle Istituzioni Pirroniane*. Florence: Le Monnier. (Italian translation of the *Outlines of Pyrrhonism*).

Bury, R. 1933–49. *Sextus Empiricus*. 4 vols. Loeb Classical Library. London: Heinemann.

Dumont, J. 1966. *Les Sceptiques grecs*. Paris: Presses Universitaires de France. (Includes French translations of selections from Sextus.)

Fabricius, J. 1718. *Sexti Empirici opera graece et latine*. Leipzig: Libraria Kuehniana. (Contains the Latin translation by Stephanus and notes by Stephanus and Fabricius.)

Ferro, A. 1944. *Tropi di Enesidemo*. Rome: Giovanissima. (Includes Italian translation of portions of the *Outlines of Pyrrhonism*).

Grenier, J., and G. Goron. 1948. *Oeuvres choisies de Sextus Empiricus*. Paris: Aubier Éditions Montaigne. (Includes French translations of selections from Sextus.)

Hallie, P., and S. Etheridge. 1964. *Sextus Empiricus, Scepticism, Man and God*. Middletown, Conn.: Wesleyan University Press. (Includes translations of selections from Sextus.)

Hossenfelder, M. 1968. *Sextus Empiricus, Grundriss der Pyrrhonischen Skepsis*. Frankfurt am Main: Suhrkamp. (German translation of the *Outlines of Pyrrhonism*.)

Inwood, B., and L. Gerson. 1922. *Hellenistic Philosophy*. Indianapolis: Hackett. (Includes translations of selections from Sextus.)

Long, A., and D. Sedley. 1987. *The Hellenistic Philosophers*. 2 vols. Cambridge: Cambridge University Press. (Includes translations of selections from Sextus.)

Mutschmann, H., and J. Mau. 1912–62. *Sexti Empirici Opera*. 4 vols. Bibliotheca Scriptorum Graecorum Teubneriana. Leipzig. (Volume 4 contains an excellent analytic index by K. Janacek.)

Pappenheim, E. 1876. *Sextus Empiricus, Pyrrhoneische Grundzüge*. Leipzig: Meiner. (German translation of the *Outlines of Pyrrhonism*.)

Russo, A. 1972. *Sesto Empirico Contro i Matematici, Libri I–VI*. Bari: Laterza. (Italian translation of M 1–6.)

Russo, A. 1975. *Sesto Empirico Contro i Logici*. Rome and Bari: Laterza. (Italian translation of M 7–8.)

Tescari, O. 1926. *Sesto Empirico. Schizzi Pirroniani in tre Libri.* Bari: Laterza. (Italian translation of the *Outlines of Pyrrhonism.*)

## Literature

Only books and papers that either are cited in the text or discuss matters plainly relevant to the topic of this book are listed. For Hellenistic philosophy generally, far and away the best bibliography is that in Long and Sedley (1987, vol. 2, pp. 476ff.). The Bibliographischer Anhang to Schmucker (1986) is useful for its references to older literature not mentioned in Long and Sedley.

Ackrill, J. 1963. *Aristotle's Categories and De Interpretatione,* Oxford: Clarendon Press.

Annas, J. 1980. "Truth and Knowledge." In *Doubt and Dogmatism.* Ed. M. Schofield, M. Burnyeat, and J. Barnes. Oxford: Clarendon Press, 84–104.

Annas, J. 1986. "Doing without Objective Values: Ancient and Modern Strategies." In *The Norms of Nature.* Cambridge: Cambridge University Press, 3–29.

Annas, J. 1992. *Hellenistic Philosophy of Mind.* Berkeley, University of California Press.

Ausland, H. 1989. "On the Moral Origin of the Pyrrhonian Philosophy." *Elenchos* 10: 359–434.

Austin, J.L. 1962. *Sense and Sensibilia.* Oxford: Clarendon Press.

Ayer, A.J. 1956. *The Problem of Knowledge.* Harmondsworth, England: Penguin Books.

Barnes, J. 1980. "Proof Destroyed." In *Doubt and Dogmatism.* Ed. M. Schofield, M. Burnyeat, and J. Barnes. Oxford: Clarendon Press, 161–81.

Barnes, J. 1982. "The Beliefs of a Pyrrhonist." In *Proceedings of the Cambridge Philological Society* 29: 1–29; also in *Elenchos* 4 (1983): 5–43.

Barnes, J. 1983. "Ancient Skepticism and Causation." In *The Skeptical Tradition.* Berkeley: University of California Press, 149–204.

Barnes, J. 1990. *The Toils of Scepticism.* Cambridge: Cambridge University Press.

Berkeley, G. 1901. *The Works of George Berkeley.* 4 vols. Ed. A. C. Fraser. Oxford: Clarendon Press.

Bevan, E. 1913. *Stoics and Sceptics.* Cambridge: W. Heffer.

Broad, C. D. 1923 *Scientific Thought.* London: Routledge & Kegan Paul.

Brochard, V. 1887; repr. 1969. *Les Sceptiques grecs.* Paris: F. Alcan.

Burnyeat, M. (1976) "Protagoras and Self-Refutation in Later Greek Philosophy." *Philosophical Review* 85: 44–69.

Burnyeat, M. 1980. "Can the Sceptic Live His Scepticism?" In *Doubt and Dogmatism.* Ed. M. Schofield, M. Buryeat, and J. Barnes. Oxford: Clarendon Press, 20-53. Reprinted in *The Skeptical Tradition.* Berkeley: University of California Press, 1983, 117–48.

Burnyeat, M. 1982. "Idealism and Greek Philosophy: What Descartes Saw and Berkeley Missed." *Philosophical Review* 91: 3–40.

Burnyeat, M. 1984. "The Sceptic in His Place and Time." In *Philosophy and History.* Cambridge: Cambridge University Press, 225–54.

Burnyeat, M., ed. 1983. *The Skeptical Tradition.* Berkeley: University of California Press.

Chatalian, G. 1991. *Epistemology and Skepticism.* Carbondale: Southern Illinois University Press.

Chisholm, R. 1941. "Sextus Empiricus and Modern Empiricism." *Philosophy of Science* 8: 371–84.

Clarke, T. 1972. "The Legacy of Skepticism." *Journal of Philosophy* 69:754–69.

Cohen, A. 1984. "Sextus Empiricus: Skepticism as a Therapy." *Philosophical Forum* 15: 405–24.

Dal Pra, M. 1975. *Lo scetticismo greco*, 2d ed. Rome and Bari: Laterza.

Deichgräber, M. 1930. *Die griechische Empirikerschule*. Berlin: Weidmann.

De Lacy, P. 1958. "*Ou mallon* and the Antecedents of Ancient Scepticism." *Phronesis* 3: 59–71. Reprinted in *Essays in Ancient Greek Philosophy*. Albany: State University of New York Press, 1971, 593–606.

Döring, K. 1972. *Die Megariker*. Amsterdam: Gruner.

Eddington, A. 1928. *Nature of the Physical World*. London: Macmillan.

Frede, M. 1974. *Die stoische Logik*. Göttingen: Vandenhoeck & Ruprecht.

Frede, M. 1979 "Des Skeptikers Meinungen." *Neue Hefte für Philosophie* 15/16: 102–29. English trans. "The Skeptic's Beliefs," In *Essays in Ancient Philosophy*. Minneapolis: University of Minnesota Press, 1987, 179–200.

Frede, M. 1980. "The Original Notion of Cause." In *Doubt and Dogmatism*. Ed. M. Schofield, M. Burnyeat, and J. Barnes. Oxford: Clarendon Press, 217–49.

Frede, M. 1983 "Stoics and Skeptics on Clear and Distinct Impressions." In *The Skeptical Tradition*. Berkeley: University of California Press, 65–90.

Frede, M. 1984. "The Sceptic's Two Kinds of Assent and the Question of the Possibility of Knowledge." In *Philosophy and History*. Cambridge: Cambridge University Press, 225–78.

Frede, M. 1987. *Essays in Ancient Philosophy*. Minneapolis: University of Minnesota Press. (Contains all Frede's papers listed here.)

Frege, G. 1892 "Über Sinn und Bedeutung." *Zeitschrift für Philosophie* 100: 25–50.

Giannantoni, G., Ed. 1981. *Lo scetticismo antico*. Naples: Bibliopolis.

Goedeckemeyer, A. 1905. *Die Geschichte des griechischen Skeptizismus*. Leipzig; repr. Aalen: Scientia Verlag, 1968.

Heintz, W. 1932. *Studien zu Sextus Empiricus*. Ed. R. Harder. Halle: Max Niemeyer.

Hallie, P. 1967. "Sextus Empiricus." In *The Encyclopedia of Philosophy*. 8 vols. New York: Macmillan, 7: 427–8.

House, E. 1980. "The Life of Sextus Empiricus." *Classical Quarterly* 30: 227–38.

Hume, D. 1888. *A Treatise of Human Nature*. Ed. L. A. Selby-Bigge. Oxford: Clarendon Press.

Hume, D. 1902. *Enquiries*. 2d ed. Ed. L. A. Selby-Bigge. Oxford: Clarendon Press.

Janacek, K. 1948. *Prolegomena to Sextus Empiricus*. Olomouc, Czechoslovakia: Acta Universitatis Palackianae Olomucensis.

Janacek, K. 1972. *Sextus Empiricus' Sceptical Methods*. Prague: Universita Karlova

Janacek, K. 1979. "Das Wort *skeptikos* in Philons Schriften." *Listy Filologicke* 101:65–68.

Kneale, W., and M. Kneale. 1962. *The Development of Logic*. Oxford: Clarendon Press.

Long, A. 1967. "Carneades and the Stoic Telos," *Phronesis* 12: 59–90.

Long, A. 1974. *Hellenistic Philosophy*. London: Duckworth; 2d ed. Berkeley: University of California Press, 1986.

Long, A. 1978. "Sextus Empiricus on the Criterion of Truth." *Bulletin of the Institute of Classical Studies* 25: 35–59.

Long, A. 1978. "Timon of Phlius: Pyrrhonist and Satirist." In *Proceedings of the Cambridge Philological Society*, n.s., 24: 68–91.

Mates, B. 1949a. "Diodorean Implication." *Philosophical Review* 58: 234–42.

Mates, B. 1949b. "Stoic Logic and the Text of Sextus Empiricus." *American Journal of Philology* 70: 290–8.

Mates, B. 1953. *Stoic Logic*. Berkeley: University of California Press.

Mates, B. 1981. *Skeptical Essays*. Chicago: University of Chicago Press.

Mates, B. 1984. "On Refuting the Skeptic." *Proceedings and Addresses of the American Philosophical Association* 58: 21–35.

Mates, B. 1992a. "Bolzano and Ancient Pyrrhonism." In *Bolzano's Wissenschaftslehre*. Florence: Olschki, 121–39.

Mates, B. 1992b. "Pyrrhonism and Modern Skepticism." In *Philosophie, Psychoanalyse, Emigration*, Ed. P. Muhr, P. Feyerabend, and C. Wegeler. Vienna, 210–28.

McPherran, M. 1987. "Skeptical Homeopathy and Self-refutation." *Phronesis* 32: 290–328.

McPherran, M. 1990. "Pyrrhonism's Arguments Against Value." *Philosophical Studies* 60: 127–42.

McPherran, M. 1991 "Ataraxia and Eudaimonia in Ancient Pyrrhonism: Is the Skeptic Really Happy?" *Boston Area Colloquium in Ancient Philosophy* 5: 135–72.

Naess, A. 1968. *Scepticism*. New York: Humanities Press.

Nussbaum, M. 1991 "Skeptic Purgatives: Therapeutic Argument in Ancient Skepticism." *Journal of the History of Philosophy* 29: 521–57.

Olaso, E. de. 1978. "Zetesis." *Manuscrito* 11: 45–73.

Olaso, E. de. 1987. "Leibniz and Skepticism." In *Scepticism from the Renaissance to the Enlightenment*. Ed. R. Popkin and C. B. Schmitt, Wiesbaden: O. Harrassowitz, 133-67.

Patrick, M. 1899. *Sextus Empiricus and Greek Scepticism*. Cambridge: Deighton Bell and Co.

Popkin, R. 1951. "David Hume: His Pyrrhonism and His Critique of Pyrrhonism." *Philosophical Quarterly* 5: 385–407. Repr. in *The Skeptical Tradition*, Berkeley: University of California Press, 1983.

Popkin, R. 1952. "Berkeley and Pyrrhonism," *Revue of Metaphysics* 5: 223–46.

Popkin, R. 1967. "Skepticism." In *The Encyclopedia of Philosophy*. 8 vols. New York: Macmillan, 7: 449–61.

Popkin, R. 1979. *The History of Scepticism from Erasmus to Spinoza*. 3d ed. Berkeley: University of California Press.

Popkin, R. 1980. *The High Road to Pyrrhonism*, Ed. R. A. Watson and J.E. Force. San Diego: Austin Hill Press.

Prantl, C. 1855. *Geschichte der Logik im Abendlande*. Leipzig: Hirzel.

Quine, W. V. 1961. *From a Logical Point of View*. 2d ed., Cambridge, Mass.: Harvard University Press.

Rist, J. 1970. "The Heracliteanism of Aenesidemus." *Phoenix* 24: 309–19.

Robin, L. 1944. *Pyrrhon et le scepticisme grec*. Paris: Presses Universitaires de France.

Russell, B. 1914. *Our Knowledge of the External World*. London: Open Court.

Russell, B. 1945. *A History of Western Philosophy*. New York: Simon and Schuster.

Ryle, G. 1949. *The Concept of Mind*. New York: Barnes & Noble.

Santayana, G. 1923. *Scepticism and Animal Faith*. New York: Charles Scribner's Sons.

Schmitt, C. 1972. "The Rediscovery of Ancient Skepticism in Modern Times." *Rivista critica di storia della filosofia* 27: 363–84. Repr. in *The Skeptical Tradition*, Berkeley: University of California Press, 1983, 225–52.

Schmucker, J. 1986. *Die Kunst der glücklichen Zweifeln*. Amsterdam: Gruner.

Schofield, M. 1980. "Preconception, Argument, and God." In *Doubt and Dogmatism*. Ed. M. Schofield, M. Burnyeat, and J. Barnes. Oxford: Clarendon Press, 283–308.

Sedley, D. 1977. "Diodorus Cronus and Hellenistic Philosophy." *Proceedings of the Cambridge Philological Society* 203 (n.s. 23): 74–120.

Sedley, D. 1980. "The Protagonists." In *Doubt and Dogmatism.* Ed. M. Schofield, M. Burnyeat, and J. Barnes. Oxford: Clarendon Press, 1–19.

Sedley, D. 1983. "The Motivation of Greek Skepticism." In *The Skeptical Tradition.* Berkeley, University of California Press, 9–30.

Sorabji, R. 1980. "Causation, Laws, and Necessity." In *Doubt and Dogmatism.* Ed. M. Schofield, M. Burnyeat, and J. Barnes. Oxford: Clarendon Press, 250–82.

Stäudlin, C. 1794. *Geschichte und Geist des Skepticismus.* 2 vols. Leipzig: Crusius.

Stebbing, S. 1937. *Philosophy and the Physicists.* London: Methuen.

Stough, C. 1969. *Greek Skepticism.* Berkeley: University of California Press.

Stough, C. 1984. "Sextus Empiricus on Non-assertion." *Phronesis* 29: 136–64.

Striker, G. 1980. "Sceptical Strategies." In *Doubt and Dogmatism.* Ed. M. Schofield, M. Burnyeat, and J. Barnes. Oxford: Clarendon Press, 54–83.

Striker, G. 1981. "Über den Unterschied zwischen den Pyrrhoneern und den Akademikern." *Phronesis* 26: 153–69.

Striker, G. 1983. "The Ten Tropes of Aenesidemus." In *The Skeptical Tradition.* Berkeley: University of California Press, 95–116.

Stroud, B. 1984. *The Significance of Philosophical Scepticism.* Oxford: Clarendon Press.

Ueberweg, F. 1926. *Grundriss der Geschichte der Philosophie* (Part 1: *Die Philosophie des Altertums,* Ed. K. Praechter). 12th ed. Berlin: Mittler.

Vlastos, G. 1973. *Platonic Studies.* Princeton: Princeton University Press.

Wittgenstein, L. 1961. *Tractatus Logico-Philosophicus.* Trans. D. Pears and B. McGuinness. London: Routledge & Kegan Paul.

Zeller, E. 1880. *Stoics, Epicureans, and Skeptics.* Trans. O. Reichel. London: Longmans.

Zeller, E. 1923. *Die Philosophie der Griechen.* 5th ed., Leipzig: O. R. Reisland.

# Index

327